BULWER LYTTON

HOC · VIRTUTIS · OPUS

Bulwer Lytton

*The Rise and Fall
of a Victorian Man of Letters*

Leslie Mitchell

Hambledon and London
London and New York

Hambledon and London

102 Gloucester Avenue
London, NW1 8HX

175 Fifth Avenue
New York, NY 10010
USA

First Published 2003

ISBN 1 85285 423 5

Copyright © Leslie Mitchell 2003

A description of this book is available from the
British Library and from the Library of Congress.

Typeset by Carnegie Publishing, Lancaster,
and printed in Great Britain
by Cambridge University Press.

Distributed in the United States and Canada
exclusively by Palgrave Macmillan,
a division of St Martin's Press.

Contents

Illustrations

Text Illustrations

For Herrattis

Acknowledgements

The production of a book draws on many talents. I have been very fortunate in this respect. I would first like to thank Lord Cobbold for allowing me unrestricted access to Edward Bulwer Lytton's papers, and for his unfailing encouragement from the very inception of the project. Henry Cobbold provided invaluable assistance in both reading the text and suggesting and supplying illustrations. Next, librarians and archivists in many institutions on both sides of the Atlantic have shown a professional competence without which authors would be lost. In particular, I would like to mention the Archivist at Knebworth House, Clare Fleck, whose patience was tried but never found wanting. I would also like to acknowledge the kindness of the Trustees of Boston Public Library and the Pierpont Morgan Library, New York, for allowing me to use manuscripts in their care. Extracts from the Parrish Manuscripts are published with the permission of Princeton University Library. As for the funding of the research of this book, I am entirely in the debt of the Master and Fellows of University College, Oxford.

Pupils and friends have gallantly supplied the deficiencies of an author who cannot drive or confront a computer. My heartfelt thanks must go to Tom Attanasio, Ross Avery, Alicia and Crofton Black, Philip Burling, Andrew Duncan, William Gore, Paulina Kewes, Matthew Hill, Emily Rose and John Wrathmell for helping to make research painless and often amusing. I hope they will feel that their efforts have had a happy outcome.

Abbreviations

Balfour — Lady B. Balfour, *Personal and Literary Letters of Robert, First Earl of Lytton* (London, 1906)

Chalon — L. Devey, *Unpublished Letters of Lady Lytton to A. E. Chalon* (London, n.d.)

Devey — L. Devey, *Letters of the Late Edward Bulwer, Lord Lytton, to his Wife* (London, 1884)

EBL — Edward Bulwer Lytton

Knebworth MSS — Manuscripts and Letters of the Lytton Family, Knebworth House, Hertfordshire

LLLR — Lord Lytton, *The Life, Letters and Literary Remains of Edward Bulwer, Lord Lytton* (London, 1883)

Life — Lord Lytton, *The Life of Edward Bulwer, Lord Lytton* (London, 1913)

Lytton MSS — Manuscripts of the Lytton family held in Hertfordshire Record Office

Speeches — Lord Lytton, *Speeches of Edward, Lord Lytton* (London, 1874)

Introduction

As with almost everything, Edward Bulwer Lytton was ambivalent on the subject of biography. At times, he demanded an approach that left nothing hidden. Writing on the death of a royal prince, he claimed to hate 'the cant of "de mortuis nil nisi bonum". Public characters *never* die; and nothing is so mischievous to mankind as to make the Grave such a "beautifier of the dead". The Duke of York was a weak, arbitrary, tyrannical bigot.'[1] At other times, he was sceptical that a good biography could ever be written:

> We die – none have known us! And yet all are to declaim on our character – measure at a glance the dark abyss of our souls – prate of us as if we were household and hackneyed to them from our cradle. One amongst the number shall write our biography – the rest shall read, and conceive they know us ever afterwards. We go down to our sons' sons, darkened and disguised, so that, looking on men's colourings of our mind and life, from our repose on the bosom of God, we shall not recognise one feature of the portrait we have left to earth.[2]

On the one hand, he was clear that, 'there is nothing in my Biography that can afford much interest to the reader'.[3] On the other, he meticulously kept papers in an archive that was to provide the means to refute any calumny perpetrated in later generations.[4] A man who was so sensitive to the opinions of those around him while alive was in fact unlikely not to protect his reputation when dead.

Certainly he, by being so multi-faceted, is a difficult subject for the biographer, and this would probably have pleased him. He was a politician, novelist, essayist, poet, commentator on European affairs and spiritualist. As he himself put it, 'the adequate biography of a life so full and various must, however, be the task of years'.[5] Otherwise, there was a danger of merely 'skimming the cream' of a life,[6] and producing a book lacking depth and balance. In an attempt to avoid this pitfall, the present book will present the man as much as the artist.

At Lytton's funeral in Westminster Abbey, Benjamin Jowett heralded him as 'one of England's greatest writers and one of the most distinguished men of our time'.[7] One hundred and thirty years later, Lytton and his work is largely unknown. Up to 1914, the sales of his books rivalled those of Dickens.

Since 1918, few people have shown any interest. Rarely can a reputation have stood so high and fallen so low. It is all the more remarkable because Lytton was a figure in so many different types of activity. His rehabilitation as an undoubtedly eminent Victorian is long overdue. It is the aim of this book to contribute to that process.

Lytton's importance in Victorian society may be measured by astonishing statistics. The market for his books was prodigious. The British Library catalogue lists 618 items under his name, and they overwhelmingly refer to books published in his lifetime. Before 1914, there were thirty-two editions of *The Last Days of Pompeii*. No other novel could match this success, and two, *Kenelm Chillingly* and *What Will He Do With It*, only managed four editions, but many others were publishing triumphs. *Eugene Aram* ran to fourteen editions, *The Last of the Barons* to seventeen, *Pelham* to fifteen, *Paul Clifford* to twelve and *Night and Morning* to ten. Nor was this acclaim limited to England. Lytton was translated often into French and German, and occasionally into Spanish, Italian, Swedish, Russian and Greek. A collected edition of his works appeared in Stuttgart as early as 1838. Even his political writings were avidly bought. *The Present Crisis* of 1834, for example, went through thirteen editions within a year. It was on the evidence of figures such as these that he based his claim that his writings could save governments.

Success bred success, and Lytton had every right to take an increasingly strong line in negotiations with publishers. At the end of his life he was unassailable. There were five editions of *The Coming Race* within a year of its publication, and 3150 copies of *Kenelm Chillingly* were sold on the day of its publication. Lytton's death in no way diminished his popularity with the reading public. A collected edition of his works in thirty-seven volumes appeared between 1873 and 1877, to be followed by a twenty-eight volume pocket edition between 1887 and 1889. An American publisher contributed a thirty-two volume edition de luxe between 1892 and 1893.

Another indicator of Lytton's reputation was the sums that he expected publishers to pay for the privilege of marketing his works. His value rose steeply, and from early in his career he rightly saw his income from writing to be as important as that from the Knebworth estate. In 1828 Henry Colburn paid him £500 for *Pelham*, a considerable sum in itself for a first novel. The astonishing success of that novel led to the same publisher having to offer £800 for *The Disowned* and £1500 for *Devereux* in 1830. Thereafter Lytton found himself being able to negotiate about contracts from a position of strength. He took such transactions very seriously. He could change and abuse publishers if they were believed to be financially or artistically doubtful, and his literary standing justified the taking of intransigent positions.

Hard-headed producers of books like Colburn and John Blackwood found him difficult to deal with, but were also aware that his books sold in huge numbers.

Quite suddenly, this interest in Lytton and his works died in 1914. He was one of the many Victorian figures who should be numbered among the casualties of the First World War. The same literary catalogues which proclaim his influence on Victorian and Edwardian society bear witness to his strange demise. *The Last Days of Pompeii* is the only novel to have had any staying-power. Editions of this book continued to appear after 1918, one of the most recent being published in 1979. With this one exception the tally is pitiable. Very occasionally an imaginative publisher has taken a chance on *The Coming Race, Eugene Aram, Pelham* and *Rienzi*, but the bulk of Lytton's enormous output has fallen away into the shadows. Quite why this should happen opens up a fruitful field for speculation.

Accounting for his success is easier. The range of his literary and political writings made him a leading commentator on many of the major debates of his time. As a practising politician for much of his life he was able, unlike most writers, to have the opportunity of translating ideas into practice. He liked to think of himself as artist and as man of action. On some issues he was a campaigner and a leader of opinion. His novels often had an enormous resonance in the anxieties and aspirations of his contemporaries.

In this sense it is possible, without undue simplification, to divide his literary production into four or five major sections, each picking up a Victorian theme of importance. The first of these sections concerned the dandy novels. *Pelham, Falkland* and *Devereux* ensured that Lytton started his life in scandal. Charges of immorality flowed freely. When the books appeared, the debate about the cult of the dandy had been in session for some years. For some this fashion was degenerate, cynical and anarchic. For others it was magnetically Byronic in its attack upon conventions. Lytton tried to claim that his hero in *Pelham* was a model for good. The young man was dandy but also the protector of women and the surest of friends. Lytton hoped that his book would stop bank clerks playing Byron. But this moral purpose was not always seen by contemporaries. They bought the book and complained about its contents. *Pelham* was a *coup de scandale*, and there are many less efficient ways of establishing a literary reputation.

No sooner had the dust of one controversy settled than another of even greater force took its place. The publication of *Paul Clifford* in 1830 confirmed Lytton's notoriety. This time his transgression was to dignify the criminal world by thinking it worthwhile to describe their values in literature. Worse, it was claimed that he put the values of this section of the community on a par with those of good society. This novel, together with *Eugene Aram*,

Night and Morning and *Lucretia,* made a major contribution to what came to be known as the Newgate school of writing. Indeed Lytton claimed to have invented the genre. Dickens and Harrison Ainsworth joined in later. Newgate had been London's principal prison in the eighteenth century. Its criminal population regularly fed the gallows. Such people normally provoked fear and revulsion, and it was therefore barely comprehensible that the Newgate writers should give them codes of behaviour that mimicked those of their social superiors.

Indeed, such writing violated contemporary canons of taste. It was a commonplace among reviewers that each level of society had an idiom that was specific to itself. Love, hate, anger and jealousy were found in all people, but their expression was different in every social group. The higher the social context, the more refined and interesting the demonstration of emotion. By contrast, the poor and the criminal reacted with nothing more than brute instinct. In this situation, writers should of course limit themselves to describing what was best and most elevating. To do anything else was simply perverse. To make a hero of a highwayman in *Paul Clifford* or to investigate the scholarly mind of a murderer in *Eugene Aram* was to affront accepted canons of taste. The dandy and the criminal both challenged society and by becoming the apologist of these Lytton made a name.

With a reputation established, Lytton drifted into the mainstream. The novels of his middle age were more accepted and acceptable to his contemporaries. The writing became more relaxed and discursive. It also began to concentrate on themes of acknowledged contemporary interest. *My Novel* and *The Caxtons* gave to the mid-Victorian reader a view of the world around him. Sixteen editions of *The Caxtons* would appear between 1849 and 1903. Affectionate accounts of village life, honest and simple values, and the importance of family ties had a real currency at a time when all of these things were thought to be under threat from a destabilising industrialisation. Such books had all the marketable qualities of topicality. Lytton the iconoclast successfully transformed himself into something respectable. He was hailed as a commentator on the age, and his novels sold as tracts for the times.

This reordering of his priorities was confirmed by delving into fashionable medievalism. Novels like *Harold, The Last of the Barons* and *Rienzi,* together with epic poems like *King Arthur,* tapped into a real Victorian preference. For those who found industrial society menacing there was solace in taking refuge in an idealised past. The middle ages were described as centuries of noble values and social harmony. Selfless heroes fought bravely for the public good. A Victorian parliamentarian could do worse than take Rienzi as his model in public life. Lytton had always admired the medievalism of Sir Walter Scott and now offered it to a new generation. In doing so he was once again picking up a theme of major contemporary concern which inevitably turned into profit. There was nothing calculated in this. Matters dealt with in the Caxton series and in the medieval novels touched Lytton deeply. Yet his new preoccupations made it easier for his popularity to be confirmed. They comforted readers and troubled them less.

Even Lytton's fascination with the occult had the same result. Novels like *Zanoni* and *A Strange Story*, which introduced Victorian readers to Rosicrucianism and other mysteries, connected Lytton with a major contemporary debate. Mid-century London was a world of seances and mediums. For some such enquiries were pure quackery, but an equal number of people took them very seriously. Scientific discoveries were being made on an almost annual basis. The scientific method of investigation was being refined. What had previously been mysterious was being made plain. Lytton and many others were open to the view that science might even make the spiritual world accessible, or allow for the indefinite prolongation of life. Elixirs were after all nothing but substances whose properties had not yet been described. There was of course potential embarrassment in all this – and Lytton hated to be embarrassed – but his writings on these subjects merely confirmed his status as spokesman for his age. Conan Doyle, Rudyard Kipling and Rosamund Lehmann would follow the spiritualist path into the twentieth century.

For sheer range of style and interest therefore Lytton was a giant of Victorian literature. His readers could be assured that he would give them something of interest on a matter of contemporary concern. His last service to them was to offer a view of the future. In old age Lytton became a prophet. His last three novels, *The Parisians*, *The Coming Race* and *Kenelm Chillingly*, deal respectively with the onset of Socialism, society after Socialism, and a restatement of what was being lost as society moved forward. The first two may be called ground-breaking in the themes they addressed. Lytton had moved beyond the role of mere social commentator. He now claimed to stand on an eminence from which he could see into the far distance. Few other Victorians could attain such heights.

As if this varied and prodigious output were not enough, Lytton had other claims on the attention of his countrymen. He was a writer who was also a politician, even briefly a Cabinet Minister. As such he was one of the few literary men who had the opportunity of putting ideas into practice. People as diverse as theatre managers, indigent writers and the population of Queensland had real reason to feel grateful for his public life. Equally, readers of scandal-sheets could feel grateful for his private life, which can only be described as exotic. One way or the other, Lytton was rarely out of the headlines. He claimed to hate notoriety but always had it. He insisted that he wanted nothing so much as a life of quiet but was always deep in controversy. In short he was a figure, and the steady success of his works reflected the fact.

Why then was this celebrity so suddenly extinguished? The simple answer is that Lytton died in the First World War. The terrible experiences of those years led to a massive rejection of the system that had produced them. Victorianism was at a discount. Lytton Strachey's accounts of Queen Victoria and other eminent Victorians held the whole period up to ridicule. Few writers survived. A list that would include Dickens, the Brontës, Trollope and George Eliot is almost complete. There was no room for Ouida or Mrs Henry Wood or Sheridan Lefanu or even Thackeray. There was certainly no place for Lytton, whose literary commentaries on Victorian preoccupations like dandyism and medievalism seemed remote to a generation which had survived the slaughter in the trenches. The very factors that had made Lytton's works so acceptable to his contemporaries worked against him in the brave new world of democracy and flappers.

Taste, too, became democratic after 1918. The reading public had new requirements. The heavyweight journals which had done so much to mould Victorian opinion, like the *Edinburgh Review* and *Blackwood's*, were doomed to extinction. So was the three volume novel. Only the giants in this genre could still command an audience. Lytton's narrative skills were certainly strong and compelling, but he made few other concessions to his readers. His books are stylistically dense. Long sentences and the use of an extended vocabulary test the reader, even though powerful story lines would otherwise hold his attention. Best-selling novelists of the inter-war years like Sapper, Dornford Yates and G. K. Chesterton offered reading matter that required less effort.

To compound the problem, Lytton's novels are almost overtly didactic. He saw them as vehicles for moral or political instruction. They are often novels with footnotes. The historical works are crammed with archaic words that would have sent an average reader in search of a dictionary. The Newgate series contains passages of criminal slang that must have had the same effect. As for the mystical novels, few readers could have shared Lytton's deep reading of books about the occult. Many of Lytton's works were therefore researched novels, and learning invaded the page insistently. This would not have been congenial to public taste after 1918, which wanted something more immediately accessible. Whether Lytton would have been surprised by his eclipse is an interesting speculation. Throughout his life he had viewed with great suspicion the onset of democracy in all its forms. He had feared a general debasement of values. If the post-1918 world had little regard for him, he would have regarded it as clear evidence of such a decline. He had often reflected that his aristocratic codes had only a limited future.

Even so, the ignoring of his work has certainly gone too far. His books still make claims on our attention. First, precisely because they are so very much of their time, they are strong evidence for what concerned Victorians. The hopes and anxieties of an age are better understood by a reading of Lytton. He was one of its principal spokesmen, and as such Jowett's words spoken at his funeral become intelligible. More important still, many of the novels have a literary merit which has been smothered in the general proscription. If not quite of the calibre of Dickens or George Eliot, Lytton is yet a powerful story-teller with the ability to shock and move. Novels such as *Paul Clifford, Eugene Aram, My Novel* and *The Caxtons,* with their compelling plots and characterisation, would be the obvious basis on which a new appreciation of Lytton's work could be founded. Such a re-evaluation is long overdue.

1

The Upbringing of a Puppy

Edward Bulwer Lytton was born on 25 May 1803, and made a pretence of regretting the fact until he met his future wife. 'I was born, darling, in Baker Street – no. 31 – the reason I suppose, for my great aversion to that street; and yet I am too thankful for my birth now, since you have made my life so happy!'[1] As matters turned out, he would have more to regret after he had met his wife. Throughout his life, his vanity was often irritated by questions about his exact age. In his mind, he was always in his mid twenties:

> I form my own idea of a man's age, and am not disposed to change it at the whim of a chronologist. It is vain to tell me that Voltaire was once young Arouet ... It is vain to tell me that Petrarch died at sixty-eight; I see him only as he first saw Laura – at the golden age of twenty-seven.[2]

The family into which he was born was dysfunctional to an astonishing degree. The history of the Lyttons and the Bulwers contained so many eccentricities and irregularities that he attempted to write about them in a fragment of autobiography. His father, General Earle Bulwer, of Heydon in Norfolk, came from a family that had held land since the Norman Conquest. He had 'a love of command',[3] and 'a self-willed nature, wholly uncultivated by literature'.[4] If asked to read aloud, he would do so as though he had been 'at the head of his regiment'.[5] A rake in his youth, Earle Bulwer turned down an heiress because he objected to the shape of her nose.[6] Instead, he eloped with a schoolmistress, and only considered marriage after her death. Of his three sons, the eldest, William, was his favourite or 'special property'.[7] Heydon would be left to him. In contrast, the youngest, Edward, was 'an object of indifference' that matured into one 'of positive dislike'.[8] According to Lytton, 'my father's aversion to me ... made my mother cling to me the more fondly'.[9] Appropriately, the General died, on 7 July 1807, after being kicked by a horse. Lytton was only four at the time, but his father's disapproval had been marked by the child: 'Peace to thy dust, O Father ... Nor do I think thou wast aware of the unhappiness thou didst occasion.'[10]

His mother, Elizabeth Barbara, was the daughter of Richard Lytton of Knebworth. A scholar and savant, Richard Lytton's unworldliness became a byword for eccentricity. Living in a world of books, he 'muddled' away a large inheritance, leaving only Knebworth itself to his daughter. He was surprised that a play written in Hebrew found few admirers. Equally odd was a decision to marry a sixteen-year old girl with no literary interests whatsoever. This misalliance quickly ended in a separation. Richard Lytton died in 1810, but not before he had dismissed Edward as so incorrigibly stupid that he 'should never know [his] ABC'.[11] His library passed to his daughter, and the young novelist was free to rampage freely among a mountain of books: 'That life in my grandfather's library was but as a vision of Khubla Khan – a glimpse of fountain and pillar, palm-tree and purple, that came and went.'[12] Grandmother Lytton outlived her husband, and settled to a life of whist and gossip in London. Admitting to 'an open aversion' to Edward, she made the second Bulwer boy, Henry, her heir.[13] When she died, in 1818, Lytton bitterly remembered that she had 'not been a good parent to me.'[14]

Caught between a remote, scholarly father and a vacuous mother was their daughter Elizabeth Barbara. She had little feeling for either parent. She was subjected to an educational programme on a Rousseauesque model that involved genuflecting to under-gardeners.[15] Forbidden to marry either of the two men of whom she was genuinely fond, she agreed to marry General Bulwer on 1 June 1798, 'perhaps with a forbidding heart'.[16] Despite the production of three sons, the marriage was not a happy one. In childhood therefore Lytton saw marriage in the separate establishments of his surviving grandparents, and in the misery of his mother coping with a bully for a husband. He was also aware that his father and grandparents disliked him. Little wonder that a recurrent theme in Lytton's novels should be that of parents losing children, or inadvertently encompassing their deaths.[17]

Faced with such hostility, the love of his mother took on a very special quality. If William was his father's darling, and Henry his grandmother's, Edward enjoyed the first loyalty of his mother. It was she who brought him up and organised every aspect of his early life. All available affection came from her. Even more importantly, she was the inspiration that directed him towards literature. In the dedication of *The Siamese Twins*, he acknowledged the fact:

> remembering, that such inclinations I owe to the interest of poetry you were accustomed to excite in me when a child, and to the patient indulgence you accorded to my own boyish imitations; I feel that this volume, containing the only verses I have written with the experience and forethought of manhood, can be dedicated to no one, so well as to yourself.[18]

The collected edition of his works of 1840 was also dedicated to her as his 'first guide', of whom he had a 'thousand memories of unspeakable affection'.[19] Elizabeth Barbara Lytton was without question the greatest influence on Lytton in boyhood and adolescence, and, since his own marriage would be a shambles, her emotional power was enduring. He himself was later to describe his feelings for his mother as 'the strongest affection my life had known'.[20] Visitors to Knebworth noted that the room in which his mother had died had been preserved as a shrine to her memory, with only Lytton himself allowed 'to move the objects within it that she valued'.[21]

Protestations of filial love are the common coin of Victorian novels, but there is a poignancy in Lytton's description of the phenomena that probably relates to his personal circumstances. In *Devereux*, a novel written when relations between Lytton and his mother were turbulent, the hero declaims:

> Yes, how fondly, how tenderly I loved her! What tears – secret but deep – bitter, but reproaching – have I ventured to shed, when I caught her cold and unaffectionate glance. How (unnoticed and uncared for) have I watched, and prayed and wept, without her door, when a transitory sickness or suffering detained her within; and how, when stretched myself upon the feverish bed ... have I counted the moments to her punctilious and brief visit, and started as I caught her footstep, and felt my heart leap within me as she approached ... O mighty and enduring force of early associations, that almost seems, in its unconquerable strength, to partake of an innate prepossession, that binds the son to the mother, who conceived him in her womb.[22]

The depth and profundity of his love and respect for his mother bedevilled Lytton's own marriage, and her death, in 1843, provoked one of the major spiritual crises of his life.

Relations with his brothers were more turbulent. It may be no coincidence that one or two novels deal famously with warring siblings. Indeed, *Devereux* contains a passionate account of fratricidal jealousy and envy.[23] Mrs Lytton's preferences were established early. In a will of 1811 she argued that, since William would have Heyden and Henry his grandmother's property, Knebworth should go to 'poor Edward'. She specifically hoped 'the two elder will treat him as a brother'.[24] At her death, her wishes were unchanged. Edward was left the bulk of his mother's estate, with only small legacies being offered to his brothers. It was not a recipe for family harmony. All the Lyttons had a real capacity for feeling slighted, and all were prepared to voice their grievances in language that stung.

William, in particular, never forgave his mother. He told Edward that he felt, with a sense of melodrama,

> most bitterly the unprovided state in which she has left both myself and my children, and I feel it the more on their account as I never could have anticipated

under any circumstances that I should be left without the means of bringing them up and living myself in the station of life in which I and they were born.[25]

In fact, he cannot have been greatly surprised. For years he had complained how 'anomalous it is, for an eldest son to have less income from family property than the younger'.[26] He convinced himself that only a lack of money had prevented him from making a name for himself in politics or the law. Pandering to the Benjamin of the family had gravely impaired William's own chances in life. He was the victim of 'the most blind partiality and the most gross parental injustice'.[27] When his mother died, he wrote a sixteen-page letter to Edward, setting out a sense of injury that was decades old. Although it talks of Edward's 'kindness' and absolves him of influencing their mother's mind, there is also reference to 'hostility' within the family, which has William as its target.[28]

Edward Lytton's response was to try to reassure his brother: 'Distinctly, unreservedly, and unequivocally from the bottom of my heart, my conscience and my honour, I declare that I have never sought in any way to exercise influence over my mother to your prejudice.'[29] As a result, there was never a formal breaking off of contact between the brothers. In many of the crises that Edward encountered, brother William would offer support and advice, not all of it helpful. But they were never to be close friends. The father's favourite son and the mother's darling had little in common, saw each other infrequently and kept their distance, one from the other. Norfolk and Hertfordshire were thousands of miles apart.

Henry complained, too, but not so loudly and with more good humour. A cheerful roué in his youth, he squandered his grandmother's money with energy and expertise, and then protested about not having any. A brief career in the House of Commons was cut short, and an engagement called off, 'on the score of money'.[30] For most of his life, he was dependent on the salary that a successful diplomatic career could earn. He ended with a peerage, and a certain financial security, but this safe haven of respectability was only reached after a bumpy journey. He insisted that 'the best understanding and closest friendship' existed between himself and his brother Edward, and there is some reason to believe this.[31] Both men had private lives that frequently led one to call for assistance from the other. Supporting Edward in 1858, when he was under attack from 'a fiendish woman', Henry expressed the hope that

> We two somehow or other may jog on sympathetically side by side thro' every transformation, for surely there is something strange which unites us and has always almost in spite of ourselves linked our destinies together. Even at this

instant we seem whirling around in some tornado of doubtful and struggling fortune, which may sink or damage our little barks (or leave them uninjured on a calm sea and sweet moonlight). Voyons! [32]

Henry, usually, felt nothing but goodwill for his brother, but often it could only be expressed in letters. Absences from England were long and meetings few.

Pride of family was a central feature of Lytton's character, but there was little to provide support or encouragement in his own personal experience of it. Grandparents and a father had disliked him. Brothers were distant emotionally, or geographically, or both. Nieces and nephews played little part in the story. Only his mother proved dependable. After her death, ties of family largely vanished. As a result, Lytton became dangerously reliant on the affections of his wife and children. His demands on them would be crippling. For the whole of his life, however, he never believed that any family member, except his mother, had given him the affection that was his due.

As his mother's son, he was brought up at her house, Knebworth, in Hertfordshire. She inherited an estate so encumbered with debt that three sides of the quadrangle that formed the house had to be demolished in 1812. The young Lytton grew up amidst a demolition brought on by debt. From this experience, he developed a parsimony and fear of indebtedness that would colour many aspects of his later life. Even so, Knebworth was a marvellous playground for a budding novelist. It had gothic darknesses and a ghostly 'Hell-hole':

> How could I help writing romances when I had walked, trembling at my own footsteps, through that long gallery, with its ghostly portraits, mused in those tapestry chambers, and peeped, with bristling hair, into the shadowy abyss of 'Hell-hole'? [33]

Knebworth became a psychological resource for Lytton. In an early essay, he talked of the estate as a pastoral idyll, peopled by happy cottagers who were protected by benevolent landlords. There was a gamekeeper, octogenarians who told him 'dim memories of former squires', and even a village idiot.[34] Returning to Knebworth was 'one of the greatest luxuries I know', and 'every year that I visit these scenes, I have more need of their solace'.[35] For the future defender of the Corn Laws, and for the future author of novels like *The Caxtons* and *My Novel*, which tell of village arcadias, an idealised depiction of life at Knebworth was an invaluable model.

There was an element of self-deception in all this. A passion for Knebworth was apparently no bar to his preference for living in London or abroad.

But, for a man who never accepted responsibility easily, there was an unusual and genuine concern for the estate. He spent large amounts of money on the house itself, gothicising its appearance with gargoyles, turrets and panelling. Matthew Arnold, on a visit, found it 'a strange mixture of what is really romantic and interesting, with what is tawdry and gimcracky'.[36] As Lytton told his daughter, all this labour was in honour of his mother:

> She died when we loved each other the most, when we best understood each other ... I turn with a kind of mournful solace to fulfil the duties she bequeathed me – to preserve and honour her memory – to make the home that she loved so much, one monument to her – to hold the property she left me as a solemn trust – and seek to emulate her active usefulness – her thoughtful benevolence.[37]

At Knebworth he played the dutiful squire, 'repairing farms, opening schools etc', quoting Goethe in justification of such activities. 'Nothing keeps the mind more healthy than having something in common with the mass of mankind. Property and politics both help to do this, whereas literature takes me away from it.'[38]

Even so, Knebworth was probably always more important to Lytton as an idea rather than a physical reality. The older he became the more French and German spa towns proved to be more agreeable as places of residence. Torquay performed the same function at the end of his life. While she lived, his daughter Emily seems to have shouldered much of the burden of day to day management. Her letters to her father revert again and again to Knebworth problems, often coupled with appeals for money in order to deal with them. After her death, Lytton managed the estate through agents and from a distance. The house itself was rarely used as the venue for large-scale entertaining. To be invited to Knebworth was a rare event, as Lytton's guests often freely acknowledged. There was no circle of acolytes or friends for whom Knebworth was a salon, on the model of other country houses. Lytton was not the man to value acolytes or to pursue friendships. Without doubt he was sincere in his lauding of the patriarchal values that an estate like Knebworth should enshrine, but he was too solitary and too foreign-living a man to perform them on the spot.

The same point holds with regard to the changes he made in and about the house itself. Medievalism was everywhere. The supposedly harmonious society of the middle ages was to be evoked in wood and stone. Knebworth's walks sprouted heraldic beasts and its staircases were guarded by gryphons. The main hall of the house, hardly baronial in size, was yet set out in the style of Warwick the Kingmaker. Running round the walls are invocations to virtue in a gothic script. Dark corridors inhabited by menacing ghosts sharpened the mood. To create effects of this kind Lytton never stinted money. His usual fear of penury was put on one side. Knebworth became a kind of stage-setting for ideas. The house itself became an argument. Those who were privileged enough to observe Lytton at Knebworth were supposed to see a baronial patriarch at his ease, paternalistically involved with all those to whom the estate owed a living. They were also expected to draw the obvious comparison between this way of living and that of the industrial world where all was self-interest and division. Knebworth was Lytton's creation as an extension of his own personality.

With pride of property went pride of family. Lytton made no secret of his fascination with genealogy and the sheer, comforting antiquity of Lyttons and Bulwers: 'In going through the ... details of family history, I am no doubt indulging my acknowledged infirmity of family pride, and, it may be, exposing myself to the contempt of the philosophical. But I am also faithfully tracing the origin of influences which swayed the character of my mother, and, inherited from her, have had a direct effect upon my own moral nature and literary productions.' [39] In protracted correspondence with the College of Heralds, he established a genealogy that went back to Cadwallader, 'the sainted, last of the kings of Britain', and, for the Lyttons, an escutcheon that had a hundred quarterings.[40] For the future author of historical novels about the Norman Conquest and the Wars of the Roses, it was a source of enormous pride that he was, in a sense, merely writing up his family's history. It was a further consolation that Bulwers and Lyttons in the past should have been so much more genial than his own immediate family.

Ancestor worship took many forms. Lytton fought tenaciously against any railway company which dared to threaten 'hereditary property', and a new line from London to York had to be moved.[41] His brother, William, wryly observed that a romantic history of the house was being fabricated, 'all which traditions have been hid in some old chest where no one ever found them before'.[42] He was proprietorial about the family's name. When Henry Bulwer was also raised to the peerage, Edward insisted that he should not take the title of Lord Bulwer for fear of causing confusion. Such confusion would be 'a perpetual blister on his mind'.[43] In the event, Henry took the title of Dalling. Even the gothicisation of the house was both a political statement and a bow to ancestral voices. Lytton hated smooth-fronted Georgian houses which separated themselves from the rest of the community with the help of unending lawns and high walls.[44] Rather, a house, covered with griffins and martlets testifying to an unchanging antiquity, should stand at the centre of a community. Knebworth was family and a view of community in brick and stone.

Most important of all, a childhood at Knebworth informed his earliest literary tastes. Adolescent poetry, written between 1815 and 1818, concerns heroism at Waterloo, Knebworth itself, fantastical tales of the Orient with heroes 'with sable brows', and, above all, a liking for the medieval.[45] Inevitably, it was Walter Scott and his evocation of the past, not Byron, who inspired. Lytton, at fourteen, wrote:

> To thee, O Scott, I tune my humble lyre,
> Who first inflam'd me with a Poet's fire
>
> ...
>
> Oh, who like thee, can waft the sense away
> In dreams divine? – and who so blind can be
> E'er to prefer that wayward Bard to thee,
> Sublime in what? – in what – Impiety!
> Yes, when oblivion o'er *his* name at last,
> Her endless and imperious shroud shall cast,
> Britons shall marvel with proud enraptur'd eye,
> Thine are the lays that shall not, cannot die.[46]

Lytton's works are full of heroes with names that evoke aristocratic credentials – Maltravers, Mordaunt, Devereux, Falkland. Contemporary critics noted that no Lytton hero would be called Smith. A 'sympathy with a chivalric age, the yearning preferment for the heroic character' seemed to 'have coloured his prose and his poetry'.[47] Lytton was very much the product of his inheritance, distinctively so.

Although he early had a private tutor called Walker, with a 'tawny complexion and a rusty wig', it was his mother who supervised his early education, reading Homer and other poets to him 'with a voice sweet with pathos'.[48] He was slow at numbers but was in every other way a prodigy. At six, he wrote his first love poem, to 'Miss Rose T.' When, in a game of blindman's buff, she inadvertently ran into his arms, he thought 'that the earth was gone from my feet, that we were both snatched up with the heavens'.[49] Hailed as precocious, he quickly developed the idea that he was no ordinary child. With self-awareness went self-importance: 'I never remember a time when I had not a calm and intimate persuasion that one day or other, I was to be somebody, or do something.'[50] But English public schools usually require more modesty in a boy, and it proved impossible to find an establishment that could cope with him. Various schools were tried, but all proved miserable experiences, punctuated by bullying.[51] From a very early age, Lytton was aware that he did not fit easily into normal patterns of education. Male contemporaries of his own social class found him difficult. An enduring sense of separateness developed that influenced his whole life. He would feel apart from his own country and the sort of men who governed it.

There began a wearying pilgrimage from one school to another. In 1812, he lasted two weeks at Dr Ruddock's in Fulham, where 'he cuffed and scratched in return for cuffs and scratches'.[52] Two years at Dr Curtis's school in Shrewsbury was not time enough 'to form a single friendship'. Dr Dempster failed to hold the boy in Brighton in 1814, and so did Dr Hooker of Rottingdean a year later. But at least Hooker understood the problem, informing Mrs Bulwer that:

> Your son is as well, and as strong, and in as good spirits, as any boy in England. But every day convinces me more and more that any Private School (whether mine or any other) will be perfect ruin to him. He has a mind of a very extraordinary compass. He has an emulation rarely found, and an anxiety and attention, and care about his business, very uncommon ... No boy can control him, and there is no comparative emulation in a Private School, or any improvement from other boys.[53]

As if to fulfil Hooker's prophecies, Lytton went on to reject Eton, finding its headmaster wanting at an interview, and to be expelled from the Rev. Burnett's establishment in Homerton for assaulting a master. Communication with masters and other boys was not made easier by the onset of the ear trouble and partial deafness at sixteen that would bedevil his later life.[54] Even so, it was a school record of rare quality.

Not surprisingly, he was left with little respect for the great public schools.[55] The fact that he was to send his own son to Harrow may indicate parental indifference rather than a change of mind. He himself had derived little benefit from English schools, of which he would be a stern critic in later life. The penalty he paid for this view was exclusion from the friendships and clannish loyalties that were formed in such places and carried over into later life. He was a late arrival in the small world of the English governing elite. He first tentatively approached it by going, in the summer of 1821, to a Mr Thomson's near Ramsgate, a cramming establishment with its sights on Cambridge. Once again, he found his fellow pupils uncongenial, asserting that they 'had not seen the world, as I had done, in boudoir and drawing room'.[56] Thomson himself excused this behaviour by admitting that Lytton was 'far beyond his years as to manners, appearance, conduct and literature'.[57] Indeed, he thought him so mature that he recommended Cambridge immediately, because 'the temptations of the University would give *me* no alarm whatsoever on his account'.[58] It is unlikely that compliments such as these endeared Lytton to his fellow pupils.

In the autumn of 1821, Lytton entered Trinity College, Cambridge. Within weeks, he had developed 'a most unreasonable disgust to Trinity', quarrelled with his tutor, and declined to accept the routine of lectures. With relief, he migrated to Trinity Hall, 'a non-reading College', where his first friend was Alexander Cockburn, a future Lord Chief Justice. Though clearly not prepared to accept overmuch academic discipline, Lytton's Cambridge career was hardly dissipated. He read widely on his own terms, and contributed to *Knight's Quarterly Magazine,* a journal which drew on the best student talent.[59] Above all, he established a reputation in the Union Debating Society that carried him to its presidency. He took a degree, though not with Honours, and carried off a university prize for poetry in the subject of 'Sculpture'. His college bills were modest, and he was not the saviour of Cambridge tailors or wine-merchants.[60] He claimed later that, at university he had at last surrounded himself with 'a circle of friends fitted to rouse ... ambition'.[61] If so, few of these friendships survived his student years. Lytton's experience at Cambridge had been reasonably distinguished, level-headed rather than scandalous, but, in terms of moulding a mind, it was much less important than other factors.

Lytton was not really educated in schools and colleges but rather by experiences that he sought out himself. In this sense, he was self-taught. This is hardly surprising in someone who found his fellows so dull and unaccommodating. For a model he looked to Germany, a practice he would continue, in many areas, for the whole of his life. The work of Goethe and Schiller had established the vital importance of the *Wanderjahr*. A would-be artist must undertake physical journeys that are also experiences in spiritual self-discovery. All future action and thought should draw heavily on these experiences. Through accident and adventure, the writer discovers his own value and limitations. This theme was to be rehearsed again and again in Lytton's novels, and in this he was the fellow of a number of Victorian novelists.[62]

Two such journeys of introspection were undertaken by Lytton himself, and their effects were long lasting. In 1819 he met a girl known only as Lucy on a riverbank in Ealing. For a few, brief weeks they were together, until an irate father removed his daughter and married her off to someone else. It was a first experience of love and a defining moment: 'I began the world at sixteen – five years before any one else ... J'ai vécu beaucoup en peu d'années et c'est le chemin des passions qui m'a conduit.'[63] He now 'longed for someone to love; I cared not whom'.[64] By 1824, Lucy was dead. When he visited her grave in Ullswater, Lytton was near to prostration. He later alleged that it was in the Lake District that he determined to be a writer. Certainly, he produced a poem called *The Tale of a Dreamer*. Although he

claimed that it was in no sense autobiographical, its themes narrowly
reflected his recent sense of loss:

> My childhood scarce had glided into Youth
> When my soul felt its secret depths – and drew
> The forms of fancy into life and truth; –
> The thousand dreams of beauty which would bless
> My musing moments, felt the spell, and grew
> Into one mortal mould of loveliness
>
> . . .
>
> Baffled and bleeding, I beheld thee born
> Away, I know not whence – but *I* was there –
> The soft stream roll'd beside me murmuring –
> And on my hot brow breath'd the air of spring –
> But the dim sense was blinded by despair,
> And I saw nought before me, like a pall
> Rayless and black spread Earth – the only light
> Which the world had for me was gone – and all
> Gloom'd in my soul, like tempests thron'd in night.[65]

Thereafter, women should always approximate to the girl on the riverbank.
When they rarely did so, Lytton was repelled. His son noted that his father
was always drawn to desolate women in need of protection. Certainly his
novels are full of childlike heroines, sometimes of such a rare purity that
they become intermediaries between this world and that of the spirits. Some
critics have seen his novels *Alice* and *Ernest Maltravers* as a working out of
the Ealing story.[66] Quite definitely, Lytton's last novel, *Kenelm Chillingly*,
was a final exorcism of an experience that had determined much of his
emotional life. The heroine, Lily Mordaunt, has 'the naiveté of a child six
years old', and is nicknamed 'Fairy'. By a small river, she meets Chillingly,
who, after Cambridge, is journeying to find 'the innermost self'. Lily,
however, is betrothed to her guardian – and dies virginally just before her
marriage. The Lytton family recorded the cost of this writing to its author:
'On the day when the chapter describing Lily's death was written, the man
of seventy was so shaken with the memory of the emotion of the boy of
sixteen, that he was seen by his son walking hurriedly out of his room in
complete self-forgetfulness, with tears streaming down his face.'[67] Quite
possibly, Lytton's disastrous emotional life was determined by an ideal of
pure womanhood branded on his mind at sixteen and never after realised.

A second journey of self-discovery, in the more literal sense, was a long
walking tour of the north of England and Scotland, undertaken alone in
1824. It proved to be full of incident. In the Lake District, he was nearly

murdered by the owner of a remote cottage in which he had sought shelter.
The experience was rehearsed in *Ernest Maltravers*. In Scotland, he narrowly
avoided a brutal assault on a lonely road, which is again used in the same
novel.[68] Allegedly, these encounters excited an interest in the criminal that
would shortly lead him to go in disguise into the 'thieves quarter' of London.
Research undertaken here allowed him to write with authority about the
criminal mind in novels like *Paul Clifford*, and, proudly, to cram his books
with the authentic *argot* of an underworld, where a magistrate was a 'cuffin'
and a gallows a 'twisting crap'. He also spent five or six days in a gypsy
encampment, as does Clarence Linden in *The Disowned*.[69] Here, his fortune
was told by a girl. Her prophecies were so to the point that Lytton recorded
them carefully. She said he would never know want; that he would be the
victim of scandal and slander; that his best friends and worst enemies would
be women; and that 'you'll hunger for love all your life, and you will have
much of it; but less satisfaction than sorrow'.[70] As a blueprint for Lytton's
life, the prophecy was impeccable. Little wonder that he would retain an
interest in clairvoyance for the rest of his life.

These forays into love and self-reliance left indelible impressions. Again
and again, in novels, he tried to work out their significance and implications.
He came back to them in the very last months of his life. As educative
experiences, they were distinctive and not generally shared by contemporaries of his social class. They confirmed a sense of separateness. With real
excitement and interest, he had brushed up against the world of the criminal
and the poor, about whom he would soon write with compassion. He had
also come to believe in a world beyond the mere material that could be
made accessible to the artist, certainly by love, possibly by necromancy. It
was this world that should enfold the creative mind. As he explored this
theme, pragmatic English souls took fright. To label someone eccentric or
exotic is the way in which the English marginalise views they do not wish
to hear. Lytton was awarded such labels.

On this pilgrimage Lytton was protected by guardian angels. A succession
of middle-aged women were recruited to guide him through a confusing
jumble of feelings and sensibilities. The first of these *amies particulières* was
Mary Porter, the widow of the Bishop of Cloyne. In 1820–21, letters passed
between the two of them which discussed the questions of the boy joining
the army, the wisdom or unwisdom of seeking Whig patronage, and the
nature of good writing.[71] Mary was allowed to scold as well as encourage:
'leave off flattery, and let sincerity for the future be your motto – I fear
you have a bad opinion of women, and think they are fond of flattery'.[72]
In 1825 and 1826 Lytton spent long periods in Paris and Versailles, preparing
Weeds and Wildflowers for publication, recasting *Falkland* and polishing

Pelham. Here he was taken up by Lady Cunningham-Fairlie, who earned his gratitude by introducing him into the best social circles and, more importantly, by taking him seriously:

> She writes beautiful poetry almost impromptu, draws charming caricatures, possesses a laugh for whatever is ridiculous, but never loses a smile for what is good. Placed in very peculiar situations, she has passed through each with a grace and credit which are her best eulogium. If she possesses one quality higher than intellect, it is her kindness of heart.[73]

He was in need of her ministrations. His stay in Paris was eventful. He became so involved with a Catholic girl that he felt honour bound to propose. His mother intervened to prevent such quixotic behaviour.[74] He had doubts about the quality of his writing and tried to work them out in solitude. In his letters to his new friend therefore, he has taken full, Romantic colouring. At twenty-two or three, he is a poet already tired of the world, mortally wounded in love, and destined for an early grave:

> Love – that of the soul, not of the senses – is dead to me for ever ... Like the burnt child, we shrink from the flame that has scorched us. And, when I perceive in myself the growth of any passion that promises to be real, I do not rest till I have destroyed it. Once only, of late, I have been in danger. But to the young and pure heart which has never awakened from the repose of its innocence, that heart would indeed have been an unworthy offering which has survived its best emotions, and sacrificed the freshness of youth above a grave in which passion has buried all that could save it from the premature satiety of age.[75]

He was 'quivering from the strain of an intense struggle' and unfit for any society.[76] Like Mrs Porter, Lady Cunningham-Fairlie countered with humour and commonsense, asking him to come out of this 'Diogenes mood', admitting that 'you will love again, and be very vexed at yourself for it'.[77] Joking, however, is not always well taken by young men in search of attention. When she dubbed him a 'Childe Harold', Lytton resented this Byronic reference. For him Byron was 'a coxcomb and a bit of a coward, very unamiable, very mean, very tyrannical, and in most matters very ignorant'.[78] Worse, he had already covered successfully ground that Lytton was only beginning to tread.

Byron was Lytton's competitor, too, in a more immediate sense. The most important confidante in Lytton's early life was none other than Lady Caroline Lamb, whose scandalous affair with Byron still echoed through the London salons, in spiteful quips and self-justificatory novels. Lady Caroline was universally regarded as unstable and dangerous. Lytton, by allowing her into his life, was touching pitch. She was the wife of Lord Melbourne, and their home at Brocket Hall was only a few miles from

Knebworth. Meetings between the two families were inevitable. When he was still a boy, she painted his portrait sitting solitary on a rock. It carried the subscription 'seul sur la terre'. An association sprang up between the two that was so important to Lytton that he tried to define it in an unpublished novel, called, 'Lionel Hastings', written in the 1840s.[79] At fifteen, hearing of an act of kindness towards an injured man at a race meeting, he penned *To Lady C.L.*:

> Thy guardian angel hov'ring near,
> Soar'd upwards with that deed of thine,
> And as he dropt the applauding tear,
> Wrote down the name of C ...[80]

Unfortunately, Caroline Lamb's good works could very easily turn into malign, and meddling interference in other people's lives.

Through Lytton's years at Cambridge and beyond there was no break in the correspondence and visiting between the two houses. Melbourne genuinely admired a young literary talent. Caroline Lamb flattered his verses, and filled him with her own prejudices against Byron and English society generally. She became his 'unique Caroline', a 'Daughter of Feeling, Queen of Love'.[81] Later in life, he described their relationship as 'a very intimate friendship',[82] which never developed beyond 'a Platonic romance'. Whether they were actually lovers is unknown, although it must be a possibility given Lady Caroline's enjoyment in seducing young men. There was certainly enough doubt in the matter to worry Mrs Bulwer, who seems to have expressed concern. In 1825 Lytton wrote to his mother to assure her that all communication with Brocket has been broken off. He admitted that he had fallen in love, 'when I saw how acceptable it would be'. It had been an infatuation that 'had little to do with the heart but a great deal with the imagination'. Now, he decided that she was 'fond of coquetry', and she took pleasure at parading rivals in front of him, and snubbing him at dances.[83] He was in fact merely one of a number of 'silly boys' who had become entangled with her.[84]

Disengagement from Caroline Lamb was an art in itself, and one that Lytton never mastered. No sooner did someone try to break free than she was all dependence and supplication. Entering her final illness in 1826, she begged him successfully to re-establish communication: 'Pray write to me as you then did even although your opinion of me and affection, boyish affection be utterly changed – your letters were beautiful and soothing.'[85] The appeal had its effect. Visits were resumed, but he found her 'fallen and degraded from all the early might have been'.[86] After her death, he reflected that 'the larger part of the World are no better than Husseys'.[87] Such philosophy would suggest a sense of calm and a little perspective. Even so, in 1829 he took the precaution of burning her letters.[88] This was an unusual act for a man whose instinct was quite clearly to preserve everything. They evidently contained points of embarrassment that he did not wish to be widely known. Everything is thereby reduced to speculation. She left him a lock of Byron's hair.

Mere death, however, was not enough to curtail her influence. Three years after her passing, Lytton was still using her references to ingratiate himself with publishers.[89] On at least three occasions he tried to exorcise her ghost in novels and short stories. In addition to *Lionel Hastings*, there were the characters of Lady Melton in *De Lindsay* and Lady Bellenden in *Greville*.[90] It may also not be coincidence that in *Timon* there is a character called Calantha, a name favoured by Caroline Lamb, who dies after being jilted. If these attributions are correct, the personality of Caroline Lamb was one to which Lytton was drawn again and again. His final judgement of her, written in 1866, was generous: 'She was very kind to me in my young days. Her natural talents were remarkable and her conversation very entertaining.'[91] Memory had smoothed away the more difficult moments.

In fact, Lady Caroline's influence was almost entirely malign. A young man, who, for all sorts of reasons, found himself at odds with mainstream society, was naturally attractive to a woman who saw herself as a victim of that same society. She encouraged his feeling of separateness. Encouraged by her, he began to frequent a literary demi-monde that clustered together in second-rate salons. It was a world of amateur poets like Elizabeth Spence, and people like Laetitia Landon, Benjamin Disraeli and Laman Blanchard, who, for reasons political, religious or sexual, were not accepted in the best society.[92] Caroline Lamb, tainted by scandal, moved among those with other stigmas. Lytton seems to have followed her. By right of birth and talent, he could easily have aspired to move in more orthodox circles. For some reason he chose other friends. It was in these circles that he was to meet Rosina Wheeler, with whom he would enter into an eviscerating marriage.

Late in life, Rosina remembered that Caroline Lamb had tried to warn her about the Lyttons, with the words, 'Don't let Edward Bulwer hunt you down – they are a bad set'.[93] But the reality had been very different. Rosina had become a protégée of Lady Caroline and was a familiar figure within the Lamb family circle.[94] They shared advanced views about the rights of women and had ambitions to be successful in literature. With Lady Caroline's connivance, Rosina and Edward often found each other in the same company. She would 'quite pine' for Rosina's company at Brocket, and then invite the family from Knebworth as well.[95] It can hardly be a coincidence that Edward Lytton proposed and was accepted in the grounds of Brocket. Apparently there was moonlight on the night in question. So began a relationship that would be calamitous for both parties and their dependents. Caroline Lamb brought devastation to her own and other people's lives. The Lyttons could be included among their number.

Lytton's fragment of autobiography ends just before his marriage in 1827. Quite rightly, he regarded that event as a turning point in his life, after which nothing was quite the same. It is a convenient moment to take stock, and to elucidate the impact of his *Wanderjahren*. Taking his own writings literally, Lytton at twenty-four was a world-weary poet, sated, expecting nothing more of the world. When he published his collection *Weeds and Wildflowers* in 1826, its frontispiece was a woodcut showing a brave little ship manoeuvring between rocks. It is a mixture of verse, much of it satirical, and aphorisms written with one eye-brow raised. Among the latter may be found such statements as: 'With women, love is often nothing but the pride they feel at being loved'; 'It is from acquaintance with vice – not virtue – that we gain experience. Knowledge of the world is the Knowledge of its sins'; and 'Vanity only sins when it hurts the vanity of others'. There was also a satiric sketch called 'Almacks' that, being a young man's calling of London society to account, was rightly branded pert. At seventeen, he affected to be bored with London:

> I was in town the greatest part of last Christmas, and found it very dull, as it is so empty. But when I say empty, I speak comparatively, since the immense numbers of all ranks which populate London, that 'Beast with many heads', are very slightingly considered and spoken of when I say the town is empty ... I intend to have my letters published after my death, like every other great man.[96]

In 1824 he wrote an essay called *Hades*, in which half the population of Hell was condemned for eternity to go to parties given by the other half.[97] As for Paris, it was 'a peopled waste'.[98]

The only escape from this tedium was death, and Lytton endlessly predicted an early demise. He warned Rosina, during their courtship that he had to be still from time to time 'to listen to the deadly pulsation of my heart'.[99] He convinced himself that his life to date had been a complete failure. Like John Ardworth in *Lucretia*, he had established a name for himself in the Cambridge Union, but had then squandered his talents. Melodramatically, he apologised to his mother for letting her down, and wished her joy of her other sons:

> For me thou never may'st behold
> The fate thy fancy once foresaw,

When Learning prais'd – and Friends foretold
The fame a Mother lov'd to draw.
But thou shal'st glad thee when the voice
Of Honour greets thine other sons,
And I for them shall still rejoice
At fame my sicklier Spirit shuns.

   ...

For darkly, like a withered tree
Which hangs along the ebbing tide,
That blighted Spirit droops to see
The waves of life so vaguely glide:
And o'er these waves like faded leaves
The germs of earlier promise stray,
And every reckless wave which heaves,
But wafts some lingering leaf away.[100]

His mother had every right to criticise and cajole, and the truth was that he believed his life to be over at twenty-four. He had degenerated into a dabbler, starting books and never finishing them.[101]

Death would be a comforting release from artistic failure, but Lytton was not in a mood to be comforted. To stoke up the gloom, he denied all ideas of heaven. In conversation with a certain Abbé Kinsala in Paris, he had been much impressed with the claims of Christian theology, but could not move beyond a belief in 'an Eternal – all perfect – provident Creator'.[102] He detested religious enthusiasm throughout his life, and reacted angrily to the idea that persecution was justifiable on religious grounds.[103] He admired non-believers like Hume and Helvétius, to whom he credited all the advances in the philosophy of his day.[104] In literature, he could be caustic at the expense of revealed religion,[105] and his sympathetic depiction of an atheist in *Devereux* was enough to unsettle the belief of George Eliot.[106] There was no hope beyond the grave, or indeed anywhere:

> There where I lie I shall moulder and mingle with the clay which surrounds me. I have no hope for that mind which seems to me inseparable with the body, alike in its life and in its decay. Darker than all, I have no hope that the grave will unite me to those from whom I shall be torn.[107]

Here was the complete picture of the doomed artist, talent unrealised, susceptibilities bruised and mangled. Damned in this world, he had no hope of the next. It was a role that Lytton played well. But it was of course a sham. In presenting himself to the world, he called on the theatrical arts willingly. He was to be playwright as well as novelist. He affected to dislike the Byronic tradition but was one of its chief exponents.

In fact, he was very clear about his own talents, and bursting with the ambition to display them. He had trained hard for future reputation. There is a notebook, inscribed 'Poetical Attempts by E. G. Bulwer', which runs to eighty pages of poetry written before the age of seventeen. He saw himself as an artist of real talent in a world of mere 'Poetlings'.[108] As such, publication could not come too soon. When the first collection of poems appeared under the title *Ismael* in 1820, he hoped it would give him an entrée into 'the first literary society',[109] and this was not the only calculation based on the book's appearance. Lytton argued that, if it was a success, it would be a foundation on which a full literary career could be built; if a failure, then youth could excuse it:

> It will be more advantageous for me to publish it now, as my extreme youth would be my passport, as the world, which generally requires some external recommendation to take up a book, would be far more anxious to see poems ... written by one at so early a period.[110]

Friends were directed to bookshops where the new volume could be obtained, and given instructions on what to ask for.[111]

Authors looking for publication and recognition needed patrons in the right places, and Lytton was happy to play this game. He became a tufthunter. *Ismael* was dedicated to the Whig savant, Dr Samuel Parr, not because Parr had been a friend of his grandfather, but because he might be able to effect an invitation to the home of Lord Holland, where books were puffed and young writers encouraged to show off. While asserting that 'my Rank in Life precludes any sinister view of Patronage or Interest', he was desperate to meet Holland, 'that nobleman whose attachment to his country has so justly and so generally procured him that appellation'.[112] Parr encouraged the young man, expressing 'astonishment at your intellectual powers',[113] but it seems that Lytton only entered the sanctum of Holland House in 1823 through the good offices of Macaulay.[114] As a young man, and throughout his life, he claimed total independence of thought and action, but, in practice, particularly in the early years, was as ruthless at manipulating patronage possibilities as any new writer had to be.

On returning from Paris in 1826, he took the most obvious route to notoriety by writing something shocking. *Falkland* in 1827 and *Pelham* in 1828 set London society by the ears. The first concerned a love affair between a young man and an older, married woman who agrees to elope with him. She is only saved from irreparable scandal by bursting blood vessels and conveniently dying. The second was denounced as a piece of foppish inconsequence, whose only long-term impact was to encase men

ISMAEL;

AN ORIENTAL TALE.

WITH

𝕺𝖙𝖍𝖊𝖗 𝕻𝖔𝖊𝖒𝖘.

BY

EDWARD GEORGE LYTTON BULWER.

Written between
The Age of Thirteen and Fifteen.

" Scribimus indocti doctique poëmata passim."

Hor. 2 Ep. 1.

LONDON:

PRINTED FOR J. HATCHARD AND SON,

No. 187, PICCADILLY.

1820.

Title page of the first edition of *Ismael* (1820).

in black dinner jackets of an evening for ever after. Both books seemed to have heroes who were contemptuous of the usual moral constraints. The outcry was loud and sustained. It established Lytton's name. He vigorously denied that there was anything autobiographical in these first novels, claiming that he had 'not drawn a person whom I should be flattered to resemble',[115] but he took to signing private letters as 'Falkland Puppy'.[116] Ten years later, he was prepared to confess that the writing of *Falkland* in particular had been personally cathartic: 'I had confessed my sins and was absolved. I could return to real life and its wholesome objects.'[117] Like Lytton, Falkland, before going to university, loves deeply and hopelessly a woman who is snatched away by circumstance and death.[118] It is the Lucy theme, the girl by the river bank, once more.

Contemporaries had no hesitation in equating the author of these books with the loosely-moralled young heroes depicted in them. Lytton thereby became an object of fascination in his own right. Salons and drawing-rooms opened their doors a little wider. But his mother was appalled:

> I take the opportunity this letter affords of saying how much I conceive it to be a matter of regret that you do not employ the talents with which you are gifted to a more noble and useful purpose than devoting them to such writing.

She saw it as an attack on Christianity itself, a kind of blasphemy. Her letter ended, 'Child, this is unworthy of you'.[119] One of Rosina Wheeler's closest friends was equally aghast at 'that horrid *Falkland*, which may be clever in point of style, but shocked us all, for the bad sentiments it contained, and infamous morals ... Alas! thought I, is this the man who is to guide poor Rosina, and counteract all the faults of her education?'[120] Clearly there was a price to be paid for bursting upon the literary scene as a supposed immoralist. Later, Lytton withdrew *Falkland* from publication, having convinced himself that it could indeed have a harmful effect on its readers. But in 1827–28, the *succès de scandale* was relished.

In answering his mother, Lytton denied that the moral basis of his writing was wobbly. Rather, 'the subject of the book is the progress and severe punishment of an unlawful passion'.[121] Ingenuously, he portrayed himself as the injured party:

> I must own that I am at a loss to conceive how by any possible ingenuity a novel in which vice is never once defended, and even the lover never attempted to do so, when it is immediately and sweepingly punished, I am at a loss to conceive how, by any possible ingenuity that novel can be called bad.[122]

To set himself up as the misunderstood writer at war with an uncomprehending world was to put a further romantic gloss on his own personality.

This would be a pose that he would cultivate and embellish in later life to great effect. In reality, he was quite unmoved by waves of public indignation. Speaking of *Falkland*, he told Lady Cunningham-Fairlie that 'the religionists and pseudo-moralists are furious with it. N'importe!' [123] To his future wife, he frankly admitted that, if readers could be drawn to these novels by any means, they might go on to investigate his poetry, which at this stage he probably regarded as more important:

> Now if *Falkland* succeeds at all, it will do so sufficiently to obtain a reading for *Poems*, and perhaps it may from its singularity gain that reading for itself which its *stupidity* might otherwise deprive it of ... I own I am exceedingly disappointed, now that I have finished it, with my attempt. Literally and seriously, it falls very very far short of the plan I had intended to execute.[124]

In other words, *Pelham* and *Falkland* were not seen as major works in themselves, but merely as devices to force himself upon the attention of the great world.

By 1827 Edward Lytton had crafted a name and reputation for himself. He was promising and talented, but also affected and unpleasantly cynical beyond his years. His upbringing and education had been a little irregular; he now moved in a literary demi-monde, overdressed, expressing more world-weariness than is common in a twenty-four year old. He had acquired a certain fame, but it was mildly tainted with doubts about its moral basis. Lytton could never be described as sound, and therefore he was to be noted but kept at a distance. It was all a little odd and ambiguous. It became a great deal more so when he united his fortunes with those of Rosina Wheeler.

2

Rosina

An early essay entitled *The True Ordeal of Love* allowed Lytton to be fashionably cynical at the expense of matrimony. Two lovers, Adolphe and Celeste, adore each other as long as parental opposition forbids their union: 'The spirit of contradiction is prodigiously strong in its effects.' After attempting suicide, the lovers at last receive permission to marry, and 'love each other so entirely that it lasted several months'. Then, 'as they had nothing to do but to look at those faces they had thought so handsome, so it was difficult not to yawn'.[1] Experience of the merciless hunting down of prospective sons- and daughters-in-law in the London marriage market stripped away any remaining sentimentality about the institution:

> This boon and bolus of the wife,
> Is England's most peculiar evil,
> Where loss of happiness for life
> Rewards the man who dares be civil!
> Where all most courteous and polite
> To such a nice excess we carry,
> That if you are not rude tonight –
> By Jove! Tomorrow – *you must marry*!
> Oh Hymen, hear thy suppliant – send
> A wife, I pray thee to – my friend.[2]

Those lines were penned three years after his own marriage, which had not been a matter of arrangement but, allegedly, a love match.

In his more serious writing on marriage, there is a disturbing schizophrenia. Lytton could never decide what sort of woman made the ideal wife. Sometimes, he insisted that she should be the intellectual equal of her husband, even if this should be construed as too 'masculine'. The hero of *The Caxtons* wanted a wife 'who can echo all the thoughts that are noblest in man'.[3] Goldophin, too, wanted 'neither a singing animal, nor a drawing animal, nor a dancing animal; he wants a talking animal'.[4] Lytton loathed Rousseau's heroines for being too good, each one a 'schoolmistress, always correcting, advising, encouraging and doing right'.[5] He repeatedly claimed that French and German women were superior to the English, because they

were not afraid of the intellect. On the other hand, many critics have
observed that Lytton heroines are often childlike, ethereal, and not much
given to rational discussion. They live on a plane of enhanced spirituality.
Alice Darvil in *Alice* has 'almost the expression of an idiot', while Fanny
in *Night and Morning* could not uncharitably be thought retarded. They
are creatures of 'a high and religious sentiment that vibrated more exquisitely
to the subtle mysteries of creation'. Marriage should be 'two immortalities,
divested of clay and ashes'.[6] In courtship, Edward and Rosina called each
other Puppy and Poodle, and used a baby language that, for example,
substituted 'oo' for 'you'. It seemed that what Lytton looked for in a wife
was an intellectual equal, a puffer of his own talents, an innocent, and a
guide to the realms of the spirit. Such people are hard to find.

More worryingly still, Lytton was aware that the act of falling in love was
less an appreciation of another person than the meeting of an inner need.
It is the supreme selfishness. Responding to the need, spouses are moulded
to a preconceived pattern. Inevitably, expectations are never realised, and
the result is misery. This rather Proustian theme is set out in *Devereux*:

> Nature places us alone in this inhospitable world, and no heart is cast in a similar
> mould to that which we bear written in us. We pine for sympathy, we make to
> ourselves a creation of ideal beauties, in which we expect to find it – but the
> creation has no reality – it is the mind's phantasma which the mind adores –
> and it is because the phantasma can have no actual being that the mind despairs.
> Throughout life, from the cradle to the grave, it is no real or living thing which
> we demand; it is the realisation of the idea we have formed within us, and which,
> as we are not gods, we can never call into existence. We are enamoured of the
> statue we ourselves have graven.[7]

Love was merely 'the *besoin d'être aimé*'.[8] Setting up impossible demands,
it was bound to prove futile. Nothing in the recent history of the Bulwer
and Lytton families would lead him to question this judgement. Brutally
and melodramatically, it would be played out once again in his own marriage.

Lytton probably met Rosina Wheeler in April 1826,[9] in the drawing-room
of a bluestocking called Miss Benger. The curiosity of each for the other
was immediately aroused. Lytton initiated enquiries about the Wheeler
family,[10] prompted ironically by his mother's comments on Rosina's
beauty, and by his own amusement at her talents as a mimic. Rosina, for
her part, made a point of calling on Mrs Bulwer next day, where she was
struck by how 'odd' her new acquaintances were. In particular, she began
to parody idiosyncrasies in Mrs Bulwer's voice patterns, in which Edward
became 'Eddard', vastly 'vaustly', and badinage 'bodinage'.[11] As it turned
out, these were the first shots fired in a lifelong battle between the two
women.

The best description of the Wheeler family comes in a fragment of autobiography, written by Rosina herself, which begins, 'The first mistake I made was being born at all ... I did not want to come into the world, neither did it appear that I was wanted in it.' [12] Between herself and her father there was only loathing. She was brought up by her mother in Caen and by a maternal uncle, Sir John Doyle, who was Governor of Guernsey. Her father refused to support his family either financially or emotionally. Mrs Wheeler had a very distinctive personality, espousing radical and feminist views far in advance of her contemporaries. Rosina inherited many of these opinions, but even she described her mother as 'strongly tainted by the ... poison of Mrs Wollstonecraft's book',[13] the *Vindication of the Rights of Women*. Dining with her was an alarming experience for Disraeli: 'Mrs Wheeler was there; not pleasant, something between Jeremy Bentham and Meg Merrilies, very clever, but awfully revolutionary. She poured forth all her systems upon my novitiate ear, and while she advocated the rights of woman, Bulwer abused system-mongers and the sex, and Rosina played with her dog.' [14] Rosina later claimed that she had been 'dragged up' by her mother, who in fact had had 'a great dislike of children'.[15] If so, this pattern would be repeated in her own lifetime. To survive, she admitted that 'how to deceive, outwit, and tell the cleverest falsehood, was one of the earliest things she had turned her thoughts and mind to'.[16] Dark stories surrounded her upbringing, including one which had her shamelessly pursuing an army officer from England to Ireland. Not surprisingly perhaps, she never possessed a Bible until she was twenty.

Some contemporaries thought that the only explanation for this exotic family history was that a strain of insanity ran through the family. Lytton himself came to think so. It became clear to him that 'the only excuse for Mrs Wheeler was that she was mad'. As for Mr Wheeler, he had been 'made dangerously mad by consistent drinking' and had once tried to strangle his daughter.[17] All of them were quick to take offence, and to feel injury where none had been intended. With manic single-mindedness, they went to law against supposed enemies and against each other. Wheeler family history was, in this respect, a chronicle of lawyers taken up, employed, and then dismissed for alleged incompetence or treachery.[18] There were moments when Rosina was at war with the whole family. She then imposed herself upon a Miss Greene in Ireland. This lady would play a central role in the lives of the Lyttons, but she was right to have misgivings about being involved with such unpredictable characters. At the beginning, she was 'far from anxious' for their acquaintance.[19]

Unorthodox upbringings reinforced the strange strain of theatricality in the personalities of both Edward and Rosina. Their courtship was unreal.

Rather, Lytton simply directed a play. He cast himself in the role as the poet who needed love for personal fulfilment. A poem of 1826 contains the lines,

> In our young days, ere yet our hearts have learned
> To blunt the feelings there be none to share
> Who, sickening in the cold world hath not sigh'd
> For some divine love? – in the deep night
> Who hath not moulded from the empty air
> A voice of music, and a shape of light? [20]

He and Rosina were both orphans, tragic children in the eye of a storm: 'We are alone in the world, let us cling to one another for support. The links and affections which belong to others, and seem from your birth to have been denied to *you* – from *me*, the dearest have been severed by death. All things, our very solitude and desolation among the world, should make us shrink more utterly into ourselves.' [21] Rosina would 'preserve' him against the world and the onset of misanthropy. In return, he would be her 'consoler from the remembrance of the past'.[22] In *O'Neill*, published in 1827 and dedicated to Rosina, Lytton told the tale of a hero who, in Ireland, finds redemption in the love of a pure woman. It was a tribute to Rosina's 'pure and warm and generous affections'.[23]

Assigning roles is not a sensible arrangement on which to build a marriage. To demand that a future wife should behave in a certain way is to invite disappointment. Indeed, Lytton's love letters are so full of personal pronouns that it seems possible to question whether he regarded marriage as involving two people at all, or as merely an extension of self:

> Now a new soul has entered within me. I have come forth, like the Grecian, from the charms of an enchantress into the glory and freshness of a new youth. I have an object alike for my feelings and my aspirations; and as men in old times chose a wilderness to erect an altar for their gods, so the sterility and desert of my heart have become at once consecrated by the altar which I have erected to you. But I recall myself from these flights. No wonder that I wander when I turn to dream over my recollections of you.[24]

In the letter to Lady Cunningham-Fairlie in which he announced his marriage, he acknowledged his fiancée to be clever, good and beautiful, but ended by describing himself as 'wretched'.[25] Doubt and anguish, the throwing of oneself against fate, were attractive emotions to someone playing the poet. It was a game in which Rosina was happy to participate.

Artificiality was everywhere. Brocket, where the marriage of Lord Melbourne and Lady Caroline Lamb had made the lives of both participants wretched for twenty years, was transformed into an Eden of 'moonlight' and 'calm', an idealised setting for professions of love.[26] Responsibility for the marriage was thrown upon fate and the workings of astrology, to which he was 'addicted'.[27] His 'adored Rose' was brought up to date with what gypsies had foretold. In this context, it is not surprising that, during the courtship, he wrote a poem entitled *The Destinies*, which warned 'maidens' of 'the voice that aye deceiveth'.[28] The success or failure of the marriage would not be the fault of husband or wife. Both would be simply accepting their fate, pitiless as it might be. Asking them to accept moral responsibility for their own choices was not in question.

Immaturity was carried over into language. Love letters may be allowed a little hyperbole, but Lytton's are outstanding in this respect. Rosina became 'my Rose of Roses', 'the Darling of Delight', the 'Quintessence of Darlingry'.[29] Both adored dogs so much that unkind contemporaries argued that they preferred them to their own children, and so he became 'Pups' or 'Puppy' and she 'Poodle'. Dinner guests were encouraged to bring their pets with them.[30] The childish nature of their relationship was confirmed by a delight in using infantile language. In 1826, for example, signing himself 'Zoo own Puppy', Lytton told Rosina that 'if oo does not love me, and feels that me cannot make oo happy, why me will leave oo and try to live as I have lived, wretched and isolated, *but alone*'.[31] Taken together, the Edward and Rosina courtship was the product of two overactive imaginations, a mere playing with emotions. That the marriage would be a catastrophe was not inevitable, but even in 1827 people in their immediate circle doubted if there was any solid basis to it.

There was trouble from the beginning.[32] Letters which lauded 'her genius for kissing' were intermingled with others that expressed doubt:

> Till very lately I always hoped that I *could* make you happy – if now, dearest, I doubt it, it is both from a knowledge of my own faults and a discovery, I will not say of a *fault* in you, but of a proud and resentful principle in your mind, which does in my opinion detract from its perfection.[33]

The same letter moved easily on to a lecturing, or a disciplining, of an actress strangely determined to play a role in her own way: 'No attachment can be permanent where the woman does not make greater concessions than the man, and does not even feel that those concessions are the most real sources of pride.'[34] He objected to 'a sarcastic positive "I'll set-you-right" sort of way, which militates strongly against the *amour propre*, tho' not the proper love, of all Masculine Puppies of every breed whatsoever'.[35] Such views could hardly be exceptional in Victorian England, but they were hardly going to be acceptable to a woman brought up with very different expectations. Peppering these lectures with endearments in baby-language was little compensation, and Rosina, shortly before the marriage, speculated about whether he would in fact come to hate her. This brought a vigorous denial. For Edward, 'she was the last anchor which attaches me to existence'. He loved 'to kiss the paper consecrated by your hand – can these signs of love ever turn to hatred?'[36] In the event, hatred would prove the more enduring. A troubled courtship, full of melodrama, was not a good omen for the future.

All might still have been well, if no other factors had been involved, but this was not the case. Lytton's mother was a major figure in the courtship. During its whole length, from April 1826 to August 1827, her son kept her fully informed of his feelings. She was made completely aware of his extraordinary mood-swings, from elation to doubt, from professions of filial piety to threats of ostracism. In response, his mother quickly formed an unshakeable view that Rosina was a human calamity. She expressed concern about her 'forlorn childhood and unguided girlhood',[37] which had blighted her reputation irrevocably. She was equally sure that marriage to such a woman would destroy her son's chances of a successful career in politics or literature. As Lytton tried to explain to Rosina, 'I am my mother's favourite son. I was brought up by her ... Her affection makes her desire that I should be happy, but her pride that I should find happiness in the distinctions of the world.'[38] To be told that you were an obstacle to advancement was not very flattering to Rosina, but it was a point that had to be explained, for his mother's views mattered. He was not only emotionally but also financially dependent on her.

In 1827 Lytton had a personal income of £200 p.a. and Rosina perhaps £80. Everything else came from his mother. It was inconceivable that two people of their tastes could live on such an income. If Mrs Bulwer could not be brought round, then all thoughts of marriage had to be abandoned: 'Upon my honour and soul, you had better learn to forget me. Much as I owe my mother, much as I might resolve not to act against her wishes, yet all obligation and resolution sink away before my love for you. But you cannot marry a beggar, nor can I see any hope of being otherwise without my mother's wishes and approbation.'[39] There was the option of living cheaply abroad, 'in some obscure corner of Italy of Switzerland', where 'one has no need of carriages or suites',[40] but neither of them had retiring personalities that welcomed obscurity. Nor were they people who would be happy with love and bread-and-cheese. It was again a kind of play-acting to pretend otherwise. So, by some means or other, the formidable problem of Edward's mother had to be confronted. A range of tactics were employed.

The first and most obvious was to be all obedience and consideration.

He promised his mother 'sacredly upon my honour as a man and my duty as a son that I will never marry without your consent'.[41] When he did so, Mrs Bulwer had some reason to complain, and was not appeased by her son grieving 'more than any human can conceive at acting against your wishes in this step'.[42] Brother Henry's support was invoked,[43] and their mother was reminded that brother William had recently been allowed to marry the woman of his choice, even though the lady in question had also not received parental blessing. Mobilising the family against his mother made real another dream. Lytton held out the possibility of a happy family life, made more harmonious after weathering a storm:

> I had a dream last night. I thought the Mother Dog found Puppy and Poodle in the same Kennel, and that there was a great scene, and Puppy said they were privately married, and then the Dog Mother consented and then they all went to a Beautiful Party.[44]

Childish language reflected the unreality of the aspiration. The Lyttons were not a particularly happy family, and Rosina's appearance on the scene would hardly improve the situation.

In September 1826 the battle had become so acrimonious that Lytton offered Rosina the option of breaking the engagement. Typically, the responsibility for ending the *affaire* was shifted onto other shoulders:

> Separate yourself from me before it is too late, and your affection has not yet become more powerful than your reason. Many bright years may be in store for you, but not with me. I know from the gloom and despondency which have become to me a second nature, I know that I am fated to be wretched; avoid me, shun me and be happy! ... I am alone, alone upon the world again.[45]

To add to this doom-laden prophecy, he intimated that he expected to be carried off by heart disease at any moment. Rosina was not to be shaken off so easily, however, and replied that all would come right – if his mother was carefully handled, with a mixture of firmness and tact.

In October the offer was renewed, with Lytton blaming the whole business on his mother's 'curse'.[46] This time, Rosina agreed to break off the agreement, sarcastically adding 'May you find in the affection of your mother all that you have lost in me'.[47] Within days of receiving this answer, Lytton was begging her to change her mind, and complaining that his mother's attitude had made him lose 'the common energies of existence'.[48] He now had no hope in the world but 'the commune of our hearts'.[49] At exactly the same time, however, he was assuring his mother that it had all been a terrible mistake. He had fallen 'in love insensibly', and now repented of it 'most bitterly'.[50] In a phrase that was hardly complimentary to himself, he admitted that he had fallen in love as the only option left, when Miss

Wheeler proved 'too feeling to flirt with and too noble to seduce'.[51] He
had had 'no other course'.[52] Up to a month before his marriage, he was
still consoling his mother with the idea that he was free of all long-term
entanglements.[53] Rarely can there have been such confusion of mind. He
was caught between two women, whose claims on him, though differently
founded, were of almost equal power.

Alongside a wish to accommodate went the determination to defy. It
seemed that Lytton had every intention of getting his own way, and that
he merely wished the rest of the world to fall in with his wishes. Letters
which praised his mother's 'penetration' of judgement went on to accuse
her of being 'blind' to Rosina's merits.[54] Mother and son traded accusations
about moments in the past when they had quarrelled about schools and
Cambridge colleges. 'Writhing beneath the sacrifice' he had made, he complained to Rosina about his mother's 'injustice and unkindness',[55]
concluding that 'It is her own fault, and she ought to see *her* loss'.[56]
Dramatically, he eventually argued that the marriage was actually his mother's doing. Only her unfairness to Rosina had determined him to stand
by his fiancée. If it turned out badly, Mrs Bulwer, not he, should take the
blame:

> You accused me of feelings and motives so unworthy that from anyone else the
> accusation would have roused my bitterest resentment; from *you* it wounded me
> to the quick in the tenderest point of what is most sensitive in my affection. It
> was this, and *this only*, which brought me again to Miss Wheeler.[57]

The logical conclusion of this type of special pleading was that, 'it will not
be my fault to have married her'.[58] Such a line was hardly flattering to
either Rosina or his mother, but it gave him a kind of absolution. He was
a man torn between two sets of obligations, and quite unable to deal with
the situation.

Mrs Bulwer, for her part, was implacable. When appeals to her son's love
and threats about financial support failed, she tried one last desperate throw.
She accused Rosina of being a congenital liar. The proof offered was that
she was in fact a year or two older than she claimed to be. Three weeks
before the marriage, Lytton agreed to call the whole affair off if his mother
proved to be right.[59] Irish and family solicitors were requested to settle the
matter. When they confirmed Rosina's story,[60] Lytton reported the fact to
his mother, merely adding that, 'it is useless to comment upon this evidence'.[61] When Mrs Bulwer still tried to raise further doubts, she was met
with a final answer: 'Enough of this. All you say makes me wretched, without
moving me one iota from the only path (thorny though it be) which I can
tread with self-respect.'[62] The enquiry into Rosina's true age is an odd

episode in a very tangled story, but the point of importance to emerge from it is, not that Lytton should have defied his mother in the end, but that he should have regarded it as important at all. Whatever the nature of his love for Rosina, it could obviously be blown off course by the slightest wind.

Edward and Rosina were married at St James's, Piccadilly, on 29 August 1827, the bride being given away by her Doyle uncle. For reasons of economy and a professed desire for seclusion, their first home was Woodcote House, near Reading. Mrs Bulwer severed all communications, and Rosina reflected that 'Toutes les Belles Mères tiennent tant soit peu au diable' (all mothers-in-law have a little of the devil in them), but that hers had '*extra* strength' in this respect.[63] Few marriages can have begun so inauspiciously. The strain on the *three* principals must have been difficult to bear.

Once the deed was done, Lytton expected his mother to accept the fact. When she declined to, he panicked. Within a month, he was begging forgiveness. When a slice of wedding cake went uneaten and unacknowledged, he became desperate: 'For God's sake write me one line – to say something – not *very* harsh! ... I could not help writing one line of remembrance, and to implore you to let me hear from you.'[64] There was no meeting between August 1827 and December 1828. Contact was precariously maintained through the intermediaries of William and Henry. Calling on the parable of the Prodigal Son, he assured his mother that 'Rose has never spoken of, or alluded to you, otherwise than in terms of goodwill and respect. Nor has she ceased to lament the breach our marriage has occasioned between you and myself.'[65] Evoking his mother's pride of family, a seventeen-page letter reminded her that the scandal was hurting the image of Bulwers and Lyttons, and damaging thereby his prospects;

> You say the world does not occupy itself on the matter, or know anything about it – In the first place the world always talks about any dissension in any family however humble, and in the next place I must be forgiven for saying I am a very marked individual. Every man who writes is talked of and when once a man is talked of every thing belonging to him is talked of also. The affront to me is therefore more glaring and more known than it would be to almost anyone else.[66]

He even tried the argument that, if he were happy, what more could his mother want. Unfortunately, Mrs Bulwer was deaf to all these blandishments.

In these circumstances, it can hardly be a coincidence that he was working on a novel for much of this period, which would be entitled *The Disowned*. In it two young men, Clarence Linden and Algernon Mordaunt, are unfairly rejected by their families, the latter for contracting an unsuitable marriage. Publicly, Lytton insisted it was a 'metaphysical' work, and that events recorded in it bore no relation to any real situations. Rather, each character was to represent an allegory of a particular vice or virtue, 'to personify certain dispositions influential upon conduct'.[67] Privately, however, Lytton was prepared to acknowledge a special affinity with Mordaunt, and that the book did indeed express 'private feelings'.[68] In early December 1828, Lytton sent an early copy of the book to his mother, linking it with yet another urgent plea for an interview: 'I cannot avoid the opportunity of adding that it is now a year and three months since you have seen me, and that I feel the most increasing concern at your continued displeasure ... I beseech you to suffer me once more to see you.'[69] To communicate by letter ran the risk of unintentionally offending with the use of the wrong phrase or an unguarded word.[70]

This time Mrs Bulwer thawed somewhat. One or possibly two meetings between mother and son took place in the first ten days of 1829. Edward described himself as being received 'very civilly and coldly', but it was a first crack in the ice. Even so, Mrs Bulwer was in complaining mood. First, she rehearsed her displeasure at what she saw as immoral in *Pelham*. Then she went on to compare William's wife, 'very ladylike', with Rosina, to the latter's obvious disadvantage. She sent a watch for a newly-born grand-daughter, in order to prove Lytton wrong when he had written that 'old women were not human'. Accusing him, above all, of loving Rosina more than herself, she absolutely refused to receive or acknowledge his wife. A present of asparagus from her daughter-in-law produced no effect.[71] On the strength of these interviews, it was clear that the Lyttons still had much humility to learn, if they were to be received back into the lady's good offices. Edward concluded that in England to be cold was to be respectable.[72]

Much later in the same year, Mrs Bulwer at last condescended to call on Rosina, but was so irritated by her reception that Edward had to rush to his wife's defence. Her strange manner was put down to nervousness, not insolence;

> I said, and I still say, that she would have been wanting in decorum, in good taste, in good feeling, ay, and also in respect both to yourself and to that disap-proval which your absence had so strongly marked, if on such an occasion she had manifested either the worldly ease of a lady receiving a stranger, or the cordial familiarity of a kinswoman welcoming a kinswoman. She ought to have been strongly affected and overcome. And so she was.[73]

As for Rosina, however deferential she was on paper, these visits were purgatorial: 'What a blessing it is that Mrs B. is not in town and thinking it necessary to make me one of her periodical ceremonious, truly-professional, mean-nothing, do-nothing visits.'[74] Both women never declared a truce. When Mrs Bulwer offered, in 1830, to restore Edward's allowance, both Lyttons flatly refused to accept what they called 'a charity' until Rosina's place within the family was clearly established.[75] The early years of the Lytton marriage was a circus involving three unaccommodating people.

Later, both woman wrote self-justificatory accounts of these events. Mrs Bulwer allowed that she 'had been very much opposed to the match and had not disguised my disapprobation', but insisted that she had been 'more lenient in my conduct that many parents thus circumstanced', not least in continuing Lytton's allowance without interruption.[76] This was memory operating selectively. She described herself as a mediator, whose efforts had been despised by both parties. Rosina's account is less circumspect:

> The sort of mother a man has had may, generally speaking, be pretty correctly known by the estimate he entertains of her sex ... if a man can only think of his mother's understanding with contempt, and her caprice with disgust, he is apt to confound the rest of her sex with her ... she is the first to wonder at the result of her own work, the worst part of which is that she, the cause of all the mischief, only suffers it in a minor degree, and it is reserved for some wretched wife to become its victim.[77]

Add Edward's insistence to these accounts that he was 'wrestling with the spirit of Demons', and that his 'prostration of mind' was such that he believed himself 'mad',[78] and it becomes evident that none of the three principals in this drama saw themselves at fault. For the first three or four years of marriage, however, the young couple would have to get by without Mrs Bulwer's emotional or financial support.

For a few months, all went well. Edward and Rosina lived happily at Woodcote, with her dog Fairy and a Newfoundland called Terror. Both dogs had calling cards printed for them, which were left with neighbours. They were encouraged to go out 'to strawberry-and-cream parties of an evening'.[79] Miss Greene was one of their earliest visitors and she reported an idyll. Rosina's

> whole object seemed to be to save her husband trouble, and she attended to every thought, word and deed of his. Upon a more intimate acquaintance I was not surprised at her devoted attention, and thought he well deserved it.[80]

As proof of compatibility, children were born: Emily Elizabeth in June 1828 and Robert in November 1831. It seemed that, against all the odds, some kind of equilibrium had been found. Unfortunately, however, neither Edward nor Rosina would be content with pastoral simplicity for long. As early as January 1828, they were looking for a London house, and two years later they moved into 36 Hertford Street. Their income could barely support London living, but further exile near Reading was intolerable. Their determination to retire from the world lasted not much more than six months.

Beneath the surface of the marriage, even in its earliest days, fault lines were appearing. Lytton never fully decided whether he wanted an intellectual equal for a wife or some incarnation of innocence. In any case, Rosina was not clever enough to be the first, and was too worldly to be the second. He invited her to criticise his work and then resented any criticism that was forthcoming. She was essentially frivolous about literature. Having dined with Thomas Moore, Benjamin Disraeli and Washington Irving, she confessed to Miss Greene, 'it is astonishing what bores I find all authors except my own husband, and he has nothing author-like about him, for this reason, that his literary talents are his very least'.[81] It is doubtful if Lytton would have taken such a remark as a compliment. Later, Rosina would claim literary distinction herself by writing a string of novels, but they were less works of the imagination than self-justificatory exercises designed to excite popular opinion in her favour. She never had the intellectual or artistic abilities that Lytton wanted and feared in a wife.

Nor was there any money in the marriage. Mrs Bulwer's intransigence on this point was her main blow against the possibility of the union being a success. Unrealistically, the Lyttons aimed to live on affection alone. When a friend tried to warn Edward about this, the reply was boyish and absurd: 'My dear fellow ... you have no need to be alarmed; so convinced am I of my own ability to make all the money I want by my writings, that, though I see the objections you urge, I am marrying without the slightest fear or hesitation.'[82] In the event, they lived in the perpetual fear of debt, which in turn led to wrangling over alleged extravagances and prodigality. Lytton was forced to supplement his income by buying and selling houses and by becoming something of a card sharp in the London clubs. It was an unenviable, slightly seedy, hand-to-mouth existence.

Above all, he had to write, not for pleasure or distraction but for survival. Between 1827 and 1837 he undertook a work load that can only be described as crushing. Eleven novels, two long poems, one play, and a history of Athens in three volumes were produced in these years, when he was also an M.P. and a regular reviewer and essayist. As Thomas Hood jokingly put it, 'Bulwer is always coming out'.[83] Without exaggeration for once, Rosina told his mother that 'Edward ... undertakes a degree of labour that, positively, without exaggeration, no three persons could have the health and time to achieve'.[84] By 1833, he was near to collapse, and had to take a long holiday in Italy to recover. Later in life, Lytton liked to pretend that his enormous literary output had been effortless. He asked an audience of schoolboys in 1854, 'what time do you think, as a general rule, I have devoted to study – to reading and writing? Not more than three hours a day, and when Parliament is sitting, not always that. But then, during these hours I have given my whole attention to what I was about.'[85] But, as his son admitted, this was mere bravado. In fact, he worked every lorning until noon and again every evening past midnight. It was a treadmill of unremitting toil that left him exhausted and ill. Quite literally, he had little time for Rosina and his family, which she took as an excuse to ignore her.

The work was admittedly profitable. Lytton's stock steadily rose with publishers. He was paid £500 for *Pelham*, £800 for *The Disowned* and the substantial sum of £1500 for *Devereux*. But there was little other pleasure in the writing. As his son pointed out, his father had to work at such a fast pace that the novels were too often 'crudely constructed' and 'the emanations of a mind which is reduced to manufacture from the want of leisure to create'.[86] Reviewing Lytton's work after his death, Swinburne agreed:

> I am not sure that the limitation of his large and vigorous qualities of intelligence may not be in part explicable by this very faculty [incessant application] carried to excess – this admirable activity which would yet have borne sounder fruit if it could have been tempered by intervals of repose in which to rest on its oars and 'wait for the grass to grow'. His intelligence had not the indispensable capacity for lying fallow, without which I do not believe that a higher prize can be won by the most versatile energy and the most studiously accomplished work than the prize of superior cleverness.[87]

Most galling of all, Mrs Bulwer was inclined to complain about the quality of her son's work, even though she, exercising financial control, was the principal reason for this. This led Edward to exasperated protest: 'With respect to my writings, such as they are, while I am flattered that you should take any interest in them, I cannot but feel that, in the first place, there is something of mockery in condemning a *class* of writing which circumstances, as you well know, have compelled me to choose. At present, I must write for the many, or not at all.'[88] Lytton's world was one of deadlines, hasty proof-reading, and the accommodation of a public taste that was not necessarily his own. For one who made the highest claims for the role and status of the artist, accepting life as a drudge was hard to bear.

In 1830 the Lyttons' expenditure rose to the enormous sum of £3000 p.a. Anxiety for the future was very real. Unfortunately, Edward could not share his concerns with his wife. Rosina spent money without plan or principle, and was wittily sarcastic about any talk of economy. Brought up in straightened circumstances as a girl, she was now impervious to requests for prudence: 'For my part, I know I should be sorry to spend more than half an hour every morning on the management of the largest establishment that ever was ... I never suffer myself to be troubled, if I can help it, with the vile details of household affairs. However, I have promised Edward to go to town next week to help him to choose a cook.'[89] Even if Rosina had been of a different stamp, it is unlikely that burdens would have been shared. Lytton's was a constructed view of marriage, where responsibilities were apportioned by gender. For good or ill, it was the husband who had to carry the whole burden. As a character in his play, *Money*, put it: 'It is his, the husband's, to provide, to scheme, to work, to endure, to grind out his strong heart at the miserable wheel. The wife, alas!, cannot share the struggle, she can but witness the despair.'[90]

With views such as these, Rosina's imperfections should have been irrelevant, because questions of financial security were a male preserve. But Lytton complained without restraint about not receiving the support and cooperation that was his due. His letters to his wife take on an overwrought, even desperate quality. The following, written in 1834 when the marriage was near to collapse, is typical:

> My dearest Rosina, believe me that I love you deeply and truly, but so many things in life fatigue, sicken, revolt me – so much do I find myself alone and unsupported in all I undertake – that I cannot help growing morbid at times, and an unkind word, sharp tone, a careless look, rankle in me for days together. Forgive this – if you know how I live and move like a man crushed by some great burden upon his shoulders, you would feel how every straw adds to the weight ... I have only the consolation of thinking that in such moments my heart turns to you, and that, forgetting all harsher recollections, all petty annoyances, I only wish now, as we all wish in the first romance of Love, that we could constitute the sole happiness of each other.[91]

The Lytton marriage was tested by strains that would have proved too much for less self-obsessed personalities. Neither could live as they had hoped and expected. Rosina complained of neglect, and Edward of being wilfully misunderstood.

Quickly, the strain translated into illness. Lytton would later become so obsessive about his health that contemporaries turned it into a long-running joke. But the collapses of 1831 and 1833 were genuine and distressing. Overwork and emotional strain had consequences. Rashes on the skin and insomnia were also the result of a 'feverish excited life'.[92] By 1834, Rosina's concern was so profound that she was reduced to begging her mother-in-law to invite Edward to Knebworth and force him to rest:

> If you could but lock up the library, hide *all* his papers, not leave a pen or pencil within his reach, and not let him have any dinner till he had ridden seven or eight miles, I am sure he would have cause to feel everlastingly obliged to you.[93]

Nothing but desperation could have led her to hand Lytton over to his mother's care. It was almost admitting that a battle had been lost.

In 1851 Rosina annotated an old letter from her husband with the words, 'on that fatal Thursday the 29th of August 1827, I was married to the man ... and *marred* as the Irish pronounce it for the rest of my life'.[94] In any real sense, the marriage was over by 1834. Hatred was replacing affection. Contemporaries began to apportion blame, and would continue to do so until Lytton's death in 1873. S. C. Hall, a close, literary collaborator of Lytton's in these years, thought that the marriage had simply been a mismatch:

> As is usually the case, the faults were on both sides; on the one there was no effort – no thought, indeed, to make home a throne or a sanctuary – a source of triumph or a consolation; on the other there seemed the indifference that arises from satiety. In many respects the sexes might have been changed to the advantage of both. Yet, although they were unequally yoked together, I doubt if either would have been made happy, or been happy with, any other man or any other woman.[95]

As the hostility developed, in succeeding decades, into grotesque pantomime, the shortcomings of both would indeed be cruelly exposed. But, as the marriage foundered, more responsibility for it was probably carried by Edward. Overwork and illness made him look 'like a man who has been flayed and is sore all over'.[96] Under extreme pressures, his behaviour became unpredictable and even threatening.

Above all, he found it impossible to modify or adapt the assignment of roles within marriage to husband and wife. Rather, each difficulty led him to re-emphasise them. The rules had been set out at the beginning and were never changed:

> No, my sagacious Poodle, no, me does not wish oo to be a bit more stupid than oo is ... but me wants to have only the perfections, not the faults of a clever woman. Me wants the companion, not the Caviller or Contradictor, which me thinks clever women generally become when the Mistress grows into the Wife, and me thinks oo has a certain independence of character which belies oo softness of temper and even oo love for me. But me won't talk of this now, prettiest.[97]

He was fully aware of the problem, but seemingly unable to do anything about it. 'Perhaps,' he reflected, 'I expected too much and yielded too little, perhaps I expected to alter your nature to suit mine, when it would have been easier and better to have adapted my own to yours.'[98] This is to present marriage as a competition between personalities, one dominant and one submissive, rather than a merging of them.[99] Further, if it became a competition, Rosina showed herself to be a world-class competitor. As their son observed, 'whether as a husband, writer or politician, she discovered and condemned his affections'.[100] If he took one side of a debate, she would take the other.

When challenged, Lytton's first instinct was to move away. From the beginning of 1829, he lived increasingly in London, leaving Rosina to vegetate in Woodcote, claiming pressure of business.[101] Guests noticed the separateness of their daily lives: 'I did not like the way things went on, as I did not see any appearance of what I would call family sociability, and Mr Bulwer always breakfasted alone in his library and she and I in her dressing room. He never dined at home unless there was company.'[102] Lytton protested that it was the pressure of work rather than inclination that kept him away,[103] but when he described life in the country he mentioned living with 'a dog, a cat and some half a dozen earwigs', but not with a wife.[104] Not surprisingly, Rosina began to complain of neglect, describing her situation as being 'in solitary confinement'. According to her, Edward only appeared infrequently and 'then invents solitary occupations'.[105] She wreaked a terrible revenge by throwing one of his favourite shirts on to the fire. It was one of the first of the 'pretty fairy tales' that began to circulate about the Lyttons, giving an insight into 'what passes behind the curtain of polished and poetical life!'[106]

Worse was to follow. In 1833 Rosina wrote an essay called *Nemesis*. It took the form of a letter from Byron to the men of England. In it she retailed her woes, thereby beginning a lifetime's hobby. She claimed that, in May 1828, Lytton had savagely kicked and beaten her, even though she was eight months pregnant. When the baby was born, its father was so jealous that he insisted on its being sent away to a wet-nurse immediately, saying that 'he would not have *my* wife's time or attention taken up with any d – n child'. Later, she would claim that Edward had also beaten his mother. On top of this, sexual irregularities were hinted at but never made explicit: 'cuffs and kicks ... of demonic passion and other little incidents which women cannot tell even to their lawyers; and which very young women, however disgusted they may be at them, are still not aware that they have *legally a right to do so*'.[107] Evaluating the truth and falsehood of this and other stories that the Lyttons would circulate about each other is very difficult. There is only Rosina's testimony for the incident, and her letters to Edward of 1828 are full of endearments. On the other hand, there would certainly be violence in the marriage later. Perhaps the main point of the story is that it symbolises the descent of a marriage into mutual loathing.

It is easier to see the same period as one in which infidelities began. Lytton, ever concerned about his public face, lectured Rosina on proper behaviour: 'That you were not acting at all different from what a girl of your age should have done with Lord Castlereagh or any one else, is of course quite clear to me – that you *appeared* to do so, is *as* evident. It is against this appearance only, I repeat again and again, that I wish to guard you.' He also warned her about consorting with female friends, who were 'much too well known' at Paris.[108] Injunctions against flirting in a wife were not expected to cover his own behaviour. While courting Rosina, he confessed to Lady Cunningham-Fairlie that he was, at the same time, involved with a woman in Paris, who was 'besieging me every hour', and also 'wrapt in a third scheme wild and foolish ... which I can scarcely with the utmost dexterity escape from'.[109] Shortly after marriage, Lytton had to deny rumours that, while at Malvern taking the waters, he had conducted an affair with a Swiss girl called Mademoiselle Pion. On a visit in 1831, Miss Greene noted Edward's absences from the family home, the lack of interest of both parents in their children, and also the strange spectacle of Rosina 'inviting ladies to her parties for him to flirt with – two in particular Mrs Hunter and Mrs R. Stanhope'. The latter will reappear in the story. According to this testimony, Rosina's 'whole time was employed in trying to anticipate his wishes and keep off violent bursts of passion, which I must in justice to her say, I then only saw her in the right and him wrong'.[110]

Miss Greene, in these years, was Rosina's confidante, not Edward's, although later alliances would change. Everyone involved with the Lyttons was on one side or the other. Their evidence is therefore always a party line to some degree. Neutral evidence from disinterested witnesses is hard to come by. Even so, it is almost certain that Edward was involved in extra-marital liaisons, as a respite from professional pressures and a home he found increasingly uncongenial. Victorian society demanded higher moral standards of a woman than a man, because every pregnancy and birth involved the smooth transfer of property rights from one generation to another. Men could deny bastards, women could not. In the social circles inhabited by the Lyttons, a mistress was almost as familiar as a bride. Rosina, however, never accepted the double standard and vigorously denounced British women who did. In challenging gender roles, she ran the risk of being ungendered. Her refusal to accept the rules drove Edward to further sexual adventures, and to the cynical observation that, 'the English find it so bad a thing to have a wife, that they suppose it quite natural to murder her, though she bring him £1000 a year'.[111] Their tragedy was that they had entered into marriage without agreeing to the ground rules that would govern the arrangement.

The explosion erupted in 1834. For a year, Lytton's affair with Mrs Stanhope had been more or less public knowledge. Then, promising to end the liaison, he asked Rosina to join him on holiday in Italy. As she recorded, it was to be an excursion of a rather extraordinary kind: 'The vessel had not sailed an hour, when who should I see but Mrs ROBERT STANHOPE sitting wrapped up – my LORD LYTTON at her feet, and her contemptible little wretch of a husband (who my LORD LYTTON afterwards told me used to sell her to men) looking on.' [112] This bizarre *ménage à quatre* travelled miserably down towards Naples, through 'plague, pestilence and famine'. Florence was thought inferior to Cheltenham, and Rome 'the most *dirty*!! barbarous and dismal place'.[113] Neapolitan society was more congenial. Lytton began a programme of serious research for a novel that would become *The Last Days of Pompeii*.[114] More dramatically, Rosina began an affair with a Russian grandee, Prince Lieven. In one account of the journey, Lytton himself referred to the prince in question as a Neapolitan, and therefore two lovers may have been in the game. It makes little difference. One lover was quite enough to push Rosina over the invisible frontier into a land beyond respectability. She herself agreed it was folly, but 'qui vit sans folie n'est pas si sage qu'il pense'.[115]

Lytton characteristically took the opportunity of transferring blame from himself to someone else. His own dalliance with Mrs Stanhope and others was forgotten, as Rosina's misdemeanour was brought centre-stage:

> The original cause of the misery that ended in separation was not in any jealousy of me, or any fault imputed to me. It was as you know in *Confidence* ... Lady L.'s attachment at Naples to Prince A. Lieven, and her avowing it openly. I knelt at her bedside and said, 'Tell me only you do not love this man and all I can do to make you happy I will do' – and she drove me away with her burst of passion. It was because I have taken her from that man that she became so outrageous, and from that day there was no peace, and no prospect of peace.[116]

When they returned to England, they separated. She took the children to live with Miss Greene in Gloucester.[117] He settled into the most fashionable of bachelor establishments in Albany. The marriage was effectively over. The auspices for its success had never been favourable. Physical separation removed the immediate sense of irritation that the one felt for the other, but disentangling emotions and feelings of accumulated resentment would prove impossible. From 1834 until Lytton's death in 1873 both he and Rosina devoted a major part of their lives to inflicting as much damage as possible on the other. It was warfare of the most implacable kind, no concessions made, no quarter given.

The destruction of a marriage always threatens long-term destabilisation of emotions, and this was certainly true of Lytton himself. There was a root-lessness about his life that in spite of a genuine regard for Knebworth, became more and more pronounced. Approaching his thirtieth birthday, in 1832, he wrote an essay entitled *The Departure of Youth*. With great self-awareness, he rehearsed the experiences of his life and the lessons that were to be taken from them:

> At the age of thirty, the characters of most men pass through a revolution … one of the most useful lessons that disappointment has taught us, is a true estimate of love. For at first we are too apt to imagine that woman (poor partner with us in the frailties of humanity) must be perfect – that the dreams of the poets have a corporeal being, and that God has ordained for us that unclouded nature – that unchanging devotion – that unalterable heart, which it has been the great vice of Fiction to attribute to the daughters of clay. And, in hoping for perfection, with how much excellence have we been discontented – to how many idols have we changed our worship.[118]

Indeed remarks such as these hit the mark. Edward Lytton looked for the ideal in marriage, and became irritated with anything less than that. Rosina was happy to indulge theatricality, until she was asked to take on uncongenial roles. Seven years of marriage would be followed by a lifetime of grinding hostility. It was said of Jane and Thomas Carlyle that their marriage ensured that two, and not four, people would be unhappy. Much the same could be remarked of the Lyttons.

Cover of Rosina Bulwer Lytton's *Cheveley: or The Man of Honour*. (*Bodleian Library*)

3

'The Misfortune of My Life'

After 1834 Lytton's youthful cynicism about marriage were confirmed by the grimmest of experiences. Attending brother Henry's wedding was to grace an 'awful ceremony', a kind of 'funeral'. There were simply no guarantees. As Lytton quaintly put it, 'one never knows what sort of wife the most charming spinster may become – the most bewitching kitten often settles into a grim Cat. *Speremus Meliora!*'[1] As the hero of *My Novel* reflected, to marry was to allow another person the chance to unsettle routines and disturb preferences: 'you have given the power to wound your peace, to assail your dignity, to cripple your freedom, to jar on each thought and each habit, and bring you down to the meanest details of earth, when you invite her, poor soul, to soar to the spheres'.[2] That person had to be a woman, and women were, by definition, changeable and impossible to understand. Madeline Lester in *Eugene Aram* was bookish, but 'the woman's tendency to romance naturally tinctured her meditations'. Aram, the scholar, loved her, but feared the truth that 'at best, woman is weak, she is the minion to her impulses'.[3] Swings in mood and temperament were difficult to follow. 'Lived there ever,' asked another fictional hero, 'a man who thoroughly understood a woman?'[4] Lytton's works are crammed with observations along these lines.

There was an allied question about whether artists should marry. As researchers of the spiritual and the immanent, perhaps they should follow the example of a celibate priesthood. To follow their trade, they had to be emotionally selfish and uncompromising. They could not be natural compromisers, particularly with each other. As Madame de Grantmesnil observes in *The Parisians*, 'Artist, do not love – do not marry – an artist. Two artistic natures rarely combine. The artistic nature is wonderfully exacting. I fear it is supremely egotistical – so jealously sensitive it writhes at the touch of a rival.'[5] A wife who was an artist was dangerous, but a wife with no intellect was worse. Such women with no feeling or 'sympathy in our better and higher aspirings' dragged the poet to the ground.[6] These doubts about marriage had a timeless quality. They were valid in Pompeii and in Victorian England:

It is not without interest to observe in those remote times, and under a social system so widely different from the modern, the same small causes that ruffle and interrupt the 'course of love', which operate so commonly at this day; the same inventive jealousy, the same cunning slander, the same crafty and fabricated retailings of petty gossip, which so often suffice to break the ties of the truest love.[7]

The anxiety could take poetic form. In *Lovers' Quarrels* Lytton wrote:

> There is no anguish like the hour,
> Whatever else befall us,
> When One the heart has raised to power
> Exerts it but to gall us.[8]

All these quotations come from literary works but they graphically describe Lytton's own experiences. Inevitably there is an element of special pleading, but the case is eloquent.

Rosina's views about marriage were less ethereal but equally pungent. For a woman to become a wife was to invite self-annihilation. As she memorably put it, a wife was no better than a cotoneaster, to be 'treated ... as ill as possible without the slightest attention, save by throwing a little cold water on it whenever it attempts to put forth anything new. Like me it is accustomed to rough it, but unlike me is extremely hardy.'[9] She hated taking the name Bulwer or Lytton, 'as a blister and a blot', because it symbolised the smothering of one personality by another.[10] She claimed what no Victorian wife could, namely equality with her husband. She wanted to be his equal, not only in the affection of their children and in the disposal of family income but also in literary production. In these areas, she was expressing views that were so foreign to contemporary opinion that she would be thought unbalanced. Relations thought her an embarrassment and she was. Law courts rejected her claims, and most people thought their judgements correct. Publishers rejected her literary pretensions. Only one weapon remained to her, but this she wielded with relish. It was to create scandal. Contemporary values were to be affronted and, best of all, Lytton's fear of exposure to ridicule could be exploited. As she observed, 'Exposure is the only thing that complex monster dreads, and consequently the only check I have on him'.[11] She became very good at it.

Between June 1834 and April 1836 they played games with no rules. Trial separations were punctuated with letters that veered from self-justification to sheer vindictiveness. Each was collecting material that could be used against the other in law. And this time there was no doubt that the violence was real. Rosina had become practised in taunting him 'in the most violent manner with everything terrible she had ever said or thought of him', and was spending without any kind of restraint.[12] Enraged by one such speech,

Lytton attacked his wife, biting her on the cheek. She claimed that he also threatened her with a knife. The letter of apology which he wrote after the incident, characteristically, started with words of contrition and ended with blaming her for pushing him into violence, with terrible consequences for his public reputation:

> You have been *cruelly outraged* ... and I stand eternally degraded in my own eyes. I do not for a moment blame you for the publicity which you gave to an affront nothing but frenzy can extenuate. I do not blame you for exposing me to my servants, for taking that occasion to vindicate yourself to my mother – nor for a single proceeding for that most natural conduct which has probably by this time made me the theme for all the malignity of London ... But I doubt whether it was humane to tamper with so terrible an infirmity as mine – to provoke so gratuitously in the first instance ... to persist in stretching to the utmost a temper so constitutionally violent.

The letter ends with the statement that he has been living in hell for the last two or three years.[13] Rosina did indeed bring Mrs Bulwer into the equation, writing a series of letters which depicted herself as unloved but resignedly dutiful, and Edward as obsessed with the burden of 'being hampered with a wife'.[14] Unhelpfully, she suggested that the only way to scotch rumour was for them to resume living together.

According to a deposition made in 1867 by a maid named Benson, the violence continued throughout the Italian journey of the autumn of 1834. In Bolzano, he 'dashed the things about, and at her Ladyship'. In Naples, 'he kicked and bang'd her Ladyship against the stone floor at the Hotel Vittoria till she was black and blue'.[15] Memory of events thirty years old can be faulty, and for some reason Rosina allowed Benson a pension of £20 p.a., when she barely had enough money to meet her own requirements. Even so, the stories fit the context. Certainly, on returning to England, both Rosina and Edward threw themselves on Miss Greene's good offices. That lady thought that Rosina's adultery had been unpardonable but accepted her claim that, on the journey home, her life had been seriously in danger. She witnessed quarrels of such bitterness that both participants were left 'exhausted with rage'.[16] What added a particular piquancy to the physical contests between Rosina and Edward was that he would sometimes come off worst. As Carlyle wryly told his wife:

> I am heartily sorry for the poor woman, for the poor man: it seems they often went to *striking*, and *she* on a free floor could dish him in that way. He and she what are they but persons swoln with wind, their natural folly made ten times foolisher thereby? God pity us all; lead us *not* into temptation.[17]

London was beginning to find the Lytton marriage amusing.

Stories about the husband's violence were set alongside tales of the wife's heavy drinking. Lytton actively sought to build up a dossier of evidence on this point. Miss Greene, in the process of changing allegiance from Rosina to Edward, reported that she was keeping company with an alcoholic named Miss Fraser, and that it was all she could do to stop the children seeing 'either of the ladies after their brandy'.[18] Servants testified that Rosina's intake 'amounted to bottles', and that, commonly, a bottle of spirits or wine would be consumed overnight.[19] By 1839 Lytton was trying to collect evidence that would prove Rosina so 'disordered of mind' that she could be committed as insane. His solicitor advised caution, but added that, if the drinking continued, it would eventually offer a chance to act: 'drinks [are] the habit of getting up a necessary consolation ... If thro' rage or drink she becomes outrageous (which is very probable) it may be both wise and merciful to place her under personal restraint.' [20] The terrible events of 1858–59 were already in rehearsal twenty years earlier. Both sides were eagerly collecting ammunition.

In these months, Edward and Rosina systematised the case that each would prosecute against the other. In a long letter of 1835 Lytton set out his grievances to his wife. While professedly hoping for 'the healing of ... sores', he in fact indulged in sustained recrimination. Rosina's deficiencies as a wife were blatant. She must stop taunting him in insulting letters. She must stop denigrating his talents. It was rumoured that she had undertaken reviews of his work that were far from favourable.[21] She must stop abusing other members of his family.[22] Above all, she had to see her fortune as linked to his:

> Among the sources of discontent we should guard against is that want of occupation which women of your talents are so liable to feel ... Would this be the case if you could learn to make my occupation yours – if you could feel that you are connected with one whose destiny it is no dishonour to share – if you could feel interest in what interests me – and in my life as part of yours? After all, what other woman would not do so? ... I stand above all those of my own age not only in literary, but political rank – if I live, my career will interest strangers – it is only my wife who yawns at its progress and sneers at its motives. Ah, how much better if you could enter into my heart – if you would see how much I desire to be good – how much I wish to keep myself unsullied and pure – and if you could sustain and support me amidst all the trials which often shipwreck the strongest ... But this is asking too much.[23]

Such remarks prompted Lytton's suffragette granddaughter, Lady Constance Lytton, to comment: 'One would think he had sufficient knowledge of human nature to realise that ... something must be conceded to her feelings, interests, weaknesses ... His letter is full of high feeling, sensitiveness, pity, tenderness but they are all for himself.'[24]

Rosina responded with spirit, equal self-obsession and sarcasm. She offered him a set of rules for her own conduct which included: 'If your project is absurd, I will never say a word'; 'You no more shall see me pout that I'm at home, while you go out'; and 'Henceforth at every ill of life, I'll first remember I'm your wife'.[25] She was as good as Edward at seeing herself as blameless and the mere victim of villainy: 'What a life has mine been! A sunless childhood, a flowerless youth, and certainly a fruitless womanhood.' She was trapped in 'that miserable, barren little segment of life, the *Present*'.[26] Melodramatically, she promised to die before the end of 1836, and gave the local sexton presents in return for a promise to cut the costs of her funeral.[27] She traded insult for insult, accusation for accusation. There was a selfishness in both their characters that transmuted into violence if not appeased. Rosina would not play by the rules of Victorian marriage and Edward would not relax them. Oddly, they sometimes relapsed into the 'Poodle' and 'Pups' language of their courtship days. They actually resumed living together from May to July 1835, but weary Bulwer and Doyle relations knew that the marriage was over. At least it excused them from the tiring business of trying to explain and excuse husband to wife and wife to husband.[28]

As the inevitability of final separation drew closer, Lytton protested that he wanted a calm and dignified agreement, which would 'render it as easy and agreeable' to Rosina 'as it may be in my power to do'.[29] It was his wish to secure her 'every comfort in my power'.[30] This was self-delusion. Expressions of concern mingled with brutal frankness: 'You have no longer affection for me – *you have completely and eternally eradicated all mine for you.*'[31] He complained to his mother that Rosina had become 'a thorn in my side',[32] and that she was the sole cause of a number of distressing symptoms: 'my career is blighted, my temper ruined, my nerves shattered, and if I am to go on for ever in this way, because she insists on continuing to force herself upon me and make my life misery, God knows what I shall do at last'.[33] Rosina, too, offered the hope that matters would be settled amicably, before relapsing into the reflection, 'How foolish it is of me to let these reptiles irritate me'.[34] Both were in several states of mind, and this explains the wearing ambiguity of these years. The consultation of lawyers ran alongside experiments in living together. A separation was agreed in 1835 and cancelled a month later. Loathing vied with the last traces of affection. There was always the temptation 'to try once more'.[35]

Matters came to a head in late February 1836. For some time Rosina had been living in Acton, while Lytton had moved into one of the apartments in the Albany, adjacent to Piccadilly. On the evening in question he had been expected to dine in Acton but had failed to appear. Rosina on impulse decided to confront him, bursting into his Albany rooms at 11 p.m. Here the story becomes confused. Rosina claimed that she saw two teacups on a table, a shawl lying on a sofa, and the figure of a woman, whom she identified as a certain Laura Deacon, disappearing into her husband's bedroom. She then made a scene that attracted the attention of the whole neighbourhood immediately and of the London press next day.[36] Both parties reacted characteristically. Edward defended himself by attacking, and demanded an apology:

> Madam, Your conduct requires no comment, your letter deserves no answer – you come to my chambers – ring violently – my sole servant is out (I am not in the habit of opening my own door) – I go at last – ill and worn out – see *you* to my surprise – you recur to your base, unworthy and most ungrateful suspicions on seeing my surprise – you recur to your base, unworthy and most ungrateful suspicions on seeing *two* tea-cups on my tray!! – make a scene before your footman and the porters of the Lodge, and expose me and yourself to the ridicule of the Town. And this is the History of your Adventures! I have only to say at present, that it furnishes another to the list of unwarrantable and unpardonable insults and injuries you have so unsparingly heaped on your husband.[37]

As for Rosina, she tried to stab herself, 'first with a Penknife, and after with a dinner knife',[38] but quickly rallied to use the incident in her singleminded campaign of revenge. Whether Laura Deacon was in the Albany rooms that night or not, she was certainly already Lytton's mistress. Rosina had acquired a real weapon with which to discomfort her husband. For ever after, political opponents of Lytton could cause him to blush by references to 'The Mysteries at the Albany'.[39]

A decision to separate settled the most pressing difficulties but set up others. Foremost among them was the question of money. By a deed of separation dated 19 April 1836, Rosina would be allowed £400 p.a., with a further £50 for each child, as long as they were in her care. When both children went to live with Miss Greene in 1838 Rosina was reduced to living on her allowance alone.[40] Lytton claimed that he had no wish to be accused of 'niggardly' conduct.[41] The sum of £500 was probably a substantial proportion of his income at the time. After inheriting Knebworth in 1843, however, which allegedly gave him an additional income of £4893 p.a., his refusal to be more generous to Rosina became a matter of family and public comment.[42] His brother William advised him to renegotiate terms, lest the Lytton case should echo 'to the scandal of society and to the surprise of wife-ridden Husbands, that a wife could be so easily provided for and disposed of'.[43] He suggested a figure of £600 p. a. But Lytton refused to budge. He took the view that William's interference in the matter was simply produced by resentment at being cut out of the Knebworth inheritance. He was also clear that Rosina was to have no share of his mother's money or of the proceeds of a steadily advancing literary reputation. His income was not great in comparison to the calls on it and did not exceed 'what a gentleman could live on'.[44]

Rosina inevitably saw the matter differently. For her, it was to open up a new front in her vendetta against Lytton. In 1847 she threatened an action in the ecclesiastical courts for non-payment of her allowance and for an increase in it. Lytton found this 'a very harassing lawsuit',[45] and counterattacked by threatening a divorce petition based on Rosina's adultery. In 1858 Rosina renewed the offensive, and again received some support from within the family. William reminded his brother that, 'anyone who knew her ungovernable temper and her violent tendencies must see that if driven to extremities by doubts and difficulties she would break out into some act of desperation'.[46] The warning was apposite, for Rosina's timing was impeccable. She chose moments to act when Lytton was most publicly vulnerable. In 1847 his political career hung in the balance as he scrambled to find a seat in Parliament. In 1858 he was even more in the public eye as he entered the Cabinet. On these occasions, it was no help to be accused of condemning his wife to poverty. He feared that 'in public life the slightest trip is as great as a stumble in private life'.[47] Knowledge of this impelled him to redouble his efforts to find evidence of Rosina's adultery. If a convincing dossier could be put together, he could divorce her and be free of all financial encumbrance. This desire set up a new theme in the marriage, namely the systematic surveillance of Rosina. Unfortunately, this would be undertaken in such a clumsy manner that it would provide many stories for the amusement and bewilderment of London society.

There would be no divorce, not because Rosina and Edward harboured a residual affection for each other but because both their lives would not bear scrutiny in a court. Before and after the separation of 1836 both had had affairs. Each therefore had much to lose. Edward would have to surrender all hope of high office, while Rosina faced penury if she lost. Oddly enough, therefore, their lovers and mistresses condemned them to each other. They discovered that they could not invoke the rules of Victorian marriage to their advantage, when they both resolutely refused to live by them on a day to day basis.

Lytton once told Mrs Disraeli that he preferred food to women: 'Young ladies have no charms for me. I prefer a patty.'[48] No one believed him. His affairs were numerous and he mocked social conventions that were overstrict. He wondered at the chastity of Edward the Confessor, concluding that, 'perhaps England at this day is the only country in Europe in which chastity in men is considered at all in the light of a virtue'.[49] Things were better ordered in France or Germany. He told his brother Henry, who was his confidant in matters of this kind, that only 'the vulgar classes' would sue a man for seducing a wife.[50] Women, after all, were 'riddles ... which elude a man's grasp or comprehension'.[51] A wife or a mistress 'makes half the sorrows which she boasts the privilege to sooth'.[52] Lytton saw himself as in a trap. Women were totally necessary to him but they would always be beyond his understanding and the source of trouble. As he wrote in a sketch of his own character in 1846: 'It has been the interchange of affection with some loving and loyal nature that has kept me from becoming a cold and ambitious egoist, and in reality reconciled me with the world with which, in seeming, it often placed me at war.'[53] At his best, Lytton would admit that his difficulties with women were not the fault of the whole gender. Rather, the conventions of English society forced them to be 'artificial'. He preferred the company of frank, confident, American women.[54] It was the fate of women 'in all the more polished circles of society ... to be unnatural and unhappy'.[55] At his worst, a strain of misogyny led him to pepper his books with cruel humour at the expense of women.

In spite of this ambivalence, there is no doubt that Lytton was very attractive to women. His correspondence contains many letters from gushing admirers, many of them young women with literary pretensions. They invited him to their 'humble abode', and refused to believe 'that you are the immoral man malice asserts you to be'.[56] Servant girls and milliners so regularly figured in his life that brother Henry, no amateur in these matters himself, warned him about their capacity 'to work mischief'.[57] The Sarahs and Mary Janes could be difficult. If uncautious behaviour stained Lytton's reputation, for some women this merely increased his attraction. As a friend explained to Rosina, a Byronic artist should have a strain of devilment in his character:

> When I have conversed with ladies about Bulwer I find that they worship him for his refinement – when I speak of his inconstancy, they smile and give me wicked looks, and so tell me with their eyes what they do not with their tongues, that a dash of gentlemanly fashionable vice is like mustard improving the flavour of the beef which they adore.[58]

In a world of womanisers like Melbourne and Palmerston, Lytton was not unique even though his taste may have been more catholic.

Society women, too, became emotionally involved. Rosina accused the poetess Laetitia Landon of being a 'cast-off' mistress of her husband.[59] Certainly, their friendship in the late 1820s was close. At various times, his name was associated with Lady Stepney, 'a wanton' according to Rosina, Lady Lincoln and Lady Stanhope.[60] To the latter he addressed poetry:

> Oh wisely thou mayst prize the minstrel's lays,
> For Poesy is present where thou art;
> And speech would turn to music in thy praise,
> If words were but the echoes of the heart.[61]

Embarrassments were always possible. In 1853 he borrowed Caroline Norton's house, in order to prosecute an affair with her cousin, a Mrs Barton. When an outraged husband appeared unexpectedly and gave Lytton 'a good horsewhipping', even Mrs Norton's broad mind was sorely tested: 'Bulwer if you are such a d—d fool that you can't manage a little affair of this sort without being found out you must carry it on elsewhere.'[62] Lytton's private life was regularly reported in the press, and where it could not be reported it was insinuated.

For most of the women playing these games the rules were well known and therefore the consequences were rarely sinister. But for the amateur or the overly sincere a friendship with Lytton could be devastating. In 1845, a certain Julia d'Eyncourt converted to Roman Catholicism and then entered a convent, shortly after confessing 'an affection' for Lytton that 'so much usurped my thoughts'.[63] Some members of her family, notably Alfred Tennyson, accused Lytton of unhinging the girl's mind. Their later, literary battles may well have been rooted in this incident. Tennyson described Lytton unflatteringly as sitting 'upon the nipple of literary Dandyism'.[64] Just as compromising was Lytton's pursuit of a daughter of Lady Glamis in 1853. This time he was so serious about the project that he informed the girl that Rosina would certainly be dead by Christmas. He also sent a lock of the girl's hair to a clairvoyant, in order to ascertain whether she would make a suitable wife. Details of this behaviour were generously circulated around London by a Mr Roebuck, a competitor for the girl's affections.[65] Although the young lady was undoubtedly infatuated with Lytton, her reputation was inevitably being compromised, and her mother cried villainy:

> I try to persuade myself that you are under a delusion and wish to dispel it that you may not allow yourself to seduce innocent girls under false pretences ... I admit that no girl is to be pitied who can listen to the addresses of a man over the contemplated tomb of a living wife. My Child is the greatest sufferer – her prospects blighted ... I am the next to suffer and much more bitterly have I suffered in mind than the misled vain girl who has been duped by your false representations ... Remember there is an all-seeing eye which brings to light

whatever it may think fit, and no excuse can be pleaded for a crime of so deep
a dye as yours on the grounds of youth or thoughtlessness, when nearly half a
century has rolled over your head.[66]

Quite simply, much of London Society would have regarded Lytton as
unsound.

His most serious attachment was to Laura Deacon, the former mistress
of a Colonel King, a neighbour of Lytton's when he lived briefly at Craven
Cottage in Fulham. He was living with her before the separation of 1836,
and she was almost certainly the mysterious lady in the Albany incident.
Three children were born to the couple as Lytton established what was in
effect a second household.[67] His mother, who knew of the arrangement,
was asked to care for all the dependants in the event of Lytton's death. She
should 'provide also for the truest and fondest friend, comforter and nurse
with which heaven ... has counterbalanced the misery of a more recognized
connection ... you cannot tell how much I owe to the soothing and devoted
love of her I speak of'.[68] As a journal of 1838 proves, his life with Laura
Deacon, who was also known as 'Mrs Beaumont' and 'Mrs Sellars', was the
closest Lytton ever came to knowing the support of a loving family. He
thought he had 'few rivals in literary reputation' and 'a not inconsiderable
station in Parliament', but all that was perishable. Only Laura Deacon's
affection was sure:[69]

> The sword hangs over my head – sooner or later the gossip and agony of a Public
> Court ... But I have a comfort even against this tho' not without sore alloy. I
> am loved I believe, honestly, deeply, and enduringly by one who is indeed to me
> a wife. It is true there is sin in the tie, and *there* is the alloy. But if ever such sin
> had excuse it is in our case. She is lone and friendless save me. [And I] utterly
> shipwrecked of all love at home, my heart bruised and trampled on – and never
> forming the tie till in despair of all harmony in one more lawful ... Blessings
> upon you L ... if Punishment must come – let it spare you.[70]

How the relationship developed is not clear. According to Rosina, in 1854
Laura Deacon and a sister were keeping a school in Kensington. Three years
later Lytton was visiting her in Boulogne, where she was living with children
whom Rosina called 'her Bastards', in a house whose walls were covered
with pictures of Knebworth. These children would be remembered in all
Lytton's wills. All of this relies dangerously on Rosina's evidence alone.[71]
What is clear is that this relationship went on for over twenty years. As
such, it was one of the most enduring in Lytton's life.

If Lytton's private life can only be described as random, Rosina's was
very similar in quality, if not quantity. None of this surprised Lytton,
because he took the view that, in matters adulterous at least, there were

no differences between the genders: 'Women are seldom systematically depraved ... In fact they are much more like *us* (especially when they have yielded) than we are apt to imagine. Directly shame is removed from Infidelity why should they differ from us – they have the same passions and are exposed to the same temptations.'[72] After all, Rosina had lived with him before marriage.[73] However, one difference between the genders was inescapable, as Lytton well know. If a woman's adultery could be proved, her husband could reduce her to poverty through divorce. She would also lose all contact with her children. A man ran no comparable risks and Lytton had every intention of exploiting this advantage. Quite simply, Rosina was put under surveillance. As she herself put it: 'Sir Liar's object is first, to worry me to death – by the mere act of *spying* which would wear anybody's life out. Secondly never to lose sight of all my movements.'[74] Lytton drafted everyone into the hunt, including John Forster, his lawyers, Miss Greene and his children.[75]

The monitoring began immediately after the 1836 separation. While staying with Miss Greene, Rosina formed a liaison with a Mr Hume, whose wife was an invalid. She then gave her children into the care of Miss Greene, and went to live with Hume in a succession of hotels. When Miss Greene protested, Rosina's answer was 'she would do it all again'.[76] The couple spent some months in Bath, so Lytton bombarded visitors to that city with requests for information that might prove useful.[77] He was particularly excited by news of her seeing a Colonel Webster as well as Hume: 'I wish to heaven we could get proof of this new liaison since to prove her guilty with *two* men would so thoroughly damn her.'[78]

In the autumn of 1839, Rosina and Hume moved to Paris, thereby initiating a train of events that were bizarre even by the standards of the Lytton family. By chance, Henry Bulwer occupied a post at the British Embassy in the city. Rosina, not unreasonably as it turned out, became convinced that Henry, 'mon animal de beau frère',[79] was his brother's willing accomplice in her persecution. She claimed that he was paying sections of the French police to spy on her and that he had tried to inveigle her into a house of ill-repute.[80] Her servants were followed and attempts at bribery made in what was a concerted pumping for information. Bonbons were dangled before cooks.[81] In October Rosina won £50 in damages from the *Court Journal*, which had reported that, at a ball, she had made faces at Henry Bulwer, 'grimaces that have scarcely been equalled since the best days of Grimaldi',[82] the famous clown. Thackeray, though no friend of Lytton's, thought this unfair because Rosina 'was the foulest wickedest libeller in England herself'.[83]

But this particular act of the comedy was by no means over. In January

1840 Lytton sent a lawyer called Lawson to Paris to collate the evidence against his wife. He was accompanied by his clerk, Tom Thackeray. Probably with the connivance of Henry Bulwer, Thackeray bribed a maid named Murray to gain access to Rosina's house. The maid then informed her mistress of what was afoot and Thackeray was caught red-handed, while rifling Rosina's desk.[84] The incident delighted her. It was proof-positive that all her accusations about harassment were well-founded. Demanding maximum publicity, she initiated an action against Lawson and Thackeray which made it necessary for Lytton to go to Paris to defend himself. Rosina was clear about what she wanted to do, cost what it might: 'nothing but exposure can do anything with the B—s ... Thanks to the spies around me, *now* I do live in a glass house. They may shiver it with their dastardly missiles, but they shall not shake me, even with the zealous assistance of Lady Blessington, or any other Messalina, old or young.'[85] The very best lawyers in France were engaged; Charles Dru for Rosina and Odilon Barrot for Lytton. In the end, the case foundered on the technicality that, in France, a wife could not bring a court action without her husband's consent, and this of course Lytton withheld. Lytton was anxious that Lawson should take the responsibility entirely onto his own shoulders, because, he claimed, he was 'not privy to it'.[86] The whole episode was grubby and humiliating, and played out before the eager press of two of Europe's principal capitals.

The consequences of this incident were, to some extent, predictable. Neither Edward nor Rosina wanted the war to end. Both saw themselves as the victims of the situation, and both were keen to carry on the fight. Rosina, with the help of Mrs Trollope,[87] continued to pursue possibilities in the French courts, while her husband investigated the possibility of divorce through the ecclesiastical courts in England.[88] He succeeded in denying her all further access to the children and, with Henry's assistance, tried to counter Rosina's appeals to the press in London and Paris.[89] It seemed that he had come round to agreeing with William Bulwer that his wife's 'vulgar, ill-bred notoriety' had inflicted as much 'discredit, scandal and disgrace' on their family as was possible.[90] Everything was now so public that silence was unhelpful. Rosina had to be defeated, at whatever cost. Bulwer's friends could only sicken at the spectacle of his humiliation:

It is a sad instance of the dreadful penalties attending an indiscretion!!! Or rather, in his case, indiscretions; for though the first includes all, his ill-advised, ill-assorted *marriage – the greatest cast in any man's life for good or ill –* yet still his infidelities since to his detestable wife, however provoked or excusable to some persons they may appear, now bitterly revenge themselves on him, in preventing him from gaining the redress he might seek, and in many cases excluding him from sympathy. A high-hearted honourable man, condemned for life to misery! *What an example!* [91]

There was no abatement in the attempted surveillance of Rosina, and little attempt to pay her allowance with regularity. Her life in Swiss hotels, from 1842–46, was full of incident. Lytton found himself sued by an hotelier for his wife's unpaid bill, while Rosina found herself nearly penniless in the unlikely context of a Swiss revolution. In 1849 her liaison with a Mr Ross in Chelsea was under investigation. Between 1852 and 1853 Lytton was employing the resources of the French Interior Ministry, his son and a clairvoyant to discover Rosina's whereabouts in France. The chase was unending.[92] Strangest of all, Rosina claimed that, while living with imposed economy in Llangollen between 1853 and 1855, the small town was visited by a succession of spies sent by Lytton and that there was a plot to poison her. She was so ill at this time that Lytton was confidently predicting her death, even though it is very unlikely that he was actually intent on engineering it.[93] Fleeing to Taunton in 1855, which she described as 'Elysium',[94] she could not shake off her pursuers. Here Lytton employed a local solicitor named Trenchard to make regular reports. He largely disappointed his employer by reporting that 'Lady Lytton leads a very quiet life'.[95] It is not difficult to imagine how damaging this kind of pressure must have been on a mind whose equilibrium was as fragile as Rosina's. Paranoia became a central feature of increasingly wild accusations. The Lord Chancellor of England was identified as one of the plotters.[96]

Rosina, too, was determined to fight with any weapons that came to hand. Her accumulated sense of grievance merely confirmed feminist leanings that she had adopted from her mother. If the courts failed her as a resource, as they did many Victorian women, she would present her case to the public in the written word. Her tactic was to appeal over the heads of official England to a wider public. She sought opinion as an ally, knowing full well how much Lytton detested the open discussion of his private life. Unfortunately, her personality hampered an effective exposition of her case. She quarrelled with everyone and accused everyone. There was not a lawyer or a publisher who was not branded a cheat, a deceiver or an incompetent.[97] More important still, she quarrelled with her family. No Victorian woman could vindicate herself without the support of her clan, but Rosina referred to 'the Noodle FitzDoodles alias Doyles'. Her uncle was 'a poor spendthrift' and her cousin, Sir Francis Doyle 'a wrecker'.[98] Significantly, Sir Francis remained on reasonable terms with Lytton even at the stormiest moments in the marriage.[99]

For the same reason, if Edward found friendships hard to sustain, Rosina found them impossible. Her self-obsession was hard to live with. In July 1838, a useful friendship with Mrs Wyndham Lewis came to an acrimonious end when Rosina admitted that the death of a dog had so prostrated her that she had forgotten to write in condolence when Mr Lewis passed away.[100] A few months earlier, there had been a rupture with Miss Greene that was never to be mended. An understanding that Rosina had once described as never having been 'shaken by the shock of contending interests, chilled by adversity, or scorched by the sunlight of prosperity',[101] was thrown away once Miss Greene took charge of her children. She was deemed to have passed over to the enemy. Every friendship that Rosina entered into was endlessly tested and strained until it broke. In this at least she was exactly like her husband. But Victorian women needed friends more than men if they were to fight public campaigns.

Nor was this the only problem. Rosina despised the very people to whom she was appealing. The British public was 'an Ass'.[102] Oddly enough, in this too she agreed with her husband. Such an opinion did not prevent her from being surprised when her work was given a lukewarm reception by that same public. For example, *Lady Lytton's Appeal to the Charity and Justice of the English People*, printed in 1857, carried an advertisement that would deter any male purchaser in language that would shock many female readers. Failing to understand this, Rosina preferred to blame an organised conspiracy, accusing her husband of having 'circled my life with a snare, and crowned it with a curse'.[103] She described her native country to her American publishers as this 'soi-disant moral and very Pharisaical England', while the editor of *The Times* was treated to the opinion that 'vice is not yet publicly chartered among English gentlemen – though like all others it exists to a fearful extent'.[104]

Obviously, the worst aspect of this English hypocrisy was the institutionalised oppression of women. Rosina saw the legal and political systems as a male plot. A woman had difficulty in making her voice heard at all. Her novels are full of digressions on this point. In *Very Successful*, she dismissed the story of Adam's rib as 'ridiculous', and merely an attempt to obscure the fact that 'injustice to our sex began with the world, and it is the *one* tradition that most men inviolately preserve'.[105] It was in England that this 'dark and Jesuitical hypocrisy in the systematically unjust conduct of men towards women' had been most vigorously pursued.[106] A woman was 'the only beast of burden not included in the Cruelty to Animals Act'.[107] Englishmen preferred women 'who are the best possible imitations of automatons'.[108] When a husband practised violence on a wife this was not only condoned but positively applauded.[109] Such vigorous writing brought the approval of early feminists like Georges Sand:

Acceptez mon amitié, lignons nous toutes deux contre un sexe qui n'a donné que deceptions et tortures; consolons nous réciproquement; et prouvons au monde que la femme jetée par la malheur au dehors de sa sphère reprend le sceptre de l'intelligence.110*

Unfortunately, very few contemporaries, men or women, would have agreed with her. The women's suffrage movement was in its infancy, and the violence of Rosina's language was offputting to some who might have generally sympathized with her theme.

Most damaging of all was the fact that, if she loathed the British as a whole, Rosina detested British women most of all. She was a feminist who roundly condemned her own gender for their passivity, and their acceptance of a code of values that made them ladies rather than women. England needed 'more *women* and fewer females'.111 Her detestation started with Queen Victoria. She expressed the hope that Prince Albert would celebrate their wedding anniversary by biting her 'till the blood streamed down her (as that *ornament* to the English Cabinet, Sir Liar, used to do mine)'.112 *Miriam Sedley* was dedicated to Henriette d'Angeville who had just climbed Mont Blanc. The comparison was all too clear. French women did everything, English women did nothing:

La *Femelle Britannique* ... est vraiment une nullité odieuse, et voilà pourquoi le commerce social est une chose incomprise chez nous; car, tandis que la France a produit tant de femmes célèbres et de grandes dames, l'Angleterre ne fit guère que *mettre bas* (et *à bas*) des femelles! des femelettes et des *fine Ladies*! La première ne sait rien, la seconde ne fait rien, et la troisième ne dit rien.113†

Accusing English women of 'an intense nullity' was a point of view, but it was hardly likely to make them a receptive audience for Rosina's grievances. To claim sympathy as an oppressed woman while detailing all the short-comings of her gender was a difficult line to take. It was intemperate and imprudent.

Rosina, however, particularly after 1840, was beyond restraint. Obsessively, she focused on one point only, namely her role as the bringer of retribution.

---

* Accept my friendship, let us both unite against a sex which has only given us deceptions and torments; let us console each other; and let us show the world that a woman who is ejected from her own milieu by misfortune takes up the wand of intelligence again.

† The British Woman ... is in truth an odious nothingness, and that is why social interaction is unknown among us; for while France has produced so many great and distinguished women England has only contrived to put women down as bluestockings, little women and *fine ladies*! The first knows nothing, the second does nothing and the third says nothing.

The storylines of her novels are endlessly interrupted by diatribes about her own case. Friends counselling moderation were swept aside. Her anguish and sense of accumulated wrong were transformed into volcanic outpourings of vituperation. She no longer had the self-respect that regarded the opinion of others as important:

> As for the iced cucumber cant of Society – more especially English Society – I despise it so cordially that, as a *choice*, I would rather outrage than conciliate it ... No, what English Society requires and bows down to and worships is a loathsome, leprous, incarnate Infamy like Sir Liar Coward Bulwer Lytton.[114]

Forthright statements such as these commanded attention, but they could be seen as so pungent as to create, in reaction, a certain sympathy for Lytton himself. More and more, everything about Rosina ran to extremes.

Her most outrageous coup was the publication of *Cheveley* in 1839, which gave her the great pleasure of setting herself up as a rival to her husband in the writing of novels. Ironically subtitled *The Man of Honour*, it is less a novel than a manifesto. In it the reader is introduced to the odious de Clifford family, presided over by an overbearing matriarch, all too recognisable as Mrs Bulwer. This character 'resembled a withered crab-apple, gifted with a parrot's beak and tongue', and spoke an affected English, with words like 'vaustly' and 'Momselle' as the stock in trade. Henry Bulwer becomes Herbert Grimstone, a rake who, having gone quickly through his grandmother's income, embarks on a career of the most unprincipled politics. Lytton became Lord de Clifford, who practised 'conjugal tyranny'. If any doubt remained about the accreditation, among de Clifford's many mistresses is listed a certain 'Laura Priest'. Cumulatively, the family was capable of anything, 'from the dressing of a child to the drowning of a puppy'. It was unsubtle character assassination that exposed Bulwer family secrets to the full scrutiny of contemporary society. Intended to do hurt, it succeeded beyond Rosina's expectations, and no doubt stung her husband's family into promoting the Paris investigation of 1840.

Inevitably the Bulwers denounced 'that most unnatural book', in which there was not 'a shadow of truth'.[115] Mrs Bulwer fell ill, and blamed the malady on 'the woman who crept into the family she maligns by sacrificing her virtue at the age of six and twenty as a trap for the honour of my son'. Henry Bulwer promised to do all in his power to stop the book being published on the Continent, complaining that he had, unfairly, been the most vilified. He advocated a severe response:

> She certainly is *the very worst woman* I ever heard of: and tho' I am of a placable disposition, and endeavour always to keep myself so, I confess that in such a case, vengeance might not only be excused, but become a duty towards society,

which can only be improved or kept up by making a distinction in our conduct towards the bad and the good. But in such a case there should be no half measures. If any vengeance were taken it should be a *tremendous one.*[116]

Lytton himself refused to allow his brother the role of principal victim. He never questioned for a moment the idea that he was most in need of sympathy. In particular, it was barely supportable that some reviewers should prefer Rosina's literary talents to his own: 'They praise the talent of the wretched trash. They who have denied ME talents! ... My God what a country this is when one who as I have – makes his age his debtors – can have no protection in public feeling from such an outrage.' Rosina's only 'distinction is the name she bares'.[117] He begged John Forster to try to stop further editions and to orchestrate hostile reviews.

No Lytton emerged with credit from the subsequent publicity. Embarrassed friends counselled moderation. Describing *Cheveley* as 'a nine days wonder', John Forster candidly told Lytton that he attached 'a vast deal too much importance to what is obviously infamous, odious, degrading, and most repulsive'. To attempt an answer was to inform the public 'that your brains had not been blown out', guaranteeing the book enormous sales.[118] On the other side, Walter Savage Landor, to whom the book was dedicated, advised Rosina to 'conciliate and not expose'.[119] If anything the publication of the book tilted public sympathy towards Lytton. Long-term critics like Thackeray and the management of *Fraser's Magazine* thought Rosina's hyperbole 'ridiculous'.[120] Had Edward been able to temporise, he might well have been able to capitalise on this new support, but, within a year, he had embroiled himself in the unfortunate adventure in Paris. In fact, neither protagonist wanted peace. The appearance of *Cheveley* merely raised the stakes of the game.

Once Rosina was established on the literary scene, she used her position to launch broadside after broadside at the enemy. Novels like *The Budget of the Bubble Family* and *The World and his Wife* lampooned the Lytton family, often with a considerable degree of wit, and, at the same time, offered platforms for diatribes about the sad conditions in which women lived. The latter, for example, has a character called 'The British Female' named Lady FitzDoodle, and an Earl of Portarjis who was 'a marital tyrant and martinet'. They take on a certain predictability of tone and theme. Lytton increasingly found his wife's productions 'a horrible bore'.[121] But he still tried very hard to put a stop to their publication and circulation. Friends with influence in publishing and journalism, like Forster and Laman Blanchard, were mobilised. Newspaper editors were lobbied and threatened. Publishers, like Richard Bentley, were warned that if they handled Rosina's writings they would never profit from Lytton's own work.[122] Throughout his life, Edward Lytton could never accept that the best way to neutralise insult and scandal is to remain silent. His instinct was always to vindicate bruised vanity in public, cost what it might.

Rosina was therefore quite right to fear the efforts of a 'Press Gang', organised by 'Sir Liar' to silence and besmirch her efforts. She identified Dickens, Blanchard, Forster and Douglas Jerrold as its prominent members. Although her judgement wobbled somewhat when she denounced the same 'Gang' for praising 'gross', 'coarse' and 'blasphemous' books by the Brontës, supreme examples in her view of vacuous British females,[123] her sense of grievance had a basis in fact; 'la camaraderie, c'est le fléau de ce pays et du siècle, toute est clique, soit en art, soit en littérature, soit en politique; et hors de la clique – point de salut, c'est à dire pas de chance'.[124]* She retaliated by using the dedication at the front of a new novel, *The School for Husbands*, to expose her persecution, and by organising a gang of her own. Her most prominent supporters were Thomas and Jane Carlyle. The latter observed that:

> When you describe that man and his treatment of you, I feel *amazed* before the whole thing, as in the presence of the Infinite; it is all so diabolical – so out of the course of nature, that I, who have mercifully had to do with only imperfect *human* beings at *worst*, *never* with an incarnate devil, cannot realise it to myself, and cannot get any more intelligent impression from it than from a bad dream, or a Balzac novel.[125]

Quite deliberately the Lyttons divided the literary world between them. In this company, too, everyone could only be an enemy or a friend. Both Rosina and Edward used the written word to demand that public opinion should not only hear their case but also agree with them. Even after her death, Rosina's son was still trying to block the publication of his mother's letters.[126]

Drink, debt, violence, surveillance, the bribing of servants and literary fisticuffs represented a steady build-up of volcanic pressure. There was no thought of surrender or compromise. When a blow was struck, the victim thought only of returning the injury with interest. A catastrophic explosion was always possible, and it happened in 1858. As early as 1839, during the *Cheveley* imbroglio, Forster had predicted that the dispute was becoming so bizarre that it would all end in 'a madhouse'.[127] He proved prophetic.

---

* Good fellowship is the scourge of this country and this century, everything is cliquish, be it in art or literature or politics; and outside the clique – no safety, that is to say no opportunity.

Rosina's behaviour became odder and odder, no doubt assisted by a heavy intake of alcohol and her fear of persecution. Public exposure remained her most effective weapon. She took to attending productions of her husband's plays and orchestrating booing and hissing.[128] She wrote volleys of letters, sometimes twenty a day, addressed to 'Sir Liar Coward Bulwer', which were distributed to clubs and hotels frequented by her husband. She tried to sue a Miss Sellars, a music teacher from Weston-super-Mare, for alienating her husband's affections. As loudly and as widely as print would carry, she accused her husband of every imaginable vice, much of it uncomfortably plausible.[129]

In May 1851 London was treated to a particularly ripe example of what Rosina could do by way of causing embarrassment. A play was to be performed at Devonshire House, written by Lytton, in aid of the newly-established charity, the Guild of Literature and Art. Queen Victoria was to attend. As an opportunity for display, it was therefore everything Rosina could wish for. She wrote to the Duke of Devonshire, warning him that she would appear disguised as an orange-seller, in order to pelt the Queen, whom she called a murderer, with rotten eggs. Devonshire was forced to employ 'detective police' to patrol Piccadilly. In the event, Rosina did appear, but only to distribute parodies of the play. The piece was entitled *Not So Bad As We Seem* and the parody *Even Worse Than We Seem*. Once again, the public character of Lytton had had mud thrown at it. He was made to look ridiculous. As a topic of conversation in the clubs and the salons, it was irresistible. Charles Dickens, one of the principal actors in the play, commiserated with Lytton and called Rosina 'the misfortune of your life'.[130]

Worse was to come. In 1858 Lytton was offered a Cabinet post in the Derby-Disraeli government. Rosina at once determined either that her allowance would be increased substantially or that she would behave in a manner that would make the Colonial Office 'rather too hot to hold him'.[131] Under the existing rules of political life, those accepting ministerial office had to seek re-election, which, for Lytton, meant fighting for his Hertfordshire constituency once more. A meeting was fixed for 8 June in the county town of Hertford and Rosina borrowed money to attend it. She arrived too late to prevent Lytton's re-election, but, as his acceptance speech was being delivered, she appeared among the crowd shouting 'Make way for the member's wife'. Lytton was so appalled by the apparition that he fell silent and then fled. Rosina mounted the hustings and regaled the voters with a speech of her own:

How can the people of England submit to have such a man at the head of the Colonies, who ought to have been in the Colonies as a transport [convicted criminal] years ago. He murdered my child and tried to murder me. The very clothes I stand up in were supplied to me by a friend.[132]

The voters of Hertford much enjoyed this impromptu entertainment and escorted the lady back to the railway station with expressions of boisterous sympathy.

The incident was more than Lytton could bear. He was less impressed by the assertions of friends that Rosina's action had been so outrageous and 'so repugnant to all womanly feeling' than by suggestions that it could only have originated in 'insanity'.[133] He determined to try to rid himself of Rosina once and for all, taking advantage of the 'facilities the lunacy law affords for disposing of inconvenient wives'.[134] Doctors and solicitors were despatched to Taunton in order to amass evidence of Lady Lytton's instability. She was then inveigled into coming to London, on the pretence of discussing her allowance. When she appeared, doctors committed her to the care of a Dr Robert Gardiner in his asylum in Brentford. Here she was kept under restraint from 23 June to 17 July.[135] For the whole of this month she was regularly interviewed by doctors, and her answers were uninhibited. She promised to murder her gaolers and to do violence to herself. She reiterated her claims that Lytton had killed their daughter Emily, possibly after an incestuous relationship, but the matter that was 'generally uppermost' in her mind was that he had committed sodomy with Disraeli, and that this was the reason why he had been offered a Cabinet post. Having had the run of the London brothels before he was thirteen years old, he was now anxious to take Disraeli's advice to travel in the East where 'seraglios of boys' awaited him.[136] The official world, represented by the Commissioners in Lunacy, now had to decide whether Lady Lytton was indeed mad, or whether a tiresome woman had been kidnapped in order to silence her. If the latter, there was the implication that some of her stories might be true. Rosina's campaign to expose Lytton to public scandal had reached its pinnacle.

Briefly, as the 'Tigress of Taunton', Rosina became a national figure.[137] Liberals in the west country took up her case as a very effective way of embarrassing the new Tory government.[138] A public meeting, held in Taunton on 6 July, decided to offer Rosina the protection of her neighbours against any further attempt to affront 'the rights and liberties of the subject'. It was rumoured that the Somerset Yeomanry were preparing to march on London. In the capital, the *Daily Telegraph* denounced the activities of 'the myrmidons of her flattered and successful husband', comparing her case with that of the Man in the Iron Mask.[139] For Rosina, all this was manna from heaven. Gleefully she joined the hunt, issuing an *Address of Lady Bulwer to the Electors of Hertford*. It was advertised as 'the extraordinary narrative of an outrageous violation of liberty and law in the forcible seizure and incarceration of Lady Bulwer Lytton in the gloomy cell of a madhouse!!!' [140] The pamphlet rehearsed all aspects of her marriage from Rosina's point of view, reaching a crescendo with the Hertford incident and her committal. It was little consolation for the new Cabinet Minister to receive letters from Commissioners in Lunacy like Lord Shaftesbury or former friends of Rosina like Rebecca Ryves, agreeing that putting her under temporary restraint had been entirely justified.[141] The humiliation was crushing and brought on illness.

In the end, Lytton bought peace, and in this respect Rosina's campaign objectives were fully achieved. Her outstanding debts of £2500 were to be paid off, and her allowance was to be increased from £400 to £500 p.a. In return, Rosina was to leave the country immediately, chaperoned by her son Robert. By 17 July the pair were at Luchon in the Pyrenees, but it was not a happy arrangement. Robert barely knew his mother, while Rosina began to accuse him to being party to the plot to incarcerate her. She called him 'that white-livered little reptile'.[142] Not surprisingly, after a few months, he retreated back to England, and allegedly never saw his mother again. Quite simply he lacked the stamina to take responsibility for his father's actions by removing Rosina from his immediate line of vision. Almost certainly, Lytton should never have asked him to make the attempt.

In fact, Lytton was never good in a crisis. Faced with scandal and difficulty, his instinct was to place the blame on other shoulders. In 1858 he tested his oldest friend, John Forster, in this way. As a result, the friendship was ruptured for three years and even when resumed, never regained its old intimacy. In October 1857 Lytton had asked Forster's advice about having his wife declared insane. His friend had, in reply, urged great caution:

> Pray, pray be careful in what you do as to the matter you mention. There is no middle way between leaving such a case altogether alone, and treating it, out and out, as a case of insanity. I have long been convinced that she *is* insane – but it is a case belonging exactly to the class which it is most difficult to get medical men to certify.[143]

When the whole project collapsed into scandal, Lytton tried to claim that the whole idea had been Forster's. In acrimonious letters, the charge was repeatedly made and just as steadily rebutted.[144] Forster insisted that 'I was not your "adviser"'.[145] The breach lasted until 1861, when Forster tried to revive 'those old times in which you had that large share in my life and thoughts', but he had to admit that, almost irrevocably, there was 'a sort of separation between us'.[146] As Rosina might well have appreciated, the undermining of this friendship hurt Lytton far more than any new arrangement about money. Forster had been the friend and factotum on whom Lytton had absolutely relied. His loss was irreparable. Lytton, who had few long-term relationships, had once again put an impossible strain on the emotions of an old friend and had lost him. Here was the real cost of the Hertford incident.

On top of all this, the drama of 1858 settled nothing. Rosina continued to launch attacks, describing herself as 'a White Slave' and 'the legal Victim of the most unscrupulous Villain and the meanest liar of even this intensely mean age'.[147] She continued to bombard everyone in Lytton's circle with accusatory letters. Others wrote to him anonymously denouncing his 'vice and profligacy'.[148] Interestingly, Lytton seems to have kept many of these letters, and could only apologise to friends who had felt Rosina's wrath. He still believed her to be insane, but the experiment of 1858 could obviously not be repeated. As he told Disraeli, 'I know not what I can do, but bear and forebear'.[149] He accepted that the scandal had brought a sudden end to all his aspirations to high office: 'Lady Lytton is a complete stopper to all my personal interest and objects in a political career.'[150] Even facing another public meeting at an election brought on nightmares. The incident had neutered Lytton as a politician.

Late in life, Rosina wrote about the necessity of forgiving and forgetting: 'pray to God, to give us that forgetfulness which will enable us, not merely in words, but in truth and spirit, to forgive those who have chronically and irreparably injured us'.[151] Her prayer went unanswered. About the same time, she wrote a poem, addressed to her husband, entitled *False Heart Beware*. It ends with the thought:

> Now the worst for me is past, and fate's bitter cup is drained,
> It was not of the gall, but the giver I complained.
> But for thee false heart beware, fate aye in a circle moves,
> And the chalice she gives back, oft tenfold more bitter proves.[152]

The lines could just as easily have been written by her husband. Both found a kind of therapy in sustained hatred. Both enjoyed heroic egoism which led them to discount and ultimately punish the views of anyone who saw the world differently. As a result, neither found friends easy to make or keep. It is pointless to apportion blame. Both had characters that could be poisonously selfish. The sadness is that each of them paid a terrible price for their behaviour. Edward suffered public humiliation after humiliation, which helped to destroy his health and career, and which confirmed him in feelings of isolation and misanthropy. Rosina continued to fling herself against convention and good taste until the day she died, worried about debt and finding a friend in alcohol. She saw herself as the victim of England's 'Political System of Sewage'.[153] She published little or nothing in the last years of her life and quickly fell into obscurity. There was no family reconciliation. It would not have pleased her that her claims to attention rested largely on the notoriety of her relationship with her husband. When he passed out of view, so in a sense did she. She died on 12 March 1882, and was buried in an unmarked grave in Upper Sydenham.

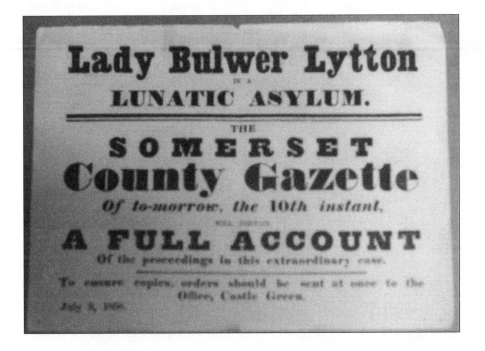

'Little Boots', Bulwer's daughter Emily, by Daniel Maclise. (*Courtesy of Knebworth House*)

4

Robert and Emily

The real victims of the Lytton marriage were their children. Neither parent had any workable relationship with Robert or Emily. It was rumoured that Rosina, in particular, preferred her dogs. Both parents made a show of affection, entering into custody battles with relish, but their aim was less to give the children security than to deny their affection to a rival. Edward, in 1840, counted it a great success to win a legal ruling which excluded Rosina from any role in the upbringing of her children.[1] But this did not mean that he wished to be unduly burdened with the responsibility himself. Instead, they were handed over to friends and schoolmasters. Both Rosina and Edward lived abroad a great deal, often in circumstances that were not appropriate for young children. They were parents who, emotionally and geographically, were distant from their son and daughter. Emily and Robert tried very hard to win their parents' support and approval with extravagant protestations of duty and obedience, but there was little affection in return. They were little more than adjuncts to the careers and ambitions of their mother and father. Friends of the family, like Miss Greene and John Forster, pitied them.

As far as Lytton himself was concerned, it was obvious that children owed their parents more than their parents owed them:

> Every nation above the savage has recognised as a cardinal law of piety the reverence due to parents from children, and said very little about the duties parents owe to children. And for a very good reason – Nature takes care that parents in general amply discharge all the elementary duties to children. But it requires a higher principle than brute nature to make children do their duty to parents, and any philosophy that should weaken by questioning that principle would be diabolical.[2]

Children should be passively obedient, so well-behaved that their parents were never troubled, and, above all, grateful for any mark of affection. Lytton claimed that he only fought Rosina to save the children and wondered, 'Will they ever thank me?'[3] Later generations of the Lytton family were puzzled by his attitude; 'why he did not take son and daughter to his heart and never part with them more is a mystery to me'.[4] Contemporaries were not so much in doubt. To them it was clear that Edward and Rosina demanded above all the gratification of personal needs, and that this fact made it impossible for them to respond to need in others. Their own children were beyond some emotional boundary.

After the separation of 1836 Robert and Emily were largely brought up by Miss Greene, with an allowance from Lytton of £100 p.a. In committing them to her charge he regarded himself as acting magnanimously, because Miss Greene was '*her* friend, not mine'.[5] Four years later, alliances shifted, and she became Edward's ally, purveying gossip about Rosina and keeping the children free of maternal influences.[6] From a distance, Lytton issued instructions on how his son and daughter were to be brought up. Governesses for Emily were vetted. French and a little history were prescribed, as well as music and drawing. Contact with Rosina was of course to be discouraged. Above all, his daughter should be prepared to fit a particular model of womanhood:

> I see an elegant gentle mind that cannot fail, under God's blessing, to obtain its own reward in the love of all who know her. I have only had occasion to find fault with her forgetfulness of order and not taking care of things, but I have spoken very severely to her on this head, and I think her already improved. But it should be kept up strictly, because want of forethought and a certain preciseness is a great blot in a woman's character hereafter in all household affairs, and there is nothing more valuable whether to her father or her husband, than the habit of order and housewifeliness.[7]

In other words, Emily was to be as unlike Rosina as possible. Instead she should be moulded into Lytton's conception of womanhood, a process which his wife had so bitterly resisted.

Supervising the upbringing of children from a distance suited both Lyttons very well. In private Rosina frankly admitted that, 'Though I do not like the society of my children, and do not know what people mean when they talk of maternal affection, I still feel that I should be glad to hear of their happiness – but away from myself'.[8] In her wilder moments, she escaped responsibility by claiming she was not their mother: 'I never want to hear anything of Sir Liar Coward Janus Allpuff Bulwer Lytton's worthy son, and would rather not be reminded that I have the misfortune and disgrace of being his nominal mother!'[9] Her attitude was so well known that few people credited her grievances as an outraged mother, even if they saw her as an ill-treated wife. Indeed Thackeray jokingly remarked that, if he really wished to hurt his wife, Lytton should send her the children:

> Hold then your news, how Lady Bulwer panted to have her children back again and everybody roared and cried fudge. The woman is known for her horrid

selfishness about the children ... and told Mrs – whom we know that seriously her daughter was the most unlikeable, ill-tempered, wicked child possible. The best thing Bullwig could do would be to send her the children, if he wanted to vex her he could not take better means.[10]

Rosina assiduously promoted the idea that chief among her sufferings was the loss of her children and the frustration of maternal feelings. In fact, nothing could be further from the truth.

In this respect, if in no other, Edward Lytton walked in step with his wife. Fundamentally, he regarded his children as threats, as competitors for affection that should rightfully be his. When Emily was born, he begged Rosina not to transfer love from him to the new baby, whom he referred to as 'it' or 'that':

Let me say one word, and make one favour, which is, that whenever oo is vexed with me, oo will not go out from me to our child! Do not say, 'This is kinder to me, or this loves me better than *he* does', do not let a being ... which is only just come unto the world in which I for three years have known and loved you, do not let it be as dear to you as me who has given and will give you proofs of affection, which *that* cannot for many years equal ... That a creature hitherto without sense, knowledge, feeling, attachment, should at once become dearer to you than I am, I do not and will not believe.[11]

The same fear of competition would later lead him to crush his son's efforts to establish himself as a poet or essayist. Any sign of talent in his children caused surprise. On seeing them after an interval of nearly two years, in January 1838, he exclaimed, they 'are so grown, so improved, so intelligent, they *can understand me now!*' [12] But neither Emily or Robert ever improved enough to make them an agreeable, daily presence in Lytton's life. Instead, they had to be subordinate and distant.

By default, the most important person in the children's early lives was Miss Greene. Living with her was the only point of stability they knew. Their mother was unknown and visits from their father were intimidating.[13] Later in life, Miss Greene wrote 'Recollection' of these years, being, like so many people associated with the Lyttons, driven into self-vindication. There is no doubt about the genuine affection she felt for the children, but there is always a hint of a growing possessiveness. She opposed proposals that Emily should be sent to school at eleven, arguing that 'she is a very peculiar child, tho conscious of my defects in other respects, I do think I can be of use to her for a little longer from my knowledge of those peculiarities'.[14] More sinisterly, she appointed herself as the children's moral guardian. From experience, she knew of Rosina's drinking and of her association with Hume and others, and she quickly came to see Lytton as even more depraved:

'Sir Edward liked doing cruel things to persons in his power.' [15] Emily and
Robert could not possibly be surrendered to him while Knebworth housed
'his second family, presided over by Laura Deacon, alias Mrs Beaumont,
alias the Vicomtesse d'Azzimart'. If Emily, in particular, came into contact
with such people, 'God knows who her father may choose to introduce her
to'.[16] Given the Lyttons' style of life, Miss Greene's reservations may be
thought justified but, in the Victorian world, to try to override parental
rights was to tread dangerous ground. Quite simply, whatever her affection
for the children, Miss Greene had no standing in the matter. Hostility
between her and the Lyttons could only engender more tension in the
children's minds.

In the early 1840s Lytton began to make determined efforts to undermine
Miss Greene's influence. In the autumn of 1842 she accompanied Emily to
Neuwied in Germany, where the girl was to go to school. Much to Lytton's
annoyance, instead of returning home, Miss Greene established herself in
Frankfurt and continued to supervise Emily's life. In response, he formally
forbade communication between the two: 'some of your letters give her
great pain, and she really needs all forbearance and sympathy in the ordeal
she must necessarily go through'.[17] Six years later, for much the same reason,
he asked her not to visit Robert at Harrow, as such visits 'rather unsettle
him'.[18] By 1849 he was formally accusing her of trying to 'insinuate an
alienation' between him and his son. He told Forster that Miss Greene's
'veracity is never to be relied upon'.[19] Her 'Recollections' were probably
written between January and July 1847, at the moment when her relations
with Lytton were fast deteriorating.

The consequences of these altercations for the Lytton children were
entirely harmful, as they became the focus for competing adult jealousies.
Both Edward and Rosina used them as bargaining counters, while Miss
Greene challenged the rights and affections of both parents. When Lytton's
grandson read the 'Recollections', he concluded that,

> Although no one really behaved well throughout this tragic story, though it is
> one long chronicle of faults in tact, judgement and character, yet I am more
> struck than I have ever been before by the redeeming features and the extenuating
> circumstances. *The pity of it all strikes me much more forcibly than the wrong of
> it all* [underlined in original].

He blamed Mrs Bulwer for undermining the marriage, a Miss Fraser for
introducing Rosina to brandy and water, and Miss Greene for being 'a
constant irritant'.[20] In such a welter of mismatched emotions, apportioning
precise measures of guilt is indeed unprofitable, but what is clear is that
the children suffered most.

A particularly ugly element in this tangle of competing claims involved money. The cost of the children's upbringing and education was cited as the reason why Lytton's allowance to Rosina could not be increased, while the profligacy of his wife was used as an excuse to keep the children on a spartan regime.[21] There was no mention of the cost of keeping up the household of his second family or of the apartment in the Albany. Before his mother's death in 1843, Lytton was probably in genuine, financial embarrassment, being reduced to borrowing five pounds from Disraeli: 'the small sum of five pounds would be exceedingly useful to me in my endeavours to regain my livelihood in the pursuits I so much love ... You will know ... that I am the *victim* of no common degree of art on the part of my destroyer ... It is my duty to myself and to an only son not to sink if possible under the shameful treachery I have experienced.'[22] But after inheriting Knebworth he had a substantial income, together with the profits of writing. At his death he left over £75,000.[23] Such figures made him a wealthy man. The memory of the poverty-stricken years of his early married life never left him, but he acted on it in ways that were unreasonable.

In particular, he never stopped preaching economy to his children, describing himself as living 'in a wretched lodging at a few shillings a week'.[24] Robert's time at Harrow was made miserable by being known as 'Poor Lytton'. The schoolboy's letters complain of being made the object of charity, even by the sons of 'poor country clergymen' and of being endlessly accused of extravagance by a father who was in fact a stranger to him; 'I am not going to harp upon that and gain for myself as I have done before from you the epithet of "conceited". I may be so. I don't deny it. It may possibly be hereditary.' The boy agreed that, if his father found him 'unintelligent, base and soulless', to expect affection was unreasonable. But, significantly, these words of grievance and defiance always gave way to appeals for regard and expressions of a willingness to help. He will leave Harrow if necessary, and make do with a private tutor.[25] Robert early took the lesson that his needs were not to be set up in competition with those of his father.

Emily was subjected to the same astringency, and responded in the same way. Lytton looked forward to the day when she could become his unpaid housekeeper.[26] She in return was all compliance. Having only one morning dress and one evening dress was bearable. As for shoes and gloves, 'one *can* do with everything if it comes to that – and I will patch up and wash what I have got'. She looked forward to the day when she could contribute to the family income by taking on embroidery or the translation of German texts. Above all, she wanted to make her father's life easier:

Why should you struggle and I not? Why in the midst of misfortune not retain at least the happiness of thinking that I have proved to you how unjust were your reproaches. Retain I entreat you, for the future the £20. Perhaps some day I shall be able to repay you what you have already expended on me.[27]

Emily, like her brother, was made conscious of how great a burden she was on her father's stock of money and affection. The children seem to have been given the notion that they were required to expiate some terrible guilt. The only way of doing so was to subordinate themselves to a father's aspirations.

Emily's childhood was predictably miserable, and subject to the strictest regulation. All correspondence between her and her mother was to be censored, in order to avoid any 'unproper tone'.[28] The giving of presents was discouraged.[29] Above all, she must not discuss her parents with any third party. It was a subject connected with too much 'terrible ignominy and disgrace'; 'This last *is* an objection that I consider binding on you – it is due to my honour and my name – to my inexpiable wrongs – to my authority as a father and my duty to preserve you ... from what I regard as contamination.'[30] Injunctions such as these placed Emily in an impossible situation. There was no way of preventing Rosina trying to get in touch but, when such attempts were known to Lytton, agonising charges of treachery were the result. 'I throw myself on the generosity of those I love or live with. Therefore my whole world seems to crumble at my feet when I find that I have been leaning on treacherous beasts ... Even then I could not ... yield you up to her ... My curse were better to you than her blessing.'[31] In Lytton's admonitions, 'ordinary good breeding' dictated that Rosina should be treated as if she had ceased to exist.[32]

Lytton saw himself in a contractual relationship with his daughter. Repeatedly he offered to be both 'Mother and Father' to her. In return, she was to acknowledge his predicament and act accordingly:

My wound never closes – it burns and rankles within me – and will to the last. But all I can ask of you my child is to look to me as *Mother* and as *Father* – to confide in me as you would in the first – never to *fear* that I will be a harsh judge. For if you *fear* me you will deceive me – and Deceit is the only thing I should find it hard to pardon.[33]

Emily tried very hard to meet the heavy, emotional demands made on her. Her letters to her father run into a hyperbole of protestation: 'I feel it as a sort of relief to let you know that in me you have a fellow-sufferer – that there is at least one heart that feels and bleeds for you – that loves you with no common affection – You Papa dearest are my all.'[34] Unfortunately, no amount of protestation could ever convince Lytton that he was the

1. Bulwer Lytton as a young man, by A. E. Chalon. (*Courtesy of Knebworth House*)

2. Portrait of Bulwer Lytton by Daniel Maclise. (*Courtesy of Knebworth House*)

3. Rosina Doyle Wheeler, who married Bulwer Lytton in 1827. (*Courtesy of Knebworth House*)

4. Mrs Bulwer, Bulwer Lytton's mother. (*Courtesy of Knebworth House*)

5. Rosina Bulwer Lytton. (*Courtesy of Knebworth House*)

6. Emily Bulwer Lytton. (*Courtesy of Knebworth House*)

7. Miss Greene. (*Courtesy of Knebworth House*)

8. Robert Bulwer Lytton. (*Courtesy of Knebworth House*)

9. Knebworth House, from Knebworth Park. (*Courtesy of Knebworth House*)

10. The State Drawing Room, Knebworth House. (*Courtesy of Knebworth House*)

11. The Banqueting Hall, Knebworth House. (*Courtesy of Knebworth House*)

12. Bulwer Lytton in his study, Knebworth House. (*Courtesy of Knebworth House*)

13. Bulwer Lytton with a pen. (*Courtesy of Knebworth House*)

object of affection. Such claims always had to be tried in the fire. He never felt reassurance.

In spite of offering total parenthood, Lytton actually saw Emily very infrequently. He could clearly live without her company, and it is even possible that the dandy in him found her deformity hard to bear. His letters to her include beauty tips. Almond powder is recommended for the hands, with lemon juice under the nails, because 'it is always worthwhile to be as *belle* as one can. And hands are a title deed to Aristocracy'.[35] The decision to send her to specialists in Neuwied and Canstatt, for the painful correction of the misshapen shoulder, was taken in the hope that she would return 'with no drawback to a shape that should be perfect'.[36] Whatever the reason, father and daughter saw each other infrequently. Lytton's letters to her mingle hopes that they will soon be together with excuses why this could not immediately happen. Literary deadlines, financial pressures and the state of his own health were all brought forward as reasons for delay. Allegedly, when dining with Victoria and Albert, 'in spite of the fine Palace and the great people', he thought only of being with his children.[37] His actions hardly bear this out. Not surprisingly, when they did meet, he complained that 'a kind of restraint' existed between Emily and himself, and that she had not yet overcome her 'old fear' of him.[38] Father and daughter both sought the other's affection, and both felt themselves disappointed.

There was little change in the situation when, in 1845, Emily returned from Germany to take up her appointed role as châtelaine of Knebworth. Lytton was elsewhere; in London for politics or in Malvern for his health. He applauded from a distance improvements that she made to the house and the estate, but also piled his own troubles on to her shoulders. He claimed that he was reduced 'to something very like beggary'. Even so, Emily was not to regard herself as a financial burden. In taking care of her he had merely 'obeyed my duty'. Grudging remarks such as these, with no mention of affection, were hardly reassuring. Equally, the trauma of his marriage still blighted his life: 'A man who has gone thro what I have of experience and emotion, has not furrows in his head – he has abysses.' All this produced 'self-absorption', for which he sometimes apologised to his daughter. It also produced illness, real or imaginary, in body and mind; 'But the *mind* – the *faculties* – that fear haunts me and makes me, I confess, an Egotist!'[39] Being quite incapable of coping with emotional and practical problems, Lytton allowed them to overwhelm him.

In 1847, therefore, Emily was asked to cope with someone who was oppressively melodramatic, or depressive, or both:

With regard to my health it is certainly much better than at Knebworth but darkness surrounds and covers me. Often in this struggle for Health, which is something like a daily war with a living foe, when I contemplate the failure that is beyond – Youth gone with all that could cheer it – a hereafter of suffering and sickness, probably to increase, as life must now tend to all decline – a desolate hearth – widowed and yet shackled ... no companionship, except my children ... and you are with me but for a while – our years themselves divide us. Before you lies the future of new ties, before me but the grave of the old. My career over ... my heart almost hopeless – When all these shadows rise before me often I am tempted to give up the strife and lie down and die. But then happily comes a better courage ... and so I march on through the valley of the shadow! If one great and terrible Affliction which now dogs me as a Ghost and makes every hour a sickness and fear be spared to me I think the world will grow bright again. But eno' of my egotisms! [40]

To the last sentence, Emily perhaps could only say amen. The self-obsession that made the writer left little space for others.

The saddest moment in Emily's wretched life was yet to come. Her death, in the spring of 1848, was tragic, not only because she was merely nineteen years old, but also because her parents absorbed the event into their own quarrel, thus robbing it of its dignity. Edward and Rosina combined expressions of hysterical grief with accusations that the other had been responsible for their daughter's death. It became so much a matter of party warfare that accounts of what exactly happened differ wildly. The only common ground is that Emily died in a lodging house in the Brompton Road, probably of consumption, and that when Rosina attempted to see her daughter, after an interval of ten years, she was ordered out of the house by Dr Marshall Hall, whom Lytton had employed to take charge of the case. Everything else is disputed. Both sides turned Emily's death into propaganda in their long-running war.

According to Rosina, Emily was 'murdered' by her husband. Lytton had compelled his daughter to labour for long hours at translations from the German, which he then claimed as his own. As Rosina graphically put it, her husband, 'that incarnate lie of the nineteenth century', knew 'that the primary cause of my poor *murdered* child's illness was the life of hard labour she led to promote her father's ill-gotten and quacky literary reputation as a German scholar (he not knowing a word of the language)'.[41] In fact, Lytton had a reasonable command of German and French. A killing routine of work was compounded by neglect. It was rumoured that Emily had owned very few clothes and had actually died wearing a borrowed nightdress. No medical attention had been offered her until far too late. This account of Emily's death was circulated in pamphlet form,[42] and particularly propagated by a friend of Rosina's named Katherine Planché.

Lytton once again saw a duel as the way of vindicating his honour and threatened to challenge Miss Planché's father.[43] Rosina's story was also oddly supported by Miss Greene, who, by 1848, seems to have switched allegiances yet again. She, too, was in the house in the Brompton Road, and claimed that Lytton hastily destroyed Emily's papers. The girl died 'neglected by all who should have cherished and taken care of her'. Unfortunately, Miss Greene's evidence is itself hardly neutral. She went on to assert that only her 'persevering love' for the girl had made her life tolerable at all.[44]

Lytton's own reaction to his daughter's death was no less colourful, but still self-focused: 'I am crushed – broken down – so young – so gentle – so pity me, pity me.' According to him, Rosina had insinuated herself into the house under a false name, and had only agreed to leave when confronted by stern, medical opinion. She must therefore 'be considered the immediate cause of my daughter's death', for 'a tone of voice would have sufficed with E's terror of her mother'. Twenty years later, Lytton still had in his possession a letter from Dr Hall, which ascribed Emily's death to the moral shock either of seeing or hearing Rosina.[45] With accusation necessarily went self-vindication. He was deeply afraid that the world would find him guilty of negligence. Miss Greene was, by his account, a liar and a hysteric. On no account should third parties interview her.[46] He told Forster that 'it is painful to me, knowing how I have ever kept before me my duty to those children to say a word that serves to vindicate oneself', but that Robert could be called to witness how much his sister had been loved. He also, without any apparent awareness of the questionable taste of the suggestion, asked his friend whether it would be prudent to insert some affectionate remembrance of Emily into the preface of his recently published novel, *Harold*.[47] As has been noted a duel was offered to anyone who questioned his role as a father.[48] He was raw on the subject of reputation. So much had already been opened up to ridicule that any new crisis, even the death of a daughter, seemed to threaten him in a way that his sensitivities could not support. The whole episode is one of violence and egotism. Everyone involved in it coloured the story to their own advantage. Oddest of all is the account given by Robert Lytton, who was in the house when his sister died. In 1848 itself, he was clear that Rosina had been most to blame: 'I don't see what new diablerie she can possibly *affect* had she the feeling of a Mother but I can only look on her almost [as] the murderess of my beloved ... Sister.'[49] Nine years later, he wrote a long account of the Brompton Road story, in which Lytton is again exonerated of all blame. This time, however, Emily was said to have died in her brother's arms.[50] But in 1865, when relations with his father were fraught, the story was completely recast. Robert told his wife that 'the memory of that murdered girl makes it sometimes all but impossible for me to forgive the man who systematically hastened and finally extinguished her existence'. Lytton's 'radical selfishness and indifference to the feelings of others' had finally proved fatal.[51]

Faced with such contradictory evidence, Lytton's grandson could only conclude that both parents 'were in a measure responsible for the unhappiness of her short life'.[52] What is clear is that Emily's life had been wretched, and that the poison within the Lytton family had made her existence sad and her death unlovely.

Many of the themes which characterised Emily's upbringing are also found in Robert's. On Lytton's death, in 1873, Robert was predictably all pious memory:

> He was more to me than a father to a son. The strongest, wisest, truest friend, and we were bound together by many peculiarities – ties woven out of very bitter circumstances, in which affection had yet learnt much sweet and tender consolation. I have been accustomed to lean so implicitly on him for guidance and support in all the difficulties and responsibilities of life, that my forty years of personal experience have virtually indeed been forty years of childhood.[53]

The dependence admitted in the second half of this quotation is more important, however, than the gratitude expressed at its opening. Sixteen years earlier he had written a poem, *To My Father*, which includes the verses:

> For thy sake, how hard have I sought
> To be patient, and earnest, and mild,
> And the pent tears that gush'd to the thought
> Of thy love, have left me a child.
>
> Thy child! … if not all that thou art,
> If not all that should spring from thy worth,
> One who yet seeks to chase from his heart,
> All that shames in its nature his birth.[54]

Very early, Lytton established an emotional domination of his son that was never broken. Robert Lytton would go on to be Viceroy of India, but in his father's presence, or even in the presence of his memory, he remained 'a child'. He always longed for paternal affection and approval, and always feared losing it. Like his sister, he was instructed that the needs of the father were the greater.

The pattern was established in boyhood. Robert adopted all his father's preferences, and hoped for a career in literature or the theatre.[55] The little boy would vehemently defend his father's reputation against any slight.[56] Quite simply, Lytton was hailed as 'the greatest man living', and his 'affection and confidence are the dearest gifts you could give me'.[57] What Robert wanted above all was to establish a firm relationship, and he was happy to be the junior partner in it. At thirteen, he wrote:

> Dearest father I cannot bear to think that you regret having opened your sorrows to me. I am your son. Oh! Let me be your friend. I see that you think me unkind though you do not say so ... I *never never* thought you exacting and if you will accept my sympathy I am ready to give it to you – if you still care for it.[58]

His greatest expression of loyalty was of course to take his father's side against Rosina. He accepted lectures from his father that argued that 'in the whole range of biography, I do not know that I ever heard of one so thoroughly wicked, shameless and debased'.[59] He returned presents sent by his mother, and flatly refused to see her when she tried to visit him at Harrow. It was terrible 'to slight a mother', but worse 'to disobey a father'. He resolved the problem by cutting Rosina out of his life, and even apologising for mentioning her name: 'I will not attempt to say anything of Lady B's character or enter into that painful subject at all, for a mother's disgrace is a fearful and a bitter thing from which every son must shrink, and the less I know of it perhaps, the less wicked I shall think it.'[60]

Filial loyalty was offered, in spite of the fact that Lytton saw his son only infrequently, and sometimes not more than once a year. There were excursions to the theatre and the seaside, but they were rare. When Lytton was abroad or engrossed in politics or writing, Robert was boarded out with friends and then dispatched to Harrow. In the schoolboy's letters there is expressed again and again the wish simply to see his father, mingled with pieces of information that Lytton would find reassuring.[61] To receive a letter from his father was exciting. It was evidence that he was still in his father's affections, though it raised doubts about how long he would stay there:

> I have just heard from my father. What an intense pleasure it gives me to receive a letter of kindness from *him* I cannot tell you. My position and my feelings are so strange, my heart is so full of love for him, full to overflowing, but it is 'darkened' and choked with the most fearful and constant doubts, the most painful suspicions, the most bitter crushing feelings ... Yet where should I garner up my heart but there! My mother is but a name and a prayer to me, and my own adored sister is in heaven. However I am like a drowning man who clutches at straws, and if this be taken from me what shall I look to? What cling to? Surely I must sink.[62]

Just as Miss Greene was the most important adult in Emily's upbringing, so John Forster was in Robert's. It was Forster who visited him in school and who organised entertainment. Lytton was happy to delegate these chores. In later life Robert called Forster 'his second father'. It was a title well-earned.[63]

As a young child, Robert conceded that his father was 'the best judge of what is right for me'.[64] The choice of school was therefore Lytton's and, in spite of the conviction that such establishments 'spoil more talent than they ever awaken', Harrow was selected.[65] The fragmented, but free-spirited, education which Lytton himself had enjoyed was not to be repeated in the next generation. On the contrary, it was to be an upbringing regulated by letter. Some friendships were recommended, others were to be abandoned at whatever cost. When Robert obeyed his father in this respect, he reported that: 'By many of my old friends and former companions ... this change has been remarked and I feel that I am no longer liked or loved as I was by them – that matters not, I should not have mentioned it.'[66] Lytton was free with advice that he himself had never followed when young. Robert, for example, should take up football, and 'amuse yourself healthfully and like a young Spartan'.[67] Always short of money and hesitant about friendships, Robert was miserable at school. Worst of all was his father's stated belief that 'your trial at Harrow has been a complete failure so far as Distinction is concerned'. The boy was repeatedly told that he was letting his father down by not establishing a reputation and a name. This accumulation of imposed guilt was borne by Robert patiently, first because his father's prescriptions were not to be challenged, and secondly because 'in gazing steadfastly on the distant star, I over look the darkness around'.[68]

Only one moment of adolescent rebellion is recorded. In 1850 Lytton, in Nice, received a number of alarming letters detailing irregularities in Robert's behaviour. On a visit to Germany and Belgium, he had 'run after low girls',[69] which left his father with the fear that he might have contracted some kind of venereal disease. From Harrow came reports that the boy had been experimenting with alcohol, tobacco, laudanum and cartharides. Lytton's reaction was unforgiving and furious. He saw himself as not dealing 'with a fault or a vice – but with a rot. Not with the excess of youth, but the morbid miserable vileness of a debauched old age.'[70] His response to the crisis was melodramatic. In his view Rosina's bad blood was coming out in the boy, which made him an object of aversion. He told Forster that

> I cannot endure the thought of seeing him. I have treated him with the greatest kindness, liberality and confidence, and now it is natural that I should remember that he is the son of his mother – it is her blood that seems breaking out.[71]

Someone else should take charge of the situation and deal with the boy, perhaps Forster or a military academy in Turin, or perhaps a curé in the depths of the French countryside where there are 'no girls in the house to fall in love with'. He must be kept 'without a shilling to spend' and 'under constant surveillance'.[72]

As in all moments of crisis, Lytton cast himself as the principal victim of the situation. Robert had injured him horribly by not consulting his father and by treating him 'as if I were in the family vault'. Worse, the boy's behaviour had gravely impaired Lytton's health, and there could be no question of leaving Nice to deal with the situation; 'while my life is of use to others, I have no right to throw it away on so worthless an object'. He asked Forster to sort the situation out, assuring him that the boy was too 'egotistical' to contemplate suicide.[73] Patiently, Forster undertook the commission, calming Lytton and counselling against undue severity. It was at his suggestion that Robert was sent off to join his uncle Henry's diplomatic mission in Washington until the scandal had subsided. It was he, not Lytton, who took the boy to Liverpool:

> We had much serious talk. Your conversation and kindness had deeply impressed him ... Whatever the result, however, you have nobly done your duty in this matter ... Your name was the last word that passed between us ... His berth was one of the best – a quite delightful berth ... He stood on the deck waving farewells till my little steamer was out of sight.[74]

Uncle Henry, no stranger himself to amorous adventures, awaited his nephew's arrival philosophically, even though American women were known to be notoriously advanced: 'I am expecting Robert. I fear his love-scrapes a little since these girls actually put their arms round an unmarried (mournful that!) gentleman's neck. But I think if he is proof against wedlock he will do.'[75]

Throughout the whole episode Robert Lytton was discussed as though he had been an unwanted parcel that somehow kept returning to the same doorstep. His delinquencies, if that is what they were, were seen primarily as inconveniencing the adult world around him. They were not enough to bring his father back to England. In spite of this, the lessons inculcated in childhood remained in place. Robert was all contrition and penitence. Writing to Forster from America, he described himself as 'wholy [sic] homeless', and begged for a reconciliation with his father, for 'if I do not garner up all that I have of home in a father's love – should I not be the cannibal of my own heart?'[76] The emotional dependence on his father was intact.

If proof of enduring loyalty was wanting, Robert's behaviour during the period of gross embarrassment in 1858–59 was totally reassuring. The Lytton

family was anxious that there should not be 'another boggle'.[77] Sending
Rosina to France, with Robert as chaperon and warder, was a crucial part
of the solution. At first, Rosina was happy with the plan. Her son was 'poor
dear Robert', who was not to be numbered 'parmi les Machiavelli Manqués
les Bulwers Lyttons'.[78] Initially, Edward too felt only gratitude: 'My own
darling boy – my noble, tender-hearted, matchless son – my all in all – the
only one in the world left for me to love.'[79] Offloading Rosina onto Robert
was a relief, but it was not thought that this placed any constraints on his
own behaviour. Robert had to protest about being followed about France
by spies in his father's employment. Continued attempts to vindicate himself
publicly about events in 1858–59 upset Rosina, as did the erratic payment
of her allowance. Inevitably, she rehearsed her grievances over and over
again, to the point that Robert's own health began to break down.[80] Eventually John Forster was forced to remonstrate with Lytton:

> I say nothing of Robert and the position in which he is placed. But in exact
> proportion to the loyalty he is now displaying to you (for I would stake my
> existence on his honour and fidelity and good faith in that respect) ... You *must*
> so far accept the consequences of your own act. You are a party to the circum-
> stances in which he is now abroad with Lady L – and you are not entitled to act
> as if you had not been.[81]

When Robert abandoned his guardianship of his mother, exhausted and
demoralised, few blamed him.

Caught between Rosina's tantrums and Edward's provoking behaviour,
Robert's choice of loyalties was unattractive. Yet he made it firmly in favour
of his father. He henceforth described his mother as 'a madwoman'. For
both of them, Rosina was now 'our Monster Plague'.[82] She was hopelessly
out of control. Her renewed campaign, in 1864, to implicate her husband
in an affair with Disraeli was gross. Her recklessness with money led Robert
to resist any thought of further increases in her allowance, for 'if she had
£40,000 a year she would spend it all on annoying others'.[83] Rumours of
her eccentric behaviour became the common coin of letters between Robert
and his own wife: 'she stays in bed all day till four or five o'clock then sits
up all night; dines at two in the morning and goes to bed at five or six a.m.
If she ever does appear in the day time she is immediately known for she
is so dreadfully scented you can smell it a mile off. I think it is a good
thing she lives at a different time from everyone else don't you.' Robert
came to fear that his mother 'will bury us all'.[84]

Robert's loyalty evoked no long-term gratitude or trust from his father.
He continued to supervise his son's life in all aspects, and took dissent as
a personal affront. In 1853, when Robert formed an attachment to a married

woman, Lytton sternly counselled 'self conquest'.[85] No doubt drawing on his own experience, he warned that 'Love is either a God or a Devil – and is often a Devil in the torture it inflicts, in proportion as it first comes with the blandishments of a God'.[86] Still insisting that the Lytton family lacked fortune, he was clear that his son should make a marriage that was financially wise. None of this advice would have jarred contemporary sensibilities. But Lytton went further. He insisted that Robert observe standards that were startlingly at odds with his own behaviour:

> Take this as a general rule – that what in the slack morality of the world are called *liaisons* in Society, tho' very pleasing excitements at first, invariably lead to anxiety, tortures, disappointments, scrapes, heart-pangs, wherever a man is not a mere cold-blooded *roué*. They may do well for a light Frenchman, they play the devil with an earnest Englishman ... Youth, I know, must be youth ... but no man ever does much, who gives up much of his thoughts and time to women.[87]

Robert was to live differently from his father, for fear of incurring the same torments.

In 1859 Lytton intervened to break off an engagement between Robert and a girl from a Dutch gentry family named Caroline de Groenix. All Dutch women, Lytton insisted, were ruled by their mothers, and this particular mother was marked by 'a coarseness or vulgarity of mind' that he found distressing. Worse, the girl had very little money. If Robert went ahead with the marriage he would have to depend on his salary as a diplomat and live, as Lytton had done, in very straitened circumstances. In sum, 'it was a very bad worldly match'.[88] This parental veto was exercised at the same time that Robert was being so helpful about Rosina. Worst of all, Lytton could only interpret his son's wish to marry a woman without fortune as a personal insult. Robert must choose between affection for fiancée and affection for father:

> If you cared three straws for the labour thro' which I have gone till at last I have succeeded, if you had comprehended how much you owed to me and to mine ... you would have felt that it was a cynical blow to my whole existence when you said 'see let me marry a Dutch woman ... who can't bring a shilling to the estate' ... Pardon me child, but this is the plain truth ... she will be eyeing the House with hereditary thoughts on my grave, sighing for the time when she and her Dutch parents may thrust me underground ... and insensibly moulding her duddle Husband to grudge the hours I have with him.[89]

The engagement was called off.

The same problems arose when, in October 1864, Robert entered into what his father called 'a very hasty marriage' with Edith Villiers, a niece of

Lord Clarendon. The family's politics were wrong, and Mrs Villiers had electoral influence in Hertfordshire which she refused to place at Lytton's disposal. In any case, he 'didn't think women should preach politics to men'.[90] But the real problem was once again money:

> I simply said that the ancient house or estate wanted money, that ever since I have had it I have sacrificed many enjoyments to myself which money would have given, if not spent on the place, as I spent it.

This explained

> why I could not feel so much satisfaction in your marriage as you seemed to think I ought to have done ... Estates need money and Knebworth consumes all I ever get and more.[91]

To mark his displeasure, Lytton refused to receive the young couple for a year after their marriage, and then only after the mediation of Forster. He played the same role that his mother had played in his own marriage. When a grandchild was born Lytton condescended to kiss it, in itself 'a wonderful act of grace', but found the idea of being a godfather 'preposterous'; and, instead of attending the christening, chose to interview railway officials about the siting of Knebworth station. Once again, he believed himself the injured party and accused his son of abandoning him: 'I resign myself tho' with a bitter pang to the conviction that you have forced upon my mind that, do what I will, there is something in your mind which renders the alienation produced by your marriage complete. And I console myself at least by thinking how little I have merited it.'[92]

Robert Lytton found it hard to cope with his father's moods, generally acquiescing and occasionally starting small rebellions. In trying to explain his father to his new wife, he perceptively, and charitably, described his own relationship with Lytton, and that of many others:

> The great defect of my father's character is a constant and excessive demand upon all those with whom he is in contact, for a degree of sympathy more delicate and intelligent than is often found, and far more patient and self-sacrificing than any which it is in his own nature to yield in return ... My father is certainly a man of genius and, like many others of that unstable race, he looks upon himself as entitled to expect from others unusual appreciation and respect for what is admirable in his mind and character, and unusually large allowances for all that is *not* admirable in his conduct and behaviour. The curse of his life has been, that a sympathy capable of meeting such demands upon it he has either not found in the legitimate social relations of life, or has alienated it at last – beyond the power of renewing it – thus unable to live without homage of some kind, and resolved to get this, like many other luxuries in life, with the least possible expense to himself, he has fallen into the hands of vulgar and unscrupulous

toadies whose permanent influence has been of the direst prejudice to all his better nature.[93]

Lytton claimed the rights and privileges of being exceptional. The artistic genius loved more, suffered more, deserved more than mere mortals. Most people, and nearly all the English, reject such claims. With enormous patience and tact Robert and Edith finally convinced Lytton that they took him at his own valuation. After 1865 relations were re-established and became even loving.

The decision to marry was not, however, the only point of conflict. Robert's choice of career was equally contentious. Lytton was adamant that the boy should not take up a literary career. He would admit that there was talent in his son. Indeed he might turn out to be 'a very *great* poet'. He was certainly sensitive enough to be given the responsibility of reviewing Lytton's own books in *Blackwoods*. His father was happy to introduce him to the gods of the literary world like Dickens, though in the unflattering phrase that 'a cat may look on a king'.[94] He was also well aware of how much the boy had a genuine longing for literature. The letters of the fourteen year old at Harrow make that clear:

> I do not ever think that I shall like to give up my old friend the poetry it cheers me when ill or unhappy and I always feel enclined [sic] to give vent to my feelings in poetry when alone, either joy or sorrow. I feel reddy [sic] to devote myself to it for life for it is almost like a companion and I feel so certain that I should make a great Poet if I ever was one at all, but I know you know best.[95]

In the boy's mind, to follow his father's profession was the greatest compliment he could pay him, and he never abandoned this ambition. His political and diplomatic career would be hugely distinguished, but he was always the aspiring writer. As late as 1886, Swinburne dismissed his efforts as those of a 'pseudonymous poeticule'.[96]

In Lytton's mind there were two reasons why his son's talent should not be realised. First, it was a talent of a particular kind. He could copy the best models but had no originality himself: 'he has *immense imitation* and small *constructive invention*'. Secondly, and perhaps more importantly, the poet must be a man apart. To live in the world too much, to follow a regular career, was incompatible with the production of high art. Lytton no doubt drew on his own struggles to do both, when he wrote to Forster to explain his views on Robert's writings:

> He does not lead the life of a poet, and does not therefore go through the actual experiences of a *poet's actual life*. No man can lead *at the same time* the poetic life and the prosaic but what one of the two must suffer for the combination. A great poet may go through all the phases of positive prosaic life and

be ultimately the better poet for it, But *during that time* the great poet does not write poetry.

Lytton even objected to the idea of his son visiting Italy 'as if the very plague of Boccacio was still to be caught there'.[97] Lytton was clear that his son was to seek a career in the diplomatic service and that this precluded all literary ambitions. Poetry was proscribed as being 'antagonistic if not altogether destructive' to this project.[98] Robert was to take what his father described as the 'prosaic' path.

The decision had been taken as early as 1841, when Robert was ten. He would become a successful career diplomat and thereby achieve that degree of financial independence which alone guaranteed an agreeable life. Without it, as his father pointed out, 'you will be discontented, dependent, sorely pinched – utterly unable to marry purely from affection and unable to gratify all the generous objects of a useful life'.[99] In this, as in much else, Robert acquiesced. Later in life he did publish poetry, under the pseudonym Owen Meredith, and enjoyed a modest reputation. But it was as an ambassador and, ultimately, as Viceroy of India, that he achieved real distinction. Long letters to his father from missions abroad reveal a mind that was intelligent and discerning. He obviously took pleasure in showing his father just how completely he was a master of the European diplomatic game. He became a success in the eyes of the world and on his own terms. The poet had indeed given way to the man of affairs. But that decision had not been his. As in so many other ways, his life had been moulded by what his father expected and desired.

When Lytton died, in 1873, Robert was bereft. It was more 'than the loss of a beloved parent, it was the loss of a great and wise friend – of an ever present help in time of trouble – of an intellectual sympathy'. Up until that moment, his whole life had been 'subordinate to the welfare and the happiness of his'.[100] Suddenly, that smothering obligation had been removed and, for the first time, he was 'alone'. Robert had finally reached a kind of maturity. As recently as 1871, the forty year old could ask for nothing more precious than 'the restoration of the light of your beloved countenance'.[101] Now he was free to make his own decisions. The presence of so much emotional dependence for so long took its toll. His marriage to Edith proved happy and fulfilling, and certainly gave him a security which neither he nor his sister Emily had ever been offered by their parents. But eccentricities of behaviour began to be noted in the official world and were attributed to his unfortunate ancestry. Lord Derby observed about him that, 'Lord Salisbury could give no explanation except that he was a little mad: and I begin to think so. With a mother insane, a father eccentric, he has every right to be in that way; and he used, like his father, to use opium.' [102] In the lives of Emily and Robert Lytton, the observation that the sins of the father are often visited on the children was profoundly vindicated. It is only necessary to add that the mother was hardly blameless.

Lady Blessington's Salon at Gore House, Kensington. Left to right, Bulwer Lytton, Count d'Orsay, Benjamin Disraeli, Countess of Blessington, Daniel Maclise, Lord John Russell and Charles Dickens.

5

Society

Before Bulwer Lytton was acknowledged as one of the leading novelists of his day, he had made a reputation as a dandy and wit, one of those endlessly up and coming young men who filled 'hot drawing-rooms', as Byron unkindly described London society. It was a world in which a well-turned phrase or a well-cut coat could carry the ambitious a long way. As Lytton recalled, 'a fine shape, with correspondent elegance of movement, was more admired than a handsome face'.[1] To be concerned about appearance was not only vanity but was also a passport to good society. It was a rule that Lytton rigorously observed throughout his life. Macaulay sarcastically noted that 'his dress must cost more than that of any five other Members of Parliament'.[2] Lytton believed that the dandyism of the 1820s was based on an aesthetic theory. Exterior elegance reflected an interior elegance of soul. As he confided to his journal in 1838:

> God gave my soul an exterior abode and the very fact there is a soul within the shell, makes me think the shell not to be neglected. There is a poetry in Dress ... A Greek was an exquisite par excellence ... So again the Romans ... I have it in my Norman Blood – the Normans were the gentlemen of the World. As for conceit in manner of conversation, of that they acquit me. Let them fall foul of the garb if they will.[3]

A well-dressed man gave evidence of an aristocratic temperament. Dandyism and pride of blood went hand in hand. Dandies were 'very agreeable men'. Straight out of Cambridge, Lytton made London notice him by dressing for attention. He became a hero of what Lady Dorothy Nevill remembered as 'the curly days when dandies flourished'.[4]

When Rosina first met her future husband, it was his costume that had caught her eye. It dazzled and amused:

> He had just returned from Paris, and was resplendent with French polish – as far as his boots went. His cobweb cambric shirt-front was a triumph of lace and embroidery, a combination never seen in this country till six or seven years later (except on babies' frocks). Studs, too, except in racing stables, were then *non est*, but a perfect galaxy glittered down the centre of this fairy-like *lingerie*. His hair, which was really golden and abundant, he wore literally in long

ringlets that almost reached his shoulders. He was unmistakably gentleman-like looking.[5]

In *Pelham*, Lytton created a hero who was the epitome of the wit and dandy. A whole chapter is devoted to 'the greatest of all sciences – the science of dress'. There are long paragraphs on waistcoats and trousers. Pelham 'had a rule never to drive out with a badly-dressed friend'. If invited to converse on a serious topic, he first rang for his poodle and some eau de Cologne, and was only then ready to listen 'from the alpha to the omega of your discourse'.[6] Elaborate manners and precise dressing marked the gentleman. In this respect, the dandyism of the 1820s followed on naturally from the beaux and gallants of the eighteenth century. In all his novels, Lytton's descriptions of male attire are lengthy and exact.[7]

Predictably, charges of unmanliness were easy to make, but they missed the point. Perfect dress expressed perfect values and perfect courage. Pelham is an expert shot, fencer and cudgeller. He is the truest of friends. To save the innocent, he thinks nothing of descending into the criminal rookeries of London, in disguise and talking 'flash', to find the evidence that will set justice right. The dandy was fop and man of action in one. By contrast, slovenliness of dress and slovenliness of character went hand in hand. The huge commercial success of *Pelham* was partly to be accounted for by the fact that the wit was also the hero.

Central too to the cult of the dandy was the cult of youth. Lytton hated the idea of ageing. 'Say what you will,' he told Lady Blessington, 'there is nothing like youth; all we gain in our manhood is dullness itself compared to the zest of novelty, and the worst of it is, the process of acquiring wisdom is but another word for the process of growing old.'[8] He regretted his youth, even before he had properly lost it. He was only twenty-four when he wrote in *O'Neill*,

> with each year's decay
> Fades leaf by leaf the Heart's young bloom away
> ... we grow
> Too cold for rapture – too obtuse for woe.[9]

According to a character in *What Will He Do With It?*, a man was too young at twenty-four and too old at twenty-eight.[10] Disraeli often remarked on his friend's preoccupation:

> Bulwer said to me one day, in his sort of confidential pompous style – perhaps, instead of pompous, I should rather say oracular, 'One of the advantages of public life is that it renews Youth. A Cabinet Minister at fifty may not absolutely be a young man, but he is a young Cabinet Minister' ... *Youth* was the master-feeling of Bulwer.

He hugely admired Palmerston, hair dyed and cheeks rouged, dominating the Commons into his seventies.[11] Editors and reviewers who announced that he was older than he actually was were reprimanded.[12] Lytton's novels are full of comfortable bachelors bemoaning the loss of their youth, like Cleveland in *Ernest Maltravers* and Beaudesert in *The Caxtons*.

Lytton dressed extravagantly for the whole of his life, often affecting styles that only much younger men could really wear: 'Bulwer is a curiosity. He arrays himself as he might have done in order to walk in Bond Street in the time of George IV's youth. His appearance is very singular.'[13] Everyone who met him made similar remarks. It was a sadness to his friends that he would not be taken seriously as long as he dressed as a guy. Dickens called him 'The Hirsute', as a tribute to magnificent whiskers, while Macready deplored his 'most lamentable style of foppery – a hookah in his mouth, his hair, whiskers, tuft etc all grievously cared for. I feel deep regret to see a man of such noble and profound thought yield for a moment to pettiness so unworthy of him.'[14] Critics were less charitable. They chose adjectives like 'ridiculous', 'picturesque' or 'tragic-gawky' to describe his appearance.[15] It was hard to take the man seriously, and to add to the sense of the exotic Lytton would often receive visitors while smoking a pipe six or seven feet in length, or taking opium through a hookah. Interviews were offered in a room decorated in the style of Pompeii and lighted by 'a perfumed pastille modelled from Mount Vesuvius'. Not surprisingly, small children found the whole effect terrifying. Sir Leslie Ward found him 'almost satanic looking', being 'touched up as the dandies of his day were'.[16] Claiming the rights of the artist, Lytton refused to live like other men or dress like other men. After meeting him for the first time, Thomas Carlyle exclaimed, 'I shall never forget Bulwer in this world. A mad world, my masters.'[17]

Predictably Bulwer Lytton was not a man's man, or at least not an Englishman's man. Apart from Forster, and perhaps Disraeli, he had no close male friends in England. He preferred the company of foreigners like Alfred d'Orsay or outsiders like the recently-Jewish Disraeli family. Others, like his Cambridge friends, Chauncey Townshend and Frederick Villiers, opted to live abroad for months on end, as did Lytton himself. The antipathies he aroused greatly amused him: 'Talking of hair, I had made more enemies in England by curled hair, than by all the superiority you are so flattering as to impute to me. I know nothing so unpopular among men, as to be born with that defect: it quite astonishes me to think of the obloquy and persecution to which it has exposed me.'[18] The British male was to be teased with remarks like, 'to make oneself uncomfortable is to be manly in this country. I rather think, too, a little mixture of uncleanliness is thought essential to merit that epithet.' The hero of *Pelham* affected not to understand why to be pleased with oneself was to offend the rest of one's gender.[19] Lytton claimed that *The Last Days of Pompeii* was his least favourite novel, because he 'could not be egotistical eno' in it'.[20] When, at Rosina's request, he cut off his whiskers, he lamented that, 'Like Ruth, I mourn for my children, and cannot be comforted, because they are not ... O Glory and Vanity of this world, where is Rome? Where is Babylon? Where are my whiskers?'[21]

There was a cost to all this. Affectation in behaviour and speech, stinging wit and extravagancies in dress were read as claims to arrogance and as an expression of superiority over others. A close literary collaborator remembered that, 'I never saw the famous writer, without being reminded of the passage, "Stand back: I am holier than thou."'[22] Thackeray, who pilloried Lytton in *Punch* and *The Yellowplush Letters*, lampooned the affectation, and regretted that it too often smothered a real talent:

> If he would but leave off scents for his handkerchief, and oil for his hair: if he would but confine himself to three clean shirts a week, a couple of coats a year, a beef-steak and onions for dinner, his beaker a pewter pot, his carpet a sanded floor, how much might be made of him even yet.

Unfortunately, it all led to 'the premeditated fine writing' that Thackeray detested.[23] None of this criticism touched Lytton. He claimed a superiority because the artist was superior to his fellows, and the great artist had the right and duty to live life by his own rules. The conventions and gender stereotypes of those around him were not relevant. Originality of mind never made for a team player.

Unsurprisingly, Lytton hated the process of ageing. Portraits painted in later life have little resemblance to the sitter. Artists prudently represented a much younger man.[24] Illness and overwork took a heavy toll. But, since he continued to dress in youthful styles, his actual appearance could be comic. In 1864 a fellow dinner guest found him looking like a scarecrow, a clown with 'Don Quixote jaws, giving the overall impression of a crapulous fossil'.[25] Lytton, too, began to dislike his own appearance. He was appalled by a photograph taken in 1871, because it made him resemble 'the ghost of a retired butler who has perished in a snow storm'.[26] For someone who could self-consciously describe himself as 'perhaps the vainest man who ever lived',[27] growing old gracefully was not an option. The passing of the years had, rather, to be resisted; but the holding them at bay with dyes and awkward styles could startle the unwary.

Throughout his life Lytton remained the dandy, making no concessions to the tastes of those around him. This behaviour confirmed his view that the artist was special. It also allowed him to affront and tease, which undoubtedly gave him pleasure. His irregular education had not drilled him in the assumptions of the men of his class. As artist and social outsider, he felt a distance from mainstream society that justified him in making his own rules. If they attracted adverse comment, this merely confirmed his belief that he stood apart. The argument became circular. Lytton as dandy was just one of the roles that singled him out, in his own estimation, from the banality of English society.

Next to the dandy stood the hypochondriac. It is perhaps not surprising that one who cared so much about external appearances should also worry about general health, and he lived through decades when valetudinarians crowded English and continental spas. But Lytton convinced himself at a very early age that he was specially afflicted: 'Hygeia ... is a Nymph singularly coy to me.' [28] An early death was endlessly predicted. When only thirty-seven, he announced that he was preparing himself for 'the Fatal Sentence of Decline'.[29] Like his clothes and mannerisms, this preoccupation with illness offered more opportunities for amused sarcasm. When Lytton complained to Disraeli that the burdens of Cabinet duties would cost him his life, the latter merely promised him a state funeral.[30] The obsession deepened with age and came to regulate whole areas of his life. He would only travel in certain months and not in others. Only 'healthful hours' during the day could be employed in social visiting.[31] He became a collector of prescriptions and medical reports.[32] There was even philosophising about disease. In January 1833 the New Monthly Magazine carried an article entitled, 'On Ill Health and its Consolations'. In it Lytton concluded that 'the time left to us for contemplation in our hours of sickness, and our necessary disengagement from the things of earth, tend to direct our thoughts to the stars, and to impregnate us half unconsciously with the Science of Heaven'.[33]

From time to time the illnesses were genuine and the suffering real. The deafness which had come on in youth became more and more of a burden. In 1840 there were chest pains, 'as if I had swallowed a bag of carpenter's tools and could not manage to get down the saw'. There were inflammations of the hands, producing rashes after only five or ten minutes of writing. There were the 'blue devils' of depression.[34] Predictably he became an expert on doctors, recommending some and gathering information on others. New treatments were always of interest, particularly if they could be related to what he would call the allied sciences of mesmerism, galvanism and clairvoyance. In 1857 he fiercely championed a doctor who had 'discovered a method of applying Electricity to Baths'.[35] Gadgets of all kinds were eagerly sought out. In 1867 a Parisian doctor was treating Lytton's deafness with 'an India rubber machine', while, just before his death, a firm in Woolwich was sending him 'a Spine Band', 'a Chest Protector', and 'Friction Gloves' for mesmerical experimentation.[36]

Like so many other Victorians, Lytton believed that health was to be found abroad, in the warmth of the Mediterranean and in the waters of the great European spas. On these he became an authority. The mineral baths at Kissingen were much to be preferred to those at Aix-la-Chapelle. Mont d'Or in the Auvergne and Eaux Bonnes and Luchon in the Pyrenees were recommended for chest infections, and Nice for recuperation: 'Nice is not good for irritable nervous cases, it is an excitable air. Bad for females, and apt to engender womb or hysterical diseases – bad for cerebral complaints ... In short Nice is good for those who want a fillip, bad for those who want soft, moist air and repose.'[37] Claiming to have 'accumulated a vast deal of general philosophy and experience as to the Medical Art and its professors', Lytton was free with advice and cautions. Carlsbad was as fatal as Cheltenham; Hastings offered some hope for sufferers from pulmonary infections; Torquay was good for nearly everything.[38] In *The Coming Race*, the advanced civilisations of the future are peopled by men and women who think that 'regular transpiration through the pores of the skin is essential for health', mixed with a little aromatherapy.[39]

Fortified by deep personal involvement in illnesses real or imaginary, Lytton eagerly joined polemical debates about new treatments. In a period when it was often difficult to distinguish medical advances from mere quackery, this was dangerous ground to tread. In 1843 his mother's death produced a nervous collapse, which was only remedied when he put himself into the hands of Dr Wilson at Malvern and his water cure, imported from Graafenburgh in Silesia. Lytton became an evangelist for the treatment. Friends were bombarded with letters recommending its advantages, and the readers of the *New Monthly Magazine* could read of them in 'Confessions of a Water Patient'. Lists of physical and mental conditions that could be alleviated are set out. In particular, the practice of 'water-packing' is much praised, in which the patient was enveloped in a damp sheet and warm blankets. 'The wet sheet', he declared, 'is the true preserver of life.'[40] But taking up causes carried risks. When he joined a campaign against homeopathy in 1853, his opponents dismissed his medical views as magnificently ill-informed.[41] Even more damaging was the ridicule that he so much feared. When he emerged rejuvenated from Malvern, one sceptical Whig lady reported to another that, 'Sir Edward Bulwer is young, blooming, and no longer deaf. The water cure ... All this was told me by the quite altered water-cured man. I expect to hear of him reunited to the wine-cured Lady B.'[42] The more Lytton fussed about his health and lectured others on theirs, the less he was taken seriously. The mocking of his ailments yet again confirmed his impression that he was not accorded the status he deserved. Long stays in the spas of France, Germany and Italy carried the added advantage of shielding him from his uncongenial countrymen.

Taken together, dandyism and a perceived crankiness about health led to charges of effeminacy which were levelled against the man and his writings. Macaulay was not alone in suggesting that 'He has considerable talent and eloquence. But he is fond of writing about what he only half understands, or understands not at all. His taste is bad; and bad from a cause which lies deep and is not to be removed – from want of soundness, manliness, and simplicity of mind.' [43] There was too much affectation and sentiment in the novels and poetry, and not enough self-controlled muscle. Lytton was acutely sensitive to this line of attack and set out to meet it head on. Again and again in his books, he presents male characters who combine delicacy of feature with firm, even heroic, temperaments. In *The Parisians* Enguerrand de Vandemar dies valiantly defending his country against the Prussians, even though his 'complexion might in itself be called effeminate, its bloom was so fresh and delicate, but there was so much of boldness and energy in the play of his countenance, the hardy outline of his lips, and the open breadth of his forehead, that "effeminate" was an epithet no one ever assigned to his aspect'.[44] The warrior Antagoras in *Pausanias* had 'features, the partial effeminacy of which was elevated by an expression of great vivacity and intelligence'.[45] In *Lucretia* the hero, Percival St John, is described thus: 'but for his firm though careless step, and the open fearlessness of his frank eye, you might have almost taken him for a girl in men's clothes, not from effeminacy of feature, but from the sparkling bloom of his youth, and from his unmistakeable newness to the cares and sins of man'.[46]

In these and many other examples, Lytton repeatedly argued that fine features, delicacy in feeling and artistic sensibility were entirely compatible with the manly qualities of courage and resolution.[47] As in *Pelham*, the dandy or the artist transforms himself easily into the man of action. But returning to the point over and over again suggests an unease in Lytton's mind. He protests too much. Perhaps the ambivalence is best expressed in his views on Byron, about whom Lady Caroline Lamb must have told him a great deal. Repeatedly, he claimed that he had no sympathy with vapid, sexually ambivalent and unstable poets. The Byronites were

> Young men with pale faces, and raven black hair
> Who make frowns in the glass, and write odes to despair.[48]

The character in his novels who comes closest to the Byronic model is Castruccio Cesarini in *Ernest Maltravers*, and he dies insane. The writing of

Pelham was specifically designed to overturn 'the Satanic Mania' of the Byron tradition, for if Pelham had foibles about dress, these 'foibles were harmless, and even more manly and noble, than the conceit of a general detestation of mankind or the vanity of storming our pity by lamentations over imaginary sorrows'.[49] Yet he occupied Byron's set of rooms in the Albany, and the poet's death in 1824 had left him paralysed: 'Never shall I forget the singular, the stunning sensation, which the intelligence produced ... We could not believe that the bright race was run. So much of us died with him, that the notion of his death had something of the unnatural, of the impossible. It was as if a part of the mechanism of the very world stood still.'[50]

Every age structures gender for its own convenience. Standards of manliness or womanliness change from one generation to another. As recently as the late eighteenth century it had been thought entirely appropriate for leading politicians to weep in the House of Commons. It suggested heightened sensibilities. The same men dressed extravagantly, perfumed and rouged themselves, and operated extravagant manners. Some continued these practises but increasingly Victorian England adopted different codes. Religious revivalism and utilitarian preferences, codified in public school life, fashioned concepts of masculinity differently. The extravagant in life or art became suspect. Lytton never sympathised with this change of mood. The artist's behaviour could not be circumscribed by convention. His special talents and sensibilities had to find free expression. Trying to convince his countrymen of this, however, was uphill work. It was a message that had more impact on German and French minds. In England it left Lytton open to charges of effeminacy which merged, in his wife's tortured mind, with sexual deviance. In trying to eliminate sensibility from the model of manliness the Victorians were fashioning a creature that was too monochrome for Lytton's taste. In his world the hero and the artist were one and the same.

Given his views and appearance, Lytton never fitted comfortably into Victorian society. He was never part of its establishment. He started life in the salons of the demi-monde, and arguably never left them. He felt himself underprized and at the margins. As a result, his earliest and deepest friendships were with people like himself, those who were by reason of race, birth or sexual history outsiders. The meeting place of such misfits was the salon of Lady Blessington. Symbolically her home, Gore House, stood not in the West End of London but in Kensington, on the site of what is now the Albert Hall. It was here that Lytton mixed with Benjamin Disraeli, Laetitia Landon, Laman Blanchard and William Macready. It was a world of penurious lady poets, Grub Street journalists, Jews and actors. In the eyes of society it was tainted, if exciting, company.

Marguerite Blessington had a past, and her presidency over the salon set its tone. Irish by birth, she had at sixteen become the mistress of an army officer. According to the unfriendly testimony of Rosina, she was then sold at an auction 'en costume de Paradis' to the elderly Lord Blessington.[51] He had the good manners to die shortly after, leaving a relatively wealthy widow to enjoy London on her own terms. For the rest of her life her companion would be Alfred d'Orsay, the epitome of dandyism and 'one of the most naturally gifted persons' of Lytton's acquaintance.[52] He added an aviary to Gore House, peopled with all 'the best dressed birds in all Ornithology'.[53] Neither Lytton nor Dickens, another habitué of the circle, thought that there was anything improper in the relationship between Lady Blessington and d'Orsay, but others speculated freely. According to Rosina, 'no decent woman ever went to Gore House' for fear of being associated with its 'brothel philosophy'. In fact, 'Messalina Blessington' and her companion became 'the cynosures of the best, bad society in London'.[54] As a consequence the Gore House Circle was largely male, a fact which almost certainly fitted in with Lady Blessington's preferences. Since she had literary pretensions herself, it was enough for her that she should have 'a brilliant circle assembled around me'.[55] Gore House was clever, stylish and not quite nice.

The biographer of Lady Blessington places her first meeting with Lytton in 1832, after she became a contributor to the *New Monthly Magazine*. But a correspondence had begun much earlier, in 1830, and a year later she was hailing him as 'the most brilliant and profound writer of your day'.[56] As relations with Rosina deteriorated, Marguerite Blessington became, after his mother, the most important female influence in his life. Sustaining a friendship never came easily to Lytton, but his association with her was the smoothest he would know. After her death, he annotated one of her letters as follows:

> Without great talents she was a remarkable woman. She was essentially sympathetic ... She had all the Irish cordiality of manner ... She understood her actual position and never tried to force herself on female society – she commanded the best male society and her House was agreeable. Whatever her faults she was undeserving of much that scandal has laid to her charge.[57]

Her friendship was 'one of the few ... he ever permitted himself to form; and one of the few out of that few, of which he has none but pleasurable and grateful recollections'.[58]

It was a collaboration based on mutual respect and sympathy. Lytton puffed Lady Blessington's literary efforts and brought her to the attention of appropriate publishers. He contributed satires and poetry to her annuals, and he widened her circle of acquaintance by introducing promising young

men like Disraeli to Gore House.[59] In return, she genuinely and effusively
lauded his talent. For a man who endlessly complained that he was not
given the recognition he deserved, this was manna. As she wrote to Henry
Bulwer: 'What a noble creature your brother is; such sublime genius, joined
to such deep, true feeling. He is too superior to be understood in this age
of pigmies [who] are jealous of the giants who stood between them and
the sun.'[60] In each emotional and political crisis, particularly those involving
Rosina, Lady Blessington was his main support and source of strength. At
moments when he felt 'like a man walking on the ice and feeling it crack
at each successive step', he was sure that her 'bright face will lay the spectres
forever'.[61] She more than met his craving for praise and sympathy, adding
breezy doses of common sense. Because nothing could 'shake my belief in
your goodness of heart, and high mindedness', and because he could 'count
on me therefore to the Death', she acquired the privilege of moderating his
language and behaviour.[62] Marguerite Blessington was a sensible woman at
moments when Lytton was badly in need of such people.

For d'Orsay Lytton felt an almost equal warmth. He regarded him as
genuinely talented and potentially as a writer of distinction. As a critic, his
views were to be respected. It was a sorrow to Lytton that his friend's
potential was never realised. *Godolphin* was dedicated to d'Orsay, and it
may not be a coincidence that it is a tale of a man of genius whose abilities
are swamped by attention to social trivialities. A heroic temperament is
undermined as 'here the Demon tempts or destroys the hermit in his
solitary cell. There he glides amidst the pomps and vanities of the world,
and whispers away the soul in the voice of his soft familiars, Indolence
and Pleasure.'[63] Alfred d'Orsay promised much and produced nothing.
Lytton pitied his friend's failure, fearing that he himself could fall prey to
the same fate. The artist who dabbled too much in society was lost. Too
many friendships might even be destructive. A standard theme in Lytton
novels is the warning given by an older man to a younger man about not
dissipating abilities in social dabbling. They are told not to become 'but-
terflies at balls' or 'the old familiar faces, seen everywhere, known to
everyone'. They were not 'to live in clubs' or 'drive about late o'nights in
mysterious-looking vehicles and enjoy a vast acquaintance among the
Aspasias of pleasure'.[64] For the whole of his life Lytton was fearful of losing
his talents. The perfectly-tailored but infertile figure of Alfred d'Orsay
compelled and saddened him.

The hostile testimony of Rosina accused the Blessington circle of acting
as a clique, promoting each other's work and egotisms. There was some
justice in this remark. The Gore House pack hunted together. When Lytton
enjoyed a publishing success they were loud in his praise. If a play flopped

they were all commiseration. Such reactions were prompted solely by the fact that he was their 'friend'.[65] Ever cautious of each other's sensibilities, there were always effusions of sympathy to rely on. D'Orsay closed his letters with '100,000 amitiés'.[66] Together they defied and teased those literary and political establishments which looked askance at their proceedings. In *The Siamese Twins* Lytton produced an extended satire on the lions and lionesses of London society. Those who, like Lady Holland, presided over competing salons were roasted:

> As they professed opinions liberal,
> And Chang was thought a youth of nous,
> They went where worthy Witlings gibber all
> Ineptitudes – at Holland House.[67]

If the characters of Lady Selina Vipont in *What Will He Do With It?* was indeed based on Lady Holland, or one of her kind, her creator could expect trouble. She was described as someone 'whose condescension would crush the Andes', and who could be 'excruciatingly civil'.[68] Taking sling-shots at the powerful was an amusing occupation but Lytton required a sure base of operations from which to launch assaults. Gore House gave him what he wanted. As his own family arrangements fell into disarray, in the 1830s and 1840s, its inhabitants became his new cousins.

In April 1849 Gore House suddenly closed. Its owner had been declared bankrupt and had fled to Paris, where she died two months later. For Lytton, 'pained, grieved and shocked', the loss was irreparable. His friends, 'the old and tried ones', no longer had a meeting place. He was genuinely moved by Lady Blessington's misfortune and bought books in the bankruptcy sales, in order to restore them to her.[69] He had lost an anchorage. What he called 'the Clique I live in', and what Rosina denounced as the 'Scratch me, and I'll scratch you, clique', was no more.[70] It had not been the most respectable society in London. Too many of its inmates had soiled reputations or were simply on the make. But for a man who never found friendship easily it had been a rare point of reassurance. Marguerite Blessington and Alfred d'Orsay were two of the very few people with whom he never quarrelled.

In Lytton's view emotional insularity was a burden that the artist had to carry, even if others thought this mere selfishness. He was therefore a social animal without intimates. The friendships he did form were always bumpy and full of recriminations. Few lasted long. In later life, some friends were women. Earlier, apart from Lady Blessington, they were almost exclusively male. The rule seemed to be that women were mistresses and men friends. Reference has already been made to the scenes in Lytton novels, in which older men warn younger against the dissipation of their talents. The point could be generalised. In particular, there is emphasis on the influence of a man with just two or three years more experience. As Lumley Ferrars observes in *Ernest Maltravers*, 'it seldom happens that we are very strongly influenced by those *much* older than ourselves. It is the Senior, of from two to ten years, that most seduces and enthrals us. He has the same pursuits – views, objects, pleasures, but more art and experience in them all.' [71]

Two men played this role in Lytton's own life. Frederick Villiers was two years older than him, and they first met at Trinity College, Cambridge. Although he was dismissed later as 'rather a bore', there is no doubt that he had been an early model for hero worship. Clever, fashionable and dissolute, he commanded attention. He specialised in 'a good-natured sneer'. Lytton chose him as a travelling-companion to Paris in 1825, and again in 1836, when his marital disasters left him badly in need of sympathy. Together they visited brothels, together they started political careers in parallel, and Lytton was happy to second his friend in a duel.[72] So great was the influence of this worldly-wise dandy that he was generally taken for the model on which the hero in *Pelham* was based. Lytton himself admitted the fact, adding only that, 'he differed from that worthy chiefly in the utter absence of the ambition which supplies motive power to *Pelham*'.[73] Villiers was another example in Lytton's circle of the promising young man who came to nothing. It was a fate that Lytton himself so much dreaded. Their friendship seems to have come to an end soon after their travels in 1836.

Predictably Rosina detested Villiers. She described him as her husband's 'amiable Epicurean debauchée [sic] friend',[74] and was sure that he exercised an influence that was wholly malign. He is pilloried in *Cheveley*, along with Lytton's family, in the character of Frederick Feedwell, a failed diplomat and barrister who had a reputation that 'was bad, even among the bad'. At one point in the book he is called 'Miss Molly', an open assertion that his sexual tastes sometimes ran in a homosexual direction. Feedwell is also accredited with a French mistress, however, and a degree of affectation that left him with 'nothing natural but his birth, his selfishness and his stutter'.[75] As Rosina collected evidence for the barrage of accusation that she would fire at her husband, his association with Villiers provided a great deal of copy.

Very similar in style, intelligence and character was Chauncey Hare Townshend. He was five years older than Lytton, and the two had first met briefly as schoolboys in Ramsgate. According to an annotation made to a letter dated 1840, Lytton remembered Townshend as follows: 'He was a young man when I was a boy at school ... His beauty of Countenance was remarkable at that time. Those who knew Byron said it was Byron with bloom and health. He grew plain in later life – an accomplished man – but effeminate and mildly selfish.' He was 'an amiable sybarite'.[76] The friendship was renewed at Cambridge, where Townshend regaled Lytton with tales of Coleridge and Wordsworth, and where 'his beauty of face ... attracted the admiration of all who even passed him in the street'.[77] Later Townshend spent most of his life in Switzerland, but he remained sufficiently close to Lytton to be involved in disentangling Robert Lytton from his escapades in 1850. Even more important, it was almost certainly Townshend who introduced the study of mesmerism and spiritualism into his friend's consciousness. The occult would become an absorbing hobby for both of them, and their shared interest would provide reassurance against charges of 'quackery and humbug'.[78] Although the documentation for the Villiers and Townshend friendships is exiguous, perhaps suspiciously so in a life that in most aspects is fully recorded, there can be no doubt that their influence had been real. At an impressionable age Lytton had been fascinated by their efficient worldliness.

More enduring and more equal were his friendships with Benjamin Disraeli and John Forster, his more immediate contemporaries. In February 1829, at a sale of Dr Parr's books, Disraeli had bought a volume of Lytton's poetry, which he returned to the author by way of effecting an introduction. He was rewarded with an appreciative, if condescending, note: 'It is one consoling property of Genius to find among strangers that interest which worth finds among friends.'[79] By the spring of 1830 they were dining companions,[80] and would soon drift together towards Gore House. Their well-wishers were clear that the two had much in common, and that each had everything to gain by association with the other. As Lady Blessington advised Disraeli, Lytton 'never appeared to more advantage than while eulogizing you ... Never suffer this friendship to grow torpid, for it is highly serviceable to both of you, and more especially, in an age, when envy, hatred, and jealousy seem to be the peculiar characteristics of literary men towards each other.'[81] She and others speculated on which of them had the greater influence. Some thought that Disraeli had the dominant role: 'Bulwer is dying of Disraeli – and yet can't be without him. The moth and the candle.'[82] Robert Lytton called Disraeli 'my father's most eminent Political Chief, and oldest personal friend'.[83] Returning the compliment, Disraeli himself reckoned his friend 'among the two or three persons whose minds had exercised a distinct effect upon the development of his own'.[84] In fact, the apportioning of influence matters little. The two men forged a bond between allied temperaments.

Both men revelled in the fact of youth and feared ageing; 'How are you old fellow? Well, strong – and hearty, I hope … one is so d-d old now – one enjoys nothing.'[85] They went to 'the Naughty House' together, and expressed pleasure in being 'shampooed and vapour-bathed'. As fashionable novelists in the dandy line, both men enjoyed their roles as *enfants terribles*:

> Quiet fellows … have a great horror of us Novel writers – they fancy, the Ninnies, we shall clap them into a Book. 'Suspicion is the badge of all our trade.' For my part, if I had not got into all my Clubs (at least the respectable ones) before I had taken to Authoring I should certainly be out of them all at this time. Campbell proposed me as one of the Committee of his Club – the refuge for the destitute – and a fat fellow from the City cried out, 'D-n his soul NO – He'll put us down in his next novel of High Life'.[86]

They puffed each other's work. Lytton described Disraeli as 'brilliant' and was in turn acknowledged as the author of 'the finest and most interesting fiction that we have had for many years'.[87] Both Disraeli and his father became contributors to the *New Monthly Magazine* under Lytton's editorship. Perhaps most important of all, both men, as aspiring Radical politicians, actively promoted each other's careers and tried to march in step in Parliament. It was a friendship that worked on many different levels and continued to do so for the whole of their lives.[88]

Inevitably there were uncomfortable episodes as well. No association with Lytton was entirely free of them. There were moments when he could become jealous and highly critical of a rival novelist. Petulantly he pointed out that half of his *Pelham* had been written before Disraeli's *Vivian Grey*, and that therefore, although published later, it was indeed the prototype for literature in the 'silver fork' genre.[89] Similarly he had no inhibitions about describing the flaws in Disraeli's *The Young Duke*:

> The flippancies I allude to are an ornate and shewy effeminacy that I think you should lop off on the same principle as Lord Ellenborough should lop off his hair. To a mere fashionable novel aiming at no high merit, and to a mere dandy aiming at nothing more solid, that flippancy or the hair might be left, and left gracefully. But I do not think the one suits a man who is capable of great things nor the other a man who occupies great places.[90]

He thought Disraeli's *Coningsby* 'full of jejeune, tinsel Schoolboyisms'.[91] Quite simply he and his friend were too close as novelists in terms of theme and style. Disraeli's ancestry provided another target. Lytton thought it 'not Ju-dicious' to 'make the Jews such a superior race', when casting a novel. In *The Disowned* he teased Jewry in the character of Morris Brown, a comic travelling salesman, not quite honest and always keen to make a sale. Playfully he told Forster that he took it 'for granted that the rising generation are circumsised'.[92] Nearly all of this was nothing more than banter, but there was also apprehension that his friend could be a dangerous literary competitor.

Disraeli, however, was more than happy to engage in the same game. At times, he found Lytton's pretensions and demands for sympathy hard to bear. He always thought his literary style overblown. To make matters worse, his friend's belief that he was destined to hold high political office led Disraeli into embarrassments with major political figures. As Disraeli recorded in his reminiscences, Lytton 'wanted to be a popular author, a distinguished orator, and a Baronet in the Kingdom of Heaven – with Knebworth Park to boot! ... He exceeded Cicero'.[93] Yet the right to be critical is one of the privileges of friendship and, for all that they were rivals in many areas, the two men held together. Poking fun at each other's mannerisms and accomplishments never came near to rupturing their friendship.

Enrolling in the small number of Lytton's friends was automatically to invite the hostility of his wife, and the virulence with which she attacked Disraeli may be taken as good evidence of just how strong their association was. In fact, the pursuit was unremitting. Even death brought no pity. As far as Rosina was concerned, Disraeli 'had had his Elysium in *this* world, and must now be prepared for the reverse of the medal'.[94] In his ugliness, she thought he resembled 'a *facsimile* of the Black Princely Devil' who wanted to 'nous Juiver'.[95] Above all, she persistently and repeatedly accused him of being homosexual, annotating a book in the library at Knebworth with the words 'I like Dizzy signing as if he were a Peer when he was only a Queer'.[96] She retailed rumours along these lines so effectively to the future Mrs Disraeli that the lady developed severe doubts about marrying at all.[97] Since Lytton himself was occasionally subjected to the same innuendoes, being compared to the homosexual Henry III of France, it was easy for Rosina to construct unpleasant assumptions about their friendship.[98]

Most of the time these accusations fell short of the target, but sometimes the discomfort they caused could have serious consequences. In 1858 Lytton had recently been appointed to the Cabinet, at the moment of his wife's internment in an asylum. Under interrogation by doctors, Rosina 'talked incessantly and vehemently, denouncing Sir Edward and Mr d'Israeli, accusing them of monstrous crimes'.[99] Letters were dispatched to her husband's 'colleagues and friends' which made the same points. She even wrote to inform Queen Victoria that, in making the two men Ministers, 'she might as well have chosen two of the inhabitants of Sodom and Gomorrah.'[100] Such behaviour was taken as evidence that Rosina was indeed mad, which also conveniently neutralised any threat to the careers of Lytton and Disraeli. But, in 1864, both men were prepared to pay a man named

John Birch to recover letters which somehow involved Rosina.[101] The steady drip of potential scandal was never quite cut off, although there is no solid evidence which would turn Rosina's fantasies into truth. What is clear is that Lytton's friendship with Disraeli survived political squabbling and literary teasing for over forty years.

John Forster met Lytton for the first time in 1832.[102] For the next quarter of a century the two men were the closest of friends. Lytton annotated one of Forster's letters as follows:

> A most sterling Man ... few indeed have his strong practical sense and sound judgement – fewer still unite such qualities with exquisite appreciation of talent ... in literary arts. Hence, in ordinary life, there is no safer advisor in literature, especially poetry, no more refined critic. A large heart ... accompanies so masculine an understanding. He has the same capacity for affection which embraces many friendships without loss of depth or warmth in one ... I am greatly indebted to his Counsels ... a nature as solid and valuable as a block of Gold.[103]

It also helped that Forster repeatedly reassured Lytton about his own talent. Immodestly, he presented Forster with a complete set of his works in 1841, inscribed 'To John Forster Esq. these volumes are presented – in token of the author's gratitude for warm friendship, and of his appreciation of genius'.[104] Forster was happy to reciprocate these compliments, protesting that 'some of the whitest stones in my memory mark the steps of our friendly intercourse'.[105] There seemed to be no limits on what could be discussed. Forster was privy to all Lytton's embarrassments, while Lytton cheerfully commented on the consequences of 'the brutal lusts' of his 'libidinous friend'.[106] Their correspondence gives the impression of two men forming an alliance against the world.

Forster, however, was more than a friend. As a lawyer with literary and theatrical tastes, he was Lytton's man of business and factotum. Simply to list the services he provided is to demonstrate how central he was in Lytton's life. He was the negotiator of contracts with publishers and theatre managers, dealing with fees, casting and the misfortunes of drunken actors. As a critic, he suggested changes to manuscripts that were acted on. Frequently he then prepared books for publication by proof-reading, deciding on illustrations, and fixing reviewers. To a very large extent Lytton's literary success and reputation was in his hands. In addition, he supervised the details of the leasing, buying and selling of houses, found tutors for Robert and visited the boy at school, and was intimately involved in the surveillance of Rosina. There was no aspect of Lytton's public or private life that Forster did not influence. More often than not, this involved pouring common sense onto inflamed situations. In return, Lytton acknowledged his dependence on his friend, even if gratitude was frequently mingled with complaints that he might have done better.

Inevitably there were moments of tension. Lytton's publication of *The New Timon* embroiled him in a public slanging-match with Tennyson, which Forster thought silly and unnecessary. Equally, after 1846, Lytton's increasing Toryism was at odds with Forster's unshakeable Liberalism.[107] But no real breach occurred until 1858, when Lytton tried to throw all the blame for the failed attempt to commit Rosina as insane onto Forster's shoulders. For once Forster refused to dig Lytton out of a hole, insisting that he take responsibility for his own actions. Relations were broken off for a number of years. When they resumed, in the early 1860s, there was still warmth and cordiality enough, but Lytton's man-of-all-work was now William Kent, and Forster could be accused of neglect: 'When I look at the dates of his friendship with Dickens, I now better understand why from these dates, Forster never once gave a help to any book of mine.'[108] Such a claim was preposterous. Forster had been a mainstay of Lytton's literary success for years. The fact that it could be made at all illustrates how difficult it was to sustain a friendship with Lytton. The demand for loyalty and unquestioning affection was a heavy burden to shoulder. To be accused of not giving enough of each was grim. Forster and Lady Blessington were the only two who came near to passing the test. Lytton therefore had few friends, and never quite trusted those who came close to him.

Dandified pretension and an explosive private life made public turned Lytton into an obvious target for the humourist. In so many areas of his life, it was difficult to separate reality from the theatrical and the fantastical. There was so much about which he could be teased, so much to snigger at. His appearance, his pronunciation of English, his fads about health and the spirit world all provided good copy. Even his name caused amusement. From 1803 to 1843 he was Edward Lytton Bulwer. After his mother's death, and at her request, he took the surname Lytton, thereby becoming Edward Lytton Bulwer Lytton. To contemporaries it seemed a little unnecessary. Then there was the overpowering sense of caste.[109] Pride in family was taken to astonishing lengths, with a slightest slur on its good name likely to provoke thoughts of a duel.[110] 'The Normans', he contended, 'are, next to the Hellenes, the most splendid people in history.' They were 'the Patricians of the World'. His own descent from these people meant a great deal, for, in his mind, 'the creed of our chivalric fathers is still ours'.[111] So Lytton developed the feeling that he was someone living in the wrong period with the wrong values.

His published work often regretted the passing of the middle ages, leaving himself open to joking on the subject. For example, *In Olden Time* included the verses:

> Alas for the days that now live but in story,
> When Chivalry reign'd in the grace of her glory,
> When Love was unsullied, and Friendship was true,
> And Fear was a meanness which man never knew.
>
> Oh! had I been born in those days, and the Lord
> Of my helm and my hauberk, my steed and my sword,
> This hand had not lost what my Fathers had won,
> Nor their scutcheon been dimm'd by the fame of their son.[112]

Many of his novels and much of his poetry were peopled with minstrels, crusaders and fair-cheeked damsels.[113] One of his favourite characters was Warwick the Kingmaker.[114] So confirmed was this preference that he seemed to take a positive delight in cramming his work with antiquarian words that would send readers scurrying to a dictionary. *The Last of the Barons* contains 'vawmure', 'dissour', 'cullions', 'bezonians', 'burgonot', 'giglet' and 'nowch'. Novels could be weighed down by learned footnotes, drawing on monastic chronicles, which ran the danger of turning a work of literature into a tract. Hostile critics amused themselves by caricaturing this pedantry.

To Lytton, however, it was a matter of importance. A feeling of living out of time, added to social insecurities, put him at odds with his contemporaries and on the margin of things. Like Lionel Hastings, the hero of *What Will He Do With It?*, Lytton 'talked about the "Faerie Queene", knight errantry, the sweet impossible dream-life that, safe from Time glides by bower and hall, through magic forests and witching caves into the world of poet-books'.[115] All this, according to Anthony Trollope, had a devastating impact of Lytton's work. He had only one hero and one heroine. The first were chivalrous, reflective, courageous, questing, and 'perfectly unnatural'. The second were all pure, featureless, and indistinguishable one from the other:

> He has conceived a character – made up of Alcibiades and Sardanapalus – and he has put the mixture on eternal stilts. This man is the same whether he be a murderer – a successful Democrat – an English nobleman – or a highway Robber. Ernest Maltravers, and Pelham. Rienzi and Eugene Aram. Godolphin and Glaucus – Devereux and Paul Clifford – are all the same person ... As to women, Bulwer has attempted little to draw their character, and in that little he is equally unnatural.[116]

Lytton did indeed want to be 'safe from Time',[117] but those who fail to adapt to the assumptions of the world around them run the risk of becoming figures of fun. In this respect Lytton offered so many targets that his detractors were almost spoilt for choice.

The baiting of Bulwer became lively sport. Macaulay poked fun at his sensitivity and liking for aristocratic names:

> After the debate I walked about the streets with Bulwer till near three o'clock. I spoke to him about his novels with perfect sincerity – praising warmly, and criticising freely. He took the praise as a greedy boy takes apple pie, and the criticism as a good dutiful boy takes senna tea. He has one eminent merit – that of being a most enthusiastic admirer of mine – so that I may be the hero of a novel yet, under the name of Delamere or Mortimer. Only think what an honour.[118]

Carlyle was more severe. Lytton's novels were 'a piece of pinchbeck', and he himself 'a quack'.[119] In *Sartor Resartus*, he provided a devastatingly funny satire on the dandyism in *Pelham*, which took the form of listing the seven rules of its hero's 'Confession of Faith':

1. Coats should have nothing of the triangle about them; at the same time, wrinkles should be carefully avoided.

2. The collar is a very important point: it should be low behind, and slightly rolled.

3. No licence of fashion can allow a man of delicate taste to adopt the posterial luxuriance of a Hottentot.

4. There is safety in a swallow-tail.

5. The good sense of the gentleman is nowhere more finely developed than in his rings.

6. It is permitted to mankind, under certain restrictions, to wear white waistcoats.

7. The trousers must be exceptionally tight across the hips.[120]

The game was so compelling that even friends joined in. In *Endymion*, Disraeli made fun of Lytton's name changes by creating two brothers called Bertie Tremaine and Tremaine Bertie, both of whom were so convinced of their talents that they marvelled that they were not Prime Minister by the age of twenty-two.

The leading tormentor, however, was William Makepeace Thackeray, who seems to have arrived at the conclusion that Lytton was a joke that could be endlessly retold. He and William Maginn turned *Fraser's Magazine* into the official journal of pleasantries at Lytton's expense. Its victim accused it of 'ribald impertinence'.[121] In *The Yellowplush Letters* Thackeray created the comic figure of 'Sir Bulwig', which allowed him to satirise Lytton's dress, accent, preoccupation with names and difficulty in pronouncing the letter 'R'. 'Bulwig' was 'slim, with a hook nose, a pail fase, a small waist, a pare of falling shoulders, a tight coat, and a catarack of black satting tumbling out of his busm, and falling into a gilt velvet weskit.' A footman was made to announce his arrival at a party as 'Sawedwadgeogeearllittnbulwig'.[122] The jokes were repeated in *George de Barnwell* (i.e. bornwell) in which Lytton is made to sign himself 'ELBLBBLBBBLLL'. The hero 'had just reached that happy period of life when the Boy is expanding into the Man', and in high-flown language with an extended use of capital letters, is made to talk twaddle about the infinite:

> What is the Unintelligible but the Ideal? What is the Ideal but the Beautiful? What is the Beautiful but the Eternal? And the sport of the men who would commune with these is like Him who ... shrinks awestruck before that Azure Mystery.

There was good reason, in the face of parodies as ripe as these, for Lytton to feel that he was not part of the literary establishment. He was rather outside it and the butt of jokes. As Thackeray admitted, 'the whole school is at you'.[123]

All this hurt badly. Lytton was never able to see the humour in a joke against himself, and to be taunted by his fellow writers was intolerable. As the object of schoolboy japes, comic verse and penetrating satire, he felt affronted, which of course made any joke the funnier. Like Algernon Mordaunt in *The Disowned*, a character for whom Lytton admitted a 'partiality', he believed that, 'there are two feelings common to all high or affectionate natures, that of extreme susceptibility to opinion, and that of extreme bitterness at its injustice'.[124] In the *New Monthly Magazine*, he wrote a short story about a Chinese writer called Fi-ho-ti, who, by being successful, attracts the malice of fellow writers, and, being 'misinterpreted, calumniated, and traduced', sinks into misanthropy and despair.[125] He simply hated bring laughed at by the English, on one occasion confessing to Disraeli that he was minded to live abroad permanently. England did not deserve him. He complained to Lady Blessington that, even if he were to die, 'four or five' people might feel a twinge of regret, but for everyone else it would only be 'something to talk about before the meeting of Parliament'.[126] Lytton knew that English philistinism mocked artists, but its unremitting hostility led him to wonder if exile might be preferable.

Lytton learned sharp lessons from all this. He convinced himself that English society disliked him, and that to indulge its fancies was to squander time and talent. He commented bitterly on acquaintances like Sir James Lake and Lord Walpole who had taken this path and had 'come to nothing'.[127]

Society figures in his novels are handled roughly, 'pecking at each other fasten nip and claw upon that common enemy, the passing friend'.[128] With every joke and rejection he withdrew trust. As he put it in an essay entitled *Infidelity in Love*, 'ceasing to be loved, we cease to love'.[129] The temptation to retreat into self-love and self-sufficiency became more and more attractive, even if this ambition could never be fulfilled. Early in life, he confessed to Lady Blessington that 'our affections are our curses. The only wisdom is to "care for nobody". Our misfortune is that, when disappointed in one place, we fly to another; we have not the courage to be alone.'[130] He was forced to the daunting conclusion that it was impossible to be loved and to be distinguished in the world at the same time. The greater an artist became, the more he ran into jealousy, malice and demeaning criticism. In his twenties he had written a short story called *The Choice of Phylias*, in which an artist has to make an exact choice between fame and affection.[131]

If the figure of Lytton in society was an increasingly isolated one, it is an open question whether he had brought solitude on himself. He had never taken criticism well. Both John Forster and William Kent found that long service to the Lytton family was no guarantee of friendship if they offered advice that was unwelcome, or asked too much.[132] Although Lytton affected to believe that bonds between fellow artists 'beget lasting friendships and bequeath imperishable results',[133] his contact with Dickens and Disraeli would hardly bear this out. Intellectually and by schooling, his preferences were not English. Much of what he claimed for art and the artist would have fallen more profitably on French or German ears. But the jibes were not confined to this type of debate. Every aspect of his personality was matter for ridicule. For someone of extreme sensitivity, the laughter of the English was insupportable. Inevitably, he was driven to seek the company of those who, like him, found themselves on the margin.

'Curse me not —
curse me not!"— cried Isabel.

Illustration by Frederick Pegram to *The Last of the Barons*.

6

A Writer and the Public

Edward Bulwer Lytton was one of the most successful writers of the nineteenth century. His sales rivalled those of Charles Dickens. He was ennobled for his services to literature and found a resting place in Westminster Abbey. Yet he was never entirely happy with his profession, and was quite sure that his native country had never properly recognised his talents. He did not always like his trade. A character in *The Disowned* bewails:

> those terrible feuds – the vehement disputes – those recriminations of abuse, so inseparable from literary life, appear to me too dreadful for a man not utterly hardened or malevolent voluntarily to encounter. Good heavens, what acerbity sours the blood of an author! The manifestoes of opposing generals, advancing to pillage, to burn, to destroy, contain not a tithe of the ferocity, which animates the pages of literary controversialists.[1]

It was no place for those 'easily wounded in the commerce of the rough world', among whom Lytton clearly numbered himself.[2] To publish was to expose oneself. Gone were the comforts and securities of private life. Instead, the author's work 'may be misrepresented, his character belied; his manners, his person, his dress, the "very trick of his walk", are all fair food for the cavil and the caricature'.[3] Macaulay and others tried to reassure him by insisting that he gave too much weight to adverse criticism when, in fact, few 'men in literary history have at your age enjoyed half your reputation'.[4] But Lytton was never comforted. He never felt secure in the literature of his own country.

The first problem was the sheer awfulness of public opinion. England was a 'land of wealth and rheumatism, corruption, vulgarity and flannel waistcoats'.[5] Unfortunately, the nineteenth century had enthroned mass opinion as the arbiter of literature as well as politics. In an article for the *New Monthly Magazine*, entitled 'Literature as a Profession', Lytton asserted that 'henceforth, all powerful opinion, that of the majority, will rule'.[6] That being so, the artist, like the statesman, would be set up and pulled down by a public opinion that was by definition fickle:

> Where in the history of the world do you find the gratitude of the people? You find fervour, it is true, but not gratitude; the fervour that exaggerates a benefit

at one moment but not the gratitude that remembers it the next year. Once
disappoint them and all your actions, all your sacrifices, are swept from their
remembrance for ever; they break the windows of the very house they have given
you, and melt down their medals into bullets.[7]

Like the hero of his novel *Rienzi*, Lytton felt that no reputation or career
was secure. What the vox populi cried out for one day, it howled down
the next. He and all artists had to live with the bitter thought that they
might be tossed aside by the vagaries of a largely philistine audience.

Unlike many of his contemporaries, who enthusiastically argued for
universal systems of education on the grounds that high art would come
to be appreciated by all, Lytton was clear that popular taste would inevitably
be debased. As he told G. H. Lewes:

> The Popular taste ... must principally bear the blame. For the Vulgar love what
> the Elevated deprecate ... the personal scurrility – the coarse slander – the artful
> misrepresentation – the audacious lie. To take these from periodical composition,
> would be to take the seasoning from the sausage.

Nothing better could be expected from 'so superficial a public as the English'.[8]
If you appease this taste they will deny you the title of artist; if you ignore
it they will leave you to penury. It was an unenviable choice.

Matters could have been organised differently. In Germany, France and
other European countries artists were the beneficiaries of state and aristocratic patronage, whereas 'In England, the author who would live on his
works can only live by the Public, in other words by the desultory readers
of light literature; and hence the inevitable tendency of our literary youth
is towards the composition of works without learning and forethought'.[9]
The main plank in Lytton's often close collaboration with Dickens was the
belief of both men that the author stood in need of protection. He repeatedly
pointed out to politicians the incongruity of, on the one hand, urging
people to enjoy the arts while, on the other, giving the artist no status or
assistance whatever:

> You count upon awakening a moral ambition for intellectual eminence amongst
> the people – you need their cooperation. Are these to be gained while you hold
> up the beggary of literature to public pity and disdainful wonder? No, my Lord;
> if you invite your acute and practical countrymen to share in the banquet of
> letters, you must give some honour to those you find at the feast.[10]

Lytton could be pathetically grateful for signs of public approval. Glasgow
became 'that wondrous city' when its university elected him its Rector.[11]
He was also quick to take offence at what he considered a slight on his
profession. The honour of receiving an honorary D.C.L. from Oxford was

ruined when it became clear that literary men would have to follow the politicians in the order of precedence. Exclaiming that he 'never wanted any of their d-d degrees', and that it was intolerable that writers should follow second to 'a parcel of political drudges', he was only dissuaded with great difficulty from simply returning to London.[12] Predictably, he was an enthusiastic supporter of any attempt by artists to help themselves. In 1832 he proposed the setting up of a 'Society of Literary Men' which would publish works of quality and come to the aid of writers in distress.[13] In 1843 he joined the committee of the Society of British Authors. All such efforts collapsed amid wrangling and backbiting, but they made the point about the deficit in channels of appropriate patronage. To be English and a writer was to be at a disadvantage.

Until the situation changed, Lytton felt that he could be popular or serious, but not both. It was an ugly tension in his mind and it presented him with problems that left him uncomfortable. In a poem entitled 'The Master and the Scholar', he pretended that there was no conflict of interest:

> Write for the pedant Few, the vein shall grow
> Cold at its source and meagre in its flow;
> But for the vulgar Many couldst thou write,
> How coarse the passion, and the thought how trite!
> 'Nor few nor many – riddles from thee fall?'
> Author, as Nature smiles – so write; – for All.[14]

But circles were not so easily squared, and Lytton was bounced between fears for his popularity and apprehension about his artistic standing. On the one hand, he thought that the serialisation of novels in reviews and journals was impossibly vulgar. On only three moments in his life did he condescend to this type of publishing.[15] On the other hand, he insisted that the subject matter of a novel should ideally relate immediately to contemporary society, thereby becoming accessible to a wide readership. He wrote of Romans and medieval warriors, but he also wrote of nineteenth-century squires and criminals. Nor was he above asking publishers for suggestions about topics that might guarantee large sales.[16] There was the additional argument that public approval neutralised the malice of critics. He told his son that critics were an unforgiving tribe, 'and the only way to conquer them is to strike at the Public and resolve to be popular. If one writes for the few and the Reviewers who represent the few turn the cold shoulder – one's works are still born for a generation.'[17] So, aspiring novelists were firmly told that 'a great writer must necessarily be a popular writer'.[18] But he only half believed this. For most of his life he wrote for an audience whose taste he despised.

Guiding public taste was the critic. In theory, this was the highest of callings. Writing 'On the Spirit of Criticism', Lytton characterised it as a priesthood:

> No science requires such elaborate study as Criticism. It is the most analytical of our mental operations. To pause, to examine, to say *why* that passage is a sin against nature, or that plot a violation of art, to bring deep knowledge of life in all its guises, of the heart on all its mysteries, to bear upon a sentence of approval or disapprobation – to have cultivated the feeling of beauty till its sense of harmony has grown as fine as the ear of a musician, equally sensitive to discord, or alive to new combinations; these are no light qualities.[19]

Unfortunately, most English critics 'would scarcely be competent to teach English to a preparatory school'.[20] For the most part Lytton despised their judgements and suspected their motives, even as their words stung and wounded him. He took elaborate literary revenge. In *The Last of the Barons*, Father Bungay is acclaimed as having all the qualifications of the critic, being faithless, hypocritical and inclined to plagiarism. In *Paul Clifford*, the unlovely character of Peter McGrawler uses his review, the *Asineum*, 'to prove, that whatever is popular is necessarily bad'.[21] A man of Lytton's sensibilities could not fail to be hurt by criticism, but the pain was made worse by the fact that it was inflicted by pygmies. He ought to have been able to ignore them but could not.

He had specific complaints to bring forward. In the first place, criticism and praise in England was too politically motivated. A work was not judged against a canon of literary values but rather on the extent to which it fell in with certain political creeds. As a young man, to be attacked by Tory critics and praised by Whigs was equally depressing if all comments were dictated by party advantage.[22] Secondly, critics seemed determined to write about his worst work while ignoring the best. How could the *Edinburgh Review* give space to a piece of nonsense like *The Siamese Twins* and yet keep silent about major novels. As late as 1864, the difficulty remained: 'When I compare the manner in which the journalism of my Country continues to ignore and disparage whatever be the position I have won, with the treatment it more graciously bestows on others – I wonder that I have any reputation at all.'[23] Worst of all, critics seemed intent on damning his writing by unpleasant personal references, as if the author's character tainted the words on the page. Inevitably, Forster had to listen to his anguish on this point: 'You have seen the obliging article in the *Times*. Firstly *Maltravers* is a wretch that should have stood in the pillory. Secondly *Maltravers* is no one but myself, ergo I am a wretch that should have stood etc. Agreeable Syllogism.'[24] None of this was the real job of the critic, which

Illustration to *The Last Days of Pompeii*.

was to elucidate the meanings of literature for their own sake. Instead critics were tasteless hacks.

Lytton liked to pretend that he was impervious to the opinions of others. In an essay entitled 'The Knowledge of the World in Men and Books' of 1831, he congratulated himself on an ability to 'forgive offences against me with ease', but such a protestation convinced no one.[25] Only a year before his death, he was sure that 'nothing I do will ever be fairly estimated by an English Public influenced by English Reviewers. I scarcely ever see a literary journal without seeing myself either insulted or ignored.'[26] He always rose to criticism, and always wanted to answer and punish it. At times he came close to being a victim of paranoia. The relative failure of his epic poem *King Arthur*, of which he was especially fond, was put down to concerted malice: 'Ever since I began what is called "a literary career", I have had against me more inveterately than any other author of my day, the cliques which supply criticism to the journals.'[27] There was 'a concealed plan in certain quarters to scare me from writing', prompted by a 'malignity' more profound than that directed against any writer in history.[28] In this at least he shared common ground with Rosina, who thought herself similarly attacked. Moments of tension in his association with Dickens came when he had convinced himself that his rival's novels were being puffed solely with the intention of downgrading his own.[29]

The problem was that Lytton was quite incapable of disentangling the written word from his own personality. To attack one was to attack the other. As he put it, an author's 'works alone make not up a man's character, but they are the index to that living book', or, to adapt the metaphor, they were 'an appendix to their biography far more valuable and explanatory than the text itself'.[30] Criticism, like so much else in Lytton's life, was turned into a commentary on his personality. A feeling of being harassed, unfairly treated, his talent cynically denied, never left him. As late as 1868, when nothing could threaten his assured position in literary life, he was still clear 'that every effort will be made by certain portions of the Press to deprecate my work'. He died in this belief. He told his son that 'I approaching my close see nothing but the impossibility of getting justice done me. I have not and never had one really useful friend in the Critical Press.'[31] So, in this respect too, he was at odds with the world around him.

Claims such as these could be dismissed as approaching hysteria, but Lytton was sure that he had good evidence for his suspicions. Specific experiences in his literary life made the point. Right at the beginning of his career *Pelham* and *Falkland* had established his reputation, but the critical response had smeared him with charges of immorality that he thought quite unfair. Respectable women wondered if it was safe to read him at all.[32] Victorian critics partly judged books by their moral or immoral content, by the extent to which they encouraged the good or discouraged the bad. Cynical heroes, who were preoccupied with collars and cuffs, were not always to their taste. To Lytton such a reaction demonstrated the limitations of English critics. They mistook the veneer for the content. As he protested in the preface to *Falkland*, his heroes were virtuous at the core, even if the reviewers were too blind to see it. Clearly they were leagued together to do down his young talent.

If the response to his society novels was blinkered, in his view, the vitriolic reviewers of his 'Newgate' novels were more bitter still. Between 1830 and 1847 Lytton produced as number of works that dealt with crime, poverty and murder. Arguably they are among his best. But novels like *Paul Clifford*, *Eugene Aram* and *Lucretia* were denounced as unsavoury. In particular, William Maginn and the battalions of *Fraser's Magazine* were appalled. To treat of low life in literature was perverse when so many more elevated themes could have been chosen. To write about the criminal with sympathy, dissecting the psychology of a murderer for instance, was inadmissible.[33] Lytton tried to deflect attacks on his 'Newgate' novels with humour. He solemnly warned his opponents that barring the criminal from the stage would mean the end of Oedipus and Othello. He promised Caroline Norton that, if he ever wrote another book about the underworld, 'the next criminal I draw shall not at least want ample chastisement. He shall write a book in three vols – and publish it!'[34]

In fact, he bled with each review. His skin was not thick enough to repel stinging words. The Newgate novels had been seriously researched. The character of Varney in *Lucretia*, for example, was modelled on the case of Thomas Wainwright, a notorious poisoner.[35] Lytton asserted, with some justice, that the books were designed to show that crime and the guilt it engenders were destructive of the finest minds and the most solid of characters. As he put it, 'guilt may not destroy the intellect itself but it destroys all its natural uses and fruit'.[36] How and why men and women descend into this abyss had always been one of the themes of great literature. The artist had a duty to continue to explore it. Criminals were 'the incarnations of Egotism pushed to the extremes'.[37] They were the moral obverse of the artist. Criminal and artist created the rules of their own morality, the one for evil and the other for truth. They were near cousins:

> The element of the highest genius is not among the village gossips of Miss Austen; it is in crime and passion, for the two are linked together. It is the art of that genius to make you distinguish between the crime and the criminal, and in

proportion as your soul shudders at the one, to let your heart beat with the heart of the other. It is not immoral, it is moral, and of the most impressive and epic order of novels, to arouse and sustain interest in a criminal.[38]

This was, however, an interpretation of morality that few Victorian critics found reasonable. To claim that the dandy or the criminal was a lesson in morality seemed to turn the world upside down.

Unfortunately, Lytton could never allow criticism to wash over him. When attacked his natural inclination was to indulge in public acts of self-justification, even if by doing so he prolonged and deepened discomfort. In 1847, for example, wounded by the reception of *Lucretia*, he issued *A Word to the Public* in which he quite literally appealed over the heads of the critics to a mass opinion he despised. He pointed out that only a tiny fraction of his literary output concerned the criminal. He argued that, since 'crime meets us everywhere', it was absurd to assert that it was not a fit subject for literature. Recent works by William Godwin, Sir Walter Scott and Charles Dickens had not met the same criticism, and he therefore asked why his should be so singled out for condemnation. Finally, his generation of writers were presented with a wonderful opportunity, for if characters in Greek tragedy committed crime at the behest of the Gods, pioneering work on criminology offered more varied and fascinating insights which the Victorian novelist would be foolish to ignore.[39] As a manifesto, this pamphlet brought together powerful arguments that had characterised Lytton's thinking for many years. But it was also evidence of real hurt. He had come to believe firmly by 1847 that the critics, who claimed not to understand his purpose, were either stupid or malevolent. In his view, they were probably both.

Battling with an untutored public opinion, and with the critics who led it by the nose, could not fail to have the most disastrous repercussions. A character as prickly and sensitive as Lytton's could only be warped by repeated belittlement. His ill thought-out responses involved him in public controversy, which only confirmed his reputation for being difficult. As early as 1843 he was threatening to abandon literature altogether. In the preface to *The Last of the Barons* he announced that it was the last time he would 'trespass upon the Public'. Robust friends like Harriet Martineau took it upon themselves to talk him out of such moods: 'Now such a being as you *must not* succumb to any discontent whatever. It is humbling to every one of us to conceive of your being in the least put out of your way by the world, by any kind or degree of opinion. Do you not feel that you can put the world under your feet? And do you not mean to do it?'[40] Lytton never did retire from writing, but the threat that he was about to do so was repeated again and again. Protesting friends then brought the reassurance he needed.

A variation on this theme was his insistence that his work should be published anonymously. He believed that anything emerging under his own name would be torn apart by the critics, so great was their animus to him personally. Often only Forster and the publisher would be in the secret. In Lytton's mind, two ends would be served by this device. First, his novels and poetry would be honestly appraised. Secondly, should they be applauded, he would have the pleasure of seeing his enemies in the reviewing world tricked into approving of him. Otherwise 'it would be highly unpleasant to have myself even suspected as author'.[41] Even late in life, when little could harm his established reputation, he still took out this insurance. It argues for a deep sense of insecurity about his position in the world of letters. Adverse criticism brought on destabilising doubt and was therefore to be avoided at all cost.

Just occasionally, Lytton chose a different response to critical hostility by taking on the editorship of a journal and turning its fire power on his enemies. But these rare moments were indicative of a feeling that he was cornered. From November 1831 to August 1833 he was editor of the *New Monthly Magazine*, writing seventy-five of the two hundred and eighty five articles that appeared in it during these months. This enormous labour was sustained by the notions that he was being revenged on those who had hurt him, and that he was establishing new standards for criticism. It was to be elevated writing. Competitors would be exposed as literary poseurs:

> The writers of that day, moreover, were miserably deficient in true taste; they had not the smallest susceptibility to genius. They were Gallicised to the core ... They cut and squared their literary opinions to political purposes. They [the *Edinburgh Review*] Whigged everything they touched ... They were unutterably smart, clever, and small ... the battledore of *The Quarterly* was merely set up to play at shuttlecock with the battledore of *The Edinburgh*.[42]

His journal, too, would be free of the malice of that 'stupid, coarse, illiterate periodical ... Mr Fraser's foetid magazine'.[43] As if to make his point, *Fraser's Magazine* greeted the news of Lytton's appointment by congratulating him, sarcastically, on moving away from fashionable novels into serious writing at last and by perpetuating the joke about his name by referring to him as 'Liston' Bulwer.[44]

Given his emotional involvement with the project,[45] it was no consolation to Lytton to preside over its failure. During his editorship, circulation fell from 5000 to 4000 copies. The *New Monthly Magazine* had had a readership of 'clergymen and steady "old-notioned" country gentlemen'. Lytton's

Illustration to the *Last of the Barons.*

attempt to interest such an audience in criticism of a highly intellectual kind, with a dash of radical politics thrown in, was unlikely to be a success. His deputy editor observed that his superior 'had a cause to advocate and uphold; he sacrificed the publication to do so'.[46] There was truth in this remark. From 1838 to 1841 the dismal experience was repeated, when, in partnership with Dionysius Lardner, he founded and co-edited the *Monthly Chronicle*. Once again it aimed to supplant politically-biased journals and to raise standards of reviewing. Once again it failed. To Lytton's way of thinking, his miserable experiences in the editorships of magazines merely proved the futility of trying to teach the English good writing. They seemed to prefer criticism based on political prejudice. As a result, the taste of the English was debased. It explained to him why his own work was received in the way it was, and confirmed in him a liking for anonymity. This view was never modified, in spite of soaring sales and the establishment of an unassailable reputation.

The saddest consequence of Lytton seeing himself rejected by critical and public opinion was that it embroiled him with his fellow writers. Quite simply, any novelist whose work was praised by critics who damned his must have had a role in the conspiracy against him. In his public as in his private life, there was no room for ambiguity in an association with Lytton. A man was either his enemy or his friend. Difficulties with those who teased him, like Thackeray and Carlyle, have already been discussed. At one point he threatened the former with a duel.[47] Even when apologies were offered 'for pelting at that poor old Bulwer',[48] they were rarely accepted. Wounds inflicted on Lytton continued to bleed. As a result, friendships with other writers, instead of being a consolation, degenerated into yet another morass of poisonous dialogue.

There should, for example, have been the strongest links between Lytton and Charles Dickens. Both men frequented the Gore House set, and both trusted Forster as their man of business. They sat on committees and on the boards of trusts designed to help their fellow writers. They collaborated on plays, and defended 'Newgate' novel writing. Lytton acted as godfather to one of Dickens's sons, who was grandiloquently christened Edward Bulwer Lytton Dickens.[49] According to a near relation, Dickens 'never had a warmer, more generous, ungrudging appreciator and admirer as he had in Lord Lytton'.[50] Unfortunately, even association on so many levels was no guarantee that friendship would develop smoothly. Lytton could not overcome the feeling that Dickens was a rival who was 'destined to eclipse me', not because he was a better writer but because he was the darling of the critics. His novels were always acclaimed while 'so little favour [was] shewn to me'.[51] Lytton was jealous of the commercial success that Dickens enjoyed. It came so easily, while his had to be fought for. 'Dickens is going to "read" in Australia in the summer. Expects to get 10,000 or 12,000 by it. I dined with him in Paris, and a very bad dinner he gave me.'[52]

Lytton sometimes praised a novel by Dickens, sometimes mixed faint appreciation with heavy criticism, and sometimes rejected works outright. *The Old Curiosity Shop* had 'snatches of the most exquisite truth and poetry', but *A Christmas Carol* was 'overrated', and *Barnaby Rudge* 'does not seem to me so good in character'.[53] In the last years of his life jealousy and complaints about ill-usage led Lytton to abandon his old friend. He told his son that he had 'deep cause for complaint against Dickens ... But a Man is never that which People think him. Dickens is *not* a great fellow. He wants heart and is a great humbug.'[54] To take the chair at a dinner in honour of his rival was torture: 'I am just come from taking the chair at Dickens dinner. It was not a pleasant position for me to go into the hornet's nest of my enemies his special friends are. They think to ignore or deny me advances him, and I suspect that he sanctions that policy.'[55] In a sense, this fear of Dickens was justified. The novels of Dickens have retained their popularity while those of Lytton have not. He was eclipsed by his rival. But it was not reasonable to attribute this fact to some preconceived conspiracy. Nor was it worth the loss of a close friend.

An even more rancorous duelling took place with Tennyson, a man Lytton once described as 'my excellent friend'.[56] With John Forster and the d'Eyncourt family from Lincolnshire as mutual friends there was every reason why the two men should have enjoyed each other's respect and support.[57] What poisoned this possibility was, once again, Lytton's belief that Tennyson was a creature of the critics, made and enlarged by their puffing. Lytton valued his own reputation as a poet as highly as that of a novelist. He saw Tennyson's fortunes growing, in proportion as his fell. Tennyson's was not a 'masculine' style, and yet the critics praised it:

> Mr Tennyson has much in him worthier of a better fate than, if he mind the pens of reviewers, he will attain to: he is full of faults; and his faults have been so bepraised, that he runs the natural Danger of thinking them beauties. He has filled half pages with the most glaring imitations, and the imitations have been lauded for their originality.[58]

Lytton was struck by 'the poverty of his conceptions'. Worse still, this effeminate 'Tennysonian Doodle' was being held up as the model for young writers to follow.[59] The world of English literature would soon be in need of 'a besom for all the small spiders weaving Tennysonian webs'.[60] It was simply incredible that critics should prefer poetry of this kind to his own.

Real battle was joined in 1846 when Lytton punished *The New Timon* as an extended satire on the leading political and literary figures of the day. It was a kind of schoolboy defiance of those who gave him no credit. With good reason, he was nervous about its reception. Not only was it published anonymously, but he even denied to Forster that he was the author. When the secret was revealed there was predictable recrimination, about which Lytton vigorously complained:

> Why, I say, I should be selected so constantly and so bitterly for the stings and slanders of the literary clique professional, I know not, except because I am a gentleman, and because I have been good-natured. I can't help being the first, but I can at least remedy the second; and wits as these persons think themselves, I will try if I cannot pay them off in their own coin. Therefore, let the hunchback look to his hump.[61]

Tennyson was singled out for special vilification. Once again contrasting the effeminacy of his rival with his own manly writing, he called Tennyson the 'school-miss Alfred', and asserted that

> No tawdry grace shall womanize my pen!
> Even in love-song man should write for men!

Tennyson countered with devastating effect in *The New Timon and the Poets*:

> So died the Old: here comes the New.
> Regard him: a familiar face:
> I *thought* we knew him: what, it's you,
> The padded man – that wears the stays.

> Who kill'd the girls and thrill'd the boys,
> With dandy pathos when you wrote,
> A Lion, you, that made a noise,
> And shook a mane *en papillotes* [paper curlers].

> And once you tried the Muses too;
> You fail'd, Sir; therefore now you turn,
> You fall on those who are to you
> As Captain is to Subaltern.

> But men of long-enduring hopes,
> And careless what this hour may bring,
> Can pardon little would-be Popes
> And Brummels when they try to sting.

> . . .

> And what with spites and what with fears,
> You cannot let a body be:

> It's always ringing in your ears,
> 'They call this man as good as *me*.'
>
> What profits now to understand
> The merits of a spotless shirt –
> A dapper boot – a little hand –
> If half the little soul is dirt? [62]

Without doubt, both men had gone too far. In later editions of *The New Timon* Lytton omitted the Tennysonian references. In return, his rival tried to make amends by publishing a kind of apology in verse, which began:

> Ah, God! the petty fools of rhyme
> That shriek and sweat in pygmy wars
> Before the strong fact of Time,
> And looked at by the silent stars.

Both men had been badly bruised in this encounter, but Lytton came off worse. What he would later call 'Tennyson's clique' had targeted their shafts well.[63] References to Lytton's vanity and jealousy of others seemed all too apt. He did resent the success of those he believed to be of inferior talent, and he did blame ignorant critics for establishing careers in literature for unworthy men.

A fear of rivals could lead to astonishing judgements, perhaps the most remarkable of which was his dismissal of George Eliot. He thought that *Adam Bede* was her only readable production, and that even that was 'third rate'. *Middlemarch* was 'a poor book'. The two novelists met only infrequently, and then Lytton was more than happy to detail the faults that stared from the page in the other's novels. George Eliot sarcastically pretended to be grateful for the advice, but declared that she would prefer 'to have my teeth drawn' rather than make any changes. With scant remembrance of his own behaviour, he also warned his son against being seen in the company of the lady while she was notoriously known to cohabit with George Lewes. But, once again, the real difficulty in his mind was that she was a talent created by critics, and 'the way in which she has been puffed up by the Critical Press is one of the many disgraces of contemporary literature'.[64]

Lytton's career was therefore punctuated by very public entanglements with many of the leading figures of the Victorian literary establishment. In each case, the reason was the same. In measuring his own talent against that of others, he felt himself superior. It was therefore incredible that critics should sometimes take a different view. Only their stupidity and malice could account for it. In England, since the state played no part in the patronage of the arts or in the arbitration of taste, callow amateurs made and broke literary careers. Little wonder that Lytton should prefer continental models. The English had no feeling for the arts and left their direction to incompetents. Predictably, none of this was likely to make him popular. After attending a meeting of the Literary Fund in 1838 he noted in his journal: 'I was coldly welcomed – authors and reviewers there who hate me.'[65] Within the literary world he felt an alienation from his kind which complemented the sense of distance in his social life.

An unresponsive state, corrupt reviewers and a debased popular taste created victims. Lytton, very much associating his fate with theirs, was prompted to take action. For the whole of his life, he became a leading figure in what might be called literary good causes. He took particular pleasure in assisting those whose work went unrecognised by critics. The theme often makes an appearance in his novels. The hero of *Ernest Maltravers* appreciated 'the vast debt which the world owes to authors, and pays but by calumny in life and barren laurels after death'. Lenny Fairfield in *My Novel* embarks on a soul-destroying battle with crooked publishers and indifferent critics. In *Eugene Aram* Lytton asserted that 'the most pitiable, the most heart-sickening object in the world, is the man of letters, sunk into habitual beggar.'[66] So pressing was this thought that it led Lytton into charitable work that was expensive both in terms of time and money. He stinted neither in terms of the artist in need.

At the most basic level there was the guaranteeing of a livelihood. Politicians would be badgered, publishers cajoled and rich patrons milked to this end. The roll-call of writers helped in this way, however, is of a very special kind. Almost without exception, they were people who were too radical, too eccentric, too nonconformist, to be eligible for the compassion of the official world. There was William Godwin, the progenitor of anarchism, penurious in old age; Albany Fonblanque, impoverished but of 'such genius'; Laman Blanchard, whose debts drove him to suicide; and Thomas Hood, who died just before the relief that Lytton had secured could reach him. Tragically, this charity work was often organised for the widows and orphans of writers whose neglected talents had never given them anything except a life on the margins of want. Lytton was tireless in helping such people. When the fortunes of Leigh Hunt were successfully put on a sounder footing, Lytton reflected that 'it is pleasant indeed to turn to any evidence of high and pure feelings in this low age of literary abuse'.[67]

Writers who fell foul of the critical consensus were especial objects of his sympathy. When Swinburne's work was denounced as immoral, Lytton's reaction was to invite him to stay at Knebworth.[68] Women like Laetitia Landon, who found it difficult to make any headway in the male-dominated world of publishing, were promoted in their lifetimes, and their dependents were cared for after their deaths. There were the whimsical oddities of Victorian literature like Thomas Hood and Mark Lemon, whose creations were dismissed as not serious. And there were giants from an earlier generation like Thomas Campbell, whose poetry was now dismissed out of hand as old-fashioned and dated.[69] All such people found in Lytton someone who shared their feelings of being excluded from establishment opinion. It was, as Hood put it, reassuring to 'accept Kindness from literary men, as from relations'. He included Lytton and himself in what he called a 'Bruderschaft', a fellowship of artists in adversity. The compliment was well made. Just as Lytton injured himself in contests with successful writers, he was held in veneration by those who were less regarded.[70] For them he was a champion and a saviour.

Lytton, however, wanted to go further. Charity extended to individuals was good in itself but was by definition random in its operation. What was really needed was a permanent endowment that would give literary men security. The setting up of such a trust could be undertaken with, or preferably without, government involvement.[71] So, in 1851, Dickens and Lytton were prime movers in the setting up of the Guild of Literature and Art. His expectations were high:

> I do devoutly believe that this plan, carried by the support which I trust will be given to it, will change the status of the literary man in England, and make a revolution in his position which no government, no power on earth but his own, could ever effect. I have implicit confidence in the scheme – so splendidly begun – if we carry it out with a steadfast energy. I have a strong conviction that we hold in our hands the peace and honour of men of letters for centuries to come.[72]

The central idea was to endow 'chairs' outside universities for writers of distinction, who would thereby be financially and critically independent of reviewers and public opinion. The model was the respected and untouchable professor in Germany. There, formal positions 'by offering subsistence and dignity to that valuable class of writers whose learning and capacities unfit them by reason of their very depth for wide popularity, had given worthy and profitable inducements to study, and more than all else had maintained the German fame for patient erudition and profound philosophy'.[73] It was a project that brought together so many of Lytton's preoccupations.

To launch the fund-raising he wrote a play, *Not As Bad As We Seem*, which was performed in the presence of Queen Victoria and Prince Albert. The cast included Charles Dickens, John Forster, Wilkie Collins, Douglas Jerrold and Mark Lemon. A national tour followed, and some four thousand pounds was raised, after which the guild was incorporated by Act of

Parliament in 1854. In addition, Lytton gave the guild land near Knebworth on which it was proposed to build cottages, 'retreats for scribblers',[74] where writers could live free of charge and devote themselves to literature. It was a romantic vision and it failed. Another Act of Parliament in 1897 wound up the guild and distributed its assets between the Royal Literary Fund and the Artists' General Benevolent Association.[75] But the attempt is more important than the failure. It was a quite genuine initiative to reorder the relationship of the artist and society. The latter was no longer to exercise financial and critical tutelage over the former. That this kind of artistic independence has never been achieved may say more about England than about Lytton. It certainly gave him new cause to doubt the good faith of his countrymen.

Lytton fought on other fronts too. If writers could not live by subvention, why should they not enjoy the real benefits of their labour in royalties. For them to do so, a major revision of the copyright law would be required. As matters stood, publishers tended to retain copyright themselves, giving writers no choice in the matter. Even worse, as soon as a book appeared, it was brought out in pirated editions abroad without any benefit to the author. It was a situation which hurt everyone. It worked 'to the disadvantage of the most eminent writers, the most standard classes of composition'.[76] The campaign to overturn Parliament's reluctance to legislate in this area occupied Lytton's attention for the whole of his life. In pushing for change he was surprisingly energetic. He was genuinely angry that the financial denigration of the writer was symbolic of a wider contempt. The copyright of his own works was vigorously defended, even if this involved initiating court action as far away as New South Wales, and he advised unworldly people like Isaac Disraeli to be firm with publishers.[77] During his years in Parliament, he was tireless in agitating for the protection of authors.[78] English legislators were simply not to be permitted to forget the issue.

Foreign governments were not allowed to doze either, particularly that of the United States. It is not overstating the case to say that Lytton regarded himself at war with a country where publishers could pirate English works without paying anything to their authors. By way of retaliation, Lytton proposed that American writers should go unprotected in England.[79] More tangibly, campaigns for a revision of the law were launched in the American Senate in 1837 and 1842. In 1852, Lytton raised over £2500 to fight a test case in the American courts, under the benign supervision of Sir John Crampton, the English Minister in Washington. He was effusive in his thanks to his ally:

> You are the first person who has taken up in earnest a question of the most vital and permanent importance to the Literature of England, and essential I believe

to the very life of Literature in America. And your success will entitle you to the
lasting gratitude of all who write in the Anglo-Saxon tongue.[80]

But, even with official help, these campaigns produced little by way of
success. Dickens and Charlotte Brontë among others feared that vested
interests in America would thwart any movement on the issue, and they
were proved right in the short term.[81] Even so, these episodes underline
the view that Lytton's demands on behalf of writers were based on a deeply
rooted feeling of injustice. His torrid arguments with rival authors should
be set in the context of a profound sense of caste. His claim that the artist
should be taken seriously went far beyond personal vanity. He wanted status
for the best of those who practised his craft.

A third way of helping the artist was to release the playwright and the
actor from the idiotic restrictions imposed by an insensitive state. Lytton
himself enjoyed considerable success with such plays as *Money* and *The
Lady of Lyons*, and he valued highly his friendship with William Macready,
the actor-manager of Covent Garden. His love of the theatre was unbroken
throughout his life. His novels are full of characters who laud its qualities.
Waife in *What Will He Do With It?* utters words that could be Lytton's
own: 'I like acting – I like the applause, and the lights, and the excitement,
and the illusion – the make-believe of the whole thing: it takes me out of
memory and thought; it is a world that has neither past, present, nor future,
an interlude in time – an escape from space.' A character in *Godolphin* was
grateful that the theatre 'awakens whatever romance belongs to our character ... the kindling exaggeration of the sentiments which belong to the
stage'.[82] The private theatricals at Knebworth acquired a certain celebrity,
performances not infrequently being used to raise money so that artists
could be made 'independent of that niggard and debasing kind of charity
which they receive from the State'.[83] The stage was an obvious attraction
to a man with as theatrical a character as Lytton's. The romantic, the heroic,
the supercharged was always congenial to him. With them, as a character
in *The Parisians* put it, the theatre allowed 'the amateur stage-player' to be
young again, to 'regain the vivacity of boyhood'.[84]

Lytton's friendship with William Macready began in 1834, but it became
more intimate when the latter took over the management of Covent Garden
three years later. As with any other involvement with Lytton, there were
misunderstandings and squabbles about money. Lytton accused Macready
of cutting his plays without consultation; Macready accused Lytton of trying
to teach him how to act. Stormy interviews would be followed by heart-
rending reconciliations, once again brokered by John Forster who had the
trust of both.[85] Ultimately, however, the friendship held. At a dinner in

1851 to mark Macready's retirement from the stage, Lytton, from the chair, attested that 'it has been the merit of our guest to recognise the truth that the actor has it in his power to assist in creating the writer. He has identified himself with the living drama of his period, and by doing so he has half created it.'[86] For Lytton to raise the actor to the level of the writer was praise indeed. He acknowledged them to be fellow soldiers in an army that had work to do.

For the theatre operated under unsympathetic laws which Lytton, as a Member of Parliament, was determined to change. He set out the problems clearly in an article in the *New Monthly Magazine* of 1832. First, there was no copyright law that protected the playwright. As soon as a piece had been performed, its author lost all control over it. Secondly, 'the pernicious monopoly' of Covent Garden and Drury Lane to produce plays restricted access to the theatre and killed off any attempt to put on serious drama in the provinces.[87] Thirdly, censorship of new plays by the Lord Chamberlain's office had been so brutal and insensitive that no playwright of note had been produced since the seventeenth century. According to Lytton, the only censorship that should operate was that 'of the spirit of the age'.[88] Lastly, Lytton refused to accept the argument that an uncensored theatre would lead to the immoralities of the Parisian stage. Quite simply, a 'higher standard of public morality' operated in England.[89] And action followed words. The Dramatic Copyright Act of June 1833 was in large measure passed by Lytton's efforts as a parliamentarian. Equally, although the monopoly of Covent Garden and Drury Lane was not broken until 1843, he was justly accredited with a role in its destruction.

Running through Lytton's charitable work on behalf of writers, and through his public statements as a politician, is a persistent, common theme. He is claiming a status for the artist that English society had never before allowed. Not only was financial security demanded but also that respect which the ordinary man owed to those of higher intellect and sensitivity. Born a gentleman and heir to a private income, Lytton could make these claims, and felt that he had a duty to do so. It was a personal crusade that quickly came to define in part his public image. Since, too, it involved the training of the English to rethink the relationship between the artist and society, it was unlikely to be immediately successful or to win him friends. To many these claims were merely arrogant pretension. But to Lytton himself they were the minimum that a civilised society should offer.

Strangely, perhaps, Lytton's greatest contribution to enhancing the status of the artist was to offer himself as a model of how to survive when surrounded by unsympathetic critics and censors. He was a ruthless businessman, a pitiless negotiator of contracts, and a jealous guardian of what was his own. Very early in life he had defined the word 'income' as 'what I receive annually, from my Books – which are to me what a rental is to others'.[90] He told his daughter that 'My hand is my only friend – and only wealth. As long as I trusted only to that all went well in the money way.'[91] The older he became, the more tenacious was he of profits. He cheerfully admitted to the editor of the *Edinburgh Review* that he was 'avaricious and literature becomes sickled over with the pale cast of business'.[92] Nor did he feel there should be any apologies for this behaviour. If publishers were mean-minded and the state unhelpful, authors had to shift for themselves.

Lytton shifted very effectively. By the mid 1840s, he was negotiating contracts with Blackwoods that brought him £3000 for each of the *Caxton* novels. In 1850 Routlege paid him £30,000 for a ten-year contract to produce his novels in cheap editions. It was one of the largest sums paid to a novelist in the nineteenth century. As Charles Kingsley observed, Lytton had achieved 'a popularity which no novelist ever before reached'. When his last novel, *Kenelm Chillingly*, sold three thousand copies on the first day of publication, Edmund Gosse observed that, 'everything he wrote sold as though it were bread displayed to a hungry crowd'.[93] Literature made Lytton rich and he revelled in the fact.

Such selling-power was also a weapon that could be used against publishers, critics and politicians, and Lytton wielded it ruthlessly. As a negotiator himself, or more likely through the agency of John Forster, Lytton tried to control not only the financial rewards of bringing out a book but also every detail of its publication. The relative merits of quarto or octavo editions were discussed, as was the most favourable date of publication and the ownership of copyright. Publishers like the Bentleys and the Blackwoods knew that Lytton gave no quarter. It was a practice started early in life, when Lytton's reputation had hardly been sufficiently established to justify his intransigence. The publisher of *The Siamese Twins*, in 1831, was threatened and instructed without mercy:

> It would be very advisable to strike off a few hundreds in Quarto as a first edition. It will be a novelty at the present time – give the poem an importance – distinguish it from the herd of little octavos that come out everyday and at once cover the expenses. I also suggest as the piece is comic – plates by any Artist you recommend ... I have agreed to the Publication of this volume on the present terms – under the *full understanding* that every pains are to be taken to promote its sale – as much as if it were a longer work ... I beg to assure you that I could only think of taking it to any other House in case it became a drag and a deadweight at yours ... I think it of the highest importance to publish the poem in the course of November.[94]

Volumes of correspondence were written covering every detail of the publishing process. At home or abroad, Lytton religiously kept track of the terms on which foreign editions of his work were to be brought out, the level of royalties achieved by performances of his plays in the provinces, and the success of prosecutions of pirated editions.[95]

He had no sympathy for publishers, who were one and all the enemies of talent. Henry Colburn was 'an energetic publisher but a quack *Jew* in many transactions'. He had 'an inherent and abstract passion for a bargain'.[96] Richard Bentley was 'the Beast' or 'the Artful Dodger'. As for John Murray, Lytton expressed himself not 'very well pleased with this specimen of the Pleasure of Publishing'.[97] The only proper way to deal with such people was to play one off against the other. Tenders would be invited and the highest bid accepted. Delinquency in performing promises would lead to work being removed to a competitor. Publishers were the mere technicians of publishing. Their first aim should be the discovery of talent and its promotion. All too often they failed in this responsibility, even daring to set themselves up as arbiters of taste. Their punishment had to come from successful writers who had the independence of mind and income that allowed them to act. Lytton set the example. He proved that financial security was possible in a literary career, but only if the writer guarded his work as a lioness her cubs.

By any criteria, Lytton must rank as one of the towering figures of Victorian literature. His sales were immense, not only in England but also in America and on the Continent. His peerage was won more for a contribution to literature than to politics. Yet none of this reassured him. For the whole of his life he felt undervalued. He wanted the artist to have a new status, respected as the interpreter of the soul's most intimate longings, with something of the prophet thrown in. In this, he was asking too much of the English. Frenchmen and Germans might listen to his claims, but his countrymen often found them eccentric and self-regarding. In Lytton's view therefore writers were endlessly confronted with a reading public that had no taste, critics who had no learning and publishers who had no pity. Theirs was an unenviable lot. He would have explained his own success in such a climate by reference to the heroic efforts he had made to have himself read, reviewed and published. Too many of his friends, with fainter hearts, had fallen by the wayside. His prickly sensibility about his work, and the failure of humour when he was teased, were both the consequences of a belief that Lytton the artist was held at a discount by those who should have known better.

7

Ghosts and Artists

If an exotic family history, literary pretension and outlandish appearance were not enough to make Lytton distinctive, there was one more thing, namely his emphasis on the spiritual. He was a man who held conversations with ghosts. His books are full of astrologers, dealers in the Kabbala, and alchemy. He was the client of mediums. To modern sensibilities this aspect of his life may appear eccentric, but in its nineteenth-century context it was strange but not beyond the bounds of reason. Scientific experimentation was opening up new fields of enquiry and discovering new forms of energy. The possibilities of electricity, for example, were only beginning to be known. Many people, including Lytton, could reasonably ask why other forces, hitherto labelled mysterious, should not come within the scrutiny of science. A mystic, in contacting the dead, might simply be exercising an energy that science had yet to identify. By this thinking, spiritualism merged into scientific enquiry. Many Victorians found the combination seductive. It was merely a question of releasing forces too long held in check. As the astrologer Volktman put it, in *Godolphin*, 'there are in the human mind two powers that affect all of which our nature is capable – REASON and IMAGINATION'. Europeans had relied too heavily on the first of these capacities. The Egyptians and other ancient peoples knew better. By cultivating the imagination, they

> not only attained to the most intimate arcana of the stars, but to the empire of the spirits about, above and beneath the earth: a power, indeed, disputed by the presumptuous sophists of the present time, but of which their writings yet contain ample proof ... By this spirit within the flesh, we grow *from* the flesh, and may see, and at length invoke the souls, of the dead, and receive warnings, and hear omens, and girdle our sleep with dreams.[1]

In this endeavour, the artist had a special role to play. Endowed with unusual powers of the imagination, he could use this 'sympathy' to transcend the body and to commune with what lay beyond. Out-of-body experiences should be part of an artistic training. On this basis, art becomes a religious vocation, in the deepest meaning of the word, and the artist becomes a priest. His special power can interpret and bring close the world of the spirit. It was a high calling. Predictably, Lytton was fascinated by death and its rituals. In a strange essay written for *Blackwood's Magazine* in 1859, entitled 'A Dream of the Dead', he reported dreaming that he himself had died: 'It was a sensation of inexpressible physical relief: all ailment, to which I had been familiarised, was gone – gone all weariness, inertness of muscle, of nerve, of spirit.' It was a world of silence, without love or affection possible between its inhabitants. More prosaically, coffee was on sale.[2] Throughout his life, he believed that all artists should pursue enquiries of this kind and that a small number of spiritualists had gifts with which to make the spirit world knowable. He would no doubt have taken great satisfaction in the fact that a photograph of his own ghost appeared in the magazine *Light* in 1915.[3]

At the end of his life, Lytton impressed on his son that all great art concerned itself with the transcendent. In its investigations it was akin to scientific enquiry:

> Science itself, even in its most material form, the mechanical, is not purely inductive – it guesses, it divines a something beyond what is yet known or proveable – Something on the other side of the Dead Wall – Art or the Poetic invention does this hourly; it is its necessity ... For myself considering how instinctively and how constantly thought tends towards a source beyond us – and how keen is the heart's appetite for prayer – I am persuaded that there is among the agencies of Nature a sort of electric link between Man (the sole animal that prays) and God.[4]

To talk in such terms inevitably brought the accusation of preaching. Critics like Leslie Stephen found it hard to take: 'The most palpable defect of his novels is their extreme self-consciousness. The writer is evidently determined that we shall not overlook his claims to be a teacher of mankind ... He aims at the Ideal, and very rightly, but the Ideal and the True and the Beautiful need not always be presenting themselves with the pomp of capital letters.'[5] In his view, too many of Lytton's characters gave themselves up to a predetermined fate and inexorable destinies. Lytton himself vigorously denied the charge of preaching,[6] but it was a popular one made against him.

Such accusations failed to move him. His definition of 'the Poetical Character' was uncompromising: 'the leading feature is that of veneration. The ideal – the visionary – the yearning – are all emanations from this principle – the vague, internal impress of something great and high above the visible diurnal sphere.'[7] Any man, artist or not, made a terrible mistake in trying to find an equivalent satisfaction or purpose in the pursuit of human love.[8] It could only be a lesser experience. As a recent writer put it, 'He recognized the supernatural to be a legitimate preoccupation of the Romantic artist, as a pivot between the inner nature of the individual and the outer nature of the cosmos'.[9] It was so noble a quest that, even if unfulfilled, it had majesty in the undertaking. In *The Disowned*, the narrative is interrupted to tell the story of a failed artist named Warner who, while accepting that his talents were limited, dies happy in the knowledge that he had at least made the attempt to live in art.

For Lytton therefore, the artist had to be a visionary whose eyes allowed him to see things other men could not. As he explained to Lord Walpole:

I am a believer in the Duality of the mind – all of us really have two minds – one which we take into the world – carry into the clubs – walk the streets with – use every day ... This is the mind that enables us to make or disposes us to squander our money ... Then there is another mind in which we pack up such sentiments as the world has not spoiled – our poetical emotions, our conceptions of what is pure or Heroic – a mind that vanishes altogether when we walk into Bond Street, and are mere men among men.[10]

The artist could not therefore be on a par with his fellows. To capture the essence of the poetical was to forego the humdrum existence. Since there was 'no chimera vainer than the hope that one human heart shall find sympathy in another', he believed that 'authors are made to be ascetics'. There was more satisfaction to be won by living in the imagination than in the company of men and women, because in 'our sleep from the passions of the world, God makes Eve to us from our own breasts'.[11] No doubt memories of his own private life would reinforce this view.

Chaste and alone, the artist must search out the spiritual world. To do so he must go beyond conviction and overcome all fear of the unknown. The investigation of the supranatural inevitably held terrors, but 'he who would arrive at the Fairyland, must face the Phantoms'.[12] All this inevitably set him apart from the world around him. When Lytton claimed special terms for the artist, as recorded earlier, this aspect of his life was of paramount importance. In his discussions of what the afterlife might be like, he was always clear that only people with certain spiritual qualities would achieve it. He did not expect to meet whole categories of people after death, among whom may be numbered savages, peasants and trades-men. Few people could be artists. Few had 'the nervous sympathy' that was transcendental. As a result, Lytton easily transferred the aristocratic notions that guided his politics into a view of the artistic world that was just as exclusive. After hearing his description of the spirit world, Harriet Martineau exclaimed, 'How aristocratic you must be!'[13] Lytton the politician wanted public recognition nearly as much as Lytton the artist, a fact which produced great tension, but the concern for his artistic reputation was always the greater. It was the superior calling.

This preference had been established early. In a poem written at Cambridge, the artist's enduring influence was contrasted to the passing pomp of the politician:

> Calm in your lofty grandeur glance below
> Unmov'd by passions which ye never know, –
> While Empires fall around you – ye retain
> Gods of the mind, your everlasting reign.[14]

Similarly, Petrarch was always a hero of Lytton's because he was thought to have been among the first to claim that 'the majesty of letters' should have the guiding of political affairs. Should it be necessary to choose between literary and political careers, Lytton had no doubt which path should be followed. He wanted public recognition in both spheres but was clear where his priorities lay. He told the Commons in 1838 that 'it is my weakness to prefer the emoluments and the distinctions that are open to me in another career to all the more dazzling honours that a Minister could bestow'.[15]

So certain was he of this point that the extent to which any writer approached the spiritual became, in his view, one of the principal yardsticks by which his or her work should be judged. Crabbe and Dickens lacked the passion which was 'the true element of fiction'.[16] Worse, Tennyson actually demoted the heroic, turning King Arthur, Lancelot and Merlin into 'a whimpering old gentleman, a frenchified household traitor and drivelling dotard'. Jane Austen was dismissed for dealing in nothing but village gossip, while Victor Hugo drew all his characters from the mud.[17] None of these understood or attempted the sublime. By contrast, the great poets of antiquity like Virgil and Homer were models to be copied, while, in the contemporary world, German literature had the surest sense of spiritual mission. Lytton wrote extensively about Goethe and Schiller. As his review of Schiller's *The Pilgrim* indicates, he thought that the Germans glimpsed a world that the prosaic English never saw:

> The Pilgrim represents the active labour of the idealist to reach the Golden Gate ... The belief in what is beyond Reality is necessary to all who would escape from the Real ... But The Pilgrim, after all his travail, finds that the earth will never reach the heaven, and the *There* can never be *Here*.[18]

Living in the imagination, German writers attained spiritual heights that English critics found it hard to comprehend. Lytton's claims for the artist were further reason why he increasingly found it congenial to live abroad.

If the writer was empowered with the duty of investigating spiritual worlds beyond earth, Lytton himself tried hard to fulfil this trust. Many of his novels explore the arcane and the occult, being peopled by characters with special powers. There are astrologers and wizards like Volktman in *Godolphin* and Alamen in *Leila*. Lytton heroines are frequently endowed with a childlike purity and simplicity that enables them to communicate with worlds hidden from the eyes of ordinary people. Even so robust a hero as Rienzi had an intellect 'strangely conjoined with a deep and mystical superstition'.[19] Lytton read extensively in astrology and in the history of mystical, secret societies like the Rosicrucians. Two novels in particular tried to give expression to the conclusions he had drawn from his reading.

The first was *Zanoni*, published in 1842. Lytton's claims for it were great:

> I conceive that work to be the truest representative of Humanity ... and opens some elevating glimpse into the sublimest mysteries of our being, by establishing the inevitable union that exists between the plain things of the day, in which our earthly bodies perform their allotted part, and the latent, often uncultivated, often invisible, affinities of the soul with all the powers that externally breathe and move throughout the Universe of the Spirit.[20]

In the author's view, there was 'nothing like it in the language'. Loftily, he acknowledged that, being an odyssey of the soul, the book 'will be no favourite with the largest of all asses – the English Public'.[21] For once, he abandoned the attempt to please critical or popular taste. For once, he was writing about what he really thought to be important: 'It shoots too much over the heads of people to hit the popular taste – But it has given me a vent for what I long wished to symbolise and typify and so I am grateful to it.'[22] It was his 'special pet production'.[23] But, in talking of 'the Ideal' and 'the Spiritual' he was importing German ideas and German language that fell oddly on English ears. Friends like Harriet Martineau recognised that it was essentially a foreign book. As such, it would be dismissed by those 'who are not conversant with German, and to whom the language of the Ideal region may be more unfamiliar than its thoughts'.[24] In spite of this difficulty, *Zanoni* remained for Lytton a kind of personal manifesto.

The plotting of the novel was 'an attempt to illustrate – I think for the first time – the Theuragia or White Magic – that the Pythagoreans and Platonists transmitted to the Rosicrucians and some other sects of amiable and noble self-delusion'.[25] Zanoni and Mejnour are the last two survivors of an ancient sect, who, by living exclusively in the realm of the spirit, have conquered time and remain forever young. Free of all earthly passions and entanglements, they have overcome death and corruption. By what precise agency this is achieved is not clear. It could be made possible by the discovery and use of an elixir or energy that was so far unknown to regular science. As Harriet Martineau noted, *Zanoni* proved that 'Science is ever striving to carry the most gifted beyond ordinary conditions – the result being – as many victims as efforts – and the striven being finally left a Solitary – his object being unsuitable to the natures he has to deal with'.[26] Alternatively, Zanoni and Mejnour were simply living in the spirit at a level only rarely achieved by the greatest saints and mystics. But, whatever the cause, there was definitely a world beyond the body, beyond death itself, that only the most spiritually advanced could inhabit.

Access to this world was impossibly difficult to discover. Would-be initiates faced daunting trials. Shapeless horrors had to be faced and overcome before entry could be allowed. More was requested than simply the denial of earthly involvements. As Lytton attempted to describe it, there also had to be inner turmoil on an unimaginable scale:

> As a patient on whom, slowly and by degrees, the agencies of mesmerism are brought to bear, he acknowledged to his heart the growing force of that vast and universal magnetism which is the life of creation, and binds the atom to the whole. A strange and ineffable consciousness of power, of the SOMETHING GREAT within the perishable clay, appealed to feelings dim and glorious – like the faint recognitions of a holier and former being. An impulse, that he could not resist, led him to seek the mystic.[27]

Even when once attained, this state of spiritual refinement is always at risk. Zanoni loses his powers by contracting an earthly love for the heroine Viola, dying on the guillotine in the French Revolution to save her life. His death could be read as a fall from grace, but Lytton would have seen it as exemplifying the difficulty of the quest. Nobility lay in the endeavour, and no final failure could detract from that. Pilgrims falter but their journeyings have grandeur.

He returned to this theme in 1862 by writing *A Strange Story*. As with *Zanoni*, he acknowledged that it was intensely personal writing: 'I have just finished my Strange Story which is the highest and deepest of all my fictions ... I think it a great vindication of Soul ... and that it solves many riddles.'[28] It is a novel packed with footnotes, which almost give it the character of a tract. References to recondite reading abound. In particular, Lytton tried to master the debate between materialists and idealists in philosophy that had preoccupied so much European writing in the eighteenth century and in his own time. In this area, he was unusually influenced by the French writer Maine de Biran, who had started out as a materialist in the Condillac line but, finding this unsatisfying, had turned to an idealism which allowed him to attain 'the Third Life of Man in Man's soul'.[29] Lytton

14. Bulwer Lytton, cartoon by Ape. (*Courtesy of Knebworth House*)

15. Bulwer Lytton smoking. (*National Portrait Gallery*)

16. Margaret, Countess of Blessington, by Thomas Lawrence. (*National Portrait Gallery*)

17. The Devonshire House performance of *Not So Bad as We Seem*. (*Courtesy of Knebworth Estates*)

18. The Institute of the Guild of Literature and Art at Stevenage, founded by Bulwer Lytton and Charles Dickens. (*Courtesy of Knebworth Estates*)

19. 'A Pair', Bulwer Lytton and Charles Dickens, cartoon 1839.

20. Bulwer Lytton, photograph. (*Courtesy of Knebworth Estates*)

21. Robert, Lord Lytton. (*Courtesy of Knebworth House*)

22. Bulwer Lytton, drawing. (*Courtesy of Knebworth Estates*)

asked that the novel be seen as a work of philosophy or theology as much as a contribution to literature.

The plot revolves around a rationalist doctor named Allen Fenwick, for whom science offers all the appropriate answers to the problems of existence. He is forced to abandon this position by meeting first Lilian Ashleigh, a childlike young woman whose 'psychic powers' allow her to channel energies unknown to science, and secondly an evil necromancer called Margrave who is searching for a compound called 'the Principle of Animal Life' or 'Life Amber' that will guarantee immortality. Caught up in a cosmic struggle between the forces of good and evil, Fenwick, in pilgrim-style again, is transformed. At the end of the book he has come to believe in the soul as something separate from corporeal existence. His affirmation that science can explain everything is revoked. Materialism is abandoned as arid and unconvincing. Fenwick, the quintessential Lytton hero, must go through stages of tormenting self-discovery, in order to achieve a full understanding of the mysterious. The story, according to Lytton, contained three images:

> Firstly, the image of the sensuous, soulless Nature, such as a Materialist had conceived it.
>
> Secondly, the image of Intellect, obstinately separating all its enquiries from the belief in the spiritual essence and destiny of man, and resorting to all kinds of visionary speculation before it settles at last into the simple faith which unites the philosopher and the infant.
>
> And, Thirdly, the image of the pure-thoughted visionary, seeking overmuch on this earth to separate soul from mind, till innocence itself is led astray by a phantom, and reason is lost in the space between earth and the stars.[30]

As Lytton conceived it, Fenwick's rite of passage is at once terrifying and sublime.

Just as much is demanded of a Lytton hero, so much was asked of any artist or writer. As people set apart by special powers and a heightened consciousness, they too had to journey in search of the immanent. Art was the exploration of the spirit or it was nothing. Lytton's voice is heard in remarks uttered by a character in *What Will He Do With It?*

> The author's temperament is that which makes him an integral, earnest, original unity, distinct from all before and all that may succeed him. And as a Father of the Church has said that the consciousness of individual being is the sign of immortality, not granted to the inferior creatures, so it is in this individual temperament one and indivisible, and in the intense conviction of it, more than in all the works it may throw off, that the author becomes immortal.[31]

To a large degree, there is a correlation between Lytton and his pilgrim heroes. His sense of spiritual mission was profound. Whether his fellow-writers or

a wider public taste would accept this self-valuation, however, was quite
another matter.

A preoccupation with things spiritual did not mean that Lytton was religious
by any conventional definition of the word. Nominally Anglican, he was
never an assiduous churchgoer and was in favour of 'the utmost liberty to
all sects'.[32] He would have been an enthusiast had he not been reined in
by scepticism about the claims of established religions. Above all, the nervousness about his public image led him to shy away from any position that
could be labelled cranky or eccentric. Such ambiguities resulted in considerable confusion. At times he was accused of being a Christian apologist,
at others of having no religion at all. Lytton thought this unfair: 'Surely
the manner in which I have treated Sabbath legislation and religion in that
part of *England and the English* addressed to Dr Chalmers must clear me
from the imputation of irreligious doctrines. The accusation startled me
not a little – for I have always been abused by the philosophers for being
a Christian' He specifically had to deny that he was a freemason.[33]

In fact, denominational controversies had no interest at all. He never
read Strauss's *Life of Jesus* or *Essays and Reviews* or any of the other books
that started intense, theological wrangling. In broad terms, he preferred
churches which emphasised faith over reason, the aesthetic over the commonsensical. Roman Catholicism has a certain attraction for this reason:

> I have the general enthusiasm of its earnest believers and the childlike faith of
> its simple flocks. I love its ascent into faith above reason. To unite, as we do,
> miracle with logic is a mistake. As I get older, and I hope wiser – I feel how little
> reason helps us ... God gave us imagination and faith as the two sole instincts
> of the Future. He who reasons where he should imagine and believe prefers a
> rush light to the stars.[34]

By contrast, Protestant churches 'are always bringing Heaven into our par-
lours – and trying to pare religion into common sense – and who can pack
the infinite into the finite – or the ocean into a silver teaspoon'.[35] Lytton's
religion was therefore part aesthetic and part spiritual. A religious system
merely had to give form to instincts about what lay beyond life. Christianity
would do in this respect. But there was also the feeling that other religions
could probably have fulfilled the same purpose. Certainly doctrinal arguments were a waste of time. As he lectured his son: 'The essential things to
hold to, you seem to hold to – God, soul, hereafter, prayer, reverence for,
and acceptance of the hopes and ethics of Christianity ... it is best not to
puzzle one's head further.'[36]

In fact, Lytton never joined a particular church. He rarely joined anything.

The supreme individualist, he crafted a religion to suit his own purposes, just as he fashioned other areas of his life. To this end, he chose two arguments and ignored all the rest. Therefore his religion was as distinctive as his clothes. First, he was hugely impressed by the fact that only mankind was endowed with an idea of God and a world beyond the senses. It was a point he reiterated again and again. This innate capacity to conceive of a God was itself a proof of God's existence:

> I have shown how the metaphysicians who have argued Man's immortality solely from mind ... must give immortality also to the brutes, for all true naturalists allow that brutes and insects have mind as well as man. Every definition of mind includes an ant and an earwig. From this I have built out a theory, not wholly new but I think never so plainly put before, viz: – that the evidence of man's soul is not in his mind, i.e. not in his ideas received thro' the senses, but in his inherent capacity to receive ideas of God, soul, etc., which capacity is not given to the brutes.' [37]

In other words, 'in the capacity of man to receive ideas of the soul lies the certain proof of his soul'.[38] Precise forms of religion mattered little because all the great systems of faith argued for a creator God, who implanted a knowledge of Himself in mankind. Being born into a Christian culture, Lytton was happy with the Christian God. But he admitted that he could just as easily have been a Brahmin.

The second element in Lytton's religion concerned prayer, which for him was to be equated with the release of all imaginative sensibilities. Just as the artist sought to contact the spirit world through the exercise of the imagination, so the believer came to God in the same way. As Lady Blessington observed: 'I perfectly agree with you that Imagination and feeling lift us higher than mere reason ever can, and these approach nearer to the Deity, to which both elevate our thoughts.' [39] Presumably, on this kind of argument, the artist, whose imaginative powers are greater than those of his fellow men, comes closest to God. Certainly, it is a view that required no priest as intermediary. By prayer the individual touches God directly. Indeed Lytton used this agency for the relief of lumbago.[40] It is also a view that equates the artistic and the religious experience. Lytton saw both as attempts to contact a world beyond reason and experience. Dissolving religious creeds into the vague workings of the individual imagination would not please orthodox churchmen, but there were virtually no clergymen among Lytton's friends or correspondents, and he was impatient with theological controversy. He was religious but only on his own terms, and these were mystical.

Lytton was nervous of his interest in the supernatural or the supranatural.

He hated to be mocked or to have his personality dissected in full public view. To add mysticism to his other eccentricities was to invite yet more adverse comment. His fascination with the subject was inexhaustible but he was always on the defensive. When attacked he was quite capable of denying any involvement in such matters, and, almost panic-stricken, would fling defiance in the faces of his critics. He carefully honed defences against unwelcome comments in this raw area and was keenly aware that it was a point of extreme vulnerability. Those who teased him should not know, for example, that at the age of twenty-five, he occasionally signed letters as 'Magus', or seer.

He was happiest when arguing that the supernatural was simply what science had not yet explored and codified. He was adamant that such enquiries should be undertaken: 'These marvels ... have been abandoned for the most part to persons who know little of philosophy or metaphysics, and remain insoluble. I wish to make philosophers inquire into them as I think Bacon, Newton or Darwin would have inquired.'[41] Other Lyttons agreed. Brother William thought that 'The progress which is now making in the science of electric agency will without doubt do much towards solving many dark problems'. Equally Robert Lytton was 'sorry to see between the Devil-worshippers and the altogether-disbelieving so little honest investigation'. For,

> As Electricity was, until, to a certain extent, captured and tamed by Science, and made to do work for man – an impalpable and useless element – a sort of mad demon, frisking in thunderstorms ... so perhaps the science of Spiritualism may in the end enable us to establish some satisfactory and wholesome communication, with that rarest material element which we call spirit, and engage it, also, to great human uses, holding it in control and obedience by a knowledge of its own laws.[42]

As these letters make clear, in Lytton's generation the line between what was science and what was quackery was unclear. If electricity and telegraphy had recently come within the notice of science, perhaps telepathy and mesmerism would be next. Lytton's experimentation in the supernatural must be firmly placed therefore in the context of George Eliot's dabbling in phrenology and the Earl of Carlisle's attempts to hypnotise his servants. One man's crankiness was another man's science.

The case was strengthened by the fact that Victorian science was, year by year, making clear what had hitherto been mystical. The establishment of hypnotism, or 'animal magnetism' as Lytton called it, was a case in point. As he observed in two articles written for the *Monthly Chronicle* in 1838, successful hypnosis depended on one individual influencing another over a certain distance. Some sort of power or energy had to be involved:

The facts thus established require the admission either of an agency in nature hitherto unnoticed, or, what is tantamount, the admission that new functions shall be ascribed to some known agent; that this agency is material, is propagated through space in straight lines; that various corporeal substances are pervious by it with different degrees of facility, and according to laws which still remain to be investigated; that it is reflected from the surfaces of bodies, according to definite laws, probably identical with or analogous to those which govern the reflection of other physical principles, such as light and heat; that it has a specific action on the nervous systems of animated beings, so as to produce in them perception and sensation, and to excite various mental emotions. Of these several propositions we cannot discover any grounds of doubt which would not shake all the foundations of physical science.[43]

If hypnosis could be so codified, there was real hope that, sooner or later, somnambulism, epilepsy and clairvoyance might yield up their secrets. All were related phenomena. If a hypnotist had special powers and released special powers, why not a medium? Lytton thought that the voices that spoke through the mouth of a medium were an 'electric or other fluid – which might telegraph from a great distance'.[44] At times, he thought of taking up 'some branch of science seriously'.[45]

Novels which dealt with the supernatural were defended with the same argument. In *The Haunted and the Haunters* a man spends a spine-chilling night in a ghost-ridden house. Tables move, doors open and close, footsteps appear from nowhere, and sudden sensations of cold envelop a room. All such phenomena, Lytton insisted, 'are but agencies conveyed, as by electric wires, to my own brain, from the brain of another ... transmitted by a kind of mesmerism'.[46] In *Zanoni* the hero's defiance of mortality makes sense if seen as a discovery yet to be made:

> Real philosophy seeks rather to solve than to deny. While we hear every day, the small pretenders to science talk of the absurdities of Alchemy and the dream of the Philosopher's Stone, a more erudite knowledge is aware that by Alchemists the greatest discoveries in science have been made, and much which still remains abstruse, had we the key to the mystic phraseology that they were compelled to adopt, might open the way to yet more noble acquisitions. The Philosopher's Stone itself has seemed no visionary chimera to some of the soundest chemists that even the present century has produced. Man cannot contradict the Laws of Nature. But are all the Laws of Nature yet discovered?[47]

In *The Coming Race* a superior civilisation has been established underground, based on the properties of a substance called vril.[48] Defined as akin to electricity, magnetic force and galvanism, it is more powerful than any of these. Its possessors can fly and tranquillise aggression. It keeps society in harmony. It was the summation of all the forces that Victorian science had brought to light.

Equating supernatural energies with forces like magnetism and electricity, or citing Faraday as an explorer of both, dissolved the boundary between mystical and scientific enquiry. A medium was simply someone of 'electric temperament'.[49] It was not eccentric to pursue such theories, because, as Lytton assured Dickens, 'the supernatural resolves itself into the natural when faced and sifted'.[50] Novels like *Zanoni* and *A Strange Story* were not to be dismissed as the product of foggy imagination. Rather, they should be received as serious contributions to an ongoing debate of great importance. As such, Lytton regarded these books as among the best and most significant he ever wrote. A hostile reception of these books was particularly hurtful.

To make the scientific claim more credible, these novels were full of footnotes citing works in English, French and German. All the works were once, or are still, in Knebworth library.[51] Some have annotations in Lytton's hand but others have uncut pages. The sequence begins with Jean Baptiste Van Helmont (1579–1644), whose *Tumulus Pestis* and *Oriastrike* argued that the principal agent in all occult practices was a gas that had so far escaped scientific categorisation. Other books on which Lytton relied heavily included *Facts on Mesmerism* by his Cambridge friend Chauncey Hare Townshend, Justus Liebig's *Organic Chemistry in its Applications to Agriculture and Physiology*, Alfred Maury's *La magie et l'astrologie dans l'antiquité et la moyen âge*, Sir William Hamilton's *Lectures on Metaphysics*, and Sir David Webster's *Letters on Natural Magic*. Lytton could claim, with some justice, that he had tried to inform himself in all the areas of scientific and historical enquiry that could have a bearing on the supernatural. Above all, he admired Alphonse-Louis Constant. His *Dogme et rituel de la haute magie* is quoted at length in *A Strange Story*, as is his *Histoire de la magie* and *La clef des grands mystères*. Constant, who changed his name to the more mystically suitable Elias Lévi, visited England in 1854 and 1861. On the second occasion he and Lytton jointly engaged in experiments in electricity on the roof of the Pantheon in London and at Knebworth.[52]

Lytton's reading was a mixture of fuzzy speculation and the most up-to-date science. With no clearly marked frontiers to delimit the end of science and the beginning of mumbo-jumbo, it accurately reflected contemporary knowledge. The only thing to do was to advocate enquiry on all fronts. Lytton congratulated Dr John Elliotson, who had founded the Phrenological Society in 1824, as follows:

> I think the manliness of your appeal one of the finest efforts on behalf of the
> only true mode of following science, viz. experiment of what is before the eyes,

with that proper mixture of faith and diffidence which teaches us both the illimitable resources of nature and the little knowledge we have yet acquired of her secrets.[53]

Therefore, to critics who were tempted to laugh at Lytton's metaphysical novels, he could reply that they were an attempt to work out in literature what contemporary scientists were actively engaged in exploring. For a man who hated to expose himself to public ridicule, it was a welcome form of defence and one which, given the state of Victorian knowledge, had plausibility.

Even so, Lytton had little courage. When teasing on this point seemed likely, he hastily retreated into professions of scepticism. For the dangers were real. Other reputations foundered on these rocks. For example, the Lytton family took a great interest in the case of Mrs Crowe, a minor novelist, who in 1854 was arrested for appearing naked in Mayfair. She informed the police that spirit voices had assured her that, if she held a card case in a particular way, she would become invisible.[54] London was of course amused, but such incidents were a warning of what could happen to those who were associated with the supernatural. Time and again, therefore, Lytton backtracked. Indian gurus and St Theresa were 'irrational visionaries'. He was 'inclined to disbelieve' astrology. As for sorcery and divination, he thought them 'dubious' practices.[55] He detested being pestered by cranks, who claimed to see in his novels arguments that were not there. Someone who thought that *Zanoni* was an illustration of the transmigration of souls was sharply corrected: 'I have only to say that I as little believe in the transmigration of souls as I do in the existence, prolonged for more than 4000 years, of Zanoni himself.'[56]

Distancing himself from enthusiastic occultists was supplemented by making jokes at their expense. He claimed to lament 'these spirit-rapping times when every day I expect to hear that Satan himself so long talked about has condescended to become visible', and asserted that only one man had ever understood the Kabbala, and that he was 'cracked – perhaps the cabbala cracked him'.[57] He also strongly advised others not to embark on these dark studies. Speaking of a proposed article on table-turnings, he observed:

I should give no theory as to where these seem to succeed for I have no theory and find all theories unsatisfactory. I should give but an accumulation of facts ... It would contain much learning. The facts themselves would shew that the most startling phenomena lead but to inconclusive and often dangerous results. And that except for strong philosophical minds, the pursuit of all knowledge 'beyond the visible diurnal sphere' seems to end in delirium and often much worse.[58]

Not surprisingly, he was usually unwilling to lend his name to public endorsements of particular psychic practices or to their exponents. Too many of them 'duped the human mind'.[59] Lytton was very anxious that he should not be numbered among those taken in.

Towards the end of his life, his scepticism on these issues may have become deeper and more genuine. His investigations had left him unsatisfied:

> I have been much pestered by letters from strangers on questions connected with special manifestations or mesmeric clairvoyance as if I were a believer in the superstitions, which subjects interesting to accurate scientific examiners are re-vered by one set of ignorant enthusiasticks [sic] and despised by another set of ignorant sceptics.

He went on to say that he had never met a clairvoyant whom it was not 'dangerous' to rely on, and that all his attempts to contact the spirit world had 'broken down when submitted to ... close cross examination'.[60] A final agnosticism on the extent to which there was a spirit world that could be made accessible by special gifts of the imagination is evident. But it should not obscure the fact that, for almost all his life, Lytton was a determined explorer of these regions. An interest in the supernatural informed the novels which he numbered among his best. He investigated phenomena at the risk of his reputation, calling on parallel, scientific experiments to justify his actions. He was very aware that, in this respect, he was walking a tightrope and that there was every risk of falling into complete nonsense.

If Lytton hoped to escape ridicule, he signally failed to do so. His interest in the occult became another target for the caricaturist. Taken with other aspects of his character and appearance, it contributed to a reputation for the eccentric and exotic that pushed him to the margins of English society. For Lytton was not someone who merely speculated about the spirit world. He was an active participant in experiments and séances designed to seek it out. Inevitably, he was sometimes taken in by fraud. Any medium or practitioner of these arts passing through London was sure of his attention. When embarrassment followed, his critics pounced.

His interest in such things had first been excited at Cambridge, where Chauncey Hare Townshend introduced him to mesmerism and somnam-bulism.[61] His friend encouraged Lytton to write a novel on the theme of mesmerism, claiming that he saw in Lytton 'a *German* depth ... peculiarly calculated to invest the mysteries of Mesmerism with solemnity and gran-deur'.[62] As early as 1826 he admitted to Rosina that he was 'addicted to astrology', and *Eugene Aram* of 1832 shows considerable interest in Lavater's theories about character being expressed in physiology.[63] These studies predictably represented a mixture of what could loosely be called science and what can only be described as mummery. But, in Lytton's view, each offered the possibility of approaching the world beyond sense, and each therefore was worthy of investigation. They could be dismissed only when they failed to produce results.

It was, however, his mother's death in 1843 that really quickened his interest. The next decade or so saw his most intense experimentation. Unlike his brothers, whose conduct Lytton condemned as callous, Lytton had kept a bedside vigil during his mother's last days. In his view, he had been the only one genuinely to mourn. His loss has been irreparable. It was 'as if my heart had turned grey'.[64] Even in a man who had a real capacity for self-dramatisation, the agony was real:

> I will not say or attempt to say what I have suffered – the ties now rent for ever were far more than those (holy as they always are) which ordinarily exist between son and mother. Whatever my sorrow – immeasurably greater than any I have yet known – I would not have it a jot less. Not for all the delights sense can dream of would I lose the remembrance of my agony when that poor hand pressed mine for the last time and the voice choked with a death that was wrestled against to the last faltered out the last 'God Bless You'.[65]

His plunging into spiritualism was an attempt to recapture maternal affection. The room in which she died was untouched as a shrine. Her name was to be remembered by changing his own surname to Lytton. And, above all, he hoped and longed for the opportunity to contact the dead.

After 1843 he began to try out on sympathetic friends the idea that communication might be possible. He speculated to Harriet Martineau that those who had enjoyed a special 'congeniality' would certainly meet again. She replied that 'those who love *each other* well enough' could certainly hope for this.[66] Christians taught that great love conquers death. Why, therefore, should not communication between this world and the next be possible, if only the right agency could be found. In particular, such contact was likely in the years immediately following a death. He had the idea that a soul journeyed from earth to heaven by stages, moving ever further away from terrestrial loves. But, early in this pilgrimage, it was still accessible to those left behind:

> He did not believe we should reach the highest Heaven when we died. 'No,' he continued, 'it is not likely that we, imperfect as we are, should suddenly be ushered into the Divine Presence on leaving this world; our minds would not be prepared for so much glory; we are too simple for that. We shall pass through successive stages of existence, rising higher and higher until we reach the fullness of knowledge and of happiness. We cannot expect instant transition from great darkness to great light, which to us would be insufferably bright. Does not everything progress? Is not progression the order of all God's works here? Why not hereafter?'[67]

Recovering his mother's love might be possible if the appropriate intermediary could be met with.

Experimentation of all kinds became part of his daily routine, providing
ammunition for anyone who wished to tease or ridicule. Least controversial
was Lytton's involvement with unorthodox medical theories. Here hypo-
chondria and a certain credulity came together. He disliked and distrusted
the medical profession, which he thought limited in outlook. Instead, he
visited healers in 'the small thoroughfares off Regent Street', and he found
their unorthodox methods exciting: 'A visit to a quack is a very pleasurable
excitement. There is something piquant in the disdain of prudence with
which we deliver ourselves up to that illegitimate sportsman of human lives
who kills us without a qualification.' [68] When a mesmerist named Mrs Mon-
tagu Wynyard effected cures on both Lytton and Harriet Martineau, the
two friends congratulated themselves on 'how we must be hated by the
medical profession – getting well without and in spite of them'.[69] He freely
recommended water cures 'for female complaints' and homeopathy as practised by a medium named Julie.[70] Further, throughout his life, he believed
in the medical properties of mesmerism, or hypnosis, and galvanism, or
treatment by electric shocks, urging them on his own family and friends:

> I should not be surprised if you found relief in Mesmerism – and sometimes
> electrics or galvanism is singularly and rapidly effective in removing congestions ...
> If you knew of an amateur Mesmerist of power it would be worth trying. The
> Mesmeric Hospital recommend Mesmerists who cure – I think for 3s. 6d. a time.
> The good of Mesmerism and Electricity or Galvanism is that if efficacious they
> do not interfere with medical treatment.[71]

The caution expressed in this last sentence is typical of a man who disliked
being thought odd, but his belief in such remedies outlived poor results.
Apparently, no mesmerist succeeded in putting him in a trance.[72]

His adventures, however, went far beyond the medical. He dabbled in
all kinds of experiments, again with little consciousness of what was scientific
and what was not. He admitted to close friends that, 'I have been pursuing
Science into strange mysteries since we parted, and gone far into a spiritual
world which suffices to destroy all existing metaphysics and to startle the
strongest person. Of this when we meet, O poor Materialist.'[73] He was
fascinated by the empathy that existed between snails. The creatures were
put into two parallel lines of bottles, each bottle being given a letter of the
alphabet. He found that by shaking the bottle in one row, labelled 'P' or
'S' or 'B', the snail in the equivalent bottle in the other row would begin
to shake in sympathy. This

> led Sir Edward to think that possibly two sympathetic compasses might be

constructed, the alphabet arranged around them, with the addition of two magnetic needles in such perfect sympathy that whatever letter one of the needles
pointed to would be instantly indicated by the corresponding needle ... the
compasses were made, but some mistake befell about the required conjunction
of the stars, and the experiment failed.[74]

Such primitive forays into telegraphy, however, went hand in hand with a
belief that the Yellow Room at Knebworth was haunted by a fair-haired
boy, whose appearance before guests foretold violent death. Castlereagh was
allegedly so visited shortly before his suicide.[75] Snails and ghosts were equally
objects of enquiry.

Just as scientific or just as nonsensical was Lytton's fascination with
phrenology, the reading of character by mapping the contours of the head.
He asked for readings of his own cranium twice, from the School of
Phrenology in King William Street, off the Strand. The first report pleased
him greatly. He wrote the word 'true' against suggestions that he was
demanding of friends and that he overestimated people, though the idea
that he had a love of moral and physical order brought the comment, 'I
doubt this'. A second reading was less satisfactory. It bizarrely credited him
with a great affection for children.[76] Even so, Lytton remained sufficiently
intrigued by the possibilities of phrenology that he warmly recommend it
to others, and had his junior colleagues in government tested in this way.
The men concerned showed real or affected gratitude.[77] To use phrenology
as a method of choosing men for high office may be thought eccentric, but
it was a practice which stood exactly on the border between science and
nonsense. Lytton was not alone in giving it credence. George Eliot and
many other level-headed people did the same.

Less respectable was simple fortune-telling. Lytton was prepared to admit
that readings quite often left the enquirer 'as much in the dark' as ever.
But there were, sometimes, 'astonishing guesses at secrets only known to
oneself'.[78] It was a service which he offered to visitors at Knebworth, calling
himself 'Le Vieux Sorcier'. His authority came from the study of the art,
'from the Chaldees to the gypsies of the present day'. Having mingled with
the latter in his youth, he claimed to have absorbed some of their secrets.
A young Welsh girl, for whom Lytton cast a horoscope that proved to be
remarkably accurate, was not alone in being impressed with his powers.
Disraeli, too, was an amused client. They were both told by their host that
they were standing in a long line of enquirers:

From the Chaldee and the Mage, from the Pythian of Greece, and the saga of
Northern Terror down to Yankee spirit rappers – hysterical clairvoyants – down
to the world weary man who makes blurred spots on a scrap of paper and startles

fair young ladies with interpretations of the characters in which a hand not visible
guides his own ... still is it not all the same – all the same mystic yearning to
pass back thro' the gates guarded by the flaming sword – see what the first father
saw – hear what the first father heard – when the stars were so new to earth that
they seemed made but as lights for man?[79]

Startling young ladies was at least an amusing pastime, and might suggest
real prophetic powers.

Most questionable of all were his attempts to contact the spirit world
directly through séances and table-rappings in all their variations. Among
the spiritualists of Belgravia and Bayswater he was hailed as 'the High Priest
and Great Wizard of our Circle'. He frequently hosted séances.[80] Even so,
he was prey for any fraudster passing through London. In 1843 he was a
patron of a Belgian boy named Alexis, who was said to have 'magnetic'
powers. Ten years later, he was intrigued by an eight-year-old girl who wrote
poetry under the inspiration of Byron's ghost: 'no child could write it but
[only] a most practised poet ... yet the sense is almost nonsense ... the
verses are like what a great poet who has lost his wits but kept the mechanism
of his craft might write in Bedlam'.[81] He and other members of his family
found it difficult to sift out the genuine from the fraudulent but they were
agreed that there was enough evidence to justify further enquiry.[82]

Inevitably he often found himself in bizarre situations. In 1853 he regularly
attended séances conducted by an American medium named Mrs Haydn
or Hayden. A disrespectful comment on her powers led him to be pinned
against the wall by a large table that flew across the room for that purpose.
He then asked to speak with the spirits of his dead mother and daughter,
both of whom dutifully appeared. Instead of enquiring about their general
welfare, he asked them to put him in touch 'with the highest and most
intellectual intelligence with which they were acquainted in the spirit world'.
Obligingly, they returned with Shakespeare and an even greater intelligence
called Raduna. Unfortunately, no record was kept about what Shakespeare
said, beyond the fact that he and Raduna had a sad tendency to contradict
one another.[83] Two years later, he was much associated with the famous
spiritualist D. D. Home, offering Knebworth as a venue for his séances.
Home, indeed, went on to claim that *A Strange Story* was written under
his influence. Lytton hailed him as 'a Magician'.[84] For the whole of his life,
the séance and the medium remained objects of fascination.

In reporting his experiences, Lytton prudently hedged his remarks around
with words of caution and even doubt. Indeed Mrs Home accused him of
not speaking out strongly enough in defence of spiritualists like her husband.
She wanted more public endorsement. According to her, Lytton was 'in
public an investigator of spiritualism, in private a believer'.[85] But this was

not a distinction that Lytton's critics would allow. For them, he was fatally compromised by these activities. He was too closely associated with quack mediums and too credulous about psychic phenomena. Flying furniture and conversations with Shakespeare were hard to accept. A man who could take such things seriously was saddled with an overripe imagination that also sadly penetrated his books. Lytton was right to fear that his interest in the occult might open his raw sensibilities to yet more ridicule.

Throughout his life Lytton could never free himself of a fascination with the spirit world. It coloured his view of the role of the artist. It occupied his leisure hours. When challenged or embarrassed, he would claim that it merely 'heightens the spirits and produces a gay humour'.[86] A more honest conclusion was offered to his friend, Macready:

> My researches have lately occupied a very interesting ground: viz inquiring into the vestiges of Ancient Magic and the old world belief in spirits, etc. I have convinced myself that there are in some organisations powers not to be accounted for by the senses, and that in short there are more things in heaven and earth, Horatio, etc. perhaps you will think from this that I am letting my fancy run very wild. But I have guarded myself against all tendencies to take any marvellous effect without strong evidence ... It is but peeps thro' the Blanket of Dark.[87]

However much his remarks were hedged about with scientific analogy and attempts at humour, there was an ingrained belief that what his contemporaries dismissed as superstition would one day be proved true. Daily life and individual character were influenced, perhaps predetermined, by a world of spirits.

His reputation was coloured by these views. He was widely thought to have dabbled in Black Magic. Madame Blavatsky the Theosophist claimed him for the Rosicrucians. Even more remarkable was Annie Besant's belief that he could make himself invisible. He was seen as the head 'of a secret school of the practical teaching of magick [sic]'.[88] Rumours of this kind were reinforced by Lytton's habit of signing letters as 'Merlin'.[89] Such affectation was a delight to his wife and a sorrow to his friends. Rosina 'recommended to Bombastes ... that he should try to believe in God, instead of in spirit rappers!', while Dickens though it 'inexplicable ... that a man of his calibre can be run away with' by quacks and fraudsters.[90] The society diarist Henry Greville marvelled that Lytton should join 'foolish women' in giving credence to such 'palpable humbug'.[91] Stories proliferated in the literary and social world of Lytton's activities, all of which were unrelieved by any sense of irony or self-parody. George Eliot, who had found A Strange Story 'unwholesome', much enjoyed one such tale:

He is quite caught by the spirit of the marvellous, and a little while ago, at Dickens's house, was telling of a French woman who could raise the dead, but only *at great expense*. 'What,' said Dickens, 'is the cause of this expense in raising the dead?' 'The Perfumes!', said Bulwer, with deep seriousness, stretching out his hand with his usual air of lofty emphasis.[92]

In 1863 his well-known interest in spiritualism landed Lytton in court. A certain Lieutenant Morrison exhibited a child of fourteen who had the power, by gazing into a crystal allegedly bought at a sale of Lady Blessington's belongings, of conjuring up such luminaries as Eve, Titania, St Luke and Judas Iscariot. A certain Admiral Belcher wrote to a major London newspaper to say that Morrison was a fraud who ought to be prosecuted as a vagabond. Lytton had the humiliation of being called as an expert witness in spiritualism, in a trial punctuated by uncontrollable laughter. One of his maidservants, who had never been to Knebworth, gave a description of the house by looking into the crystal. Asked to comment, Lytton tried to extricate himself from association with such doubtful practices by saying that the girl might have seen a print of his home. The jury found for Morrison, but only awarded damages of a pound and no costs. Lytton's stay in the witness-box had been mercifully brief, but London had enjoyed the spectacle. It was made funnier by the fact that 'he evidently disapproved of the levity exhibited in court'.[93]

Treatment such as this inflicted terrible scars. Lytton became nervous about publishing on the occult and about using it as a literary theme. He needed reassurance from Dickens before allowing *A Strange Story* to go to press at all. In the event, his fears were more than justified. The public could not understand it, and the critics were too stupid to give a lead:

> It is just one of those things in which I did want some aid from critics, to explain and vindicate it to the Public. But the critics seem to attack it ruthlessly ... The Public don't know exactly what to make of it, whether to admire or condemn. A powerful review by a great critic, such as a German might write, would at once decide the public in its favour – none such is likely to appear.

Instead, the book's reception proved 'the dislike of our practical public to mysticism and allegory'.[94] With no qualified critics to tutor them, 'that most august of all Apes – the English Public' turned away.[95] Too pragmatic to follow him into the spirit world, the English also denied his claim for special status for the artist as the interpreter of that world. They waved such arguments aside, reinforcing Lytton's feelings of exclusion. In his view, the English laughed at him too much.

8

Europe

In 1833 Lytton wrote a book entitled *England and the English*. It consists of a series of essays, which reflect, very critically, on English attitudes and institutions. The author was just thirty years of age but already he was an outsider. At a tangent to the English way of life around him, he was able to stand back and look at his fellow countrymen quizzically. Numbering himself among 'the Citizens of the World',[1] he compared them to the French and the Germans, and often found them wanting. He chose to live abroad more and more. This partly reflected a cosseting of his health, but it was also simply more congenial. Foreigners were rather more willing to honour the artist, as Lytton demanded, and to think as Lytton thought. They saw no reason to laugh at him. It may be significant that one of the dedicatees of the book was Talleyrand, then French Ambassador in London, whose views on the English could be undiplomatically caustic. All over France, Germany and Italy there were long-established communities of English who for one reason or another found their homeland uninhabitable; the debtor, those of shady reputation and the artist looking for recognition. Lytton joined them.

To fit himself for this role he armed himself linguistically. Although he claimed that he was 'a poor proficient in modern languages',[2] what he meant by this was that his ability to speak foreign languages was in no sense comparable to the ease with which he read them. For example, by his own admission, he spoke German 'very ill', but read it with such fluency that he had no hesitation in taking on translations of Goethe and Schiller.[3] Rosina's spiteful assertion that he sent his daughter to Germany only for the purpose of supplying his own linguistic deficiencies is unfair. He was happy to have his translations checked by academics, but these generally applauded his efforts. He was even more confident in Italian, and novels like *Rienzi* drew on Italian sources.[4] His French was weaker. He read the language but, in conversation, while understanding what was said, preferred to answer in English.[5] French friends tried to encourage him by saying that his writing was 'si française, si française de toute façon et dans le sens le plus aimable du mot',[6] but his nervousness never entirely disappeared. In all three languages, his knowledge was literary rather than conversational.

This fitted neatly with other preferences. His long sojourns abroad did
not mean that he garnered large numbers of new friends. He had no more
friends abroad than he did in England. In particular, 'it is my misfortune
not to be much acquainted with the actual Literary World of Paris'.[7] He
rarely met the giants of European literature. His liking for the Continent
was not based on a network of friends. Rather it focused on an appreciation
of the ideas which preoccupied the writers of Italy and Germany. Lytton
believed that they were similar to his own. To talk of the ideal or the
spiritual did not lead to incomprehension as it did in England. His preferences were therefore artistic, rather than social or political. He liked
countries where the artist was given his due. He despaired of the English
ever doing this.

Just as French was his weakest language, so France was the country about
which he had most reservations. In this he was once again singular. The
francophilia which influenced so many of England's social elite passed him
by. The problem was partly literary. The French were too firmly the heirs
of the Enlightenment's rationality for his taste. But a greater objection lay
in politics. The boy who had written a poem glorifying the victory at
Waterloo never overcame his suspicion of French objectives. With a population three times that of England, France would always be a threat. Lytton
remembered the first Napoleon, and was an acquaintance of that Emperor's
nephew. Therefore, although he lived in France a great deal, knowing the
spas of the Vosges, Auvergne and Pyrenees intimately, these sojourns never
translated into a trust of French politicians. Sometimes, as a young man,
he wrote in different terms, but then he was merely being diplomatic in
corresponding with people he barely knew, referring to

> your enlightened and enlarged view of the true policy to be maintained between
> France and England. Unfortunately those two countries have been too often
> hitherto misled by the propagators of an error as ridiculous as it has been popular,
> viz – that there has been something in their relative situations to render them
> 'natural enemies'. The map of the whole world cannot indicate two powers of
> whom this assertion can be less truly made. We have nothing to gain from each
> other in war – we have everything to gain in peace. That the Grand Truth may
> at last be permanently acknowledged is the sincere prayer and will always be the
> warm endeavour of one who has studied the national character – and brought
> from that study hearty admiration, of that great change which Revolution has
> wrought within it.[8]

Such remarks were polite, but almost entirely misleading.

In fact, a fear of French expansionism was a theme that ran through his
whole life. From 1823, when he praised Spanish resistance to French invasion,

to 1870, when he distrusted a possible French victory in the Franco-Prussian War, his concern never changed. In the first year, he wrote:

> Tho' our homes in the dust be laid low,
> Tho' our Children be crush'd in the fall,
> Tho' all Spain be a camp for the foe,
> Yet we never will crouch to the Gaul.[9]

In 1870 he warned his son: 'Reflect. France could at this moment and for six months to come destroy us – outnumber our Channel fleet – throw a force into Ireland ... and could threw [sic] also 50,000 men into England ... All I say is Arm, Arm, Arm.'[10] The French believed that there was no world outside France. This self-obsession turned them into armed missionaries, forcing others to share the culture and politics of their great Revolution. According to Lytton, a central aspect of 'Frenchmen' was 'that rude fault which prevents [the French] from understanding any national character but their own'.[11] He was hugely amused when a French writer described a cottage in the middle of Piccadilly, whose extensive rose garden also contained a palm tree.[12]

Until 1870 France was universally regarded as a world superpower. Its military potential was enormous. The memory of the Napoleonic Wars never left Lytton's generation; or, as he succinctly put it, 'France is strong. Europe weak'.[13] Wellington's victory at Waterloo had been a great achievement, but it was only a pause in a much longer campaign. Sooner or later, there would have to be a final reckoning: 'the time will come when the preservation of Europe will force the great Powers to destroy France as a nation, to parcel it out ruthlessly and to Polandise it. France must ultimately engulf Europe, or Europe will France; of this I am certain.'[14] The establishment of the Second Empire under Napoleon III in 1851 seemed to bring that final battle closer. Lytton had met him at Gore House in 1839, and remembered frank conversations:

> I knew Louis Napoleon well once; I recall his conversation with the more alarm, seeing how tenacious he has been of the idea as to Government But his strongest idea was that of 'effacing the stain of Waterloo'. Give us fair play and I should apprehend no power [but] shall we have fair play? ... I own I breathe very much as if there were an avalanche in the air.[15]

He knew the man to be unpredictable. Someone who had 'invaded' France by landing at Boulogne from a steamboat was capable of anything. He suffered from what Lytton called 'the splendid fantasies of a child of fortune and genius'.[16]

In this situation England's duty towards Europe dictated policy. Only

English watchfulness could save the Continent from French domination. As he informed the Commons in 1857, 'England is in every way most fitted to check the preponderance of France; because whilst she has the permanent interest, she has also, more than most nations, the permanent power to do so. And that not only by her fleets, but also by the superiority of her fiscal resources.' [17] The logic of the situation had not changed since Waterloo. The alliance with Prussia, which had secured that victory, must be maintained. To talk of keeping France under control by allying with it was self-delusion: 'England with popular assent may join with France against Prussia. But how will England look if France only uses England to grab the Rhine frontier. Alliance with Napoleon where wars are possible is very much like the hunt of the lesser beasts with the lion. They help in the hunt and the lion takes to himself the prey.' [18] Episodes like the Crimean War, in which England and France found themselves as allies, seemed to Lytton nothing more than an aberration.

In his view, there had been no hope for France ever since the great Revolution of 1789. It was a subject on which he was something of an expert. In writing about it in essays or in novels like *Zanoni*, he drew extensively on his grandfather's papers and on the accounts of eye-witnesses he had heard on his visits to Paris in the 1820s.[19] His judgement on the Revolution was final and clear. It had been a 'misfortune' from which the French 'have never recovered and never I fear can. The Revolution destroyed all the great foundations of calm and durable Government – all that stands between a popular passion and a Master ... it rendered a Republic and a Constitutional Monarchy alike impossible ... This is always the case where Philosophy unites with the working class.' [20] In an essay entitled 'The Reign of Terror' of 1842, he agreed with Edmund Burke that the whole business had been 'the work of amateurs carried away by a fit of drunken inspiration', and with his contemporary Alexis de Tocqueville that it had left France with 'scarcely one guarantee, either for permanent government or liberal institutions'.[21] Worst of all, the Revolution's descent into 'a butcherdom of devils' was unpardonable.[22] It destroyed all hope of political consensus among the French, replacing it with ingrained hatreds. These in turn undermined all attempts at political stability.

Two consequences of the Revolution were, in Lytton's view, of particular significance. The first was the destruction of the French aristocracy 'by that fiction of law called égalité'.[23] Never were Lytton's aristocratic prejudices so clearly affronted. In his view, aristocratic values, such as disinterested public service and rational decision making, were essential if any state was to escape the twin dangers of tyranny and mob rule. Otherwise politics became the preserve of adventurers and the self-seeking. Men of birth and education like himself should not be replaced by those who only lived on their wits. In his novel *The Parisians*, which is set at the time of the Commune and the Franco-Prussian War, the only characters to show self-sacrifice and a true patriotism are drawn from the ranks of the old aristocracy. Lytton's own pronounced sense of hereditary right and duty created a natural bond of sympathy between himself and those who had been dispossessed in France.

The second baleful result of the Revolution was the importance that it had given to Paris. The capital dictated politics to the rest of the country unmercifully. It was Paris which had destroyed the Bourbon monarchy in 1830 and that of Louis Philippe in 1848. It had created Louis Napoleon and it had given Europe the Commune in 1870. The city's turbulence gave the rest of France no peace. As a character in *Alice* put it, 'Paris is the tyrant of France'. It was a matter of surprise that 'the French should still persist in perpetuating this political vice; that all their policy should still be the policy of Centralism – a principle which secures the momentary strength, but ever ends in the destruction, of States'.[24] It was an unenviable legacy. Mercifully, London had never achieved the same predominance.

Put these two trends together and there was, in Lytton's view, an end to all possibility of stable government after 1830. He had no liking for the regime of Louis Philippe, nor any confidence that it would prove durable. Watching the opening of a session of the Chamber of Deputies was merely depressing. There was nothing to see but 'the King's shrugs and grins, and the *vives émotions*, which replied to his well-tuned periods'. The monarch was 'not fit in honesty ... to be an elector in England'.[25] The French seemed to think that the exercise of liberty meant nothing more than 'bring rude and wearing a beard'.[26] The theatricality embedded in their character made politics a matter of 'either laughing or crying'.[27] The Revolution had made it impossible for them to live by commonsensical pragmatism. Worse, the habit of overthrowing governments by force, of which 1830 was the most recent example, gave no government a claim to legitimacy. On his frequent visits to Paris in the 1830s and 1840s Lytton's views on the matter solidified.

Quite simply, the real victory of 1830 was that of the demands of trade over the values of aristocracy. No one of Lytton's temperament could sympathise with such a change. In his opinion, it merely reduced politics to vulgarity and corruption:

> The people triumphed – what do they possess?
> A venal Chamber and a shackled Press!
> On the scar'd ear of earth for this alone
> Crash'd the great ruins of the Bourbon throne.

> All France herself one standing army made,
> All freedom fettered, to the fears of trade! [28]

The aristocrat guarded liberty as a duty, while the tradesman regarded it as a commodity. Even more alarming was the proud boast of Louis Philippe that he was king by the will of the people. For Lytton this claim was madness. Once the people were hailed as the arbiters of politics instability was assured. He foresaw the Revolution of 1848, which brought in the Second Republic and universal male suffrage:

> What a *bouleversement*! I content myself with saying that all which I prophesied has come to pass. I enjoy the triumph over the incredulous donkeys to whom I have (within the last twelve months) said so often – 'Louis Philippe must crash, if he live; if not, the dynasty is gone.' [29]

Inevitably, it was the work of the 'disagreeable' part of the population, which lived in Paris. These he had long feared. Equally, since 'there are no republicans except thugs and fanatics', the prospects for France and Europe were irredeemably gloomy.[30]

In these circumstances, Lytton could only reluctantly welcome the *coup d'état* which established Louis Napoleon's authoritarian regime. True, most forms of liberty had been snuffed out. But at least order, religion and property rights were guaranteed. Louis Napoleon's flamboyance suited the French:

> Remember the secret of his nature and success is that he is theatrical. Grandeur, nobility, disinterestedness – France the Arbiter of Nations etc. etc. These are to him worth more in phraseology and attitude than any *material* gains. He deals with a theatrical race. Tho' I believe in every country, the man will seem taller who stands upon stilts.[31]

Since the Revolution had left the French unable to exercise a rational liberty or live by consensus, order imposed from above seemed to be the least awful option. Lytton gazed at France, 'as on a playground of children without Master or usher, and I haven't the slightest idea what game they will play next – saying to myself "Children will be Children"'.[32] His novel *The Parisians* was in part an apology for Bonapartism, but only because it was the least damaging of the options. There were 'a thousand phantom forms of LIBERTY – but only one living symbol of ORDER'.[33]

For Lytton, France represented the unfortunate combination of enormous military potential and political instability. The country was a threat to the rest of Europe, both from the revolutionary ideas it generated and from the power at its disposal to enforce them. The Revolution had 'destroyed all desirable elements of good government'.[34] With it had gone self-restraint and the most elementary maturity. Europe could only look to its own defences, and that fact placed particular responsibilities on England. Lytton lived French in many aspects of his life, and lived in France for long stretches of time, but neither point could overcome a basic fear and distrust.

There were far fewer reservations about Italy. It was a country that Lytton knew well and loved deeply. At ease with its own antiquity, Italy offered the visitor a kind of idyll, warm, relaxing and artful. Visits to Naples in 1833–34 and again in 1846 allowed him to tour the ruins of Pompeii in the company of experts like Sir William Gell. True, creature comforts were not always on hand. He battled with the mosquitos and the trickster. True too were the deficiencies of the local population. But these were minor irritations when set against the idea of Italy, past and present. As he confessed to Forster, 'the *dolce far niente* gains upon me as I breathe the relaxing airs of Parthenope and look on the vacant faces of this lazy population'.[35] Under the Italian sun, the English could shed inhibitions and reserve and wallow in unaffected beauty. There was much of Lytton in the character in *Godolphin* who noted that

> It is impossible ... to compare life in a southern climate with that which we lead in colder countries. There is an indolence, a *laissez aller*, a philosophical *insouciance*, produced by living under these warm suns ... it is like living amidst perpetual music – a different kind of life – a soft, lazy, voluptuous romance of feeling, that indisposes us to action – almost to motion. So far from a sojourn in Italy being friendly to the growth of ambition, it nips and almost destroys the germ.[36]

As this quotation suggests, lotus-eating had its dangers. Both his Italian novels, *The Last Days of Pompeii* and *Rienzi*, are to some extent about the consequences of decadence. Upper lips could be fatally unstiffened. But, by way of compensation, Italy offered a life in the imagination that was quite unobtainable in England.

For most of his life, the Italy that Lytton watched over was a peninsula containing a jumble of independent states, ranging from great kingdoms like Piedmont-Sardinia in the north and Sicily-Naples in the south, through the holdings of the Papacy, to small duchies and city states. The questions which preoccupied statesmen were whether a united Italy could be forged out of such diversity and by whom. In that it would involve the ejection of the Bourbon dynasty from Naples and the Austrians from a large part of northern Italy, violence was almost certainly to be part of the equation. Lytton himself was sympathetic to the project on certain strict terms. First, unification must not be a populist venture leading to the sort of democratic republicanism which had ruined France. Secondly, there must be no forcing of the issue. A feeling for an Italian identity had to precede action. In 1848 he wrote as follows in a preface to a new edition of *Rienzi*:

> But it is still a grave question whether Italy is ripe for self-government – and whether, were it possible that the Austrian dominion could be shaken off – the very passions so excited, the very bloodshed so poured forth, would not ultimately place the larger portion of Italy under auspices less favourable to the same growth of freedom, than those which silently brighten under the sway of the German Caesar.[37]

He wanted the national movement to be in safe hands, and to be led by social elites. Mass participation jeopardised both the venture itself and the kind of political settlement that might come later. After all, 'We all know what the people are without leaders, or with only such leaders as lawyers and professional men, literati etc.'[38]

He could only be hugely relieved when Charles Albert of Piedmont-Sardinia offered himself as the leader of the nationalist movement. In his hands it would be free of democratic appendages. The king became one of Lytton's greatest models of heroism. He was 'nobly and pre-eminently national'.[39] With prescience he had written in 1846 that, in Turin, 'the foundations of a great state are being surely and fairly laid. The King himself approaches to a great man, and tho' priest-ridden is certainly an admirable Governor and Monarch. I venture to predict that Sardinia will become the leading Nation in Italy.'[40] Charles Albert's failure to unite Italy in 1848 in no way diminished Lytton's respect. He made a point of attending his funeral in Turin a year later. The great thing was that the Italian nationalist movement was now in the hands of the Piedmontese dynasty, and that 'People don't care a button for chamber or franchise. Democracy is not popular in Piedmont.'[41] As a result, the national idea would come about in Italy through the actions of the peninsula's elites. The noisy populism that underpinned French nationalism could be avoided.

When the Italian state was finally put together, in 1859–60, under the watchful eye of Charles Albert's son, Victor Emmanuel, Lytton was therefore generally sympathetic, even though he detected imperfections. Garibaldi was 'the best fellow going', but it was a mistake to force the Sicilians to join the new state. Victor Emmanuel was a hero, but he was wrong to force himself on Venice and the Papacy, and very misguided to annex the kingdom of Naples. Lytton told the House of Commons publicly, and Gladstone privately, that the southern half of the peninsula had nothing in common with the north. To absorb it was to create problems analogous to those which Ireland endlessly presented to England. He predicted that the south would only be held by some kind of military occupation, and in this he was right. He wisely pointed out that the borders of the new Italy went far beyond any real feeling for the concept.[42] Overall, though, there was cause for relief. The Italian state had been achieved, in stark contrast to France, without the systematic subversion of the past or a lurching into a democratic future. It could remain a country of artists and patrons and aristocrats; men like himself in fact.

Without doubt, however, Lytton's greatest admiration was reserved for the German-speaking world and its leading state, Prussia. In *England and the English* the Prussian model is endlessly held up as the one England should follow. This was particularly true in the field of education and the arts, but the preference extended to other areas as well. Quite simply, a man who distrusted popular taste and the advance of democracy saw merit in a system where enlightened government oversaw everything. The educated bureaucrat was to be preferred to the populist politician:

> In a well-ordered constitution, a constitution in harmony with its subjects, each citizen confounds himself with the state; he is proud that he belongs to it; the genius of the whole people enters into his soul; he is not one man only, he is inspired by the mighty force of the community, he feels the dignity of the nation in himself – he beholds himself in the dignity of the nation. At present, my friends, you only perceive the Government when it knocks at your door for taxes ... but I wish that you should see the Government educating your children, and encouraging your science, and ameliorating the condition of your poor ... Reform should seem ... the legitimate offspring of one faithful and indissoluble union between the Power of the People and the Majesty of the State.[43]

To argue in this way was profoundly unEnglish. The English tradition trusted to change emerging from the clash of interests in healthy debate in a Parliament. For Lytton to pass so much of that activity over to the state and its officials was highly controversial and very distinctive.

All these prejudices were confirmed by the revolutions in Germany in 1848–49, of which he was an eye-witness. Their futility and failure were due to the fact that the people as a whole were 'unfit for constitutional liberty', being led by politicians with 'an utter absence of practical views'. As in France, inexperienced and non-consensual parliamentarianism was hopeless. As he concluded, 'one's experience of popular triumph abroad does not tend to radicalise one overmuch at home'.[44] Unlike the French, however, the Germans learned the lesson of 1848 well. They turned their backs on the new and looked for leadership to the old elites. He perceptively noted that: 'Here the sense of a great blow to the New Elements – that have sprung up against the repose of old systems – is unspeakably profound among men of all politics ... there is a new lease given to thrones and their tenants have time to look about and breathe.'[45] This reaffirmation of regal and aristocratic principles in the German world after 1848 could only be welcomed by someone of Lytton's temperament. In his view it made Prussia, and later Germany, the obvious ally for England in Europe:

> Every cultivator of literature and science much cherish a deep and grateful affection for the German people, and a warm hope in their ultimate coalition with ourselves ... Between ourselves and the German people, of which Prussia is one of the great representatives, there is so kindred a community of race, of commercial interests, of all that belongs to intellectual interchange.'[46]

As a practising politician himself, he therefore detested anything that threatened Anglo-German understanding. When the Schleswig-Holstein question blew up in 1864, for example, his main concern was to express his dislike of 'any thing that can embroil us with Germany our only real barrier against France, and for the sake of a "Scandinavian principality"!' He promised to do all in his power to maintain England's neutrality on the matter.[47] Even the Franco-Prussian War of 1870, which allowed Germany to replace France as the greatest power on the Continent, was only of interest in so far as it brought about a cooling of English sympathy for Berlin and its ambitions.[48] By contrast, the outcome of the war in no way changed Lytton's views. For him, Germany remained an essential counterweight to democratic, and increasingly socialistic, France. It was the great example of how the introduction of a parliamentary system could leave aristocratic leadership largely untouched. Populist politics was moderated through an educated bureaucracy.

In his novel *The Parisians*, which is set in the time of the Franco-Prussian War and the Commune, there is a moving description of a Te Deum being organised in Rheims Cathedral by the German victors. In the very building, where legitimate kings of France had been crowned until 1830, German soldiers concluded the service by singing 'Nun danket alle Gott'. Hearing this, an English visitor is made to observe, 'What a difference between the two nations, the Marseillaise and Luther's Hymn'.[49] The symbolism was obvious. Lytton saw two options in Europe. On the one hand, there was the French tradition of democracy, irreligion and socialism. On the other, Germany offered popular politics diluted heavily by aristocracy, together with a reverence for religion and property rights. Lytton never doubted far a moment where his preferences lay.

Even more compelling than the direction of German politics was the grandeur of German literature. Lytton was convinced that, in Goethe and Schiller, Germany had produced the two writers on whom all lesser men should model themselves. Goethe was 'a giant beside all other fictionists', a producer of 'perfectly pure art'. As for Schiller, he was 'the greatest Poet that ever existed' and 'the most enchanting writer next to Shakespeare'. He was really 'GREAT'. Not surprisingly, their works were undervalued and little read by a philistine English public, whose taste was more earthy:

> The crowd of readers would call it the most ridiculous nonsense! I mean of course English readers. Our countrymen only understand the broad splash – the thick brush – lots of outline – and a burly chap in the foreground.[50]

The same readers and critics, who so misinterpreted his own work, predictably found Lytton's German masters heavy-going. The English seemed to suffer from a kind of allergy to anything beyond the pragmatic that put Goethe and Schiller quite out of reach.

What intrigued Lytton about these two men was their 'intense perception of self – this earnest, haunting, consciousness – this feeling of genius as a burden, and of life as a religion'.[51] They, like him, believed that the artist must investigate the world of soul and spirit. Of course their works were carefully and expertly crafted, but only so that this higher mission could be undertaken. Both men also accepted that art should be didactic and the artist a teacher. The pursuit of the beautiful had to involve moral decisions. In the preface to *Night and Morning*, Lytton discussed the question of whether literature should entertain or instruct, and argued that the second function was quite as important as the first. It also followed that, if the artist had special gifts in interpreting the beautiful and the immanent, then he should have the status of sage. The Germans revered their poets and they were right to do so.

By contrast, in Lytton's view, French literature never raised its eyes to the hills and beyond. The influence of the French Revolution had been too great. It had given the people as a whole such claims and pretensions that they even demanded to be the subject of literature. There had been an 'abrupt intrusion of the People upon our thoughts and dreams even in our closets'.[52] As a result, French writers became bogged down in the mire of everyday life. They had neither time nor inclination to look for anything higher. Little wonder therefore that Victor Hugo, whom Lytton called 'the great Bombast furioso' should be so popular.[53] His world of thieves and revolutionaries suited the French mood. Once it had also been Lytton's too. As a young man, he had written of criminals and poverty. But by middle age he was demanding that 'there must be something practical kneaded up with the ideal', and, at the end of his life, the ideal alone was his priority. In making this progression, however, he was acutely aware that neither the French nor his own countrymen would follow him: 'Books which dispose the mind to abstract reverie or speculation, exercise a greater influence over the Germans than they do over us; a theory appears to them the more seductive in proportion as it is detached from the experiences of practical life.'[54] Englishmen and Frenchmen seemed to prefer 'the vulgar' to 'the heroic',[55] and both were ineducable on this point.

The influence of Goethe and Schiller on Lytton's own writings was enormous. He would inevitably be drawn to a tradition that gave the artist the status of priest or holy man. He translated Schiller and wrote essays on Wieland, Lessing, Herder and Klopstock among others. Critics have been quick to point out just how much he owed to German masters. For example, the influence of a single work, Goethe's *Wilhelm Meister*, has been discerned in *The Disowned, Godolphin, Alice* and *Kenelm Chillingly*.[56] All these works emphasise the importance of the *Wanderjahre* or *Lehrerjahre*, years taken out of a young man's life, in which he travels in search of experience and spiritual self-discovery, often under the guidance of an older man. Lytton had attempted this journey in his youth. As he tried to explain to an English audience in the preface of *Ernest Maltravers*:

> For the original idea, which, with humility, I will venture to call the philosophical design, of a moral education or apprenticeship, I have left it easy to be seen that I am indebted to Goethe's *Wilhelm Meister* ... But I do not mean by 'life as it is', the vulgar and the outward life alone, but life in its spiritual and mystic as well as its more visible and fleshly characteristics. The idea of not only describing, but developing character under the ripening influences of time and circumstance.[57]

Under German influences the writer, who had once concerned himself with everyday issues like crime and poverty, had been transformed into something altogether more visionary.

Friend and foe recognised the change. Hostile critics of Lytton's play *La Vallière* thought it filled with 'German horrors'.[58] On the other side, Louis Napoleon flattered him by comparing his work to Schiller's, and Mary Braddon likened his conversation to a 'wandering away into all manner of dreamlands ... whither scarcely any but Germans would have the strength of wing to follow you'.[59] In a similar vein, Caroline Norton teased him by asking, 'Do you not wish instead of an English baronet, you were Edward von Bulwer?'[60] For once, it was the sort of pleasantry that Lytton might have found amusing, for there was no hint of apology in his admiration for Germany. He made extended visits in 1833, 1840, 1847, 1848, 1849–50, 1859 and 1862. It was a country where he felt properly appreciated. He deeply regretted the fact that in England 'Science ... is not in its right level', and hoped 'that it should receive from the state that grateful recognition, and that marked honour which befits its rank in what Germans call the Spiritual Kingdom'.[61] Lytton increasingly wanted nothing more than to be accepted as a leading citizen of that same 'Kingdom'.

There was, too, a more prosaic reason for Lytton's admiration for Germans. They liked his books and they bought them in large numbers. Lytton's reputation in Germany was established early. *Pelham*, published in 1828, was in German translation within a year, and this pattern was repeated with all Lytton's works. By 1831 he was being hailed as the new Walter Scott. German publishers competed for the rights to bring out his books individually or in collected editions.[62] German critics reviewed his work with more warmth and understanding than their English counterparts. As one of them remarked, 'Wir wünschen es, denn Bulwers Romane sind um vieles besser, als das gewöhnliche Lesefutter'.[63]* Surrounded by chilly English criticism, it was warming for Lytton to be told by friends returning from Germany of his success there. The publisher John Murray, for example, reported that: 'I have recently returned from a journey of some extent in Germany, where I assure you without exaggeration I found your name in every body's mouth and your works in their English or German dress in every bookseller's shop.'[64] Another traveller reported that, in Munich, 'the Germans worship Bulwer – call his productions Shakespearean'. Equally, German visitors to England marvelled that Lytton should be more highly regarded in their country than in his own.[65]

Lytton himself pondered the same point. The difference between his reception in England and his welcome abroad was too glaring to ignore. While Germans thought him 'a demi-god',[66] Tennyson satirised and Thackeray teased. Even those like G. H. Lewes, who admitted that 'if you were speaking to a foreigner on the subject of English literature, Bulwer's would be the first name which both of you would pronounce', went on to argue that Lytton's frosty relations with his own countrymen were his own fault. His books were marred by

> a certain Walpole-foppery of wishing to be considered rather as a gentleman than as an author. It is a foppery which sits very ungracefully upon him. There are few authors of any station who have worked harder or reaped more substantial pudding and praise from their labours. Why, then, this otiose assumption of superiority – this impatience with Grub Street?[67]

Lytton's answer to this question would have been robust. He despised much English writing because it rarely aspired to a high calling. It refused to take on the mission of spiritual investigation. Grub Street and its earthy

---

* We wish it because Bulwer's novels are much better than the usual reading fodder.

preoccupations was indeed on a lower plane than himself. The Germans
understood this. The English did not.

Not surprisingly, Lytton frequently wondered whether life in England was
possible at all, particularly for any kind of artist. There were moments,
admittedly, when he could play the patriot. He thought the English were
pre-eminent in the writing of history, for example.[68] He could assure Lady
Blessington that 'while I have joked at the English, I love England. What
a country! What force! What energy! What civilisation.' The members of
the Hertford Literary Society must have been pleased to be told that England
'had a literature more splendid than that of Greece; an empire more colossal
than that of Rome; and a political constitution, which still towers aloft'.[69]
But, in giving such reassurances, Lytton was bluffing. From the publication
of *England and the English* on, he was much more often a systematic critic
of his own country. Its deficiencies were dissected and put on view in a
manner that seemed to give Lytton positive pleasure. Speaking of England,
he claimed that there was 'no place more deserving to be a desert. The
worst climate and the worst society, the dearest necessaries and the least
attainable luxuries are its chief characteristics.'[70]

There was first of all the problem of where to live in England. The
countryside was of course out of the question for a man of taste and culture.
It was too 'fatiguing'. But equally to live in a great city like Birmingham
was to reside in 'a vast sort of kitchen covered with red flock paper – a
pewter substance glaringly blackened – Italy or Yankee and vicious all over'.
He thought that there was a real danger of the whole of England being
'Brummagemed'.[71] Added to this, the British Isles laboured under a climate
that made any valetudinarian despair. When a German doctor advised him
to pass the winter in a mild climate, Lytton could only throw up his hands
in astonishment: 'I am ordered to find a mild climate in England for the
winter! Had it been the philosopher's stone I should not have minded. But
a mild climate in England!'[72] In old age Torquay provided some consolation
in this respect, but even here there was much to be desired: 'I am at the
moment deposited on a shelf under glass – thro' which the sun comes as
well as he can in *Perfide Albion*.'[73] For Lytton much of England was quite
literally uninhabitable.

The deficiencies of his native country went, however, beyond the climatic.
For the whole of his life Lytton was a determined critic of English views
on education. He loathed public schools and their determination to produce
sportsmen and construers of Greek and Latin. It was a syllabus without
philosophy, ethics or use. There was not even anything that could be called
religious in the larger sense of the word, merely an unthinking subscription

to a conventional Anglicanism. The 'sixth-form ornament of Harrow and Eton' had no knowledge of 'the principles of jurisprudence, the business of legislation, the magnificent mysteries of commerce', and absolutely no knowledge of figures. There was nothing artistic, spiritual or utilitarian. It was all so unlike German schools, which offered their pupils 'the full appreciation of the dignity and objects of men – of the duties of citizens – of the powers, and equality, and inheritance of the human soul'.[74] The cult of the amateur and the denial of anything intellectual was excruciating to behold.

With his keen interest in European affairs, Lytton was particularly depressed by the inability of the English to speak any language but their own, and to take a certain pride in this ignorance. Few members of the elite even spoke French 'with accuracy and elegance'.[75] Fewer still had that fluency which allowed them another homeland. Instead they were trapped in Englishness. In recommending French and German to his daughter Lytton observed that:

> It's good to be able to speak other languages because it makes one throughout life independent even of one's own land. How often have I sighed to quit this dull, envious, vulgar, heartless English people, with no nobler thoughts than eternal money-making – and their loud squabbling party politics. And though my affection for my mother would have been reason eno' to chain me to my country ... what would I not give now to have had, in my young years, the advantage you possess of acquiring that glorious facility of expressing thought in other languages than one's own sub-division of the varieties of Babel.[76]

He gravely told the readers of the *New Monthly Magazine* that, whenever anything ridiculous or impertinent happened in Europe, 'its perpetrator is an Englishman'. He then tried to amuse them with tales of ignorant English travellers being bamboozled by people calling themselves the Prince of Seidlitz Powders or the Duchess of Epsom Salts.[77] The cry of the hero of *Pelham* was undoubtedly Lytton's own: 'O! English people, English people! why can you not stay and perish of apoplexy and Yorkshire pudding at home?'[78]

To add to the misery, badly-educated products of public schools married women who had barely been educated at all. Lytton thought it a wasteful scandal that 'the mental powers of women, in all classes, from the highest to the lowest, are not brought under their fair share of cultivation'. Rather, the whole matter was regulated by chance.[79] As the new editor of the *New Monthly Magazine*, he announced that 'One among the designs in the ambition entertained by the present conductors of this Magazine, is to support that wise and enlarged social policy which would give to one sex the same mental cultivation as to the other. Of all cant in this most canting country, no species is at once more paltry and more dangerous than that which has been made the instrument of decrying female accomplishment.'[80] His preference was for women like Madame de Ventadour in *Ernest Maltravers*, who could preside gracefully over a salon and converse knowledgeably 'on a hundred topics'.[81] Lady Blessington came nearest to his ideal in England. Her house and its habitués proved just how important and congenial a woman's mind could be. The tragedy was, of course, that there were so few women like her in England. The powerful salon-holders of Paris and Berlin had only rare counterparts in London.

The matter of improving female education was the more urgent, in Lytton's view, because, until substantial progress had been made, English women were not just dull but rather a positive menace. They made up a large section of the reading public, and Lytton feared that they would not understand his novels. As he put it, 'They don't appreciate elaborate plots and artful management'.[82] Equally, their untrained minds were incapable of concentration or the taking in of complicated ideas. Before giving a lecture in Edinburgh, Lytton gave the following instructions to its organisers:

> Pray let me express a hope that the Music Hall will not be overcrowded with Ladies – they always throw a chill upon every audience. Accustomed to talk, it bores them to listen; and their unaccustomed and frigid silence stifles every attempt at a cheer which the labouring orator vainly endeavours to provoke. If these fair refrigerators are to be multitudinous, I hope they will be ranged together and not interspersed throughout, so as to leave the whole assembly despoiled of any spark of electricity by non-conductors of silk or muslin.[83]

In this unflattering description Lytton and Rosina for once agreed. His wife thought that English women were ignorant of their rights, and he thought them ignorant about everything else. Both looked for an urgent remedying of the situation.

As these examples indicate, Lytton had little compunction about lecturing the English on their own shortcomings. Society diarists regularly recorded his sallies. The English lived in such 'moral air' that 'mirth would be altogether out of character'; in England intellectual life consisted of making 'short speeches on the weather and long odds upon horses'; all his countrymen aimed at nothing higher than to be thought 'generous, a bold rider, and a bit of a fool'.[84] In plays, reviews and articles, the nagging never stopped. In England everyone suffered from a 'commercial aversion to the Poetical and Imaginative'.[85] Religion was a passionless social convention. Status was as long as a rent roll. Respectability 'has been another word for money'.[86] Morality itself had been reduced to a set of rules that 'might induce a tradesman to trust us'.[87] Taken together, by irony and straight-forward observation, Lytton compiled a damning indictment of his own country that did little to endear him in London society. To complain of being slighted and undervalued by a people he roundly lectured was unfair. He could hardly expect gratitude. Those who show up the deficiencies of the world around them should probably reconcile themselves to standing alone.

For Lytton himself the greatest problem about England was that, in a country where 'Money is the weightiest of all deities', there was no room for the artist. Writers and their kind had no status: 'In the great game of honours, none falls to their share.'[88] It was a theme that permeated so much of his thinking. What passed for intellectual life were the aphorisms of a few 'scattered witlings'.[89] In the *New Monthly Review* of 1830 he identified the three unforgivable 'sins' committed in English society. The first was to be poor, the second to be civil, and the third to claim originality. As he wrote:

> And sin the third is – to aspire
> From 'vulgar flight of low desire',
> Leave the dull paths by others trod,
> And dare with ... to be odd.
> For independence all condemn,
> To please *oneself* displeases *them*.
>
> But if you must talk – talk of cooks,
> But never say a word of books;
> Descant upon your poodle's tricks,
> But mum on those of politics;
> And prate with persons of a pigeon,
> But shun, oh shun, the rock – religion.
> In short, if any nobler lore,
> Your hearers could suspect you knew,
> Then, if a man, you're dubbed a bore
> But if a woman, damn'd a blue.[90]

Little wonder that he should spend more and more time abroad. By the 1850s he only returned to England 'with a reluctant spirit', describing England as a 'hard stepmother'. There was so little by way of recompense for putting up with 'the fogs and east winds of the White Isle'.[91] He had few friends there, and the English gave him no credit for pointing out their deficiencies. In *The Pilgrims of the Rhine*, Lytton recounted the tale of an English fairy who marries a German fairy and abandons his homeland forever. It could easily have been his own story. In England, as the fairy explains,

> The mortal poets are dumb, and Fancy, which was then priceless, sleeps hushed in her last repose. New and hard creeds have succeeded to the fairy lore ... The wheels of commerce, the din of trade, have silenced to mortal ear the music of thy subjects' harps ... For, despite our diviner nature, our existence is linked with man's. Their neglect is our disease, their forgetfulness our death.[92]

At odds with the mainstream in so many aspects of English life, Lytton finally came to separate himself from it almost completely. His countrymen had laughed at his appearance and personality, and had made light of artistic claims to which he attached the greatest importance. All this may help to explain why Lytton, the most status-conscious of men, yet had no wish to be buried in Westminster Abbey.

9

Radical

Lytton was a political figure for almost the whole of his life. But someone who saw himself so firmly on the margins of his own society was never going to find a political party that was entirely congenial. It is hardly surprising, therefore, that he should start life as a Radical, be flirtatious with the Whigs for a decade or two, and end it as a Tory. None of the mainstream options in British politics quite suited. Even so he was determined to make his mark, not least because his mother had indoctrinated him with the idea that someone carrying their name had to have a public career, and, since significant sums of money would be required to support such a move, to encourage political ambitions in her son was to give Mrs Bulwer yet more control of his life.[1] He believed that the artist had to be a man of action as well as a contemplative. Sometimes he thought literary recognition more important than politics. Sometimes, particularly as a young man, he might reverse these preferences. In 1826 he told Rosina that 'Literary honours are not therefore so desirable as Political rank but they must not for that reason be despised – they are the great stepping stones to our more material object – to get power I must be in the House of Commons ... I shall therefore directly the winter begins commence *regular Author* ... I expect before *the end of* the same spring to be in the House.'[2]

He was aware that such a purpose would involve much that was disagreeable. He would have to 'fag night and day at parliamentary history and political economy'.[3] But there was the consolation that, in the generation that lived through the excitement of the first Reform Bill of 1832 and its aftermath, politics was suddenly in vogue. Lytton told the readers of the *Edinburgh Review* that:

> Young men, formerly contented with the honours acquired from horses and hats, and the golden opinions of club window loungers, have caught the political fervour that pervades the working classes themselves. Parliament presents a cheaper opening and a more exciting field than heretofore. Politics is no longer a thing apart from the ordinary pursuits and occupations of society; it enters into the ideas, it pervades the conversation, it colours the opinion of whole classes of men, who, ten years ago, would have voted 'all politics a bore'.[4]

The long wars against the French Revolution and Napoleon had frozen domestic politics, but the thawing in the late 1820s opened up possibilities of every kind. It was a moment for the artist as well as the statistician and political economist.

As literary critics have pointed out, a recurring theme in Lytton's work is that of the young man with literary pretensions being lectured by an older mentor about the absolute necessity of going into public life. True virtue was only to be expressed in action. The man who merely reflected had no moral or useful impact. Algernon Mordaunt, Ernest Maltravers and Clarence Linden are among the heroes who are informed that 'knowledge beneficently employed is virtue', and that 'in morals ... we have no such thing as a distinct or divided interest from our race'. As a result, they were to embrace 'the virtue of Action – the obligation of Genius – and the philosophy that teaches us to confide in the destinies, and labour in the service, of mankind'. By contrast, other characters are condemned for self-obsession. Godolphin 'soured by disappointment' was 'inert, and his very wisdom taught him to be useless'. Similarly, Castruccio Cesarini had black Byronic curls and a passable sneer, but was 'of no *use* to anyone'.[5] In short, the special insights of the artist had to find expression in being of benefit to mankind. Rosina may therefore have been right in suspecting that Lytton's very limited success in politics 'supplies the bitterest drop in his cup of disappointment'.[6] Quite simply, his attempts to play the artist as legislator were less than heroic.

Lytton sat in the Commons as MP for St Ives in Huntingdonshire from 1831 to 1832 and for Lincoln from 1832 to 1841. In these years, he claimed to hold Radical opinions, and there is a plausible case for accepting his claim. In answer to a taunt in 1834 that his Radicalism was lightly held and recently acquired, he insisted that his views had not changed since his Cambridge days 'as all my Contemporaries might avow'.[7] In university debates, his record was impressively consistent. He argued against the Game Laws, the suspension of Habeas Corpus, the pressing of seamen, and the character of George III. All proposals to extend the scope and variety of education received his enthusiastic support.[8] During the travelling of his *Wanderjahr*, he had been much impressed by Robert Owen's utopian settlement at New Lanark:

> I listened with wonder to his projects for upsetting society and remodelling the world. To upset society and remodel the world might be very desirable. I did not wonder at the idea: I wondered at the sublime confidence with which Mr Owen anticipated its speedy realisation.[9]

A few years later, he admitted that Owen's views were 'visionary' and 'grounded on erroneous estimates of our nature', but, even then, he still wanted to contribute to 'an extensive but safe change in many of the great features of our social system'.[10] Attending Owenite meetings convinced him that there were unlimited resources of talent and moral purpose in working people that had to be released.[11]

Early associations and experiences therefore allowed Lytton to enter Parliament with clear, if rather raw, Radical sympathies. He was a believer in the inevitability of major change, and saw himself as belonging to a society in movement. As he told a friend, 'There are times in which we may labour, I think, with hope as well as zeal in the cause of human improvement, and I feel convinced that we shall live to see the triumph of the opinions for which both of us are fighting'.[12] During the Reform Bill agitation, he formally warned his mother not to stand out against change. Not surprisingly, John Stuart Mill saw Lytton as a promising recruit to the staff of the *Westminster Review*, the Bible of radical thinking, flattering his writing and perception. These compliments from serious men were not misplaced. Lytton worked hard to master the Radical creed, immersing himself in facts and figures, and absorbing the prophecies of Malthus. For a moment, he was identified as a rising star on the left of politics.[13]

In his earliest parliamentary speeches this reputation was confirmed. He spoke against sabbatarianism and religious tests for entry to Oxford and Cambridge, as well as the practice of flogging in the army as unacceptable 'amongst the freest people of the globe'.[14] He was radically sound on the issue of slavery, denouncing the attempts of white planters in the West Indies to undermine the emancipation laws of 1833. The final liberation of black apprentices in Jamaica and other colonies, in 1838, was celebrated by a party in the grounds of Knebworth during which the poor of neighbouring parishes were, without irony, treated to 'bread, meat and ale'.[15] Parliamentary debate also allowed him to follow up his educational interests. He took Southey to task for doubting whether an artisan was capable of poetry, while puffing Brougham for promoting new schools and a wider literacy:

> Let the people fairly into the road for discovering truth; we don't care who starts them upon it; as they travel on, they will acquire confidence in their own judgement and discretion. Their views will enlarge; the means will open to them of looking fairly on the different modes of government in church and state. They will not adopt violent (moderation is the distinctive mark of knowledge) but they will, we believe, adopt honest and correct opinions of both.[16]

His Radical credentials were not apparently dented too much by mixing admiration for Brougham with a little teasing. In a novel, he caricatured

Brougham's Society for the Diffusion of Knowledge as the Society for the Diffusion of General Stupefaction.[17]

Two other major issues led contemporaries to take Lytton's Radicalism seriously, the first of which was Irish affairs. On an extended visit to that country in 1834 he discovered that 'the misery of the people makes your heart ache'.[18] The bulk of the population seemed to have no steady occupation 'beyond an occasional shot at a parson – an employment, though animated, not lucrative'.[19] His summing up of the Irish situation was perceptive, even prophetic:

> Prosperity and intelligence all on one side. Ignorance, Pauperism, and the Irresistible People on the other. The course of things imperatively demands moderation, and yet moderation is but a licence for two parties to shoot – Capital! Sooner or later this must end in a Despotism or a Republic. Perhaps both. The Orangemen are the true link between the English Government and the Irish; and yet that *link* must be broken. The time is not yet come when a great statesman could save Ireland – I mean reform it. It can't support bad, and it won't appreciate good government.[20]

He repeatedly warned the House of Commons that the unfeeling behaviour of the landlord class, coupled with the denigration of majority Catholic opinion, would produce a catastrophe. Ireland, in fact, was 'Naples without its heaven'.[21]

The concern for Ireland was genuine, no doubt fortified by the fact that both Rosina and Lady Blessington were Irish. Some of his earliest poetry addresses these problems. In *O'Neill*, of 1827, he described the desperation of the Irish peasantry as follows:

> The want which links the wretched to his kind
> Shakes all control save Nature's from his mind
> Wild from the laws whose mercy only gave,
> Rest in the gaol and shelter in the grave.[22]

He was alive to both the deficiencies of the Irish themselves, and of their representatives at Westminster, whom he accused of bringing 'that moveable bog into our two houses'.[23] But he never wavered in his opposition to the coercive legislation against Ireland which was put through by Whig governments after 1833. In parliamentary speeches he argued again and again that, however intractable the problem, government-sponsored violence could never be a solution.[24] In his implacable hostility to the privileges of the Anglican Church in Ireland and in his sympathy for its Catholic peasantry, Lytton was as Radical as anyone could wish.

Even more significant than Ireland was Lytton's wholehearted involvement in the cause of Parliamentary Reform. At the age of seventeen, the venality and corruption of the electoral process had profoundly shocked him. He talked of borough electorates being 'bought and sold like cattle'. Members of Parliament, as a consequence, were either 'the tools' of governments which found them seats, or 'mercenary and base' characters who had simply purchased political power.[25] Between 1830 and 1832, when the heated debates on Reform were held, Lytton was totally engaged in the struggle for change. In the same years, as editor of the *New Monthly Magazine*, he used that journal to promote the appropriate arguments. Reform was an issue that aroused in him 'a fever of expectation'.[26] In his maiden speech in the Commons, he begged the governing elite to use Reform to re-establish its links with a broader constituency urgently, because its legitimacy 'was only in proportion as it lost or gained in public opinion'. The recent example of the French Revolution underlined what happened when those links snapped.[27] The new suffrage was excellent in its creation of 'a numerous constituency' of middle-class and aristocratic property owners that would offer educated and informed debate.[28] He expressed contempt for the House of Lords for showing 'a lamentable want of discretion' in trying to stop the measure. In direct contrast, he did nothing to save his own constituency of St Ives from abolition, since 'by sacrificing local to general interests, he believed, that the welfare of all would be most promoted'.[29]

What Lytton meant by 'the welfare of all' is clear. Once Parliament had been cleansed, once men of privilege had given way to talent and expertise, that body could take on an extended legislative role. All Lytton's German preferences led him to see the state as the proper promoter of change. In his view, amateur administration by squire, parson and parochial officials should be replaced by the order of the bureaucrat. The new Poor Law Act of 1834, for example, was splendid because it put an end to 'the jobbing of parish officers'. He himself, on a modest scale, undertook the kind of research into social issues which he wanted the state to sponsor much more widely.[30] In *England and the English* and in the *New Monthly Magazine*, he demanded immediate action in the fields of education, the regulation of female and child labour, and poor relief. Quite simply, 'the physical condition of the Working Class in Manufacturing Towns is more wretched than we can bear to consider'.[31] To call for an enhanced role for the state, through the agency of a reformed Parliament, in areas traditionally controlled by local hierarchies, was authentically Radical.

Very much complementing his contribution as a foot soldier in the army for reform was his high-profile reputation as a Newgate novelist. The Newgate school of the 1830s, which included Dickens and Ainsworth as well as Lytton, was one which chose to investigate social issues through literature.

The writers of these novels were convinced of their close relationship with politics. Artists were the harbingers of change. Their sensitive noses sniffed the wind and registered the first indication of changing moods in society. The legislator only had to respond to their perceptions. As Lytton himself put it in 1848: 'The heart of an author is the mirror of the age. The shadow of the sun is cast on the still surface of literature, long before the light penetrates to law. But it is ever from the sun that the shadow falls, and the moment we see the shadow, we may be certain of the light.'[32] Lytton had no doubt that novels which exposed social evils had a real impact on politics and the moulding of opinion.[33] In his view, this sequence gave proper status to the artist as someone with special gifts. He was delighted that *Paul Clifford* had 'its share in the wise and great relaxation of the Criminal Code' and that 'the Lawgiver is compelled to redress what the Poet has lifted into esteem'.[34]

To make such claims was controversial. According to contemporary ideas, writing about the criminal and the poor ran the danger of dignifying those ways of life, at least with interest if not with sympathy. The moral purpose of literature was thereby threatened. Worse still, any attempt to argue that crime was the result of poverty, not sin, again undermined moral standards and, at the same time, raised large questions about how society was organized. Critics could not understand why Lytton and the other Newgate novelists chose such themes when much more elevated ones were so readily available. Once again, Thackeray led the attack. Talking of *Eugene Aram*, he thought it 'very forced and absurd taste to elevate a murderer for money into a hero'. It was 'eloquent clap-trap'.[35] In his view, criminals were born as well as made. Sin, original or otherwise, came into the equation somewhere. For him, Lytton's description of the criminal as someone who quoted Plato and had the instincts of a gentleman was 'humbug'. In a wicked satire on the Newgate school, Thackeray wrote *Catherine*, the story of 'a poor, illiterate country wench, who has come from cutting her husband's throat; and yet, see! she talks and looks like a tragedy princess, who is suffering in the most virtuous blank verse'.[36]

Lytton was happy to meet this charge head on. He told Forster that,

> on the score of *Immorality*, i.e. that it is both dangerous and immoral to excite any sympathy for or interest in a Criminal ... to me this dogma seems to strike down at a blow the grandest privilege and the grandest masterpieces of Art.

Macbeth and Othello alone proved that crime was properly of interest to the writer.[37] He was further convinced by a certainty that, in adverse circumstances, he himself 'could commit any crime'.[38] He felt criminality to be innate. The personal histories of notorious contemporary criminals, like the murderers Wainwright and Thurkell and the embezzler Fauntleroy, were studied as illustrations of this view. The heroic but murderous hero of *Eugene Aram* was drawn on a man of the same name who had been a tutor in the Lytton family in the eighteenth century. It was a point of pride that Lytton's views on the nature and causes of crime were based on research.[39] In the 1820s, he moved in disguise among London's criminal classes, learning their argot and listening to their tales. Everything conspired to confirm him in the belief that the criminal was the victim of upbringing and circumstance. In the preface to the 1853 edition of *Lucretia*, he frankly admitted that the villainy in that novel should be contrasted with the virtue in *The Caxtons*. One set of characters were made bad by unhappy circumstances, while the others were good because they had known nothing else: 'The two fictions were intended as *pendants*: both serving ... to show the influence of home education – of early circumstance and example upon after character and conduct ... One shows the evil, the other the salutary influences of early circumstance and training.'[40]

Four novels, among Lytton's most powerful, established his reputation as Newgate novelist and reformer: *Paul Clifford* (1830), *Eugene Aram* (1832), *Night and Morning* (1841) and *Lucretia* (1846). They were all avowedly didactic in purpose. In *Paul Clifford*, a project possibly undertaken at the suggestion of the anarchist William Godwin, Lytton set out to rework the subversive theme of Gay's *Beggar's Opera*. The corruption, venality, bribery and violence of Clifford's gang would be mirrored in the world of high fashion and politics. The criminal and the lord would be shown to operate the same values. As he explained to his publisher, it was 'rather a piquant and original idea ... to satirise and expose the various objects and methods of rising which are emphatically called "worldly" – to make a kind of ludicrous resemblance between great men who are thought honest and Rogues who are hung'.[41] To make the connection clear, the gang members are given nicknames which immediately identified them with a major figure in public life, so 'Gentleman George' equated with George IV, 'Batchelor Bill' with the Duke of Devonshire, and 'Fighting Atty' with the Duke of Wellington. Actions which were denounced as criminal among the lower orders were received as mere worldliness among the social elite.

The point was brutally made. Introducing *Night and Morning*, Lytton wished

> To deal fearlessly with that universal unsoundness in social justice which makes distinctions so marked and iniquitous between Vice and Crime – viz between the corrupting habits and the violent act ... Let a child steal an apple in sport, let a starveling steal a roll in despair, and Law conducts them to the Prison, for evil commune to mellow them for the gibbet. But let a man spend

an apprenticeship from youth to old age in vice – let him devote a fortune, perhaps colossal, to the wholesale demoralisation of his kind – and he can be surrounded with the adulation of the so-called virtuous, and be served upon its knee, by that Lackey – the Modern World.[42]

One of Lytton's most engaging creations, Augustus Tomlinson in *Paul Clifford*, was a whimsical rogue much given to philosophising. His reflections lead him to compare the trade of politician and that of cut-throat: 'Have we not both our common vexations and our mutual disquietudes? Do we not both bribe ... our enemies, cajole our partisans, bully our dependents, and quarrel with our only friends, viz ourselves? Is not the secret question with each – "It is all confoundedly fine; but how long will it last?"'[43] To make such comparisons was subversive of social hierarchy. Lytton won few friends for undertaking the task.

Even more radical was the manner in which characters from the lower orders were depicted. They were not only objects of interest but invitations to pity. In *Lucretia*, for example, Lytton offered his readers a poignant description of a poor crossing-sweeper:

> There he was, then, seemingly without origin, parentage, or kindred tie, a lonesome, squalid, bloodless thing, which the great Monster, London, seemed to have spewed forth of its own self – one of its sickly, miserable, rickety offspring, whom it puts out at nurse to Penury, at school to Starvation, and, finally and literally, gives them stones for bread, with the option of the gallows or the dunghill, when the desperate offspring calls on the giant mother for return and home ... this living reproach, rising up from the stones of London against our social indifference to the souls which wither and rot under the hard eyes of science and the deaf ears of wealth.[44]

Little wonder, therefore, that a Lytton hero would be made to utter remarks disrespectful of the law. Paul Clifford acknowledged 'no allegiance to society ... openly I war against it, and patiently will I meet its revenge'. For Philip Morton in *Night and Morning* the law seemed 'as it ever does to the ignorant and the friendless – a Foe!'[45] Lytton's social novels of the 1830s and 1840s were as powerful as those of Dickens in disturbing consciences and irritating authority. They should be read as agenda for action as well as literary productions.

As a result, the careers of Lytton the novelist and Lytton the parliamentarian ran in parallel. As his novels argued, there was so much to be done. Criminal codes needed to be softened; poverty had to be relieved effectively; education had to be taken in hand. The life of the poor had to be regulated by something more substantial than the threat of the gallows. Lytton very much felt that his was a generation which would take change seriously and that his was a society in movement. It was a campaign in which the artist-legislator had a special role to play. The preface to the 1848 edition of *Paul Clifford* defiantly announced that:

The true movement of the last fifteen years has been the progress of one idea – Social Reform ... Let us do justice to our time ... there is no time in History in which there was so earnest and general desire to improve the condition of the great body of the people ... it unites in one object men of parties most opposed – it affords the most attractive nucleus for public meetings – it has cleansed the statute book from blood; it is ridding the world of the hangman.[46]

The Newgate novelists helped to mould opinion into a willingness to look for solutions to social problems. Lytton the radical played an honourable part in this process.

As a young man, Lytton was a Radical by conviction. But there was also a sense in which he was Radical because he could not be anything else. The other options, Tory and Whig, were unpalatable. For him, a Tory was a mixture of provincialism and bigotry whom he delighted in caricaturing. As he told Forster, 'there is nothing thoroughly good, bold or manly to be got out of the Galilee of Toryism'.[47] His early writings are full of jokes at the Tories' expense. In *Falkland,* the hero remarks that his father was 'a great country gentleman, a great sportsman, and a great Tory: perhaps the three worst enemies which a country can have'. Readers of the *New Monthly Magazine* in April 1830 were treated to schoolboy rhymes describing a Tory squire:

> Take some thick skull, as thick as you
> Can get, or it will never do;
> Fill it with Christian lore – for horses;
> With honour – for Newmarket courses;
> With sound unerring views – for pheasants;
> With disregard of death – for peasants.
> Mix in some bright divine confusion
> Of 'Eighty Eight' and 'Revolution';
> Of 'corn-laws' and of 'innovation',
> Combined with 'ruin of the nation'.[48]

If an idea were to enter a Tory mind it caught its owner unawares, entering 'like a stray sunbeam on a cave full of bats'.[49] The very Englishness of the party was offputting. As such, it was an obvious target for Lytton's satirical catapult.

For a young man embarking on a political career in the late 1820s or early 1830s, caricature and real life seemed to come together. Clever men

like Peel were discounted. Instead, military roués like Wellington were
preferred. Lytton enjoyed debunking national heroes. The schoolboy who
had written poetry extolling the glory of Waterloo had grown into a young
man who teased its victor:

> With a simper and a bow,
> And a look the Lord knows how
> On a girl the Lord knows who
> Moves the chief of Waterloo –
> Alas.that heroes should decrease
> To such a slender size in peace.[50]

Predictably a party led by such men had no time for intellect or art. They
treated 'literary men as a class with the same discouragement and neglect'.[51]
Over and over again, Lytton feasted on Tory faults and deficiencies. Enemies
were accordingly made, and they had long memories. When Lytton ironically
turned Tory himself, in 1852, he could not expect to be received with open
arms by his new allies. Wounds caused by the teasing of Lytton the Radical
had not closed.

It was clear that the young Lytton could not be a Tory. He could not
be a Whig either, but the reasons for this are more complicated. After all,
he and the Whigs had much in common. Led by the greatest aristocrats,
Whigs had a profound sense of caste and a contempt for the pretensions
of new money. Metropolitan, cosmopolitan and well-read, they took intellectual life seriously and patronised artists. There was much in this list with
which Lytton could identify. Not surprisingly, his description of Whig
grandees in his early novels is almost admiring.[52] The novice parliamentarian
praised the Whig leader, Lord Grey, and hailed him as a liberator:

> If to enforce those ends, the Hour
> Hath sceptered Liberty with Power,
> May we not hope from thee for more
> Than Might ere gave to Right before? [53]

He dined with Whigs, dedicated books to them, and went frequently to
Holland House, the Mecca of the creed.[54] More prosaically, for much of
his early career, he was not above soliciting 'some distinction' from the
Whigs, through Dr Parr in 1820 and Lord Melbourne in 1837.[55] Much of
the time he found their company congenial. They were, after all, well-read
men with aristocratic attitudes, like himself. They had a range that few
Tories could match. In spite of this, however, Lytton was never a Whig,
and his reasons for never enlisting under their banner were cogent.

Quite simply, the Whig sense of caste was theoretically admirable, but not if it was so rigidly defined as to exclude the Lyttons. For a man like Lytton, who bristled with pride of ancestry, it was galling to be told that his family were neither rich enough or distinguished enough to stand among the Whig leadership. The place they were offered was that of a faithful lieutenant. Repeatedly, between 1830 and 1841, Lord Melbourne, Lytton's near neighbour in Hertfordshire and competitor for the affections of Lady Caroline Lamb, lectured the young man on the realities of the situation. In the Whig world precedence was decided by name, birth and wealth. Those who lacked any or all these qualifications could only advance by showing unquestioning obedience.[56] Men who claimed the right to follow an independent line should look elsewhere. It was not enough only occasionally to vote with the Whig governments of these years. More consistent loyalty was required. Lytton, however, confided to his journal that 'I will not be a subordinate'.[57]

Above all, he could not admit that his own family was lower than his own estimation suggested. It was a vital problem if the Whig party itself was nothing but 'the interests of cliques and families'. They were certainly richer than most people, married each other incestuously, and behaved like 'the Hebrews in politics' in their exclusiveness.[58] They patronised and condescended in both meanings of those words, but, for Lytton, 'the condescending with a man of genius' was 'a thing not to be forgiven'.[59] A family which proudly traced its origins back to the Norman Conquest and beyond had no need of Whig charity, when many Whigs were the descendents of Tudor sheep farmers or Charles II's mistresses. When the Melbourne government took office in 1834 Lytton was only offered a lordship at the Admiralty, and he promptly declined it as an insult.[60] He took a sort of revenge in *England and the English*, by asking his readers 'to direct the spirit of the age ... against a very peculiar and all-productive organisation of the aristocratic spirit'.[61] This could only have been a euphemism for the Whig party. As a result, Lytton, who was aristocratic by every instinct, felt rejected by the party of aristocracy. This difficulty made it no easier for him to find a comfortable niche in English politics.

Predictably, his responses to Whig governments between 1830 and 1841 followed a distinctive pattern. He was inclined to vote against them at will, but also to rally to their defence in a crisis, for, after all, they were to be preferred to Tories. The result of this behaviour was that the Whigs accused him of disloyalty and he accused them of ingratitude. He complained constantly about the indifference of Grey and Melbourne: 'I can say safely that I have buried a thousand public – a thousand private causes of complaint in serving the Whigs.'[62] He chose colourful metaphors to describe the relationship between Radicals like himself and the Whigs. The latter were either disorientated sheep whom 'we sheepdogs try our best to drive strait and right', or well-meaning employers who forgot to pay any wages to those that followed them.[63] He listened, with irritation, to dinner-table conversation at Holland House on the subject of 'getting rid of the Radicals'.[64] Whigs needed Radical votes but gave them no countenance. It was intolerable hauteur on their part. Lytton fully agreed with John Stuart Mill when he warned that Radicalism must not become the mere 'tail' of Whiggery.[65]

And yet the Whigs were better than the Tories, and, for the moment, England would always be governed by one or the other. Lytton was faced with 'the Whigs' return or Tory ascendancy'.[66] Swallowing his pride, Lytton had to help Whigs in difficulties. Twice he made a significant contribution to their survival. There were moments when 'all men not against us are for us'.[67] In November 1834 William IV summarily dismissed the Whig government of Lord Melbourne, even though it still enjoyed a Commons majority. Lytton quickly penned a pamphlet denouncing the King's actions, *A Letter to a Cabinet Minister*. It was written in two days. In it Lytton argued that, although Whig government since 1830 had been disappointing, monarchs had no right to remove those chosen by the electorate. Wellington was identified as the real villain of the piece, being categorised as a friend of obstructionist Orangemen in Ireland and of would-be despots in England and France. The pamphlet went through twenty-one editions in six weeks, with Lytton proudly noting that its sale exceeded that of Burke's *Reflections on the Revolution in France*.[68] It provoked at least ten replies in pamphlet form. Typical of these was *A Calm Consideration on the Present State of Public Affairs*, which described the crisis as a battle between 'the Destructive Revolutionists and the Conservatives'.[69] In retrospect, Lytton firmly believed that his writings largely accounted for the Whig victory in the election of March 1835. He was inordinately proud of making a major contribution to what he called 'the great March'.[70]

In the summer of 1839 the Whigs were once again in trouble. This time their position was threatened by the Radicals themselves indicating that their disappointment with Whig inactivity would end in the withdrawal of their support for the Melbourne government. Lytton fully shared the disillusion of his Radical friends, but the awful prospect of Tory government forced him to ride to the defence of the Whigs yet again. He wrote a carefully crafted essay for the *Edinburgh Review*, the proofs of which were vetted by Holland and Melbourne before publication. His aim was 'to make a complete and triumphant vindication of ministerial policy' and 'to keep Whigs and Radicals on good terms with each other'.[71] Significantly though, he complained to the *Edinburgh*'s editor that all he could expect in return was Whig 'Ingratitude'.[72] In fact, the article is much less pro-Whig than anti-Tory. He defended Whig policy on colonial and constitutional points, but spent more time underlining divisions within the Tory party. These conflicts, and a basic Tory inability to meet the demands of the new middle-class electorate, would lead to inept government and the prospect of real disorder.[73] Once again, Lytton convinced himself that his efforts had saved the day and that the Whigs had rewarded him badly. He accepted a baronetcy with an ill grace. He thought he was worth a peerage. In 1834 and 1839 the Whigs snubbed him. He could never feel comfortable in their company, and so a Radical he had to remain.

A Radicalism that was rooted in a distaste for the other options, rather than a conviction that certain views were right, is a doctrine lightly held. Lytton was in politics because he believed that he had a duty to family to be a public man, and because the artist was required to bring his special insights into politics. Unfortunately, Lytton was uncomfortable with the English and uncomfortable with English parties. He was never emotionally involved with any of them. The detail of his actual parliamentary performance more than proves the point.

First and foremost, the House of Commons only rarely heard his voice at all. He was most active in 1834, when he made eight significant speeches, and in 1859, when, as a Cabinet Minister, he was frequently required to answer questions. But there were no speeches at all in 1840 and 1861–64, and only one in 1839, 1841, 1853, 1857, 1860, 1865 and 1866. Lytton in fact had a fear of speaking. Nearly every performance was a nightmare. His high-pitched, rather squeaky voice, which tended to drop in volume at the end of sentences, often made him inaudible. The same defects were mercilessly parodied by his enemies. He took lessons in elocution and enlisted the help of his actor friend Macready, but entries in his journal record how much the problem worried him; 'Reporters complain of my dropping my voice at the end of a sentence. Must master the knack. I have a good voice when well managed – but so bad an ear, that I don't often do it.'[74]

The problem was made worse by other factors. An advancing deafness made it hard to gauge the reaction of an audience, or to answer objections appropriately. Even more inhibiting were mannerisms that invited ridicule. Lytton's speeches were accompanied by such wild gesticulations that Palmerston teased him by saying that he had to be seen rather than heard.[75] The total effect was described by a parliamentary reporter as follows:

> He always walks about in that abstracted manner, rather stooping, hat on the back of his head, his hands thrust into his trouser pocket, and his eyes cast downwards – looking for all the world as if he fancied he had lost something, and was searching the ground and feeling for it in his pocket at the same time.

It is generally known about the house when he is going to speak, as he then wanders about more abstractedly than usual. The Hon. Baronet is not an effective speaker; not, however, because his matter is not good, but because his action spoils all. It is well known that he studies his speeches carefully beforehand – would that he would, under proper guidance, study how to deliver them! His manner is this: he begins a sentence, standing upright, in his usual tone; as he gets to the middle he throws himself backwards, until you would fancy that he must tumble over, and gradually raises his voice to the higher pitch. He then begins to lower his tone and throws his body forwards, so that at the finish of the sentence his head nearly touches his knees, and the climax of the sentence is lost in a whisper.[76]

The same reporter thought that only a diagram could properly describe these movements. Their impact on an audience was unfortunate. Macaulay thought Lytton had the manner of 'a bad actor'. A visiting German poet thought he was drunk.[77]

Not surprisingly Lytton was always apprehensive about platform performances. The Disraeli correspondence is full of notes from him explaining why he would prefer not to speak. A doctor's prohibition was often used as an excuse, or 'spasms in the teeth'.[78] At no stage in his career did he ever find confidence in debate. Speeches would be written out in full, because spontaneity was too dangerous, but still they came out oddly. A speech of 1852 'left out what I had meant to say and said some things I never meant to say – was disgusted with my own manner and delivery etc etc.' Twenty years after making his maiden speech he was still hoping for 'self-confidence and a knowledge of the House'.[79] When, occasionally, a debate went well, it was such a relief that he could not retire for the night without writing to brother Henry with the news.[80] As late as 1865 he would sadly inform his son that 'it is an uphill matter to argue in Parliament'.[81] For someone with ministerial ambitions, it was a severe handicap, and one which he never came near to overcoming.

Even more compromising for his Radical reputation were the issues on which he did rise to his feet in the House. There are notable single speeches on such major issues as Parliamentary Reform, slavery and the Corn Laws, but the issues which most preoccupied him as a parliamentarian were those that touched him as a writer. Such issues could easily be seen as part of a Radical agenda but were in no sense a central feature of it. Campaigns to break the monopoly of London theatres in the presentation of plays, and to give copyright protection to writers, have been dealt with already. They were long and time-consuming. Equally so was his crusade to abolish stamp duty on newspapers, which increased costs so much that they were priced at levels which many among the reading public could not afford.

By sponsoring serious parliamentary initiatives on this issue in 1831–32, and again in 1834–35, Lytton made it his own. Friends in journalism like Edwin Chadwick and Albany Fonblanque were drafted into the battle.[82] The argument was simple. After 'the blessing' of the 1832 Reform Bill, the new electorate should be as informed as possible.[83] It was absurd to put 'taxes on knowledge. A newspaper should be on every breakfast-table.' When all such duties were finally lifted, in 1855, Lytton spoke in the debate and expressed himself fulfilled.[84] The establishment of a free press was undoubtedly the attainment of a Radical ambition, but it was the only reforming issue with which Lytton was intimately associated.

Further, if he was a reluctant parliamentarian, Lytton was even shyer of contact with the electorate. If he was serious about his Radicalism, it was a creed that preferred to talk about the people in abstract rather than shake their hands. Finding a constituency was a bore. They were either too expensive, too riotous or not respectable enough. At the beginning of his career he flirted with an impressive list of boroughs which included Marylebone, Southwark, Truro, Penrhyn and St Albans. Courting their electorates he found expensive and 'very fatiguing'.[85] Even when he had secured a reasonably sound tenancy in Lincoln he rarely went there, preferring to deal with his constituents through the intermediary of his solicitor or of the local d'Eyncourt family. It is no coincidence that his novels are full of descriptions of the miseries and indignities suffered by candidates. The borough of Lansmere in *My Novel* exacted a high price from its would-be representatives:

> The candidates had to speak – at the close of each day's canvass – out from wooden boxes, suspended from the windows of their respective hotels, and which looked like dens for the exhibition of wild beasts. They had to speak at meetings of Committees – meetings of electors – go the nightly round of enthusiastic public-houses, and appeal to the sense of an enlightened people through wreathes of smoke and odours of beer.[86]

A Radical by instinct might have found all this rather exhilarating. Lytton found it only wearing.

In the face of evidence such as this, it is possible to describe Lytton's early Radicalism as rooted in not much more than hero-worship of one man. The Earl of Durham, colloquially known as 'Radical Jack', dictated Lytton's views and was hailed by him as a messiah. His correspondence with Lady Blessington is full of remarks which catalogue Durham's talents and prophesy about the brilliant future that lay ahead: 'Durham has written his Horoscope in People's hearts – they only want the occasion to tell him of his destiny.'[87] In speaking in this way Lytton betrayed his political naivety.

True, Durham was rich and, as Grey's son-in-law, moved within the innermost circles of Whiggery. But he was erratic and unpredictable. The Tories detested him and his Whig relations regarded him as a maverick. They preferred to use him on diplomatic missions in Russia or Canada, far away from the mainstream of English politics. It was understandable that Lytton should have fellow-feeling for someone who was also on the margins of acceptability, but to think that Durham could overcome his critics and attain the leadership of politics was eccentric to say the least.

For much of the period 1831–35, Lytton wanted nothing more than to be a foot-soldier in the political army that advanced Durham's career, patching up quarrels and writing apologias.[88] So keen was he about the project, that he argued for the formation of a new party, if the existing ones could not promote Durham's ambitions: 'You are probably aware that arrangements are making for the formation of a new party ... I think the notion of this party is admirable.' In contemplating such a move, Lytton agreed to be entirely governed by Durham's opinion. He disowned all other labels. He clearly was no Whig or Tory, and he 'did not call [himself] a Radical'.[89] As early as 1833, in *England and the English*, he had argued that 'an independent party ought to be formed'.[90] Even when Durham poured cold water on the idea, Lytton remained faithful to him. He lectured his constituents at Lincoln on the need for a new political configuration and on Durham's virtues. In 1838 he was actively canvassing J. S. Mill on the proposal. He hoped that 'a party can be formed for the Durham policy', which would at once defeat the obscurantism of Tories and the dilatoriness of Whigs.[91]

All of this was nonsensical, with no grounding in the realities of politics. Tensions within both the Whig and Tory camps were certainly severe, but they remained coalitions loose enough to accommodate the views of most Englishmen. It would take something as explosive as the Corn Law issue of 1846 to blow apart existing structures and thereby raise the possibility of new parties. It was even more quixotic to continue to invest Durham with a glorious destiny. Few men in official politics liked or trusted him. As the 1830s closed, he had never moved from the margins of politics, becoming frustrated and a little shop-worn. Lytton's campaigning for the man tells little about the state of politics, but a great deal about his own relationship with English politics. Men call for new parties and idolise mavericks when they feel dispossessed themselves. Lytton operated under the label of Radical because it was the best of those available. Sometimes he rejected it as uncomfortable. Like Durham, Lytton was homeless in English politics. He had a real desire for change. He had a real sympathy with the poor, even if they were more congenial as characters in books than as participants at election meetings. But no established party gave him satisfaction.

Not surprisingly, some of those who were closest to him in the 1830s were intrigued by the incongruities in Lytton's politics. S. C. Hall was the sub-editor of the *New Monthly Magazine* in Lytton's time, and described his views as follows:

> Bulwer could hardly be said to entertain settled political opinions. It is sufficiently notorious that he began life – politically – as a Liberal of very advanced type, and, in fact, sought to enter Parliament under Radical banners. I can never imagine him soliciting the 'most sweet voices' of the multitude otherwise than with awkward constraint – as a gentleman out of his sphere ... He was thoroughly an aristocrat; all his affinities were with his 'order', although he sought, and thought, to connect himself with the hard-handed men of the working classes. I could fancy him scrupulously washing his hands after a meeting with his constituents – where he had been condemned to exchange greetings with them. He could scarcely have done that which, undoubtedly, he would have preferred to do – put on his gloves before he entered a meeting of Radicals.[92]

There was evidence to justify such cynicism. In novels, Lytton's respect for the poor is genuine but his description of Radical agitators is not flattering. Wolfe in *The Disowned* is a cold, humourless prig who, incompetently, murders the wrong man. He was a dangerous, amateur 'Demosthenes'.[93] Coming face to face with rioters in 1830 dismayed Lytton. He deplored their 'disgraceful habit of throwing stones at old gentlemen on horseback'. Injured by one of the missiles, he returned home 'with his head tied up in a handkerchief'.[94] It was a hard lesson in popular politics.

In Parliament, Lytton supported the first Reform Bill in 1832 and also spoke in favour of a secret ballot at elections. Beyond these changes, however, he had no constitutional ambitions. After 1832 'he was not anxious to have a new Reform Act ... and had many objections to the popular scheme of household suffrage'.[95] Similarly he spoke up for the Tolpuddle Martyrs, while, at the same time, expressing distaste for the trade unionism that had entangled them with the law.[96] When, in 1838, he became the proprietor of the *Monthly Chronicle*, that journal was committed to 'a medium policy' which seemed to include sustained attacks on the demands of the Chartists. Working men could not claim the vote unless they could 'prove that they are fit for it'. As for the social programme of Chartism, it enshrined nothing more than 'the right of the sturdy beggar to pick the pockets of industry'.[97] If the amelioration of working men's lives was to come about, it should not do so through their own initiatives. The direction of affairs should remain in the hands of gentlemen.

With reservations such as these, the tailing off of Lytton's parliamentary activities is easily understood. He made no apology for what he called 'Parliamentary indolence'.[98] Increasingly the only label he liked to be given, as he told the Commons in 1834, was that of 'an independent Member, attached to neither of the two parties'.[99] He was never a convincing Radical but nor could he be a convincing anything else. Politics began to bore him. He told his daughter that he considered 'Parliament as I dare say you considered school – and don't like it at all. It is very hard work – worse than lessons'. By 1841 the fag of regular attendance was overwhelming:

> So Parliament has met – and it will be 'votes, riddles and botheration' for some time at least. – Adieu Comedy – Farewell Schiller! – No more Cakes and Ale – Hail the more lulling pleasures of hearing Sir Robert and cheering Lord John – I have been complaining of want of sleep. I must be Argos himself if I don't sleep now.[100]

As in much else, Lytton really wanted politics on is own terms. He searched in vain for a party that would narrowly agree with him and value him by his own estimation. Such a consummate individualist could never be a party man. On the evidence of 1830 to 1841, neither Radicalism nor Whiggery could offer him a long-term home. It remained to be seen whether advancing age could turn him into a plausible Tory.

10

Tory

By 1850 a great change had overtaken Bulwer's politics. The so-called Radical had become something of a Tory, though whether his new allegiance was any more deeply rooted than the old was a matter of debate. If some of his friends now numbered him among 'the red-hot Tories',[1] a more likely description would be that there had only been a change of mood, a settling into middle age. The letters of that year are philosophical in tone. He told his friend Lord Walpole that

> The real secret at our age (if I may, sinking some years' difference, indulge in that phrase) would be the proper arrangement of one's life into something like orderly method, avoiding the passions, but not the affections, getting rid of false excitements and the necessity of that stimulant – change – whether in persons or things. In short, trying to concentrate one's existence so that one might get into the circle of enjoyments most to our individual tastes, and least injurious to other people.[2]

New possibilities in life had led him to 'cease almost to care about politics'. With resignation and a quieting of life, the Radicalism of his youth appeared less and less congenial. Looking for political company there seemed to be 'none for my doubts but in good old Toryism'.[3] There was no zealotry in his conversion. It was rather an easing of his mind.

In the early 1850s an apocalyptic element begins to appear in his correspondence which confirmed his drift towards the party of order and tradition. He believed that 'the nation is divided into two great parties'. One would lead England towards democracy and the social and cultural values that went with it. The other would build on aristocratic tradition. In his view, there could be no accommodation between these two forces. One would certainly destroy the other and, since men of conservative temperament could not work together, Lytton thought it likely that a democratic future, with all its uncertainties, was the most likely outcome. Gladstone and Disraeli were both suspicious of democracy, but loathed each other.[4] Palmerston was an aristocrat to his finger tips, but a perverted 'self-will' led him to flirt with the Radicals.[5] Saddest of all were the Whigs, who eagerly seemed to promote moves towards democratic values without apparently being aware that they were contributing to the destruction of their own world. Very soon they would be 'as the fossils which speak of the race before the flood'.[6] If the natural defenders of established forms behaved like this, Lytton despaired of any defence 'against Extreme Democratic government'. He lamented the fact that even the word 'Antireformer' had become 'an odious title'.[7] The time had come for a liberal aristocrat like Lytton to decide whether he was a liberal or whether he was an aristocrat.

In 1853 Lytton contributed a series of articles to the Tory newspaper *The Press* under the name of 'Manilius'. They took the form of an appeal to the Whigs to wake up to the dangers that faced them and their kind. He asked them to defend the Reform Bill of 1832 and to resist calls for a further extension of the suffrage. Instead, they seemed paralysed between 'those two contending powers ... Monarchy and Popular Suffrage'. He begged them to forget the past and the agendas which had divided Whig and Tory. Since he stood 'somewhat distinct from the ordinary relations of party', he thought himself well-qualified to ask this favour: 'I see the sole hope of England in the union of those men who will defend England as she is. History has buried in the past all the old feuds between Tories and Whigs save that mere emulation for power which hunts out pretexts for unsubstantial differences.'[8] Sadly, the writer had no real hope that anyone would hear his words. The democrats would prevail because their opponents spent their days navel-gazing, ruminating on old hatreds. Lytton took on the role of Cassandra.[9]

By the time these letters were being written Lytton had a clear mind about his preferred model of society. It was one based on a working aristocracy which set values for the whole community. 'Show me,' he wrote, 'a class of gentlemen, an Aristocracy in short, and I will form a conjecture as to the duration of any free constitution; without that, between Crown, soldier, traders and mobs, I am all at sea.'[10] Aristocracy, for him, was a word with a broad definition. It meant more than the House of the Lords. Rather it described a governing class generally, and one that lived and acted by the creed of obligation. There was obligation to country, to a disinterested political life, and to lower social groups. Lytton praised the novels of Sir Walter Scott for, among other things, compelling 'the highest classes to examine and respect the lowest'.[11] Social harmony lay in an interchange of respect. The lower orders deferred to educated gentlemen. They, in turn, protected the interests of those below them. His concern for the poor earlier in his life had been based on the idea that aristocrats had a duty to behave in this way. His early Radicalism did not allow the poor to make demands on their own initiative. Rather they should receive benefits from well-intentioned and hard-working aristocrats. Lytton's values were always patriarchal. In the 1820s and 1830s social change was managed by people like himself. Radicalism could be gentlemanly. After the experience of Chartism and the Revolutions in Europe of 1848 this was less and less true. Working people now demanded things as of right and not as a gift from their benevolent superiors. Lytton's gentlemanly philanthropy could no longer be accommodated within Radicalism and had to find a new hiding-place.

Unfortunately, Lytton's model of social relationships only fitted the agricultural England which existed before the Industrial Revolution. There were no equivalents of dutiful aristocrats and patriarchal squires in sprawling conurbations. Lytton mourned this development. In *The Last of the Barons*, which he acknowledged as one of his favourite productions, the sense of loss is rehearsed again and again. Village greens, once the scenes of merrymaking, were 'now foul and reeking with the squalid population whom commerce rears up – the victims, as the movers of the modern world'. Where gin-shops now stand, there was once a monastery 'and the chime of its heavy bell swung far and sweet over the pastoral landscape'.[12] In this world noblemen who were truly noble, like Warwick the Kingmaker, prided themselves in having 'the reverential and yet affectionate admiration which he inspired amongst the yeoman, peasants and mechanics'. When England was governed by men such as this, 'what need', Lytton asked, 'of a poor law then! The baron and the abbot made the parish.'[13]

Throughout his life, even in the days of his political Radicalism, Lytton's novels repeatedly extol the values of a pre-industrial world. In *Ernest Maltravers* (1837) and *Alice* (1838), books for which Lytton claimed a particular affection, the eponymous hero shows, among many other qualities, an inbred desire to be an exemplary landlord. He establishes a village school and allotments, and is clear that 'individual want had to be looked out for and relieved by private charity'. As a result, 'Age, infirmity, temporary distress, unmerited destitution found him a steady, watchful, indefatigable friend'. Crucially, he was as spiritually benefited by these acts of benevolence as those he materially helped.[14] In *Lucretia* (1846) the idyll of agricultural England is described in loving language:

> It is market-day, at a town in the midland districts of England. There, Trade takes its healthiest and most animated form. You see not the stunted form and hollow eye of the mechanic – poor slave of the capitalist – poor agent and victim of the arch disequaliser – Civilisation. There, strides the burly form of the farmer; there, waits the ruddy hind with his flock; there, patient, sits the miller with his samples of corn; there, in the booths, gleam the humble wares which form the luxuries of cottage and farm. The thronging of men, and the cracking of whips,

and the dull sound of wagon or dray, that parts the crowd as it passes, and the lowing of herds and the bleating of sheep, all are sounds of movement and bustle, yet blend with the pastoral associations of the Primitive Commerce, when the link between market and farm was visibly direct.[15]

It was a world that England was losing or had already lost.

By 1850, when he began to rough out ideas for *My Novel*, he made no secret of his wish to write something that was specifically 'anti-Socialist or Antirevolutionary'. Evoking memories of the healthy values of pre-industrial England would cheer 'all sound-hearted Britishers' and 'strengthen the old English cordial feeling – and bind together those classes which the Manchester school are always trying to separate and the French school would dip into the fusing pot altogether'.[16] In the novel, characters with pastoral surnames like Dale, Fairfield and Hazeldean live in pleasantness with one another under the caring eye of parson and squire. The novel was overtly a political manifesto too. It was an appeal to the gentlemen of England to defeat the prospect of revolution by behaving well: 'Don't suppose that any scribbling and typework will suffice to answer the scribbling and typework set at work to demolish you – *write* down that rubbish you can't – *live* it down you may. If you are rich, like Squire Hazeldean, do good with your money; if you are poor, like Signor Riccabocca, do good with your kindness.'[17] The novel was an urgent and insistent call to arms.

For the dangers were all too obvious by 1850. In Lytton's view industrialising England was replacing the harmonious relationship between squire and tenant with a poisonous competition between capital and labour. Value based on birth, long-ownership and education were being subverted by a preoccupation with profit. The unbending rules of political economy were everywhere, but Lytton was unimpressed. He thought Adam Smith 'a very shallow, though a very original thinker'. He wondered 'if that dismal science is compatible with the agricultural interest'. Certainly Liberal governments, acting on Smith's principles, seemed determined 'to legislate against the cultivators of the land'.[18] Lytton's most successful play, *Money*, gleefully satirised a society which worshipped no other god. At one point a character named Stout, a political economist, explains his late arrival for a meeting by saying that it had taken 'me an hour and a half to beat it into the head of a stupid widow, with nine children, that to allow her three shillings a week was against all the rules of public morality'.[19] It is unlikely that Lytton had any clear alternative to offer, beyond a return to the past, but that in no way eased the situation of a man who felt his values to be increasingly at a discount.

There was an urgency in the matter too. Warfare between capitalists like Richard Cobden and working men could have the most terrible

consequences. The revolutions in Europe in 1848, which Lytton had witnessed at first hand, might have their counterpart in England. Lytton
complained to Forster about

> These miserable Cobdens ... What fools they are, and these are the men by whom
> England herself has been half driven to the brink of revolution. Wise Daniels
> indeed ... A Republic is cheap, but if ever that hour arrives it shall not be, if I
> and a few like me live, a Republic of millers and cotton-spinners, but either a
> Republic of gentlemen or a Republic of workmen – either is better than those
> wretched money spiders who would sell England for 1s. 6d.[20]

It was quite literally a case of 'England versus Cobden'.[21] To avoid a tearing
of the social fabric, the country had to turn away from materialism and
recapture at least some spiritual values. The nervous and intellectual energy
of the English was running in the wrong channels: 'We as yet live under
the influence of the philosophy of Adam Smith. The minds that formerly
would have devoted themselves to metaphysical and moral research, are
given up to inquiries into a more material study. Political economy replaces
ethics, and we have treatises on the theory of rents, instead of essays of the
theory of motives.'[22] The leadership of Radicalism had slipped from the
hands of people like Durham and himself, and had become the preserve
of lawyers, journalists and professors. It was no longer safe. By 1850 Lytton
was sure that he should look elsewhere.

In Lytton's mind one issue above all encapsulated the conflict between
countryside and city, between harmony and discord, between ethical and
materialist assumptions: the Corn Laws. He fairly owned to the House of
Commons that it was the issue which had 'estranged' him from one party
and which had led him to cohabit with another.[23] The laws in question
guaranteed agricultural prices. No corn could enter the country from abroad
until the price in England had passed a certain point. Critics rightly pointed
out that such restrictions artificially raised the price of bread, the staple
diet of working people. But defenders of the laws not only argued that a
viable agriculture guaranteed that the English would never be dependent
on foreigners for food but also that they underpinned a model of living
that was morally superior. The Squire Hazeldean of *My Novel* could never
have been in a position to exercise his patriarchal benevolence without an
income made certain by the Corn Laws. The symbolism invested in this
legislation was therefore incalculable. Lytton was not alone in seeing the
laws as a benchmark against which his own conduct would be regulated.
It was by far the most pressing motive for his drift to Toryism.

When he re-entered Parliament, in 1852, he sat not for a populous borough but for the agricultural county of Hertfordshire. Immediately he began to use phrases like 'we, the country Gentlemen'.[24] He repeatedly claimed that, for almost the whole of his political life, even in his Radical days, his affection for agricultural society and its interests had never wavered: 'even since 1834, when I voted against Mr Hume's motion I remained invariably opposed to the repeal of the Corn Laws ... The fact is, that I had never thoroughly considered the questions connected with the Corn Law till Mr Hume's memorable motion, and my convictions were decided by the arguments employed in the debate.'[25] Any suggestion to the contrary that appeared in a journal or newspaper was swiftly rebutted. One offending editor was chastised as follows:

> It may be that my political career has been inconsistent but that is not the way to put it. I had always while representing Lincoln been opposed to the total abolition of the Corn Laws – in this I had agreed with the Whigs – when they changed I did not – and thus came to act with Lord Derby. I do not consider this inconsistent.[26]

In the polishing of his political reputation, his steadfastness on this point concerned him greatly.

Although protesting too much, Lytton's claims should be allowed. Even when a Radical he had cautioned Durham against attacking the Corn Laws, and had argued that 'for any party to be permanent and powerful, great care must be taken not to alarm the Agriculturalists'.[27] Just before the abolition of the Corn Laws, in 1846, he gave an impassioned speech to the Hertfordshire Agricultural Society which insisted that 'it is in the quiet strength of her agricultural population that the bulwark of England has been found'.[28] The defeat of both the Armada and Napoleon were cited as examples of what a compact and harmonious community could do. Squires and yeomen had been the managers of England's greatness. To challenge that relationship with other values was madness. The owner of a great estate at Knebworth understood what was at stake.

Predictably, therefore, the abolition of the Corn Laws in 1846 came as a terrible shock. Agriculture would be totally exposed to foreign competition and the values it supported would be destroyed. That a Tory, Sir Robert Peel, should have been the instrument of this change was, for Lytton, 'stupendous treachery' which 'excites my gall'. It was 'perfidy' on such a scale that no honourable man should seek his company thereafter.[29] He went so far as to describe Peel's behaviour as tantamount to a *coup d'état*.[30] In the run-up to the final debates Lytton could still discuss the issue in balanced language,[31] but when the blow fell he was outraged. There was not 'the least excuse or necessity' for what had been done.[32] When the bulk of the Tory party repudiated Peel and his attack on agriculture, Lytton's sympathy was immediately engaged. Former Radical colleagues like Charles Gore were dismayed by Lytton's change of front:

> I cannot bear to think of you among these people. It is all very well for Lord G. to patter to his father's tenants like St Anthony preaching to the fishes. Or for Dizzy who if he had lived in the middle ages would have been a Sir John Hawkwood leading a band of mercenaries ... But it really riles one to think of a man of your great powers and great name and great position embarking in – I will not say a sinking vessel – but going down in a diving bell to embark in the wreck of the *Royal George*.[33]

If Lytton ever became a Tory, it was the Corn Law issue that made him one.

His friends were convinced that he had made a fatal mistake. He seemed to have tied his career to a lost cause. The Corn Laws had been buried in 1846 and would never be resuscitated in their view. There was more than an element of gloating when Henry Brougham wrote to Lytton to say, in 1852, that 'I suppose that you are now full of protection – and probably are beginning to perceive how compleatly [sic] you have been thrown over – to the great satisfaction as you may believe of us free-trade men'.[34] Lytton did not agree. He regarded 1846 as merely a serious defeat in an ongoing battle. It was not a final statement. He was sure that, sooner or later, one way or the other, agriculture would have to be rescued in the national interest. It could not be allowed to founder, and the calamities inflicted on it would have to be reversed. His correspondence of 1850–51 chronicled agricultural distress. His own estates at Knebworth produced little income, and all around him there were 'farmers breaking in all directions'. He had two farms without tenants, and those that were worked were a drain on resources. They were 'more ruinous even than children'.[35]

To continue to argue for the Corn Laws and Protection after 1846 has for long been thought eccentric. Recent research has, however, modified this view. Lytton was not alone in continuing the campaign.[36] He was sure that large sections of the electorate could see the madness of destroying England's agricultural base. He lectured his brother on this point in January 1850:

> Verily agricultural prospects are in that state that I must look to my brains for rent. It is wholly impossible that Corn can remain at its present prices without ensuring the ruin of the present agricultural generation. And if an Election were to come tomorrow with the present constituency ... I firmly believe that free trade would be doomed. It is for this reason only, I suspect, that Johnny Russell is about to bring forward a new Reform Bill, with an increase of franchise, to drown the agricultural cry.[37]

How agriculture was to be protected was open to negotiation. As he pointed out to a Hertfordshire Tory, there were many ways of doing this: 'Protection may come through other quarters than a tax on foreign grain. Protection is not thrown over, if one mode of seeking it be substituted for another.'[38] Perhaps the malt tax on barley could be cut. Perhaps the poor rates in agricultural districts could be reduced. Perhaps there could be a sliding scale of duties on the importation of cereals. But something had to be done. Otherwise there would be terrible consequences: 'If the present prices continue there will be such a burst of distress from existing farmers as will endanger the country in the disaffection of its only conservative class.'[39]

After 1850 the rescuing of agricultural England and its values became a major, if not the central, element in Lytton's politics. To the dismay of liberal economists like J. R. McCullough he seemed to be impervious to argument on the point. McCullough asserted that agriculture had known worse periods of distress when Protection was in force, and that the downturn of 1850–51 was a localised phenomenon. As a result, there had to be something 'peculiar' about Hertfordshire if its farmers were unhappy. Equally, to tamper so soon with the decision of 1846 was 'folly'.[40] Lytton heard the words, but could not accept the argument:

> I remain as convinced as ever that a duty must sooner or later be put upon Corn – as part of a general revision in the principle of taxation. My common sense is persuaded of this. And the recusancy of Chiefs may damage themselves and delay the hour. But as sure as I write these lines that hour will come – and perhaps Whigs after all may do the work, if the Conservatives choose to abandon it.[41]

To plan determinedly for the reimposition of Corn Laws was distinctive but not eccentric. Shortly after Lytton's death much of Europe and America would return to protectionism.

In the spring of 1851 Lytton went public with his concerns. He published three *Letters to John Bull*, much to the delight of 'the large-acred squires'.[42] On one level, these essays were an appeal to relieve the 'very critical and dangerous state' of agriculture. On another, they were a public declaration of his separation from a Radical past and of his determination henceforth to work with the Tories. He had become an apologist for the land and its way of life:

> I speak of the class which cultivate the land we live in; I speak of the interest which comprises a vast mass of the real property of the country: an interest which supports the bulk of our poor; which maintains the clergy and defrays the costs that uphold civilisation in rural districts; which, whether it be or be not disproportionately taxed does at all events contribute towards the state to so large an

amount, that it cannot be materially injured, nor depressed, by any change in the law, without affecting the very capital upon which depend the income of the fund-holder and the solvency of the nation.

He went on to insist that, since the Corn Laws guaranteed this world, their abolition in 1846 could only be seen as temporary. 'The Corn Laws settled! No! Free-traders and Protectionists alike feel in their heart of hearts that it is not settled.'[43]

The arguments rehearsed in these *Letters* had been prefigured in private correspondence from the late 1840s or even earlier. They were a curious mixture of points that were the common coin of Protectionist writers and thoughts that were peculiarly Lytton's own. In the first category came the warning of the danger of relying on foreigners to feed the nation. Self-sufficiency was common sense. The Napoleonic Wars had proved the point within living memory, and those with a classical education would not find it difficult to produce other examples. In his history of Athens, Lytton had already suggested that breaking this rule had contributed to the destruction of that civilisation: 'Dependence on other resources than those of the native population has ever been a main cause of the destruction of despotisms, and it cannot fail, sooner or later, to be equally pernicious to the republican that trusts to it.'[44] A living agriculture had to be preserved, so that the nation would not starve.

A more distinctive preoccupation was Lytton's concern about the radicalisation of the countryside. He believed that, if agricultural concerns were continually bruised, those who worked in the countryside would turn to desperate measures. The opinions of these people had always been of interest to him. When editor of the *New Monthly Magazine* in 1832, he had commissioned an article on this precise point:

> I want particularly to bring this subject – in a clear-lucid familiar yet practical manner – before the attention of the Public! I wish not only the actual State of the Poor to be considered – but also their feelings, the opinions current among them – the influence of the Dissenters – of the Owenites – of the state of Education, their feelings to the Clergy etc – and it might not be amiss to touch upon the causes of that marvellous respect which the Agricultural Labourer seems to feel in excited times for the Mechanic. It is here, I suppose, that 'Knowledge is power'.[45]

If the farmer and the labourer felt abandoned by the legislator, their reactions were dangerously unpredictable. As if to underline this point, Lytton had a frightening experience at a meeting he chaired in September 1851. A farmer made a violent speech attacking landlords for various forms of alleged delinquency. Lytton's reaction was a mixture of defiance and alarm:

Nuts to them! It is true that a meeting so mixed gave no fair representation of Farming Feeling but still there were a dogged strength in the speaker and a savage sympathy among such farmers who were present, that alarms me more than the voices of the free traders – for it shows the Democratic spirit strongly rising in the Agricultural Class – and if Protection be not restored, there will even be a fusion between the farmer and the Democrats.[46]

In Lytton's view, the Corn Law debate was about more than mere economics. It threatened to put all established patterns of social and political life in motion, with wholly unpredictable results.

Elaborating this point, Lytton insisted that, in giving industry preference over agriculture, 'the real consequences had been overlooked by both parties'. They were nothing less than altering 'for the worse the staple character and spirit of the people'.[47] The stakes simply could not have been higher. As he told Lady Blessington, he thought 'the question ... one in which political economy – mere mercantile loss and gain – has least to do. High social considerations are bound up in it.'[48] Belittling the farmer and the tenant was to undermine 'the class that acts as a Constitutional Counterpoise to the classes which inevitably tend towards democratic innovation'.[49] In other words, the conservative and settled instincts of the countryside would no longer be available to act as a moderating influence on politics. As a result, no institution, no property, no useful tradition would be safe. At the height of the Corn Law debates, Lytton published a poem called *The Crisis*, which set out apocalyptic prophecies:

> 'Move on', 'Move on there!' – decked in proud array
> The Anti Corn Law 'Bus' stops up the way!
> Ten thousand levellers on the roof may ride
> And twice ten thousand malcontents inside!
> The 'ribbons' grace a cotton-spinner's hands,
> With beck and call behind the Quaker stands; –
> 'Corn Law Repeal?' 'Free Trade?' but soon the cry
> Will be 'No Church?' 'Confusion?' 'Anarchy?'
> Poor fated Realm! e'en now distinct and true,
> Rises the mournful epoch on my view!
> O'er Agriculture waves the cypress-bough,
> And the State's pillars all have crumbled now!
> Dimly remembered through the mist of years –
> Bishops and bullocks, topboots and the Peers.[50]

With consequences such as these in prospect, a change in party allegiance was more than justified. In long, valedictory letters to former political allies, Lytton explained his defection to the Tories in forthright terms. He insisted that the Corn Laws promised to alter the very concept of Englishness.

Aristocratic values and a secure agriculture stood or fell together. Therefore, he now differed from Radicals and Whigs

> as regards the maintenance of an Established Church, upon the danger of a household or democratic suffrage – upon the importance of our Colonial Empire; and I differed from them especially and fundamentally as to their belief that popular liberty can be permanently promoted in any old constitution by the destruction of what is called 'Aristocracy'. I hold the Aristocratic Element on [sic] a State to be vitally essential to all elevation of social thought and all durability of free institutions. I would infinitely prefer an Aristocratic Republic to a Democratic Monarchy. And connecting with this theory, whether erroneously or correctly, the peril of disaffecting or greatly impoverishing the party in the State that counterbalances the inevitable democracy engendered in manufacturing populations (I mean the Agricultural) I have ever been opposed to the total repeal of the Corn Laws.[51]

This was not a majority view in the 1850s, and some thought it alarmist and eccentric, but it had an inner coherence. The evolution of Lytton the Tory was based on something real.

The turmoils of the 1840s upset and rerouted lots of political careers. In this muddle, Lytton was not alone in finding it difficult to present an electorate with a clear image, or even to discover an appropriate political label to operate under. In 1841 he lost his seat at Lincoln because its 'addle-headed' electors wrongly concluded that, because he had voted to reduce duties on the importation of sugar, he was actually an opponent of the Corn Laws.[52] When he tried Lincoln again, in 1847, no one was clear where he stood. Lytton himself was far from sure. He told one friend that to ally with Tories rather than Liberals 'would be against my feelings of right'. He told another that he was 'not against either Tories or Radicals'. He thought of standing as a 'Liberal Protectionist', apparently unaware that many people would find that a contradiction in terms. It seemed to leave him 'half-Tory, half Protectionist'.[53] His electoral agent in Lincoln reported that his playing with party labels promoted a rumour that 'your Politics had changed, that you were no longer a reformer, but a conservative, and that you were brought down by a section of the liberal party for the purpose of injuring the liberal cause'.[54] Inevitably Lytton complained that these stories maligned him, but the electors of Lincoln had a point. Someone calling himself Radical or Liberal, but who yet defended the Corn Laws, was a strange beast. They had every right to be confused. With an ill grace, Lytton withdrew from the poll.[55]

To complicate matters even further, the events at Lincoln in 1847 revealed that Lytton still maintained a highly ambiguous relationship with the

Whigs, even after the Corn Laws had been repealed. On the one hand, he accused them of contributing to his humiliation at Lincoln by drafting in the brother of a Cabinet Minister, which had had the effect of splitting the anti-Tory vote to his disadvantage. The Whigs were guilty of 'an act of political discourtesy and ingratitude without parallel'.[56] On the other hand, within months of his defeat, Lytton was brazen or naive enough to ask a Whig Prime Minister either to find him another seat or to promote him to the House of Lords.[57] It did not seem to occur to him that his defence of the Corn Laws had made any association with the Whigs impossible. After 1846 Lytton had lost whatever anchorage he had ever had in Radicalism and was adrift. He had no clear political definition in the eyes of the electorate, or perhaps even in his own mind.

Much of 1847–52 was spent by Lytton looking for a new seat, all the while trailing ambiguities. The venality of the electors of Leominster revived what remained of his Radicalism. The town seemed to be 'in about the same state of civilisation as it was when Leofric Earl of Coventry first ruled over it'.[58] A few months later he was the aristocrat again, telling his old constituents at Lincoln that he would only consent to be their representative again if he could be elected in absentia, without trouble or expense. He absolutely refused to run the risk of being 'pelted'.[59] He was more compromising when considering the possibility of Marylebone. The constituency was so prestigious that he expressed real interest in becoming its Member, even though it was 'dear' and 'more democratic than I like'. To secure it, in 1847, he seemed to be prepared to stand on his head. Within one year of the Corn Laws being abolished, Lytton, their champion, denied their claims and much else:

> With regard to my poll opinions as agreeing with the Maryleboners, I can only refer to my past votes. I am for ballot and shorter Parliaments – the same as ever – for an encreased [sic] suffrage proportional to Education, not property. For encreased facilities to education, without making it compulsory. As for the Free Trade in Corn, this question is over, and I should certainly not sanction any attempt to disturb the experiment made. My attachment to liberal principles is as strong as in my youth – but I wish to be quite independent of compromise to *Men.* I have no love for Party whether Whigs or Radicals. *Voilà* tout that I can say on this head.[60]

Apart from the disavowal of party allegiance, nearly everything else in this manifesto flew in the face of his publications at the time and his private statements. Little wonder that few people were confident about his politics.

Within three years, 1846 to 1848, Lytton had asked the Whigs for a seat, publicly sided with the Tories on the Corn Laws, and presented the electors of Marylebone with a Radical programme. Lytton expressed a

distaste for party because none existed that suited his mood. He wanted
to be in politics but only on his own terms. In theory this ambiguity
ended in 1852, when he was elected as a Conservative for Hertfordshire, a
constituency he would represent for the next fourteen years. But, in fact,
the fuzziness about his principles was never entirely resolved. He kept in
touch with Lincoln, and described his Hertfordshire constituents as 'a
perfect Mob'.61 When the Conservatives briefly took office in 1852, Lytton
was not clear that he would automatically support them. It would all
depend on 'what Lord Derby does or intends to do'.62 Evidence such as
this counsels caution. Just as he had only been a Radical on his own
definition of Radicalism, so his Toryism was quaintly personal to himself.
Some Tory leaders, notably Derby, doubted that he was ever seriously to
be numbered among their following. In investigating Lytton's Toryism after
1852 one must remember that it was as distinctive as his dress or his voice
patterns.

Mordant comments on the futility of pursuing a political career are a
consistent theme in Lytton's novels and correspondence. They are often
interspersed with reveries about the attractions of withdrawing from public
life. But, after 1846–47, these remarks become more pronounced. After the
Corn Law disaster and his rebuff at Lincoln, Lytton claimed 'to loathe
politics – it is associated in my mind with the most bitter feelings. I am
much out of my sphere in this. I have met with what I call gross ingratitude
from the leaders and the people.' Leaving 'the filthy career in public life',
he determined 'to shut myself in my shell'.63 Talk of retirement became
more and more convincing in letters to friends. Winning elections gave
him less and less pleasure because, having won, 'the worst part is now to
begin viz. the House of Commons'.64 He was sure that friendship was more
important than politics. In 1851, he assured Forster that their diverging views
on the Corn Laws and much else in no way threatened their regard for
each other. For him politics was 'but one (tho' large) element in human
thought and human happiness – and this is natural to me who has had to
divide thought among so many topics. Therefore, let us differ ever so much
here, it cannot shake my really brotherly love for you.' 65 The urgency which
had taken Lytton as a young man into politics, as an arena in which the
artist could influence events, had disappeared.
    This reassessment of values is worked out in a long poem on politics
called *St Stephen's*, published in 1860. The statesmen of Lytton's generation
are passed in review and judged. Whig, Tory and Radical are described
as aspects of human frailty. Bitterness and resignation compete in the
delineation of a politician's life:

> Few, who at ease their Members' speeches read,
> Guess the hard life of members who succeed;
> Pass by the waste of youthful golden days,
> And the dread failure of the first essays –
> Grant that the earlier sleeps and sloughs are past,
> And Fame's broad highway stretches smooth at last;
> Grant the success, and behold the pains:
> Eleven to three – Committee upon drains!
> From three to five – self-commune and a chop;
> From five to dawn, a bill to pass or stop;
> Which, stopt or pass'd, leaves England much the same,
> Alas for genius staked in such a game! [66]

With every year that passed after 1847 Lytton was more and more torn between wanting a role in politics and hating the duties and pretensions that went with it.

After 1852, however, he could not escape the fact that he was a Conservative, even if he described himself as having been 'driven by circumstance into Lord Stanley's party'.[67] Continuing concern for the reimposition of the Corn Laws in some form left him no other choice. But his language on joining the Tories was neither jubilant nor enthusiastic. Interestingly, Gladstone chose the same verb as Lytton to describe Lytton's change of politics. Protectionism 'drove him to the Tories'.[68] In talking about his new allies, Lytton sometimes uses inclusive words like 'my' and 'our'. Just as often, he employs terms that suggest a greater emotional distance. Equally telling was the fact that he had few friends among the Tory leadership. He and Derby eyed each other with mutual suspicion, and Lytton had teased his new leader joyfully:

> Nor gout, nor toil, his freshness can destroy,
> And Time still leaves all Eton in the boy.[69]

Even his old friendship with Disraeli was sorely tested in real politics. In 1851 Lytton complained that he was 'vexed to see that Disraeli is leading the Protectionists all askew'. His renowned Budget of 1852 was nothing but a 'snake-cloud'. Lytton doubted if a Tory party led by his old friend 'could long command the confidence of the Country'. Indeed, in 1868, he was convinced that the only hope for the Tories was to find themselves a new leader.[70] If his long association with Disraeli could not bind him more tightly to Conservatism nothing else would. He fought under the Tory banner but his politics remained Lyttonite.

Not surprisingly, Lytton often broke ranks in parliamentary divisions and rather gloried in the fact. On issues big and small, he claimed the right to an independent opinion. In particular, he was at odds with the Tories for almost three years on the great challenge of the Crimean War. First and foremost, in his view, a war 'in the Dismal Swamp' of the Crimea should have been avoided. Its outbreak represented a level of diplomatic failure that deserved the severest criticism:

> As to the War – Now it is begun, I think we cannot draw back without dishonour and worse danger from France than Russia. But where it may end – and what it will produce Heaven knows. If the least diplomacy had been managed by every straightforward plain manly intellect, I cannot conceive that the war would ever have occurred.[71]

The descent into miserable conflict was Palmerston's fault. He had 'embroiled and bedevilled us with all powers'. Lytton was furious that, instead of being brought to book, Palmerston was treated like 'Mama England's spoilt child'. As a result, 'smash goes the crockery'.[72]

An unnecessary war was then being fought, according to Lytton, with a degree of incompetence that was almost criminal. He felt this point deeply. His speeches on the Crimean War are among the best he ever made, being full of informed argument. He was fearless in condemning the declaration of war, 'in the utter ignorance of the power and resources of the enemy you were to encounter, the nature of the climate you were to brave, of the country you were to enter, of the supplies your army would need'.[73] By June 1855 he was taking a lead in calling for an enquiry into the whole fiasco. The conduct of the war had been so inept that it was suggesting to public opinion a degree of rottenness at the heart of government that could only be cured by radical change. There was 'a danger to the fundamental principles of representative government'. To stave off further upheaval, government had to admit its mistakes and do better. The matter was urgent.[74] This speech put the Whig-led administration under such pressure that it agreed to adopt the wording of Lytton's resolution on the war as its own. It argued

> the necessity of a careful revision of our various Official Establishments with a view to simplify and facilitate the transaction of public business, and, by instituting judicious tests of merit, as well as by removing obstructions to its fair promotion and legitimate rewards, to secure to the service of the State the largest available proportion of the energy and intelligence for which the people of this Country are distinguished.[75]

If linguistic concessions of this kind were intended to silence Lytton they singularly failed in their purpose. He kept up his criticisms throughout the war and re-established himself as a public figure by doing so. Even with peace in sight, ministers continued to be punished in debate: 'Not a step do you take, not a conception do you originate, not a strategy prepare until you are overwhelmed by the logical consequences of your own improvidence.'[76] Predictably, government supporters tried to dismiss Lytton's remarks as 'a tissue of foul abuse with the grossest and most wilful misrepresentations',[77] but their attacks on him were a backhanded compliment to the success of his campaign. His relentless exposure of the diplomatic failures that had led to war, and the bungling that had characterised its prosecution, revived his claims to be taken seriously as a politician. His speeches on these issues would be referred to appreciatively when he was offered a Cabinet post two years later.

Lytton's protestations were the more convincing in that he never had any doubt that the purpose of the war was correct. Russia had to be stopped from dismembering the Turkish Empire. Its ruler Nicholas I was 'the author of great calamities to the human race', while Russia itself was a power that 'threatens all that is dear to civilisation and freedom'.[78] At the very least, the Black Sea had to be demilitarised to prevent the Russians gaining access to the Mediterranean. In this sense, the conflict was 'a war waged on behalf of posterity' to 'preserve Europe from the outlet of barbarian tribes'.[79] The longer the crisis lasted, the more consolation Lytton took in the fact that Russia was being disproportionately weakened. Every battle and engagement 'consumes her vitals'.[80] Lytton wanted no peace until Russia had been thoroughly muzzled and had no sympathy for peacemakers like 'that little beast Lord John Russell'. Mercifully, England seemed to be 'warlike to the backbone'.[81] Lytton therefore believed the war to be just and purposeful. But the same ends could have been achieved by capable diplomats without war at all; equally, the conflict, when it came, had been mismanaged on a heroic scale. It was a set of views that had resonance with opinion outside Westminster. His assessments were not peculiar to him but they were distinctive. The Crimean War rehabilitated him as a public figure.

These opinions, however, in no way endeared him to the Tory leadership. The Conservatives were widely believed to have ducked the issue of war against Russia in 1852–53. As a result, as Disraeli sharply lectured his friend, they had to be a peace party, arguing that the war was unnecessary:

> There appears to me in your views of the subject ... the omission of an important element in forming an opinion as to the practical conduct of a political party. You are apt to forget ... that you are an eminent member of a great party which has shrunk, or which at any rate is believed by the country to have shrunk, from the responsibility of conducting the war. One might be inclined to believe that a party in this pitiable position, were bound to prepare the public mood for a statesmanlike peace. I do not very clearly comprehend how a war ministry and a war opposition can coexist.[82]

Lytton could not agree. The country was properly bellicose. What the Tories had to do was to prove that they could fight the war better. It was madness to leave Palmerston with a 'monopoly of the War Cry'. He was horrified to hear rumours that Disraeli and Stanley might be thinking of joining Gladstone and Bright in a peace initiative. Lytton's feelings on the subject were 'of the strongest'. So much so, in fact, that he threatened to abandon the Tories, although he had only just joined them: 'I should be sorry to find myself splitting from Dis, and any of the Conservative leaders ... But England and England's honour are my first thought.'[83] On the first great test of party loyalty after his re-entry into the Commons Lytton had refused to toe the line.

Nor was he entirely in step on the other great issue of the 1850s and 1860s, namely a further extension of the franchise. For a party which had been out of majority government since 1846, changing the composition of the electorate or redistributing seats had to be a matter of interest to the Tories. Some would argue that to continue to be a party narrowly associated with agriculture was to invite extinction. An accommodation with industrialisation had to be made. Others believed that the predicament the Tories found themselves in was so grim that they had quite literally nothing to lose by changing the rules. Neither argument appealed to Lytton. In his view, the values of industrial England were anathema. Equally, to change constitutional procedures merely on the off-chance of securing party advantage was irresponsible. Therefore, as the Tories squared up to the challenge of another Reform Bill, it was unlikely that their association with Lytton would be an easy one.

On a superficial reading, Tory leaders like Disraeli might have hoped that Lytton could be persuaded to move on the issue. He had supported the Reform Bill of 1832 enthusiastically. He had also seemed to take the point that one Reform Bill might lead to another:

> The moment you widen the suffrage, you may date the commencement of universal suffrage. He who enjoys certain advantages from the possessions of ten acres, will excite a party against him in those who have nine; and the arguments that had been used for the franchise of the one are equally valid for the franchise of the other. Limitations of power by property are barriers against a tide which perpetually advances.[84]

But ominously, as early as 1833, in *Godolphin*, he was able to expound the anti-reform case with conviction, through the mouth of one of his characters:

> I am for *popular* governments, though I like *free* states. All the advantages of democracy seem to me more than counterbalanced by the sacrifice of the peace

and tranquillity, the comfort and the grace, the dignity and the charities of life
that democracies usually entail. If the object of life is to live happily – not strive
and to fret – not to make money in the market-place, and call each other rogues
on the hustings, who would not rather be a German than an American? [85]

Playful restatements of the joys of aristocratic government such as these
gave the clue to Lytton's real instincts, even in his Radical days.

By 1846 he had convinced himself that the limits of constitutional change
had been reached, and, eleven years later, that a great disaster threatened:
'New colonies alone can deal safely with Democracy. But if we are to have
a Democratic suffrage here – it gives power to the party least national –
Manchester is not patriotic, and I shall look upon the fate of England as
sealed.' [86] Gladstone was 'unsafe' on the issue. As for the Tories, their attempts
to come to terms with working people were futile. He doubted if a new
newspaper directed at such an audience would succeed. In 1860 he was
publicly embroiled in a controversy about whether he had or had not called
English labourers 'boors'.[87] In short, his thinking on the question of reform
had hardened.

When Tory governments brought forward Reform Bills, in 1859 and 1867,
Lytton's support for them was firmly conditional. He could see that a
redistribution of seats would be done more effectively by Tories rather than
by Liberals. But the franchise was another matter. He never allowed that
men should vote as of right. That was the French model, and he had
witnessed its baleful effects in 1848–49. Rather, any extension of the suffrage
should be on the same principles as those of 1832. Property and education
were absolute prerequisites for making political choice. Universal education
must precede universal suffrage. The object of any change should be 'to
widen the franchise the middle class now enjoys', but only to turn artisans
into middle-class people. On this basis he hailed the 1859 Bill as 'emphatically
a Bill for the middle class'.[88] On these terms he was a reformer.[89] On any
others he was not. The granting of household suffrage, in 1867, was a step
too far. It would 'disembowel' the Tory party: 'What is to become of the
poor Conservative Party I don't know. I could never defend the Bill or
their management of it in Parliament. But don't say that.' [90] Since he had
been elevated to the Lords a year earlier he could hide his dissent, but his
loathing of the measure was real. Household suffrage cut the links between
property and the franchise in a manner that would inevitably lead to full
democracy. Lytton's feeling of separation from Disraeli and the Tories was
once again linguistically expressed. It was 'their' Bill, not his.

Lytton's Conservatism, like his Radicalism, was peculiar to himself. He was
no friend of Derby and was suspicious of Disraeli. He had no sympathy

with the idea of changing tack to meet the wishes of a changing electorate. His values were always agrarian, hierarchical and bound by aristocratic instincts. He wanted a Radicalism led by the Earl of Durham and a Toryism preserved by an Earl of Derby. He feared giving the broad mass of the population the upper hand. French and American models were not inviting. He talked of Conservatism less as a movement to win votes and elections than as a philosophy:

> All that Conservatism regards is duration for the body politic. It is not averse to change – change may be healthful; but it is averse to that kind of change which tends to disorganisation. Whatever there be most precious to the vitality of any particular State, becomes its jealous core. As but one thing is more precious to a State than liberty (social order) so where liberty is established, Conservatism is its stubborn guardian, and never yields the possession, save for that which it is more essential to conserve ... And if it seems at times opposed to the extension of freedom, it is not on the ground of extension, but from the fear that freedom may be risked or lost altogether by an incautious transfer of the trust.[91]

This is the language of the study, not the hustings. Canvassing and speech-making were not to his taste. Lytton was never really a practising politician at all. When, as will be seen, he briefly entered the world of real government, it led to attacks of the vapours. He was more seer than statesman.

11

Cabinet Minister

For almost a year, in 1858–59, Lytton found himself at the heart of government. In the administration led by Derby and Disraeli he was invited to
look after the British Empire, as Secretary of State for the Colonies. The
appointment surprised everyone, including Lytton himself. Many people
rightly suspected that the challenge would starkly underline his virtues
and limitations, and their prophecy was quickly justified. He worked with
diligence and dedication. His period in office was notable for the number
of imaginative decisions that were implemented. On the other hand, Lytton
found the pressure of work overwhelming, and, as usual, his skin was not
thick enough to deflect criticism. Within seven months of joining the
government he was asking to resign. It was bad luck that Rosina should
have been at her most energetic during these months, but, even without
her assistance, it is unlikely that he could long have withstood the heat of
office. Temperamentally Lytton was unsuited to high political office. A
hundred years earlier, in the closed aristocratic world of the eighteenth
century, things might have been different. But he was lost in a world of
Chartists, journalists and the pressing claims of democracy.

Shortly before accepting a place in government, Lytton assured a visitor
to Knebworth that he had lost all taste for public life. 'I do not care for
such things now; I have no political ambition; all I ask is rest.'[1] After a few
months in post, he told another visitor that his life was miserable; 'But,
well a day, my life has passed out of all holidays – all glimpses of Fairyland.
I feel as if the Colonial Empire would go smash if I were out of reach of
the mails and messengers two days together ... there is more to pity than
to envy in place and power.'[2] The offer of office was only accepted with
reluctance and a kind of pantomime coyness. It was first made by Lord
Derby in February 1858. Derby had doubts about Lytton's personality but
had been much impressed by his campaigning on the issue of the Crimean
War. In any case, the Conservative government he now led was noticeably
short of talent. Lytton's temperament was questionable, but no one doubted
his intelligence or distinction.

Lytton agreed to accept the post, then changed his mind a few days later.
He agreed with John Forster that to exchange literature for politics would

be a mistake. It was literature after all which had brought out his 'greater qualities', and had made his 'name familiar and honoured all over the world'.[3] There was also the additional problem that what Lytton really wanted out of politics was not office but a peerage. When he made this a condition of his accepting the Colonial Office, Derby was simply exasperated. Angrily, he wrote to Disraeli about Lytton's demands:

> Another hitch! Lytton informed Joliffe, at 11 o'clock last night, that he could not face his County election! The fact is, he wants to be made a Peer – which I will not do for him. *If* he is to be of *any* use, it must be in the H. of C. They parted on angry terms ... call on your refractory friend, and get him straight again. I must have his answer *at once*, Aye or No: and I think it would not be amiss to hint to him that we are not without resources.[4]

Henry Bulwer was called in to remind his brother that peerages had to be earned 'by doing well'. Lytton refused to be cajoled or persuaded and declined Derby's offer. His prevarication plunged the relationship between the two men into a pit of distrust.[5]

A Cabinet reshuffle, in May 1858, led Derby to renew the offer of the Colonies. This time Lytton accepted without hesitation. Disraeli welcomed his decision by asserting that it brought into government 'a name of European celebrity'. Lytton returned the compliment by saying that he wished only to stand shoulder to shoulder with his old friend: 'Believe me sincere from the bottom of my heart when I add that in accepting office I have no sensation so pleasurable as that of sharing in any difficulties that may beset you; and in the easier opportunities, so afforded, of removing any misconceptions which may yet leave a shadow over the affectionate friendship which I intend to carry with me to the grave.'[6] Courageously, Lytton offered himself for re-election in Hertfordshire, a requirement at the time for those taking office. The price to be paid for his boldness was the gross embarrassment of Rosina's most intense campaign against him. As a result, he began his official duties in a state of nervous prostration. Rosina gleefully reported that he 'was as mad as Bedlam'.[7] No ministerial career opened under worse auspices.

Even so, Lytton immediately set out to prove to himself and to a wider public that he was of the calibre. Throwing himself into work, he tried hard to master his brief, wishing all the while that he 'could feel less strange as to the simplest question in the Colonies'.[8] His feverish activity was a nightmare for his subordinates. In his haste, Lytton was not above putting letters in the wrong envelopes, or mixing confidential documents with run-of-the-mill state papers. One of his clerks called him 'insolent, wild and reckless'.[9] If such criticism is justified, it was the result of a man trying to do too much rather than too little. There was the added tension of having to appear and speak more frequently in the House of Commons. The old terrors about debating had not gone away, and each performance was carried off at a terrible cost. Friends reminded him that a Colonial Secretary 'should have a constitution of iron'. After eleven months of unremitting activity, they feared that he was 'if not deranged, so much overworked as to be quite *hors de combat*'.[10] Lytton tried to do well but seemed to lack the capacity to pace himself.

By December 1858 Lytton wanted to resign. He had convinced himself that his health was deteriorating to the point of collapse. He complained of 'the wear and tear' of office-holding and feared that he might 'suddenly give way'. When Disraeli unsympathetically suggested that he took too much notice of doctors, Lytton was not pleased:

> I have studied pathology eno' to know how this must end if it cannot be set right; it ends but in three ways. Firstly consumption, to which I have so far a tendency that one lung is affected, and for the last three years I have been compelled to take great precautions during the Winter; secondly organic heart disease most probably inducing rapid termination by dropsy. Thirdly and most dreadful and in case of nervous excitement perhaps the most probable of all – sudden paralysis.[11]

As a self-diagnosed compendium of disease, he thought himself too weak even to write his own letter of resignation. He asked Forster to draft something suitable.[12]

When Derby received the letter of resignation his reaction was less than sympathetic. Calling it 'Lytton's curiously pathological epistle', he sent a copy to Disraeli, adding that he was 'inclined to think that he is seriously worried about his health ... I have another letter from him in which he tells me he is going to Malvern to try hydrotherapy, from which he has before derived benefit (he will probably kill himself).'[13] He begged Disraeli to persuade Lytton to stay on until April 1859, as a favour to government, and this request was granted. He therefore served for eleven months when his own inclination was to leave after six. Disraeli, like Derby, had run out of patience. He thought Lytton's decision to leave office was 'suicidal'. Sarcastically, he observed that his friend's real reason for retreating to Knebworth was to see 'the trees bowing to their Lord'. With an even heavier humour, he told Lytton that, if he did indeed die in office, he would give him a public funeral.[14] It was an inglorious departure.

In the event, Lytton stayed on until April 1859 in order to prevent a government crisis. He loathed every minute of it. He complained to Disraeli that 'complete repose with change of scene and thought' offered him 'the only chance of preserving life itself'.[15] Every extra hour spent in government was described in terms of the greatest self-sacrifice. The moment that his resignation became effective he fled to the German spa of Wildbad, vowing never again to enter public life:

> As to my health, it continues very weak and variable. I never intend to take office with Lord Derby again. My present interest and ambition in politics are gone. Of course, I feel for the country, but it will probably be long before I am well enough to take any active part ... I am disenchanted in all ways with politics, public and private.[16]

To Derby, and, to some extent Disraeli, Lytton's behaviour was hard to bear. The prima donna seemed to have conquered the statesman. They were even more shocked when Lytton proved to be so unconscious of the impression he had made that he renewed his request for a peerage.[17] This second application was turned down even more firmly than the first.

Lytton's ministerial career, like everything else about him, was distinctive. It was short and stormy. It embroiled him in arguments with friends and with men he barely knew. He was too conscientious, overworking and not delegating enough. The old fear of public ridicule followed him into the House of Commons, and the shadow of Rosina followed him everywhere. A real or imagined breakdown in health was the result. Lytton simply could not cope with the rough and tumble of politics. Public life involved other people evaluating his talents and worth, and sometimes those judgements fell short of his own. Altogether, it was a miserable experience. It was all the more astonishing therefore that, in terms of objectives achieved, his time as Colonial Secretary should have been so completely successful.

In imperial debates Lytton had always shown an energy and interest that was sometimes lacking in other areas. How an empire should be run, or indeed whether it was wise to have an empire at all, were questions which preoccupied Lytton's generation, and never more so than in the wake of the Indian Mutiny in 1857–58. These were debates to which Lytton was happy to make a contribution and, in public, his views on the subject read as follows: 'I say that our colonies repay England not in hard money alone, not, if you please to say so, in hard money at all, but by the rank and dignity, by the moral power, by the weight in Europe, which are due to a sceptre that casts over earth a shadow so vast and so tranquil.' [18] But patriotic remarks were usually followed by important qualifications that substantially modified his views. A more rounded description of his position on Empire was set out in a speech to his constituents at Lincoln in 1838:

> England is essentially a colonizing country – long may she be so! – to colonize

is to civilise. Be not led away by vague declamations on the expense and inutility of colonies. When you are told to give up your dependent possessions – consider first whether you wish this island, meagre in its population, sterile in its soil, limited in its extent, to hold a first rate empire, or to constitute a third rate nation ... But would I maintain a colony by force of arms when that colony desires to be free, *and can support itself*? No! [19]

Lytton saw the imperial purpose in moral rather than economic terms. The historian of Athens and her empire found it easy to see colonization as a civilising process bounded by clear ethical assumptions. It followed, as the Lincoln speech suggested, that empire could not stand on force. When a colonial people fairly felt themselves ready for independence, their request should be granted. Bringing them to that sense of moral and political self-sufficiency was a vital aspect of the whole venture. Lytton was therefore an imperialist, but only on certain conditions. In 1857–58 for example, just before taking up the post of Colonial Secretary, he expressed grave doubts about the British government taking over the whole administration of India from the East India Company. He agreed that the recent mutiny had shown 'misrule' in the subcontinent, but he disliked the idea of London becoming more intimately involved. Without doubt greater regulation of the affairs of India was urgently needed, but formal empire threatened that country with 'favouritism and jobbery'.[20] This caution about enlarging Britain's colonial responsibilities would follow him into office. It was ironical that his own son would become Viceroy of India. A character in *My Novel* could refer to 'the empire on which the sun never sets. Poor Sun, how tired he must be – but not more tired than the Government.'[21]

These nuanced views brought him into collision with politicians who advanced straightforward expansionism. In 1857 he took Palmerston to task for bullying the Chinese, suspecting him of hoping to establish yet more colonies: 'In dealing with nations less civilised than ourselves, it is by lofty truth and forbearing humanity that the genius of commerce contrasts the ambition of conquerors.' He doubted 'the ultimate success or benefit' of a forward policy in China.[22] In his view, a severe pragmatism had to govern colonial policy. New colonies should not be established unless the consequences were clear and beneficial. As Colonial Secretary, he had grave doubts about Sarawak on this score: 'If England takes as a colony a corner of that great island, we may regard as inevitable in the course of time the encroachment of the more civilised settlers on the possessions of the less civilised natives. India again on a smaller scale!'[23] It was no coincidence that, within months of taking office, Lytton had asked for a balance sheet to be drawn up on all existing colonies. Profit and loss, moral, financial and strategic, would be set out. It would for example answer the question,

'What does the Gold Coast really cost us?' 24 Lytton was no unthinking patriot on imperial matters. His approach was half that of the accountant, half that of the moral philosopher.

Perhaps his views were best set out in a letter sent to Sir George Bowen, who had been appointed the first Governor of the new colony called Queensland. It is a sustained argument for the management of empire on certain terms:

> There is much to learn before hand for your guidance in this new colony. The most anxious and difficult question connected with it will be the squatters. But in this, which is a conflict between rival interests you will wisely abstain as much as possible from interference – avoid taking part with one or other – ever be willing to lend aid to conciliating settlement, but to secure that end you must be strictly impartial. Remember that the great care of a governor in a free colony is to shun the reproach of being a party man. Give all parties and all the ministries formed the fairest play.
>
>   Let your thoughts never be distracted from the paramount object of finance. All states thrive in proportion to the Administration of the Revenue.
>
>   You will as soon as possible exert all energy and persuasion to induce the colonists to see to their self-defence internally – try to establish a good police if you can, then get the superior class of Colonists to assist in forming a Militia or Volunteer Corps – spare no powers to do so ...
>
>   Education the Colonists will be sure to provide for – so they will for religion. Do your best to keep up the pride in the mother country. Throughout Australia there is a sympathy with the ideal of a gentleman – this gives a moral aristocracy – continue it by shewing the store set on integrity honour and civilised manners ... the more you treat people as gentlemen, the more they will behave as such. After all men are governed as much by the heart as by the head. Evident sympathy in the progress of the Colony – traits of kindness and generosity – devoted energy where required for the public weal, a pure exercise in patronage, an utter absence of vindictiveness or spite, the fairness that belongs to magnanimity are the qualities that make governors powerful ... courtesy is a duty Public Servants owe to the humblest member of the Public.25

A catechism that mixes prudence in financial matters with injunctions to foster aristocratic virtues precisely mirrors Lytton's priorities. Classical models were probably more influential on his thinking than the nineteenth-century emphasis on racial destiny or economic power.

On assuming office Lytton confronted and dealt with three pressing problems. As it happened, they were all concerned with the future of colonies of white settlement: Australia, Canada and the Ionian Islands. Unfortunately there is simply not enough evidence to decide whether Lytton would have offered the same prescription of self-reliance and aristocratic virtue to black or brown populations. In the climate of thought pervading mid-Victorian England it is unlikely, though his doubts about English involvement in India are of note. Logically there was no reason why non-white peoples should not eventually be trained up to meet the levels of self-awareness that he required.

In Australia the separation of the Moreton Bay Colony from New South Wales, under the name of Queensland, was supervised by the new Colonial Secretary. He appointed Bowen as its first Governor. Brisbane was originally to have been called Lytton, and, although that project failed, a new township called Knebworth was established. Lytton relished his popularity in the new colony, and, significantly, employed the Greek word 'Oikist' or 'colony-founder' to describe his role. London and ancient Athens were associated in his mind. He told Bowen that, 'It is indeed a grand thing to have been the Oikist, the founder of the social state of so mighty a segment of the globe as Queensland'.[26] In surveying his handiwork, he was moved to prophesy about a future world order, which was more than fulfilled in 1914 and 1939:

> The time will come when these new Colonies will be great States; when they will find it easier to raise fleets and armies than they now find it to raise a police ... It may so happen that in that distant day England may be in danger, that the great despotic and military powers of Europe may then rise up against the vulnerable mother of many free Commonwealths. If that day should ever arrive I believe that her children will not be unmindful of her, and that to her rescue, across the wide ocean, ships will come thick and fast, among which there will be one cry, 'While Australia lasts, England shall not perish.'[27]

As with Australia, so with Canada did he apply the principle that a colony should become self-regulating as soon as possible. As early as 1838 he had congratulated government on responding to Canadian representations not with troops but with sensible, constitutional adjustments. He told the Commons that he looked forward to the day when they had 'educated the Canadas to that safe and gradual independence which should be the last and crowning boon that a colony should receive from a parent state'.[28] He was clear that it was unwise 'to lecture any free Colony'.[29] In dealing with the Canadian crisis that unexpectedly blew up, he therefore tried to find solutions which the Canadians themselves would suggest or see as acceptable. In old age the memory of the success of his approach gave him much pleasure:

> When I came in I found the question in that state that any declaration of opinion one way or the other by the Home Government would do great mischief – and set the different provinces by the ear. I said it was a question in which the

provinces should judge for themselves – that the interest of England was to see them strong and contented in the way that pleased themselves best. My career gave unusual satisfaction.[30]

The crisis in question was provoked by the discovery of gold in the far west of Canada in 1856. Thousands of people poured into an area with only rudimentary administrative structures. Lytton was firm about 'the necessity of providing at once for the government of a country threatened by so many disturbing elements'.[31] He approached the problem clearheadedly, following certain imperial principles. First, he was unusually sensitive to the claims of indigenous peoples. He told the Commons that, whatever was done with British Columbia, the native Indians had to be protected 'from terrible demoralisation'.[32] This was not a new concern. One of the reasons he had given for arguing that the management of Indian affairs should be left to the East India Company was that it understood Hindu and Muslim culture better than any London-based government. By contrast, he accused the Hudson's Bay Company of putting profit before any consideration of the interests of the Indians. He allowed that they had trading rights in the west of Canada but refused to allow them the privileges of government. Claims of that kind were 'a mere usurpation'.[33]

Lytton's solution to the problem was to create the colony of British Columbia, with a governor appointed by London who was to act as an umpire among the competing interests of Indians, prospectors and the employees of the Hudson's Bay Company. This was, however, only an interim measure, to run for five years. He retained the conviction that 'all healthful colonies should be self-supporting'. The hope was that, as soon as the new settlers had had time to think out their future, self-government should follow. By 1862 or 1863, the assumption was that London would be seen 'yielding sway at the earliest possible period to those free institutions'.[34] Above all, everything that was done should be done with a sense of civilising mission in mind. A boatload of Royal Engineers, about to embark for Canada, must have been bemused to hear certain parts of a farewell speech that Lytton made to them:

> You will carefully refrain from quarrel or brawl. You will scorn, I am sure, the vice that degrades God's rational creature to the level of the brute – I mean the vice of intoxication. I am told that this is the vice which most tempts common soldiers. I hope not – but I am sure it is the vice which least tempts thoughtful, intelligent, successful men. You are not common soldiers – you are to be the Pioneers of Civilisation.[35]

He offered them books from his own library for entertainment on the long voyage. Headmasterly speeches, drawing heavily on classical models of empire as a civilising force, should not be treated with cynicism. Lytton meant every word. His was an empire of moral purpose as much as economic advantage.

The third pressing problem concerned the British Protectorate of the Ionian Islands. Here insensitive behaviour on the part of a governor, Sir John Young, had led to the formation of a party within the islands which called for their unification with Greece. Once again, Lytton's priority was to respond to local opinion. He determined to send out a commission of enquiry, which, while not criticising Young openly, would sound the views of the islanders and come up with appropriate recommendations.[36] It was a stroke of genius to persuade William Gladstone to go out to the islands as head of the commission. A classical scholar of note, he shared Lytton's reverence for Greece. Like Lytton too, Gladstone brought to imperial questions a moral dimension that not everyone in politics shared. It was a strange and singular pairing. There was so much in Lytton's private life and public views of which Gladstone would disapprove. But in talking of the purpose of empire, particularly in relation to Greek-speaking peoples, the two men stood on a narrow strip of common ground.

Without tying Gladstone's hands unduly, Lytton set the parameters for his thinking. First, any proposal to give the islands to Greece would provoke a great deal of trouble. It could not be done without consulting the views of Russia and Turkey at least, probably within the forum of a specially convened conference. There was the further problem that 'neither the English Public nor the English Parliament like a policy that "gives up"'. More importantly, Lytton found it hard to believe that some association could not be found between a nation which had invented liberty and one which was, by empire, in the process of disseminating its benefits around the world. It simply could not be 'a hopeless task to link the safety and prosperity of a race, that boasts descent from the parents of civilised liberty, with the might and intellect of a nation, that has planted civilised liberty among new communities'.[37] Even so, nothing could be done without the consent of the Ionian Assembly. The wishes of the islanders were paramount.

As a starting point, Lytton suggested to Gladstone that some significant readjustment of existing arrangements might be the answer: 'I would desire first to see whether our present protectorate could not be made congenial to the feelings and in harmony with the genuine liberties of the islanders.'[38] If not, perhaps some form of home rule could be devised which gave wide powers to an elected legislature. Whatever scheme was proposed, however, there was to be 'nothing sham on the side of liberty'. The only caveat that Lytton entered was that any new electorate should reflect propertied rather than democratic values. He told Gladstone that:

Even England is not yet for a universal, or manhood suffrage. Even France has shewn that with such a suffrage, liberty is a shuttlecock. Of all class legislation, none I believe to be so adverse to solid liberty and rational progress, as that in which the neediest class, however large, overbear the others ... If the Constitution be in any way altered or redrafted I should be certainly glad if the aristocratic element could have whatever healthful and legitimate influence may be afforded to it by the hearts of the People. I believe that nothing has saved England from mob leaders, than the large share in political life, which is taken by persons of property, birth and refined education.[39]

Preferably, the Ionian Islanders should in fact adopt England itself as a model for constitutional development.

In the event, Gladstone was hugely successful. He produced a scheme which allowed the islanders a large measure of self-regulation through an elected assembly. Demands to join Greece faded away, and a potentially disruptive issue in European diplomacy was put to rest. Lytton was full of congratulations for Gladstone's work:

I don't know what the Assembly has done or may do – I know that we have succeeded. We have vindicated the Honor [sic] of England in the eyes of all free nations. I know that I have now the right to say to Despotic Sovereigns, 'what we have preached to you we have practised ourselves' ... you have made immense sacrifices for a noble object – you will stand higher in England than ever.[40]

He never became Gladstone's friend. Political differences ensured that they remained 'mere acquaintances'.[41] But there was always a sense of indebtedness and appreciation. At times in the 1860s, Lytton flatly refused to join his Tory colleagues in attacking Gladstone's policies because he liked the man 'so much'.[42]

All this euphoria was somewhat dampened, however, when Lytton paid a visit to the islands in October 1860. Instead of meeting the descendants of Pericles and Socrates, he found people living in towns and villages that were 'wretched, like a wild village near Naples with a mixture of the back slums of Portsmouth'. Shortly after, he gave up the chore of learning modern Greek as 'too arduous'.[43] Even so, a happy resolution of the difficulties in the Ionian Islands, set alongside successful policies in Canada and Australia, marked Lytton's period of office as one of distinction. The cost to his own sense of well-being was considerable but he had also won a certain eminence.

This success, however, brought with it one bizarre consequence. In the spring of 1863, while Lytton was once again nursing his health on the French Riviera, he was approached by a group of Greek exiles and asked to become their king. To be offered a throne, even in this very unofficial way, could not fail to excite his vanity. He immediately asked Forster to make enquiries and to determine 'whether you think there is any substantial chance of the option being freely ... before me, or whether the whole thing is a dream'.[44] He was flattered enough to start debating the pros and cons of acceptance in his own mind. On the one hand, a king could do great things: 'I have reason to believe that if I cared for and tried for it I could be elected to the Kingdom of Greece. And, certes, if I were and if I took it, I should defy "the great Powers" to turn me out. And I would if I served ten years, make Greece a very important state.' On the other hand, all this would take time, money and a lot of effort: 'A country without roads, without revenues, over head and ears in debt, an unhealthy capital subject to fevers, a language one could never learn to speak, a horrible travesty of a free constitution; with subjects profoundly orientalised, corruption universal – all this looks dismal beside the calm Academe of Knebworth.'[45]

Predictably the plan came to nothing. There had never been the slightest chance that the European powers would have accepted an Englishman on the throne of Greece. Equally someone who had found eleven months in the Colonial Office a purgatory was unlikely to find the larger problem of running Greece very congenial. But this comic episode is evidence both that Lytton's work had been recognised as important, and that his perennial lack of self-awareness could lead him to think that he was a serious candidate for a throne. He seemed unmoved by the fact that some Greeks had turned to him only after Lord Derby and Gladstone had turned down a similar offer.

Lytton's short period in office proved that he could be a very effective administrator. Clear about his objectives, he was also hard-working and keen to master his brief. He knew the detail of great issues involving Canada and Australia, and he was equally expert in smaller matters concerning Ceylon or Mauritius. Unfortunately, he never developed comparable political skills. He was an excellent administrator but a badly flawed politician. His success in office lay in conversations with officials within his department, and in the scrutiny of memoranda. By contrast, his public presentation of policy was halting and unsure. Inevitably, the exercise of power revealed the strengths and deficiencies of the man.

On the debit side, Lytton never felt comfortable in Cabinet or Parliament. He never made any mark in the former, complaining that decisions were apparently 'the exclusive appanage of two or three of my colleagues'.[46] Part of the difficulty lay in the fact that he never established any real rapport with Lord Derby, the head of government. He was happy to admit that his leader was 'the *cleverest* public man I ever met', but that 'his mind is more critical than inventive, and thus he is more formidable in opposition than

in office. His favourite companions are not literary men. He is not at ease
with them ... I have never been very intimate with him, perhaps because
we are both proud and both somewhat shy. But I like him well and admire
him extremely.'[47] Derby, for his part, never understood or sympathised
with Lytton's affectations, which seemed to him more the mark of a prima
donna than a politician. Meetings between the two men in Cabinet were
therefore difficult.

Nor was Parliament any more congenial. All the old fears about debating
were rehearsed. As a Minister of the Crown, Lytton was forced to perform
in the House of Commons on a regular basis, but he spoke as little as
possible, and then in paragraphs rather than full speeches. Major expositions
of colonial policy were extremely infrequent. A short explanation of why
the government had refused to extend the frontiers of Cape Colony in
South Africa would be followed by an equally short account of the collection
of guano in the Kooria Mooria Islands. In addition, voice and gesture were
still not under control. A Liberal opponent admitted that he could at times
be 'very brilliant', but that this was unusual. More often, his parliamentary
appearances were unfortunate:

> Bulwer Lytton made a stilted, pompous, seriocomic and prolix reply. He has
> everything to learn in the art of answering questions in Parliament. Disraeli's
> face it was painful to behold. Lord Stanley smiled, but smiled as though it was
> no smiling matter. The worst is that Bulwer Lytton, being deaf, was not aware
> that the House was at length fairly bored with a general buzz, in which it was
> evidently impossible that the reporters could catch the orator's words ... The
> real wit of Bulwer Lytton certainly failed to redeem a manner unpardonable in
> a Secretary of State.[48]

It was perhaps not surprising that an individualist like Lytton, thin-skinned
and self-referential, should never have found the right idiom for persuading
and accommodating other men. Here was a basic art of the politician that
was never in his repertoire.

By contrast, Lytton's management of day to day, departmental affairs was
almost universally commended. Delane of *The Times* found his written
submissions 'admirable both in expression and sense'. Lytton's publisher
was delighted by the competence that Lytton displayed as a man of business,
observing that 'very few have any idea what a shrewd practical man he is'.[49]
After a few months in office, Henry Bulwer consoled his brother about
the embarrassments of Cabinet meetings by assuring him that he heard
'from all sides that you have done admirably in the Government and
established as I knew you could, a reputation for business ability'.[50] These
accolades were well-deserved. From small matters concerning patronage to

large decisions on the management of empire, Lytton was intelligent, dutiful and precise.[51]

As a Minister Lytton won the ungrudging respect and admiration of his subordinates. His Permanent Undersecretary, Sir Frederick Rogers, was astonished by his industry, and noted that he wrote 'volumes of minutes'. He remembered him 'as a chief whom it is impossible to serve under without admiring and loving; and who has imported into official drudgery a charm which I, at least, will never forget'.[52] Lytton's junior colleague at the Colonial Office, Lord Carnarvon, was even more effusive. He became a sort of acolyte who continued to feed him titbits of gossip and information as long as Lytton lived.[53] In return, Lytton thought his junior 'very accomplished, very honourable, very hardworking, very ambitious, very sensitive to praise or censure', though sometimes missing 'a virile grasp of thought in difficult occasions'.[54] Not a man who usually found delegation easy to exercise, Lytton made an exception in Carnarvon's case. The young man was allowed a wide discretion on matters great and small, and was trusted to sign letters on Lytton's behalf.[55] It was the happiest of working relationships.

The acquisition of new friendships was consoling but it in no way compensated for the wearing stress of office-holding. Lytton was teased about his parliamentary performances. He was vigorously tossed around by the London press when secret papers concerning the Ionian Islands question were stolen and sold to the *Daily News*. Improbably, the thief was called Greville Wellington Guernsey.[56] However complimentary the remarks of those who worked with him closely, in his own mind they never outweighed the coldness of Cabinet colleagues. His application and intelligence and success were not given their due reward. In his view, he was ruining his health for the pleasure of being brought into ridicule. When he finally succeeded in resigning, he told his son, unsurprisingly, that he was 'disenchanted in all ways with politics, public and private. Nothing but a strong conviction that I should do any good to the Country, or that the Country was in danger would urge me into much activity.'[57] The ambition that had led the artist and aristocrat into public life had drained away. After 1859 he spent little time at Westminster, and less and less as time went on. In many ways, he had been a capable Minister, but he now turned back to literature with an audible sigh of relief.

12

Prophet

Lytton's experiences of politics had proved that he was not a party man. He was an indifferent parliamentarian and an unhappy minister. In spite of very practical contributions in the colonial sphere, his real role in politics was that of the prophet. His last three novels, *The Coming Race* (1871), *The Parisians* (1873) and *Kenelm Chillingly* (1873) are all overtly didactic in intention. As he himself put it, they 'constitute a special group distinctly apart from all the other works of their author ... Each of them is an expostulation against theories, or a warning against the influence of certain social and political tendencies upon individual character and national life.' They were designed to investigate the impact of 'modern ideas' on the individual and on the community as a whole.[1] At the end of his life, Lytton saw the world as a dangerous place. Visiting Paris, shortly after the revolution which had brought the Commune to power, was a determining experience. He became an old man in a hurry to point a finger of suspicion at the future.

First and foremost, there was the challenge of socialism. In using this word Lytton more often meant the Jacobin inheritance from the French Revolution than Marxism. It was defined for him in demands for equality rather than in large schemes of economic reorganisation. Even so, for someone whose preferred model of living was an agrarian world of paternalist hierarchies, it was menacing enough. He had seen socialism in action in the Midi in 1850 and had not enjoyed the experience: 'I never can find anyone to explain what he means by it – or rather such men explain it differently ... a proof that there is a great sore in the social state – when people applaud against all morality.'[2] In *The Caxtons* of 1849 there is an intrusive appearance by a character called Miles Square, a peripatetic who preaches to agricultural workers 'that dead flat of social equality, that life in its every principle so heartily abhors'.[3]

None of this made Lytton the friend of the capitalist. The greed and self-interestedness of the banker and the businessman were as destructive of harmony in social relationships as the egalitarian claims of the socialist. In 1867 he was outraged to be asked to attend a City dinner:

I will not propose the health of the City. I detest and scorn the City – and I should say that the City was the focus of the most unfounded jobs, the reason why London was the ugliest malefactor in the world and that the greatest humbug in clothes was the Lord Mayor. Find someone else to give the City.[4]

In his view, the struggle between capitalist and workman was poisonous. The hatreds and jealousies of the industrial world were to be contrasted to the quiet of a pastoral England, which is so often praised in his novels. As he saw this world slipping away, he could only fear the worst.

He saw the evidence of disintegration everywhere. The Paris Commune, which had left at least twenty thousand people dead in Europe's most sophisticated capital, had opened 'a new page in History and Heaven knows what or when may be the stop to that'.[5] Anarchism, socialism and syndicalism were all now firmly on the agenda. The Lytton family was appalled. As Robert wrote to his father: 'France ought to be an awful warning to every nation not to break up its social foundation in a hurry'.[6] *The Parisians* therefore, which covered these events, was a novel of purposeful topicality. In it Lytton described barricades manned by 'the philosophical atheist, sundry long-haired artists, middle-aged writers for the Republican press, in close neighbourhood with ruffians of villainous aspect, who might have been newly returned from the galleys'.[7] The sad consequences of a French obsession with equality was to be contrasted with the hero of *Kenelm Chillingly*, who personified the very best kind of English paternalism. The two novels should be read together as a commentary on the drift of European politics: 'I am not without hopes that *Chillingly* may do some good and have an influence on the usury generation against certain of those new ideas which are to my mind as dangerous as when closely examined they are absurd.'[8]

Calls for equality naturally accompanied the march towards political democracy. The voices of the people were becoming louder and more insistent, and Lytton heard them with suspicion. After enthusiastically supporting the Reform Bill of 1832, he opposed further changes. The shift from aristocratic to democratic values was fraught with danger and had not been thought out. In *Ernest Maltravers* the hero is made to reflect on this point:

'But while a nation has already a fair degree of constitutional freedom, I believe no struggle so perilous and awful as that between the aristocratic and the democratic principle. A people against a despot – that contest requires no prophet; but the change from an aristocratic to a democratic commonwealth is indeed the wide, unbounded prospect upon which rest shadows, clouds and darkness. If it fail – for centuries is the dial hand of Time put back – if it succeed ...' Maltravers paused.

'And if it succeed?' Said Valerie.

'Why, then, man will have colonized Utopia!' replied Maltravers.[9]

Lytton saw his generation as that in which the transfer from aristocratic to democratic would begin, and it was merely the speed of the victory of 'the Great Popular Creed' that was in doubt.[10] What the consequences would be no one could accurately discern.

The problems presented by this change were particularly acute for men of aristocratic temperament like Lytton himself. Ideally they should be the arbiters between capital and labour, rich and poor, despot and parliament. Without such arbitration there could only be calamity: 'destroy an aristocracy and between throne and mob – between wealth and penury – between thief and till – what do order and property invoke to their aid? The answer is brief – an army! In every European community soldiers appear in proportion as aristocracy recedes.'[11] A Europe of Napoleons was in prospect. To avoid this, men with aristocratic feelings should offer to lead popular movements, channelling their demands into safe and workable schemes. The trouble with this notion is that democracies gratefully accept such guidance, quickly grow impatient and envious, and end by murdering those who try to help them. Two characters in Lytton's novels meet this fate. The eponymous hero of *Rienzi* 'fell from the vices of the People'. In *The Parisians* Victor de Mauléon discovers that 'in the first stage of revolution the mob has no greater darling than the noble who deserts his order, though in the second stage it may guillotine him at the denunciation of his cobbler'.[12] Both men learned the following rule of politics by tragic experience:

> Such is the eternal doom of disordered states. The mediator between rank and rank, the kindly noble – the dispassionate patriot – the first to act – the most hailed in action – darkly vanishes from the scene. Fiercer and more unscrupulous spirits alone stalk the field; and no neutral and harmonising link remains between hate and hate – until exhaustion sick with horrors, succeeds to frenzy, and despotism is welcomed as repose.[13]

Detailing the destruction of Italian and French patriots in democratic excess was intended by Lytton to act as a warning to his own countrymen. He and his kind in England were under the same threat. Their blindness, by which men of aristocratic temperament connived at their own destruction, was incredible to witness:

> In England, potent *millionaires*, high-born dukes, devoted Churchmen, belonging to the Liberal party, accept the services of men who look forward to measures which would ruin capital, eradicate aristocracy, and destroy the Church, provided these men combine with them in some immediate step onward against the Tories.[14]

In Lytton's view, it was probably futile for an aristocrat to resist democracy and fatal to flirt with it. Such a man had only a narrow strip of political territory on which to stand.

Nor was it reassuring to observe those countries which had experimented with popular government. France, in Lytton's lifetime, had lived through two empires, two monarchies and a republic. Instability seemed to have become a system of government. As a result it had subsided into universal suffrage, 'which gives to classes the most ignorant a power that preponderates over all the healthy elements of knowledge'. Little wonder that, in the Franco-Prussian War, France had yielded the title of the Continent's super-power to Prussia, 'the coming Giant', which had tempered a democratic franchise with all manner of constraints.[15] American democracy was more hopeful, but only because it enjoyed special advantages that were not available to European states. Being a new country, it did not have to graft democracy on to old structures. Being a huge country, it brought property ownership within the range of most of its citizens. Since these circumstances were unique to America, it was absurd to take that country as a model:

> These servile imitators of America imitate none of its *safeguards* while enjoying none of its peculiar advantages – they do not see that America practically resolves her electoral democracy into an administrative *oligarchy*, that she despises her representative Chamber and places the Government of the Nation in the hands of the Senate. They do not understand too – that in all cases of difficulty she has the land of a vast continent for her bank – in fact all modern liberals are the dullest of asses.[16]

Even with advantages, America descended into Civil War. Lytton watched its slaughter without surprise and thought that four separate states would probably be the result. Perhaps, he reflected, this might be no bad thing. Otherwise, America 'would have hung over Europe like a thunder-cloud'.[17] Democracy in action, in France and America, offered examples of popular autocracy, civil war and red republics. It was unappetising and probably unavoidable.

As England edged nearer and nearer to democracy, Lytton was predictably fascinated by the likely consequences of such a drift. He wrote about them obsessively, and in these essays and speeches there were moments of op-timism. He told an audience at the Leeds Mechanics Institute in 1854 how wonderful it was to see 'the recognition of intelligence as the supreme arbiter of all those questions which, a century ago, were either settled by force or stifled by those prejudices which are even stronger than the law'.[18] He also reflected that 'the idiosyncracy' of England might be strong enough, even to absorb democracy without danger: 'this characteristic of Englishmen – this desire of the individual rather to raise himself to the height of others more favoured by fortune or culture than to drag them down to his level – separates our English system of freedom from the levelling attributes of a democracy'.[19] And, where optimism failed, there was always fatalism. Political health demanded a constant search for improvement, for 'whenever progress ends, decline invariably begins'. He told a friend in 1859 that 'Democracy in England is as sure as that we are in this room'.[20] Fatalism, tinged with fragments of optimism, sometimes resigned Lytton to make the best of it.

More often he despaired. He could not really believe that England would be exempted from the general contagion: 'I doubt not the success of any republican or revolutionary experiment in any of the great old European States – even England', which would also see 'a general plunder'.[21] Not surprisingly, he identified the rot as starting with the repeal of the Corn Laws in 1846. Their loss had 'altered for the worse the staple character and spirit of the people'.[22] As agriculture and its values gave way to 'the dense population of manufacturing towns', democracy would grow and become ever more rapacious.[23] In the last decade of his life, he thought Parliament was full of 'visionaries' who resembled the men who led France into Revolution in 1789.[24] It was gloomy, but not surprising, to see that a further extension of the franchise in 1867 led immediately to the confiscation of the property of Anglican Church in Ireland in 1868. For Lytton, 'it is an awful thing to begin confiscation of private property', and it was an omen of what lay ahead in the democratic future.[25]

Such musings led to the sad conclusion that the arrival of democracy in England would be disastrous, and that it would hold no place for men of aristocratic temperament like himself. He told his son in 1866 that 'I agree with you that Democracy is in the future, and will be succeeded on the Continent by imperial despotisms, in England by ruin as a first rate or second rate power'.[26] He played less and less of an active role in politics after leaving office in 1859, and this withdrawal was the easier in that he felt that men like himself were not wanted. It was an obvious conclusion to reach for a man who had often felt marginalised by the society around him. The projected arrival of democracy merely brought yet another form of exclusion.

Beyond personal interest, there was the larger question of whether the Tory party, of which he was 'obliged' to be a member, had any serious prospects in the new order of things.[27] Under pressure of events, in 1858 Lytton attempted to define the essentials of Conservatism, to which he later gave the adjective 'high-minded'.[28] He thought that, in all communities, there were 'certain organic principles' peculiar to that community. If those principles were affronted, 'the society begins to decay'. In England those principles were still aristocratic, by which he meant a union of 'energy and character with property and station'. He believed that such had been the governing idea in English politics since Anglo-Saxon times. It was 'the genius of Conservatism' and peculiar to England.[29] French and American models were irrelevant, not only because they seemed to end in despots and civil war, but also because they were the product of different cultures and moods. English Conservatism was aristocratic, in the widest definition of that word, or it was nothing.

Lytton believed that his kind of Conservatism was killed off, once and for all, by the extension of the franchise perpetuated in the Reform Bill of 1867. Tragically, it was a Tory government led by Derby and Disraeli which had committed this dark act. Lytton took the view that Derby was almost criminally unknowing about the consequences of his own actions, and that 'the Conservative party suffered much under his guidance'. As for his old friend Disraeli, he could only feel 'steely' towards him. The two men seemed to be engaged in the euthanasia of their own party.[30] Lytton was actually relieved when Gladstone and the Liberals returned to power, because an incubus had been lifted from his shoulders.[31] Disraeli had 'smashed the numerical strength of his party'.[32] Conceivably, a new form of Conservatism might emerge, which would have a certain resonance with the new electorate, but it would be an unwelcome mutation, in Lytton's view, of something that had once had real worth. As he told a friend in 1869:

> Conservatism pure and simple is among the things before the Deluge. And I suspect that the Party which adopts the name must enter boldly into the lists with all other parties for the favour of the Household Democracy it has established, since it has chosen to be Frankenstein and create a giant ... it can't escape from that giant and had better make a friend of him than an enemy.[33]

As this quotation suggests, the opening up of politics to mass participation in 1867 was, in Lytton's view, quite literally monstrous.

Parliamentary Reform reached the surface of politics with uncomfortable regularity in the period 1858 to 1867. Whenever it did so, it left Lytton 'plagued, unsettled, moving about and absorbed in anxieties political'.[34] He warned the House of Commons in 1860 that a democratic suffrage had destroyed Athens and was in the process of destroying France.[35] Six years later, he lectured the same audience on the dangers of making 'the urban working class ... the arbiters of all that concerns the system of this elaborate monarchy and this commercial system'.[36] When the Derby-Disraeli Bill came before the Lords, Lytton was almost paralysed with indecision. On the one hand, he was sure that it would obliterate Conservatism as he valued it. On the other, the agitation for Reform had reached such a pitch, that a measure of some sort might be unavoidable. He chose to remain mute. In a speech which was written but never given he expressed a determination to 'consent, or rather submit to it with great reluctance', and then only because the clamour for change had become deafening.[37]

Throughout these years, Lytton could not understand why the political elite in England should be so anxious to dig their own graves. He was sure that the 1867 Act would sweep away Gladstone and Lord John Russell, Disraeli and Derby, just as his literary heroes like Rienzi and Victor de Mauléon were destroyed. His view of the probable future grew darker and darker. In the years before his death, it became positively apocalyptic:

> As to 'Party' I confess that my ardour is chilled. I do not join in any attack on the *honour* of the Government that passed the Reform Bill. So far as the *temporary* interests of the party are concerned perhaps they may have done a clever thing. *But* where is Conservatism henceforth? Men die – Ministers go out. Principles of conduct are more lasting – who can tell me now what a Conservative is except a somebody who is in opposition to a Whig? And far beyond all that, this is the question to be applied to the most artificial empire ever built up – can that empire long last when you place its destinies in the hands of men who live upon weekly wages? Yes, possibly for a time – How? Because a Conservative is a richer man than a Radical and in a contest may thro' himself or his supporters corrupt a majority. Believe me there is no other means – and for these means there is no other cure. But when you come to wholesale corruption – in quiet times a state rots – in stirring times the state ignites – it is rot or combustion. I have been a great liberal in my day, but I never was in favour of a very low suffrage – never could favour the theory that poverty and ignorance massed together in towns should govern an empire founded on intellect and wealth – and once injured – ruined for ever. Henceforth Great Britain will be *so* governed. Pardon these croakings.[38]

As a reading of how a democratic system would operate, this prophecy may be thought unduly pessimistic, but the sternest critics of Lytton's views would have to admit that it is not all wrong. It was certainly a future for which Lytton himself had little appetite.

If the immediate democratic future was forbidding, speculation about the far future, beyond the democratic phase, might be consoling. Certainly Lytton found it so. His penultimate novel, *The Coming Race*, is a truly remarkable production. Lytton himself called it 'an odd sort of thing'. In one sense, it was one of the earliest examples of modern science fiction writing. In another, it resembled *Gulliver's Travels* satirising of Victorian trends in politics and society by talking of them in an imaginary society which was geographically and temporally remote. As Lytton observed, the book was 'satirical upon many things now discussed political and social but very gravely so'. He was so nervous about how his satire might be received that he not only insisted on publishing the book anonymously, as usual, but he also dedicated it to someone he had never met by way of distracting attention from himself. As he told his publisher, 'I could not publish it if I thought I should be detected; and whatever its success I doubt if I should ever own it'.[39] Anonymity had always covered his extreme nervousness about criticism. It now allowed him to publish something which was a kind of revenge on contemporary ideas which he found absurd and threatening.

In the novel a man falls, like Alice, down a cavernous hole to find himself the guest of a superior race who have advanced beyond democracy. Elsewhere underground the democratic force still exists under the name of Koom-Posh, but it is dismissed by his hosts as an old form of barbarism:

> They pretend to be all equals, and the more they have struggled to be so, by removing old distinctions and starting afresh, the more glaring and intolerable the disparity becomes, because nothing in hereditary affections and associations is left to soften the one naked distinction between the many who have nothing and the few who have much. Of course the many hate the few, but without the few they could not live. The many are always assailing the few; sometimes they exterminate the few; but as soon as they have done so, a new few starts out of the many, and is harder to deal with than the old few ... In short the people I speak of are savages.[40]

The visitor is suitably impressed by the arguments against Koom-Posh and by the superiority of the society in which he finds himself.

To argue for government by the few was not simply to restate the case for Victorian aristocracy, although a number of Lytton's critics plausibly accused him of doing so. Rather, the advance from democracy had been made possible by a new form of energy called Vril. When human beings came into contact with it they cease to be jealous, competitive and aggressive, and become instead, quite literally, a new and superior species. Vril literally cured democracy. In the underground language, 'vril' was synonymous with civilisation and 'vril-ya' signified the civilised nations. In the opinion of those who enjoyed the benefits of Vril, democracy had been

> the age of envy and hate, of fierce passions, of constant social changes more or less violent, of strife between classes, of war between state and state. The phase of society ... was finally brought to a close, at least among the nobler and more intellectual populations, by the gradual discovery of the latent powers stored in the all-permeating fluid which they denominate Vril.[41]

This was not Lytton the aristocrat voyaging into the future but Lytton the spiritualist. Science would tame the worst excesses of democracy. A new force would lead to the government of a new few. Improbably, it also gave its name to Bovril, which was advertised as a drink with new and marvellous properties.

But the satire went further still. Living in a period when demands for female suffrage were growing ever louder, Lytton, no doubt with Rosina in mind, took the opportunity to comment on the issue. In his underground society women, absorbing Vril more easily than men, have the dominant position. All the citizens of this world are winged, but women are stronger and fly higher than men. Equally, they are pre-eminent in intellectual life and alone decide on marriage partners. Once married, however, woman flies no more and her wings are removed: 'she suspends them with her own hands over the nuptial couch, never to be removed unless the marriage tie be severed by divorce or death'.[42] Having chosen a mate, a woman had to be 'lenient to his faults, consults his humour, and does her best to secure his attachment'.[43] Divorce would be possible after three months of cohabitation, at the request of either party. In Lytton's utopia marriage was still to be managed on patriarchal lines, but women were free to choose about entering into the arrangement and could dissolve it at will. Whether Rosina would have regarded these rules as satisfactory is debatable, but they were certainly different from those which governed Victorian society. Lytton, half mocking and half serious, offered a view of what might be the outcome of 'that very delicate question, urged of late as essential to the perfect happiness of our human species by the most disturbing and potential influences on upper-ground society – Womenkind and Philosophy. I mean the Rights of Women.'[44]

Speculation about the future, inevitably fanciful, fulfilled a satirical purpose but also had a more serious justification. Lytton was convinced, in almost Darwinian terms, that human society was undergoing quickening evolution. A new race and new ideas about social organisation would emerge: 'The only important point is to keep in view the Darwinian Proposition that a Coming Race is destined to supplant our races – that such a race would be very gradually formed – and be indeed a new species developing itself out of the old one – that this process would be invisible to our eyes and therefore ... unknown to us.'[45] Lytton delighted in every new fad and theory. When great claims were made for the medical properties of electricity, he bought 'electric gloves', wore 'electric papers' on his back and experimented with 'a pair of electric flesh brushes'.[46] His discussion of the political and social consequences of new forms of energy like Vril dovetailed with his interest in the forces which might underpin spiritualism. The world was full of unknown agencies with unknown properties. Their discovery would so change man that he would quite literally become another species. He tried to explain the interrelation of the various strands of his thinking to Forster:

> I do not mean Vril for Mesmerism. But for electricity developed into uses as yet only dimly guessed and including whatever there may be genuine in mesmerism, which I hold to be a mere branch current of the one great fluid pervading all Nature ... I am by no means wedded to Vril, if you can suggest anything else to carry out the meaning, viz that the Coming Race tho' akin to us, has nevertheless acquired by hereditary transmission etc certain distinctions which make it a differing species, and certain powers ... so that this race would not amalgamate with, but destroy us ... Now as some bodies are charged with electricity like the Torpedo or Electric Eel and never can communicate that power to other bodies, so I suppose the existence [of] a race charged with that Electricity ... in a word to be the Conductors of all lightenings.[47]

Before the new race established itself, however, the choppy waters of Koom-Posh or democracy had to be negotiated. Even when this was done, even when aggression and class hatred had been removed, Lytton envisaged only a society that was calm but excruciatingly grey: 'Assuming that all the various ideas of philosophical reformers could be united and practically realised, the result would be firstly, a race that must be fatal to ourselves ... Secondly, the realisation of these ideas would produce a society which we would find extremely dull, and in which the current equality would prohibit all greatness'.[48] It was, in a sense , consoling to look beyond the horrors of the approaching democracy. It was fascinating to observe the discovery of new forces in nature. But Lytton was under no illusions that the values he cherished had a place in the future. Democracy had no place for heroic or aristocratic colour. Nor did a futuristic world where the emotions were controlled by the agencies of science. Therefore Lytton turned into satire and speculation a terrible sense of loss for a world that was passing. Just as *The Parisians* underlined the dangers of democracy and socialism, *The Coming Race* was intended as a warning of what lay even further in the future.

A future that was at once so dark and so inevitable bred fatalism and a wish to withdraw. After leaving office in 1859 Lytton thought of retiring from party politics altogether and 'acting singly'.[49] By 1866 he was clear that he never again wanted a significant position in public life. Two years later, he had 'quite given up all taste for politics'.[50] He lived in London less and less, adopting a lifestyle that was increasingly reclusive. If he agreed to attend a social function, he believed that he conferred 'a great obligation'.[51]

The offer of a peerage, in 1866, flattered his instinctive sense of dynasticism and he reflected pleasurably on how much it would have delighted his mother. But he was under no illusions about its implications. Going to the Lords was 'a fall. One ceases to be a power. One is shelved. A member for the smallest boro' who has the ear of the House of Commons has more influence with the public than the richest peer.' [52] He took comfort, however, in the thought that the Upper House had a more relaxing atmosphere than the Lower: 'I might not be strong eno' for the Commons. I might be strong eno' for the Lords (where I suppose Hercules is a rare God).' [53] Never the most robust of politicians, he took his easing out of public life with due philosophy.

In the last decade of his life, Lytton's correspondence takes on an increasing world-weariness. He saw a world spinning out of control, and saw himself as powerless to do anything to stop it. The French Revolution had, quite simply, 'destroyed all the great foundations of calm and durable government – all that stands between popular passion and a Master'.[54] Passively, he chronicled the extinction of his world. It was in this mood that he wrote his last novel, *Kenelm Chillingly*. Its hero, after investigating the thinking of his day, comes to grim conclusions:

> We are living in an age in which the process of unsettlement is going blindly to work, as if impelled by a Nemesis as blind as itself. New ideas come beating in surf and surge against those which former reasoners had considered as fixed banks and backwaters; and the new ideas are so mutable, so fickle, that those which were considered novel ten years ago are deemed obsolete today, and the new ones of today will in their turn be obsolete tomorrow. And, in a sort of fatalism, you see statesmen yielding way to these successive mockeries of experiment.[55]

Chillingly's answer, like Lytton's, was to withdraw into a world of art, following Schiller's verse:

> Aber in den heitern Regionen
> Wo die reinen Formen wohnen
> Rauscht das Jammers trüber Sturm nicht mehr.[56] *

Lytton's life had come full circle. As a young man, he had believed that to live in art was preferable to all other kinds of existence. He had made great claims for its practitioners. Now, that idea was his defence against a future that was bleak. He told his son, above all else, 'to hold fast to the conviction of soul'.[57] A man who had convinced himself that his work had

---

* But in the merry regions, where pure forms live, the moanings of the murky storm roar no more.

never been taken seriously was also sure that his advice would not be taken or his warnings heeded. His son agreed:

> I live in a sort of nightmare of horror about the political, or rather social, state of the world. I see no future – absolutely none – in any direction – but I feel everywhere an abyss of chaos – into which it seems to me we are rapidly travelling – and of all communities in Europe, our own in England seems to me the most threatened and the least capable of resistance.[58]

In these circumstances, the artist could only draw deeply on his philosophy, and withdraw from a world that had grown cold.

The last two of three years of Lytton's life were spent at Torquay nursing deteriorating health. Two new friends, Mrs Halliday and Lady Sherborne, did much to make his life agreeable. In his description of the latter, he outlined a portrait of the wife he should have had:

> Lady Sherborne is an enigma. She is not young. She would generally be considered very plain. She is not clever. She is not a flirt. She is very good with a religious temperament. But she certainly has charm. She is so quiet and feminine, with a wonderfully sweet voice in talk as well as song. We are great friends. Lord Sherborne is, however, an infliction – dull and cross, but a fine man, and she seems a very good wife, takes his scoldings and governs him with a silk vein.[59]

In short, Lady Sherborne was the precise opposite of Rosina. In her company Torquay was particularly restful.

The year 1873 opened uneventfully. Lytton read chapters of *Kenelm Chillingly* to his daughter-in-law, Edith, who had become a constant companion.[60] At a dinner early in January he had been delighted to meet the formidable Benjamin Jowett at a dinner party. The two men took walks on the beach and talked of Plato and spiritualism.[61] But soon after Jowett's departure Lytton began to feel unwell. A week or so earlier he had undergone an operation designed to help his deafness. An abscess formed in his ear and then burst. He wrote his last letter to his publisher on 16 January: 'I am suffering terrible agony from a species of tic, and am utterly unable to look at any proofs or do any business today, or for some days, the pain I have been suffering is very trying.'[62] Within two days, he was dead. He expired at two a.m. on Saturday 18 January, with Robert and Edith at his bedside.

Quite what killed him is not clear. Mrs Halliday put it down to 'a local affliction of the ear spreading to a *vital organ* with *fearful* rapidity'. His son thought death had come from 'an inflammation of the membranes of the brain, resulting from a disease of the ear which he had suffered a long time'. The doctor in attendance blamed 'an irritation of the brain' which had led to a coma and finally to death by choking. Symptoms in the last illness included total blindness, nearly total deafness, spasms that were described as epileptic and incoherent movements of the limbs. One such simulated Lytton's old habit of cleaning his ear with the help of a four inch needle, the end of which was tipped with lint.[63] Many of these symptoms would be consonant with the onset of a stroke. But, whatever the exact cause of death, it came after a week of intense suffering.

Lytton drew up three wills during his lifetime. In each his son was the residual legatee and main beneficiary. Lytton's sense of dynastic obligation would have dictated this decision. Of more interest are the minor bequests. In the 1848 will £2000 is left to a Mrs Grant and her three daughters, and a similar sum to a Marion Wolstonecraft Waller, 'now Mrs Lowndes', and her son Arthur. Six years later, the Lowndes bequest held, while 'Mrs Grant' and her three daughters have been replaced by a 'Mrs Beaumont' and three daughters. Almost certainly Mrs Grant and Mrs Beaumont were one and the same person, and both names were aliases for Laura Deacon.[64] Other letters make it clear that this Mrs Grant and one of her daughters named Gertrude had been set up in a school in Vienna by Lytton.[65] In the will that was executed after his death, large sums were left to a considerable list of beneficiaries; Marie de Rosset (£1500), Gertrude Sherwood (£500), Mary Anne Sherwood (£5000), Henrietta Vansittart (£1200), Georgina Grant (£1500), Gertrude Grant (£1500), Violent Gaunter (£1500), Arthur Lowndes (£1500), Lucy Lowndes (£500), William Henry Sherwood (£100), Frederick Vansittart (£300), Louis de Rosset (£500).[66]

Quite who these Vansittarts, de Rossets, Grants and Sherwoods were is not clear. They were not servants or estate workers, because such people are mentioned elsewhere in the will. It is quite probable that they were all illegitimate children. Indeed the list may not be exhaustive. The critic Edmund Gosse identified the minor poet Arthur O'Shaughnessy, a fellow Keeper at the British Museum, as Lytton's son.[67] There may also have been two children, Edward and Alice, born to one his housekeepers, Eleanor Thomson. New claimants to kinship with the Lytton family continue to come to light. Rosina was right to suspect that her husband had more than one family. He may well have had many.

Lytton had asked to be buried at Knebworth but his wishes were ignored. Such was his stature as a man of letters that a final resting place in Westminster Abbey became unavoidable. The funeral took place of 1 February 1873. It was bitterly cold and the ground was covered with snow. Benjamin Jowett was asked to give the eulogy, a slightly strange choice in that he and

Lytton had not known each other for long. He took as his text the opening lines of the Nunc Dimittis, and, in his address, had two clear objectives: to acclaim Lytton as a towering figure in English literature and to reclaim him for religion. He told the congregation about conversations he had had with Lytton in Torquay only a few weeks earlier, in which his new friend had said that: 'Faith is something wiser, diviner, happier than we see on earth. The artist calls it the ideal, the truest, purest faith, but the ideal and faith are in reality one and the same.'[68] Lady Sherborne also believed that Lytton was 'never without thought of the World to come'.[69] Few in the congregation could have accepted this. That Lytton believed in a world of the spirit and the artistic ideal is undeniable. To what extent this dovetailed with any kind of conventional Victorian piety is difficult to evaluate. Probably the answer is not very much.

The grandeur of a funeral in the Abbey represented the public recognition of his worth which Lytton had always despaired of receiving. But, almost immediately, many people found it impossible not to speak ill of the dead. His old political associate, Lord Derby, found 'his strange ways of living' odd, and deplored the fact that 'he smoked so much, used opium, [and] took little exercise.'[70] S. C. Hall, who had known him for forty years, was even more lukewarm:

> I believe Bulwer to have been a man made to be admired rather than loved. He achieved fame, but I am not sure that it brought him happiness. He seldom gave one the idea that he was in earnest: the good he did seemed rather the result of calculation than of impulse. I believe there would have been even among his friends and admirers a greater number to rejoice at his failure than triumph at his success.[71]

This chilling summing-up had more than a grain of truth in it. Lytton had not been loved. His wife despised him, his children feared and respected him, and his contemporaries found him insufferably quirky.

Lytton would have eagerly embraced this assessment. He complained of neglect and a lack of appreciation throughout his life. He was clear that 'life is a War' and that he had been sidelined in the conflict.[72] It is perhaps no coincidence that *Ernest Maltravers* was the creation for whom he felt the greatest personal affinity. Maltravers believed that 'half our life is consumed in longing to be nearer death'. He has the instincts and preoccupations of a solitary. Above all, Maltravers is acutely aware of how transient a literary reputation could be; 'every age has its own literary stamp and coinage, and consigns the old circulation to its shelves and cabinets, as neglected curiosities'.[73] Lytton's works, hugely popular in his day, are now little read or discussed. This is unfair and a slight on their real talent, but it was an outcome that would not have surprised him. Like Maltravers, he felt alone in his own generation and had very little hope that a later one would be more understanding.

Even more revealing is *Pausanias*. It was a work composed with great seriousness of purpose. Benjamin Hall Kennedy, the Regius Professor of Greek at Cambridge, was enlisted as an amanuensis. It was also the book that gave Lytton the most trouble. Begun in 1856, it was still unpublished at the time of his death. This was very unusual. Lytton wrote quickly as a rule, and, even though he always enjoyed anonymity in publishing, not to bring the book forward at all was very odd. Perhaps he felt it to be too self-revealing. Pausanias, after all, was an heroic figure who, feeling rejected by his countrymen in Sparta, was tempted into treasonable negotiations with the Persians. As Lytton put it: 'The more he felt himself uncom-prehended and mistrusted by his countrymen, the more personal became his character, and the more unscrupulous the course of his ambition.'[74] The last seventeen years of Lytton's life were spent in honing and refining the story of an outsider.

As Pausanias stood to the Spartans, so Lytton to the English. In so many aspects of his life, he was not of their company. They looked at him askance as dandy, spiritualist, Germanophile and artist. His dress was unEnglish, and so were his voice and mannerisms. These deficiencies, if deficiencies they were, had not been corrected in the rough and tumble of a great public school. Instead, they had been confirmed by a disastrous marriage that had made him notorious. In short, he lived a life that confronted his contemporaries. Few of them offered him friendship, and fewer could cope with him over a long period of years. Predictably he spent more and more time abroad, nursing both his health and his bruised susceptibilities. He suspected correctly that his literary reputation would not survive. As he warned Laman Blanchard: 'prose is very doubtful material for the artist to leave behind – its colour soon fades and its texture rots ... the prose of one generation is prosy to the next'. He pointed out, by way of example, that no one now read Richardson's *Clarissa*, so 'what hope for us moderns? None.'[75]

The more he felt rejection, the more his ambition to force himself upon the attention of the English became insistent and sour. He became self-obsessed to the detriment of his friendships and family ties. In his repeated invocation of the blessings of death there is affectation and truth in equal measure:

I look upon leaving life, as upon leaving school, a yet more wide and active existence fairly spreads beyond. The oldest of us has never trained a tenth part of his faculties. All the good and unexpected remainder must have its opening somewhere ... And if any part of us survives the rest it must be the Afflictions.[76]

Since his death, the English have taken the ultimate revenge of unfairly ignoring his books and of demeaning the major role he played in so many aspects of Victorian life. They insisted upon putting him into their Abbey where he had no wish to be while savaging his reputation. It was a terrible, final irony that he died not in Wiesbaden – or Nice – but in Torquay.

Notes

Notes to Introduction

1. EBL to Rosina Lytton [1827], L. Devey, *Letters of the Late Edward Bulwer, Lord Lytton, to his Wife* (London, 1884), 94.
2. 'Want of Sympathy', Lord Lytton, *Miscellaneous Prose Works by Edward Bulwer, Lord Lytton,* (London, 1868), ii 110.
3. EBL to W. Kent, 2 November 1851, Boston Public Library, Kent MSS, C.1.41.2.
4. Knebworth MSS, 04408.
5. Lord Lytton, *Speeches of Edward, Lord Lytton* (London, 1874), i, preface vii.
6. Rosina Lytton's Journal, 23 December 1836, Devey, 314.
7. Lord Lytton, *The Life of Edward Bulwer, Lord Lytton* (London, 1913), ii 491.

Notes to Chapter 1: The Upbringing of a Puppy

1. EBL to Rosina Lytton [1827], Devey, 140.
2. Lord Lytton, *The Life, Letters and Literary Remains of Edward Bulwer, Lord Lytton* (London, 1883), i 75.
3. Ibid., i 73.
4. Ibid., i 14.
5. Ibid., i 73.
6. Ibid., i 13.
7. Ibid., i 77.
8. Ibid.
9. Ibid., i 78.
10. Ibid., i 83–84.
11. Ibid., i 88.
12. Ibid., i 108.
13. Ibid., i 88.
14. EBL to Mrs Bulwer, 2 November 1818, Knebworth MSS, P4, box 68. His grandmother was a woman of some spirit. Having defeated the efforts of three highwaymen on Hounslow Heath, she announced that 'a woman with her wits about her, and the whip hand disengaged, is a match for three men any day of the year'.
15. *LLLR*, i 20.
16. Ibid., i 72.
17. This theme is found in *My Novel, Lucretia, Timon, Calderon* and *Paul Clifford.*

18. Dedication, *The Siamese Twins* (1831). Lytton's wife later argued that he was his mother's favourite only because his real father had been a Mr Rawlings, one of the men of whom Barbara Lytton had been genuinely fond. Rawlings, however, appears to have died four years before Lytton was born. See Rosina Lytton's annotations to the copy of Lady Blessington's Memoirs in Knebworth Library.

19. T. Cooper, *Lord Lytton*, 17.

20. *New Monthly Magazine*, 175, September 1845, 3.

21. Lady Hills-Johnes, Recollections of a Visit to Knebworth, 1857, National Library of Wales, Dolancothi MSS, 8103.

22. *Devereux*, book 1, chap. 15.

23. Ibid., book 6, chap. 4. See also the hostility between Philip and Robert Beaufort in *Night and Morning*.

24. Barbara Lytton to Elizabeth Lytton, 1811, Knebworth MSS, box 55A.

25. William to Henry Bulwer [1843], ibid., box 56.

26. William Bulwer to Mother, 12 March 1833, ibid. See also ibid., 14 May 1832, ibid.

27. William to Henry Bulwer [1843], ibid. In fact, Mrs Bulwer left Henry £1000 p.a. and William the interest on a capital sum of £16,000.

28. William to Edward Lytton [1843], ibid.

29. Edward to William Bulwer [1843], ibid., P4, box 69.

30. Henry Bulwer to Mother; 8 March 1833, ibid., P4, box 58.

31. H. Bulwer to Princess Lieven [1844], British Library, Add. MS 47376, fos 211–12.

32. H. Bulwer to Edward Lytton, 16 January 1858, Norfolk Record Office, Bulwer MSS, BUL 1/140/39a.

33. *LLLR*, i 36.

34. Knebworth MSS; Lord Lytton, *Miscellaneous Prose Works of Edward Bulwer, Lord Lytton* (London, 1868), ii 60.

35. Ibid., 54 and 56.

36. M. Arnold to Mrs Arnold, 12 May 1869, *Life*, ii 452–53.

37. EBL to Emily Lytton, 7 January 1844, Knebworth MSS, P5, box 88. See also EBL to Mrs Hutton, 6 May 1845, C. H. Beale, *Reminiscences of a Gentlewoman of the Last Century* (London, 1891), 223. When only fifteen years old, Lytton wrote a poem entitled 'To K. The Seat of Mrs ...' It contains the lines:

> Then, then, arose the last of all her race,
> To join each pow'r, her native house to grace;
> Again to raise the beauties of thy pile,
> With added lustre, make her K. smile;
> Again thy halls, the graceful dance shall bear,
> And heavenly music charm the thrilling ear;
> Again thy doors shall open to receive
> The lordly noble, and the poor relieve;
> Again shall taste and eloquence impart
> Each varied scene to charm the captive heart.

38. EBL to Lord Walpole, 2 August 1850, *Life*, ii 130–31.

39. *LLLR* i 45.

40. Ibid., i 41. For some of his genealogical work, see Knebworth MSS, Q3 01450 and 01488.

41. EBL to Benjamin Disraeli [1845], Bodleian Library, Hughenden MSS, BXX 104/1, fol. 81. See also W. Gravatt to EBL, 9 August 1844.

42. W. Bulwer to H. Bulwer [1850], Knebworth MSS, box 56. See also *LLLR*, i 248.

43. Henry Bulwer to Robert Lytton, 25 March [1870], ibid., box 58. See also, Henry Bulwer to EBL [1869 and 1870], ibid.

44. In book 5, chap. 1 of *What Will He Do With It?*, there is a description of a Georgian house, 'built in the reign of George I, when first commenced that horror of the beautiful'.

45. *Ismael*, 1818, published 1820.

46. *Address to Sir Walter Scott*, 1816.

47. M. Rochester, *The Derby Ministry* (London, 1858), 148.

48. *LLLR*, i 95–96.

49. Ibid., i 97.

50. Ibid., i 99.

51. In *Devereux*, book 1 chap. 20, there is recounted a story of playground bullying that some critics believe was taken from Lytton's own experiences.

52. *LLLR*, i 116.

53. Dr Hooker to Mrs Bulwer, 18 September 1815, ibid., i 121.

54. Ibid., i 149.

55. EBL to Robert Lytton [1856], Knebworth MSS, P5, box 72. This letter reports a speech given by EBL at Bishops Stortford School.

56. *LLLR*, i 170.

57. J. Thomson to Mrs Lytton , 5 June 1821, Hertfordshire Record Office, Lytton MSS, K610.

58. Ibid., 7 August 1821, ibid., K611.

59. T. Pinney, *The Letters of Thomas Babington Macaulay* (Cambridge, 1974–81), i 188 n i.

60. See Lytton MSS, DEK 633.

61. *LLLR*, i 231.

62. A. M. Brown in an unpublished Cambridge Ph.D. thesis entitled 'The Metaphysical Novels of Edward Bulwer Lytton', chapter 7, identified the following novels as among those exploring the *Wanderjahr* theme: *Contarini Fleming* (Disraeli), *Mandeville* (Godwin), *Wotton Reinfred* (Carlyle), *Eustace Conway* (Maurice), *Ranthorpe* (Lewes) and *Arthur Coningsby* (Sterling).

63. EBL to R. Cunningham [*c.* 1826], Lytton MSS, DEK c26/20.

64. *LLLR*, i 159.

65. *The Tale of a Dreamer*, 1824. See also *Farewell to Lyra* (1818).

66. In the preface to *Ernest Maltravers*, Lytton noted that the character of Alice Darvil was based on 'a person I never saw but twice'. He adds that she 'was

no longer young', but this could easily be mere camouflage. As for Maltravers, 'he loved – and forgot all but that love. He was eighteen.' (Book 1, chap. 7).

67. Balfour, i 290.

68. *Ernest Maltravers*, book 1, chap. 1. See also *LLLR*, i 293–300 and 308.

69. *The Disowned*, vol. 1, chap. 1.

70. *LLLR*, i 316. See also *Eugene Aram*, book 4, chap. 9.

71. M. Porter to EBL, 24 December 1820 and 14 January 1821, Lytton MSS, DEK, fos 17–21.

72. Ibid., 15 January 1821, ibid., fol. 22.

73. *LLLR*, ii 21.

74. Ibid., i 365–69. Socially, Lytton seems to have preferred the *salons* of the pre-revolutionary aristocracy. Their memories were useful for his description of the Revolution in *Zanoni*, and their characteristics, in idealised form, are set out in *The Parisians*. Lytton did not share his mother's dislike of Catholicism, and one of his guides in Paris was a certain Abbé Kinsala, confessor to the Polignac family. See also *LLLR*, ii 18.

75. EBL to Lady Cunningham-Fairlie, February 1826, *LLLR*, ii 45–46.

76. Ibid. [March 1826] and 17 April 1826, ibid., ii 54 and 56.

77. Lady Cunningham-Fairlie to EBL, February 1826, ibid., ii 46.

78. EBL to Rosina Lytton, 2 January 1828, Devey, 228. In *The Disowned*, the character of Castruccio Castrucani, whom some take to be modelled on Byron, descends into insanity.

79. *LLLR*, i 176 seq.

80. To Lady C.L., 1818, Lytton MSS, DEK c28/9.

81. L. G. Mitchell, *Lord Melbourne*, 82. See also Lady C. Lamb to EBL [1823] and 23 May 1823, Lytton MSS, DEK C24/21/1–2. *LLLR*, i 328–31.

82. Ibid.

83. EBL to Mrs Bulwer, 1825, Knebworth MSS, P5, box 68.

84. J. Preston, *That Odd Rich Old Woman* (Dorchester, 1995), 156.

85. Lady C. Lamb to EBL, August [1826], Lytton MSS, DEK c1, fos 7–8.

86. EBL to Rosina Lytton [*c.* 1826], Knebworth MSS, P4, box 70.

87. Ibid., 11 February 1827, ibid.

88. Ibid., 25 February 1829, ibid., P4, box 71.

89. EBL to John Murray [1830], Princeton Library, Parrish MSS, AM 16335.

90. *LLLR*, i 337.

91. EBL annotation, 1866, Lytton MSS, DEK c1, fol. 4.

92. In the Parrish MSS there is a copy of a second edition of *Ismael* (1821), inscribed to Elizabeth Spence by EBL

93. Devey, 15 n. i.

94. Rosina Lytton to Augustus Lamb, 31 August 1826, Lytton MSS, DEL6, F78/17.

95. EBL to Rosina Lytton [1826], Knebworth MSS, P4, box 70.

96. EBL to Drake Garrard, 21 February 1820, *LLLR*, i 150–51.

97. *Hades or High Life Below Stairs*, 1824.

98. *To My Mother*, 1826.

99. EBL to Rosina Lytton, 17 September 1826, Devey, 45.
100. *To My Mother*, 1826.
101. *LLLR*; ii 100–1. Among works which were started but not completed were 'A Sketch of the Progress of English Poetry', 'A History of Portugal', and 'A Satire upon England and the English People'.
102. EBL to Lady Cunningham-Fairlie, 25 February 1826, Lytton MSS, DEK c26/20/2.
103. *LLLR*, ii 14–15.
104. Ibid., ii 98.
105. Describing the reaction to the death of a spouse in the futuristic society outlined in *The Coming Race*, he observed that 'the survivor takes much more consolation than, I am afraid, the generality of us do, in the certainty of reunion in another and happier life.' (Chap. 17).
106. G. Eliot to M. Lewis [31 March 1840], G. S. Haight, *The George Eliot Letters* (New Haven, 1954–78), i 45.
107. EBL to Rosina Lytton, 17 September 1826, Devey, 45.
108. EBL to M. Napier, 8 September 1830, British Library, Add. MS 34614, fol. 389.
109. EBL to Mrs Bulwer, 2 April 1820, *LLLR*, i 142–43.
110. Ibid., Knebworth MSS, P5, box 68.
111. EBL to Drake Garrard, 2 April 1820, *LLLR*, i 151.
112. EBL to S. Parr, 4 February 1820, Bodleian Library, M. Eng. Misc., d 590, fol. 23.
113. S. Parr to EBL, 26 April 1821, *LLLR*, i 157–58. See also ibid., 9 April 1821, Lytton MSS, DEK c25/6.
114. T. H. S. Escott, *Edward Bulwer, First Baron Lytton* (London, 1910), 44.
115. EBL to Rosina Lytton, [1826], Devey, 76.
116. Ibid., 154.
117. *Life*, i 186.
118. *Falkland*, book 1.
119. Mrs Bulwer to EBL, n.d., Knebworth MSS, P5, box 68.
120. Miss Greene's Memoire, *Life*, i 187.
121. *LLLR*, ii 105.
122. EBL to Mrs Bulwer, 17 June 1828, Knebworth MSS, P5, box 68.
123. EBL to Lady Cunningham-Fairlie, 1 May 1827, *LLLR*, ii 145.
124. EBL to Rosina Lytton [*c.* December 1826], *Life*, i 185–86.

Notes to Chapter 2: Rosina

1. *The Ordeal of Love*; Lytton, *Miscellaneous Prose Works*, ii 94 seq.
2. *New Monthly Magazine*, 28 (1830), 329.
3. *The Caxtons*, part 18, chap. 7.
4. *Godolphin*, chap. 2.
5. *LLLR*, ii 51.
6. A. M. Brown, 'The Metaphysical Novels of Edward Bulwer Lytton' (unpublished Ph.D. thesis, Cambridge University, 1979), 150–54.
7. *Devereux*, book 2 chap 7.

8. *LLLR*, ii 36.
9. Though Rosina dated the first meeting in December 1825, Devey, 63. See also *Life*, i 155.
10. EBL to Lady Cunningham-Fairlie, 25 June 1826, Lytton MSS, DEK c26/20.
11. Devey, 63.
12. Ibid., 1.
13. Devey, 8. Rosina insisted that she had been 'neglected, hated, and ill-used, owing to her mother's vanity and ill-temper, and the amiable weakness of her good old uncle in submitting to her mamma', *Life*, i 160. As for her father, she only saw him once after the age of three and then thought him 'very vulgar'. Her father left his estate to another daughter, Henrietta.
14. Benjamin Disraeli to S. Disraeli, 29 January 1833, W. F. Monypenny and G. E. Buckle, *The Life of Benjamin Disraeli* (London 1910–20), i 223.
15. Miss Greene's Recollections, Knebworth MSS.
16. Ibid.
17. EBL Deposition [1858], Knebworth MSS, P2, box 142.
18. For Mrs Wheeler's attempts to sue Edward and Rosina, see Sir F. Doyle to EBL, 9 January 1832, Lytton MSS, DEK c22/156/3; and W. Loaden to EBL, n.d., ibid., c24/41. All lawyers failed Rosina's expectations, see Devey, 340, 352, 358, 360, 368.
19. *Life*, i 159.
20. *Monos: A Meditation*, 1826; Knebworth MSS, P5, box 68.
21. EBL to Rosina Lytton, 1826, Devey, 19.
22. Ibid. [1826], ibid., 50–51.
23. *O'Neill*, preface. Much the same theme is retailed in another work of the same period called *Glenallan*, *LLLR*, ii 79.
24. EBL to Rosina Lytton [1826], Devey, 16–17.
25. EBL to Lady Cunningham-Fairlie, 1 May 1827, *LLLR*, 144–45.
26. EBL to Rosina Lytton, 12 March 1827, Devey, 141–42.
27. Ibid., [1826], ibid., 17–18.
28. *The Destinies* or *Magus*, Knebworth MSS, box 13.
29. Devey, 85, 87, 90.
30. EBL to Sir W. Gelling, 2 December [1833], British Library, Add. MS 50135, fol. 9.
31. EBL to Rosina Lytton [1826], Devey, 27. See also ibid. [1826], Knebworth MSS, P4, box 70.
32. Although the evidence is far from conclusive, there is some evidence that there was cohabitation before marriage. See C. W. Snyder, *Liberty and Morality: A Political Biography of Edward Bulwer Lytton* (New York 1995), 25.
33. EBL to Rosina Lytton, n.d., Knebworth MSS, P4, box 70.
34. Ibid., 11 February 1827, Devey, 114–15.
35. Ibid., 18 March 1827, ibid., 148.
36. EBL to Rosina Lytton [August 1826], *Life*, i 168–69.
37. *LLLR*, ii 39.

38. EBL to Rosina Lytton, April 1826, Knebworth MSS, P4, box 70.
39. Ibid., Devey, 23.
40. Ibid., 13 March 1827, ibid., 143–44.
41. EBL to Mrs Bulwer, 1826, Knebworth MSS, P5, box 68.
42. Ibid., August 1827, ibid.
43. H. Bulwer to Mrs Bulwer, 1827, ibid.
44. EBL to Rosina Lytton [c. 1827], ibid., P4, box 70.
45. Ibid., 13 September 1826, *Life*, i 172.
46. Ibid., 12 October 1826, *Life*, i 177.
47. Rosina Lytton to EBL, ibid., i 179.
48. EBL to Rosina Lytton, 12 October 1826, Devey, 57.
49. Ibid., *Life*, i 175.
50. EBL to Mrs Bulwer, 1827, *LLLR* ii 142.
51. Ibid., 21 October 1826, Knebworth MSS, P5, box 68.
52. Ibid. [1827], ibid.
53. Ibid., July 1827, *LLLR*, ii 147. See also ibid. [August 1827], ibid.
54. Ibid., [1827], ibid., ii 149.
55. Ibid., 21 October 1826, ibid., ii 137.
56. EBL to Rosina Lytton, March 1827, *Life*, i 192–93.
57. EBL to Mrs Bulwer, 21 October 1826, *LLLR*, ii 137.
58. Ibid., 16 April 1827, ibid., ii 143.
59. Ibid., 2 August 1827, ibid., ii 148.
60. W. H. Palimore, 6 August 1827, Knebworth MSS, P5, box 68; and W. Loaden, 13 August 1827, ibid., P2, box 41.
61. EBL to Mrs Bulwer, 18 August 1827, *LLLR*, ii 149. Interestingly, however, EBL returned to the question of whether Rosina was lying about her age in 1832, when the marriage began to falter; F. Arthur to EBL, 16 January 1832, Lytton MSS, DEK c22/12.
62. Ibid., 16 August 1827, *LLLR*, 150–51.
63. Rosina Lytton to A. E. Chalon, 26 February 1855, L. Devey, *Unpublished Letters of Lady Lytton to A. E. Chalon* (London, n.d.), 140.
64. EBL to Mrs Bulwer, *LLLR*, ii 174.
65. Ibid. [c. Jan. 1828], *Life*, i 226.
66. Ibid., 1828, Knebworth MSS, P5, box 68.
67. *LLLR*, ii 206.
68. EBL to Mrs Bulwer [1828], Knebworth MSS, P5, box 68.
69. Ibid., 1 December 1828, *LLLR*, ii 203.
70. Ibid., 23 December 1828, Knebworth MSS, P5, box 68.
71. For accounts of these interviews, see *LLLR*, ii 212–15, and Devey, 254–58.
72. EBL to Rosina Lytton, 14 January 1829, Devey, 258.
73. EBL to Mrs Bulwer [1829], *LLLR*, ii 228.
74. Rosina. L to ?; 1832, J. Preston, *The Old Rich Woman* (Dorchester, 1995), 202.
75. EBL to Mrs Bulwer [1830], *LLLR*, ii 288. See also ibid., ii 221–25, 229–30.
76. Mrs Bulwer's Notes, Knebworth MSS, box 58 no. 3.

77. Rosina's Journal, 13 December 1835, Devey, 308.
78. EBL to Rosina Lytton [1827], ibid., 124
79. *Life*, i 258–61.
80. Ibid., i 208. See also *LLLR*, ii 199.
81. Rosina Lytton to Miss Greene, 26 May 1830, *Life*, i 253.
82. R. Nevill, *The Reminiscences of Lady Dorothy Nevill* (London 1906), 37.
83. P. F. Morgan, *The Letters of Thomas Hood* (Edinburgh 1973), 307.
84. Rosina Lytton to Mrs Bulwer, 1831, *LLLR*, ii 165.
85. *Life*, ii 15.
86. *LLLR*, ii 234.
87. A. C. Swinburne to F. G. Waugh, 27 March [1873], C. Y. Lang, *The Swinburne Letters* (New Haven, 1959–62), ii 235–36.
88. *LLLR*, 17 June 1827, ii 180.
89. Rosina Lytton to Miss Greene, n.d., ibid., ii 158.
90. Ibid., ii 231.
91. EBL to Rosina Lytton, May 1834, *Life*, i 281–82.
92. Rosina Lytton to Mrs Bulwer, 15 August 1832, *Life*, i 257.
93. Ibid., 28 May 1834, *Life*, i 283.
94. Annotation on EBL to Rosina Lytton, 29 August 1827, Knebworth MSS, P4, box 71.
95. S. C. Hall, *Retrospect of a Long Life* (London 1883), i 266.
96. *LLLR*, ii 218.
97. EBL to Rosina Lytton [1827], Devey, 185.
98. Ibid., [1827], Devey, 158–59.
99. Defining roles and areas of activity for women extended to objecting to them being allowed in the Athenaeum on Wednesdays: 'I think it quite imprudent in the women to force themselves thus daringly on our retirement and our strictures', *New Monthly Magazine*, 28, April 1830, 363.
100. *Life*, 279. For example, Lytton sat as a Radical in the Commons, while Rosina loathed 'beastly Radicals'; Rosina Lytton to Benjamin Disraeli, 13 August 1837, Bodleian Library, Hughenden MSS, BXX 140/3, fos 159–60.
101. EBL to Rosina Lytton, 25 May 1829, Devey, 277.
102. *Life*, i 248.
103. EBL to Rosina Lytton, 30 May 1829, Knebworth MSS, P4, box 71.
104. EBL to ?, 31 January 1831, Princeton, Parrish MSS, AM 16308.
105. Devey, 307. See also *Life*, i 255.
106. A. Kenealy, *Memoirs of Edward Vaughn Kenealy* (London 1908), 94–95.
107. Devey, 80–82 and Rosina Lytton to A. E. Chalon, 17 March 1855, Chalon, 150–51.
108. Devey, 193 and 209.
109. EBL to Lady Cunningham-Fairlie [1826], Lytton MSS, DEK c26/20/3.
110. EBL to Miss Parsons, 28 May 1828, ibid., c28/44; and Miss Greene's Recollections in the Knebworth MSS.
111. EBL to Lady Blessington, 5 October 1836, Lytton MSS, DEK c26/35.

112. R. Lytton, *A Blighted Life* (London, 1880), 77.
113. *Life*, i 263–66.
114. On returning to London, Lytton persuaded his mother to pay for one of the rooms in his London house to be furnished in the style of an apartment in Pompeii. T. Escott, *Edward Bulwer, First Baron Lytton* (London, 1910), 180–81.
115. Devey, 332.
116. EBL to Robert Lytton, n.d., Knebworth MSS, P2, box 142.
117. Although he would very much change his opinion later in life, EBL at this point referred to Miss Greene as 'a most malignant and dangerous enemy', Devey, 271–72.
118. Lytton, *Miscellaneous Prose Works by Edward Bulwer, Lord Lytton*, ii 271.

Notes to Chapter 3: 'The Misfortune of My Life'

1. EBL to C. d'Eyncourt, November 1848, Lytton MSS, DEK c26/21.
2. *My Novel*, book 2, chap. 6.
3. *Eugene Aram*, book 1, chap. 1, and book 1, chap. 6.
4. *What Will He Do With It?*, book 4, chap. 19.
5. *The Parisians*, book 4, chap. 3.
6. *The Pilgrims of the Rhine*, chap. 20.
7. *The Last Days of Pompeii*, book 1, chap. 6.
8. *Lovers' Quarrels*.
9. Rosina Lytton to A. E. Chalon, 26 November 1852, Chalon, 72–73.
10. Ibid., 26 February 1856, Chalon, 248–49.
11. Ibid.
12. *Life*, i 289.
13. EBL to Rosina Lytton, July 1834, Knebworth MSS, P4, box 31.
14. Rosina Lytton to Mrs Bulwer, 11 October 1834, *Life*, i 290. See also letters of 3 and 5 July, ibid., 286–88.
15. Mrs R. Benson's deposition, 1867, Devey, 324–25.
16. Miss Greene's Recollections, Knebworth MSS.
17. T. Carlyle to J. Carlyle, 16 April 1839, C. R. Sanders, *The Collected Letters of Thomas and Jane Welsh Carlyle* (Durham, North Carolina, 1970–97), xi 87–88.
18. Miss Greene's Recollections, Knebworth MSS.
19. EBL to Miss Greene, n.d., ibid., Q5, box 118; and EBL to Rosina Lytton, n.d., ibid., P2, box 41.
20. EBL to Miss Greene, 22 July 1839, ibid., Q5, box 118; and J. Beaven to EBL, n.d., Lytton MSS, DEK c22/33/8.
21. A. Fonblanque to Lady Blessington, 31 March 1836; A. Morrison, *The Blessington Papers* (London 1895). 'Mrs Bulwer has attacked her husband in *Fraser's Magazine*. This must surely make the case between them understood ... the woman who could take such a step must have in her a fund of ungovernable malice, accounting for all antecedents.' See also Devey, 292–93.
22. Sometimes the Bulwers acted as intermediaries, with little thanks for their

pains. H. Bulwer to Mrs Bulwer [5 July 1834], Knebworth MSS, box 58 no. 7; and *Life*, i 305–7.

23. EBL to Rosina Lytton [22 January 1835], ibid., box 13.

24. Lady C. Lytton to Lady B. Lytton, 4 March 1902, ibid.

25. 'Rules to be adhered to strictly, in the year of 1836, if I live to the end of it by RLB', Knebworth MSS, box 42/94.

26. *Life*, i 328–29.

27. Ibid., i 322–23.

28. Ibid., i 308–9. See also H. Bulwer to Mrs Bulwer, 28 January 1836, Knebworth MSS, P4, box 58; EBL to Miss Greene, 27 March 1836, ibid., Q5, box 118; and Miss Greene to EBL, 13 April 1836, ibid.

29. EBL to Miss Greene [1836], Princeton, Parrish MSS, AM 19180.

30. EBL to Rosina Lytton, 30 December 1834, *Life*, i 291–92.

31. Ibid., 21 December 1835, *Life*, EBL's italics i 315–16.

32. EBL to Mrs Bulwer, 20 December 1835, Knebworth MSS, P5, box 68.

33. Ibid., January 1836, ibid.

34. *Life*, i 318.

35. EBL to Rosina Lytton, 18 January 1836, Knebworth MSS, P4, box 31.

36. For Rosina's account, see *Life*, i 333–34, and Devey, 110–11.

37. EBL to Rosina Lytton [1836], Devey, 291.

38. Miss Greene's Recollections, Knebworth MSS.

39. EBL Journal, 1 June 1838, ibid.

40. Deed of separation, 19 April 1836, Devey, 300.

41. EBL to Rosina Lytton, 16 January 1835, *Life*, i 292.

42. W. Bulwer to EBL [1843], Knebworth MSS, box 56.

43. W. Bulwer to EBL, 19 January 1844, Knebworth MSS; also 9 June [c. 1843].

44. EBL annotation on W. Bulwer to EBL, n.d., ibid.

45. EBL to G. H. Lewes [December 1846], Bodleian Library, MS Eng. Litt. d 40, fol. 74. See also Devy, 230.

46. W. Bulwer to EBL, 11 August [1858], Knebworth MSS, box 56.

47. Ibid. See also J. Addams to EBL, April 1847, Lytton MSS, DEK c22/3/2.

48. EBL to Mrs Disraeli [1843], Bodleian Library, Hughenden MSS, 190/3, fol. 111.

49. EBL to ?, 10 February 1851, Princeton, Parrish MSS, AM 8581.

50. EBL to Henry Bulwer, 17 January 1850, Knebworth MSS, P4, box 69.

51. EBL to Mrs Halliday, n.d., Lytton MSS, K 28/10.

52. *What Will He Do With It?*, book 1, chap. 6.

53. *Life*, ii 503–4.

54. EBL to Mrs Halliday [July 1872], Lytton MSS, DEK c28/10.

55. *Godolphin*, chap. 24.

56. C. Bisset to EBL, 1843, Lytton MSS, DEK c22/43/26.

57. H. Bulwer's annotation on W. Bulwer to EBL, n.d., Knebworth MSS, P4, 69A.

58. W. Reade to Rosina Lytton, 17 May 1860, Bodleian Library, MS Eng. Litt. e 7, fol. 5.

59. Rosina's annotation of Lady Blessington's *Memoires* in Knebworth Library.
60. Lady Blessington to Benjamin Disraeli, n.d., Bodleian Library, Hughenden MSS, 119/2, fol. 156; EBL to H. Brougham, n.d., Princeton, Parrish MSS, AM 17260; EBL to Mrs Disraeli, 4 October 1853, Bodleian Library, Hughenden MSS, 104, fos 138–39.
61. EBL to Lady Stanhope, 15 March 1839, Kent Record Office, Stanhope MSS, U1590 C347.
62. Rosina Lytton to Miss Ryves, 31 August 1853, Huntingdon Library, Bulwer MSS, 10013.
63. J. d'Eyncourt to EBL, 4 September 1845, Lytton MSS, DEK c22/145/2; EBL to C. d'Eyncourt, 20 October 1845, ibid., c26/21. It should be noted that Charles d'Eyncourt's friendship with Lytton was unaffected by these events.
64. A. Tennyson to R. Monckton Milnes, 8 or 9 January 1837, C. Y. Lang, *The Letters of Alfred Lord Tennyson* (Oxford, 1982–90), i 147–48.
65. EBL to Lady Glamis, 8 October 1853, Knebworth MSS, P4, box 69A. This box also contains love letters from the girl. EBL to ?, 2 September 1853, ibid., P5, box 72.
66. Lady Glamis to EBL [1853], ibid., P4, box 69A.
67. Rosina Lytton, *A Blighted Life*, 23; and Rosina Lytton to Miss Ryves, 7 September 1854, Huntingdon Library, Bulwer MSS 10018.
68. J. Preston, *That Odd Rich Old Woman*, 211.
69. EBL, Journal, 25 May 1838, Knebworth MSS. On his birthday, he found every step on the great staircase at Knebworth strewn with flowers and verses.
70. Ibid., 22 May 1838, Knebworth MSS.
71. Rosina Lytton to Dr Price, 3 November 1857, Devey, 270–72; Rosina Lytton to Mrs Jermyn, 21 August 1857, Harvard, Houghton Library, autograph file; Rosina Lytton to A. E. Chalon, 10 June 1854, Chalon 92–95.
72. EBL to H. Bulwer, 22 August 1837, Norfolk Record Office, Bulwer MSS, BUL 1/3/33. A subscription on this letter reads 'Burn this'.
73. EBL to J. Beavan, 5 June 1847, Lytton MSS, DEK c26/4.
74. Rosina Lytton to Miss Ryves, 20 Jan 1854, Huntingdon Library, Bulwer MSS 10014.
75. EBL to John Forster, 1 September 1839, Lytton MSS, DEK c27 642; EBL to Miss Greene, 20 November 1839, Knebworth MSS, Q5, box 118; EBL to Robert Lytton, n.d., ibid., P5, box 72.
76. Miss Greene's Recollections, Knebworth MSS.
77. EBL to John Forster, n.d., Lytton MSS, DEK c27, fol. 301.
78. EBL to Mrs Bulwer, 3 October 1838, Knebworth MSS, P5, box 68.
79. Rosina Lytton to A. E. Chalon, 15 February 1852, Chalon, 55.
80. Ibid., 29 February 1856, ibid., 256–57. Rosina's annotation in Lady Blessington's *Memoires* in Knebworth Library.
81. Devey, 170–73.
82. Ibid., 161.
83. W. M. Thackeray to Mrs Carmichael-Smyth, March 1840, E. F. Harden, *The*

Letters and Private Papers of William Makepeace Thackeray (London, 1994), i 434–35.

84. This story can of course be presented from many points of view. See EBL – M. Lawson correspondence in Lytton MSS, DEK c28/32; EBL to O. Barrot, 14 April 1840, Knebworth MSS, P2, box 41, and Devey, 170–90.

85. W. Koff, 'Recollections of an Idler', Bodleian Library, Hughenden MSS, 140/3, fos 143–51.

86. EBL to M. Lawson [15 February 1840], Lytton MSS, c28/32.

87. Frances Trollope, the novelist, is an interesting witness because she claimed, unusually, to be a friend of both parties. F. Trollope to C. Trollope, 13 February 1840, F. E. Trollope, *Frances Trollope* (London 1895), i 308.

88. EBL to John Forster, [30 March 1840], Lytton MSS, DEK c27, fol. 748; EBL to Adams and Austin, 1840, ibid., c26/4; EBL Deposition, 1869, Knebworth MSS, P2, box 42.

89. EBL to Henry Bulwer, 13 January 1840, Knebworth MSS, P4, box 69.

90. W. Bulwer to EBL, n.d., ibid., box 56.

91. W. Toynbee, *The Diaries of William Charles Macready* (London, 1912), ii 54–55.

92. Devey, 218. EBL to H. Bulwer, 19 March 1849, Norfolk Record Office, Bulwer MSS, BUL 1/86/11; EBL to Robert Lytton, 14 December 1852, Knebworth MSS, J2, I, fol. 40; Robert Lytton to EBL, 13 November 1853, Knebworth MSS, P5, box 95; Devey, 255–56.

93. Ibid., 211.

94. Ibid., 220.

95. H. Trenchard to EBL, 17 November 1857, Knebworth MSS, P2, box 42, fol. 81.

96. Lord Lyndhurst was forced to exculpate himself before the House of Lords from a charge of 'having treated a lady with a want of proper courtesy'. *Parliamentary Debates*, 19 May 1857, vol. 247, 481–82.

97. T. Trollope to Rosina Lytton, 9 July 1840, Devey, 203; J. Beavan to EBL, 1848, Lytton MSS, DEK c22/33/1.

98. Rosina Lytton to A. E. Chalon, 11 September 1856, Chalon 270–71.

99. Lytton MSS, DEK c22/156. Letters between Sir F. Doyle and EBL.

100. Rosina Lytton to Mrs W. Lewis and vice-versa, 12, 15 and 18 July 1838, Bodleian Library, Hughenden MSS, 190/3, fos 179, 206–8, 212–13.

101. Ibid., 23 May ?, ibid., fos 219–20. Devey, 131.

102. Rosina Lytton to Mr Harness [1850], BL, Add. MS 45918, fol. 57.

103. Devey, 397.

104. Rosina Lytton to American publisher, 6 February 1850, Boston Public Library, MS Griswold 705; Rosina Lytton to editor of *The Times*, 17 January 1857, Knebworth MSS, P2, box 42.

105. *Very Successful*, i 167.

106. *Cheveley*, i 3.

107. *Miriam Sedley*, i, chap. 9.

108. *Cheveley*, i 271.

109. Rosina Lytton to A. E. Chalon, 28 February 1852, Chalon 57.

110. G. Sand to Rosina Lytton, 6 December 1842, Devey, 206.

111. Rosina Lytton to A. E. Chalon, 2 April 1856, Chalon 265.

112. Ibid., 10 February 1855, ibid., 122–23.

113. *Miriam Sedley*, dedicace. See also Chalon 197.

114. Rosina Lytton to A. E. Chalon, 15 June 1854, ibid., 98–101.

115. EBL to Lady Blessington, 6 April 1839, Lytton MSS, DEK c26/35.

116. EBL to Mrs Bulwer, 23 April 1839, Knebworth MSS, P5, box 68; H. Bulwer to Mrs Bulwer, May and 29 May 1839, ibid., box 58.

117. EBL to John Forster, [6 April 1839], Lytton MSS, DEK c27, fol. 626; also 1 and 10 April 1839, ibid., fos 625, 631, Devey, 147 seq; EBL to Mrs Bulwer, 1839, Knebworth MSS, P5, box 68.

118. John Forster to EBL, 1839 and 9 April 1839, Lytton MSS, DEK c14, fos 9 and 23; Rosina Lytton to R. Bentley, 21 February 1839, Bodleian Library, MS Eng. Litt., d 90, fol. 339. Rosina tempted the publisher by saying 'the additional circumstance of its being opposed – or prosecuted – is at once a safe guarantee of an enormous sale'.

119. W. S. Landor to Lady Blessington, 8 February 1839, A. Morrison, *The Blessington Papers*, 138.

120. W. M. Thackeray to J. Fraser [1839], E. F. Harden, *The Letters and Private Papers of W. M. Thackeray*, i 41; *Fraser's Magazine*, 19, May 1839, 618.

121. EBL to John Forster, 1 September 1840, Lytton MSS, DEK c27, fol. 690. See also ibid., 14 September 1840, ibid., fol. 699.

122. John Forster to EBL, 10 September 1840, ibid., DEK c14, fol. 42; EBL to editor of the *Morning Post*, January 1852, G. Storey, *The Letters of Charles Dickens*, March 1840, v 14 n 3.

123. Rosina Lytton to A. E. Chalon [April 1854], Chalon, 81–85; Rosina Lytton to R. Ryves, 16 June 1854, Huntingdon Library, Bulwer MSS, 10016.

124. Rosina Lytton to A. E. Chalon, 24 January 1852, Chalon, 47–48.

125. *The School for Husbands* was dedicated to Carlyle. J. Carlyle to Rosina Lytton [*c.* 1847], Chalon 25–26; T. Carlyle to Rosina Lytton, 7 January 1851, C. R. Sanders, *The Collected Letters of Thomas and Jane Carlyle*, xxvi 11; Devey, 265–66.

126. Knebworth MSS, P4, box 71.

127. John Forster to EBL, 21 March 1839, Lytton MSS, DEK c14, fol. 22.

128. EBL to Mrs Bulwer, 5 May 1838, Knebworth MSS, P5m, box 68.

129. EBL to Robert Lytton, 2 February 1858, ibid., J2, vol. I, fol. 123.

130. C. Dickens to EBL, 9 May 1851, G. Storey, *The Letters of Charles Dickens*, vi 379–80. See also EBL Deposition, Knebworth MSS, P2, box 41.

131. Rosina Lytton to F. H. Thornton, 1858, ibid.

132. Rosina Lytton to A. Boys, 11 June 1858, Devey, 282–88; *Life*, 8 June 1858.

133. W. Blackwood to EBL, 1 August 1858, Lytton MSS, DEK c22/45/1.

134. C. Reade to Rosina Lytton, 28 February 1864, Huntingdon Library, Bulwer MSS, 10097.

135. For accounts of her abduction and confinement, see Knebworth MSS, P2, box 41; EBL to J. Blackwood, 4 August 1858, National Library of Scotland, Blackwood MSS, fos 251–54; Devey, 288–95. With considerable plausibility, the incident is

claimed to have inspired *The Woman in White* by Wilkie Collins. Rosina thought so. The book is dedicated to Bryan Waller Proctor, Chairman of the Commissioners of Lunacy. I am grateful to my colleague, Dr John Mee, for bringing this point to my attention. Rosina Lytton to Dr Price, 26 September 1860, Devey, 364.

136. Mr Hill's Journal, Knebworth MSS, P2, box 41.

137. *Life*, ii 274.

138. H. Drummond Wolff, 12 July 1858, Lytton MSS, DEK c25/172/2.

139. *Somerset County Gazette*, 13 July 1858; *Daily Telegraph*, 15 July 1858.

140. Knebworth MSS, V2/29.

141. Lord Shaftesbury, 29 July 1858, National Library of Scotland, Blackwood MSS, 4130, fol. 89. See also Lytton MSS, DEK c25/46.

142. *Life*, ii 275.

143. John Forster to EBL, 11 October 1857, Lytton MSS, DEK c23; EBL to John Foster, 7 October 1857; ibid., c27.

144. John Forster to EBL, 27 July 1858, 12 March 1859, 2 April 1859, ibid., c23 and c27; and EBL to John Forster, [July] and 10 September 1858, ibid., c27.

145. John Forster to EBL, 25 March 1859, ibid., c23.

146. John Forster to EBL 27 July 1861 and 27 July 1862, ibid. c14. There seems to be a resumption of a closer friendship after 1865.

147. Rosina Lytton to ?, 14 October 1861, Boston Public Library, Ch.H.10.39.

148. 'John Smith' to EBL, 8 November 1860, Bodleian Library, Hughenden MSS, 104/2, fos 109–10. See also Knebworth MSS, Q5, box 117.

149. EBL to Benjamin Disraeli, 20 January 1864, Bodleian Library, Hughenden MSS, 104/3 fos 1–2.

150. EBL to Robert Lytton, n.d., Knebworth MSS, J2, i 307; and EBL to John Forster, 20 January 1864, Lytton MSS, DEK c27.

151. 'Forgive and Forget', in *Shells from the Sands of Time* (London, 1876).

152. 'False Heart Beware', Bodleian Library, Hughenden MSS, 190/3, fol. 228.

153. Rosina Lytton to editor of *Once a Week*, 14 December 1872, J. P. Morgan Library, M.A. unassigned.

Notes to Chapter 4: Robert and Emily

1. Predictably, he was not sympathetic to the campaign being run by his friend, Caroline Norton, to give wives more rights in custodial disputes. C. Norton to EBL, 2 March 1838, *Life*, i 517; ibid. [1839], J. O. Hoge and C. Olney, *The Letters of Caroline Norton to Lord Melbourne* (Ohio, 1974), 13.

2. EBL to Robert Lytton, 9 October 1865, Lady E. Lutyens, *The Birth of Rowland* (London 1956), 239.

3. EBL to Miss Greene, 1840, Knebworth MSS, Q5, box 118.

4. Lady B. Balfour to Lady C. Lytton, 5 March 1902, ibid., V3/9.

5. EBL to Miss Greene, 1838, ibid., Q5, box 118; Miss Greene's Recollections, ibid.

6. EBL to Miss Greene, 14 July 1838, ibid., Q5, box 118; EBL to Miss Greene [1840], Princeton, Parrish MSS.

7. Ibid., n.d., Knebworth MSS, Q5, box 118. See also ibid., 4 March 1837, 31 May 1838 [??1839] and 7 June 1839, ibid.

8. Miss Greene's Recollections, Knebworth MSS.

9. Rosina Lytton to A. E. Chalon, 2 November 1856, Chalon, 277–81.

10. W. M. Thackeray to Mrs Carmichael-Smythe, 20 December 1839, G. N. Ray, *The Letters and Private Papers of W. M. Thackeray* (Oxford, 1945–46), i 398.

11. EBL to Rosina Lytton, 16 January 1829, Devey, 260.

12. EBL to Mrs Bulwer, 12 January 1838, Knebworth MSS, P5, box 68.

13. Knebworth MSS, P5, box 88 contains the early letters from EBL to his children.

14. Miss Greene to EBL, 3 June 1839, ibid., Q5, box 118.

15. Miss Greene's Recollections, Knebworth MSS.

16. Ibid.

17. EBL to Miss Greene, 20 September 1843, Knebworth MSS, Q5, box 118.

18. Ibid., 14 February 1848, ibid.

19. EBL to John Forster, 22 June 1849, Lytton MSS, DEK c27, fol. 257.

20. Lord Lytton to Lady B. Balfour, 2 May 1903, Knebworth MSS, box 13.

21. EBL to Miss Greene, 20 November 1836, Knebworth MSS, Q5, box 118; EBL to Robert Lytton, 11 February 1862, ibid., J2, i 363.

22. EBL to Isaac Disraeli, 30 May 1838, Bodleian Library, Hughenden MSS, 244/5, fol. 108.

23. EBL, Notes [c. 1843], Lytton MSS, DEK, fol. 52, and Knebworth MSS, 04408.

24. EBL to Emily Lytton [c. November 1847], Knebworth MSS, P5, box 88.

25. Robert Lytton to EBL, 6 May 1845, Lytton MSS, DEK c41.

26. EBL to Emily Lytton, 8 March 1844, Knebworth MSS, P5, box 88.

27. Emily Lytton to EBL, n.d., ibid.

28. EBL to Miss Greene, 1839, Knebworth MSS, Q5, box 118.

29. Devey, 208–10.

30. EBL to Emily Lytton [10 March 1843], Knebworth MSS, P5, box 88.

31. EBL to Emily Lytton, n.d.; ibid.

32. EBL to Emily Lytton [15 April 1844], ibid.

33. EBL to Emily Lytton [22 March 1843], ibid. See also ibid., 20 June [1844], ibid.

34. Emily Lytton to EBL [10 April 1843], ibid.

35. EBL to Emily Lytton, 11 February 1842, Knebworth MSS, Q5, box 118.

36. EBL to Emily Lytton, 21 May 1844, ibid., P5, box 88.

37. EBL to Emily Lytton, n.d., ibid.; also 19 January 1844, ibid.; and Miss Greene's Recollections.

38. EBL to Emily Lytton [14 October 1844], ibid.

39. EBL to Emily Lytton, 12 May, 19 July, 15 October, 13, 21 November, 5 December 1847, Knebworth MSS.

40. Ibid., 1847, ibid.

41. Rosina Lytton to Dr M. Hall, 17 July 1848, Devey, 250.

42. Charles Kingsley was one of the embarrassed recipients of this pamphlet. C. Kingsley to EBL, 21 February 1850, Lytton MSS, DEK c24/13.

43. Devey, 316–23.

44. Knebworth, Miss Greene's Recollections.
45. EBL to Lady Blessington [1848], Lytton MSS, DEK c26/34; EBL, deposition, 1869, Knebworth MSS, P2, box 142; EBL to C. d'Eyncourt, n.d., Lincolnshire Record Office, d'Eyncourt MSS, TdE/H/160/42; EBL to John Forster, n.d., Lytton MSS, DEK c27/150–51.
46. EBL to C. d'Eyncourt, n.d., Lincolnshire Record Office, d'Enycourt MSS, TdE/H/160/42.
47. EBL to John Forster, 22 March and May 1848, Lytton MSS, DEK c27, fos 155–56, 165–66.
48. Ibid., 26 June 1848, ibid., fos 185–87; EBL to C. d'Eyncourt [1848], Lincolnshire Record Office, d'Eyncourt MSS, TdE/H/160/44 and 50.
49. Robert Lytton to EBL [1848], Knebworth MSS, P5, box 97.
50. Ibid., 20 October 1857, ibid., P5, box 96.
51. Robert Lytton to Edith Lytton, 31 July 1865, Lady E. Lutyens, *The Birth of Rowland* (London, 1956), 89.
52. *Life*, ii 103.
53. Robert Lytton to ? [1873], *Life*, ii 496.
54. *To My Father*, Knebworth MSS, P5, box 97.
55. Robert Lytton to Emily Lytton [26 January 1843], ibid., P5, box 88.
56. EBL to Mrs Bulwer, 4 September 1835, ibid., P5, box 68.
57. Robert Lytton to EBL, 15 May and 26 July 1846, Lytton MSS, DEK c41.
58. Ibid., January 1844, Knebworth MSS, P5, box 98.
59. EBL to Robert Lytton, 17 July 1846, ibid., V2/45.
60. Robert Lytton to EBL, 16 and 20 July 1846, Lytton MSS, DEK c41; EBL to Mr Harris, 28 June 1849, ibid., DEK c28/41; Robert Lytton to EBL, n.d., Knebworth MSS, P5, box 97.
61. EBL to C. d'Eyncourt, 22 November 1845, Lincolnshire Record Office, d'Eyncourt MSS, TdE/H/160/16; Robert Lytton to EBL, 22 July 1846, Lytton MSS, DEK c41.
62. Robert Lytton to Dr Perry [1851], Balfour, i 24–25.
63. Robert Lytton to ?, 1873, Huntingdon MSS, Bulwer MSS.
64. Robert Lytton to EBL, n.d., Knebworth MSS, P5, box 98.
65. EBL to Miss Gordon [1841], Princeton, Parrish MSS, AM 18689.
66. Robert Lytton to EBL [1849], Lytton MSS, DEK c41.
67. EBL to Robert Lytton [14 October 1846], Princeton, Parrish MSS, AM 17982.
68. Ibid., n.d.; Knebworth MSS, J2, vol i, fol. 7; Robert Lytton to EBL [1846], Lytton MSS, DEK c41.
69. EBL to John Forster, 18 March 1850, Lytton MSS, DEK c27, fol. 344. He had been opening his son's letters.
70. EBL to John Forster, 25 February 1850, ibid., fol. 315.
71. EBL to John Forster, February 1850, ibid., fol. 326.
72. EBL to C. d'Eyncourt, 16 September 1851, Lincolnshire Record Office, d'Eyncourt MSS, TdE/H/160/29. EBL to John Forster, 25 February 1850, Lytton MSS, DEK c27 fol. 315.
73. EBL to John Forster, 10 and 25 February 1850, ibid.

74. John Forster to EBL, 4 March and 7 October 1850, Lytton MSS, DEK c14, fos 155 and 180.

75. Ibid., 26 October 1850, ibid., fol. 197.

76. Robert Lytton to John Forster, 10 May 1850, ibid., c40 A, fol. 6.

77. H. Bulwer to Benjamin Disraeli, 12 May 1858, Bodleian Library, Hughenden MSS, 121/3, fol. 128.

78. Rosina Lytton to Dr Price, 21 August 1858, Devey, 332; Rosina Lytton to Robert Lytton, 6 April 1859, Knebworth MSS, box 13.

79. *Life*, ii 381.

80. Robert Lytton to EBL, 1858–59, Knebworth MSS, P5, boxes 95, 96, 98.

81. John Forster to EBL, 28 July [1858], Lytton MSS, DEK c23.

82. Robert Lytton to EBL, 25 January [1864], Knebworth MSS, P5, box 67; EBL to Robert Lytton, 20 January 1864, ibid., J2 ii 555.

83. Robert Lytton to EBL [1867] and 16 January 1868, Knebworth MSS, P5, boxes 97 and 96.

84. Edith Lytton to Robert Lytton, and vice-versa, 4 and 11 August 1865, Balfour, 114, 116.

85. EBL to Robert Lytton, 6 April 1853, Knebworth MSS, J2 I, fol. 23.

86. EBL to Robert Lytton, 15 September 1853, ibid., JIV 2042.

87. EBL to Robert Lytton, 7 October 1853, *Life*, ii 387–88.

88. EBL to Robert Lytton, 2 December 1858, Lytton MSS, DEK c28/34; ibid., 4 March and 25 May 1859, Knebworth MSS, P5, box 72.

89. EBL to Robert Lytton, 2 April 1859, ibid.

90. EBL to Robert Lytton, July 1865, ibid., J2 ii 817.

91. Ibid. [1865], *Life*, ii 360.

92. Robert Lytton to Edith Lytton, 3 October 1865, Lady E. Lutyens, *The Birth of Rowland*, 182; Robert Lytton to John Forster, 4 July 1864, ibid., 23.

93. Robert Lytton to Edith Lytton, 12 July 1865, Lady E. Lutyens, *The Birth of Rowland*, 63.

94. EBL to Robert Lytton, November 1862, Knebworth MSS, P5, box 72; Robert Lytton to J. Blackwood, 21 April 1862, National Library of Scotland, Blackwood MSS, 4171, fol. 299.

95. Robert Lytton to EBL [1845], Lytton MSS, DEK c41.

96. A. C. Swinburne to J. C. Collins, 16 June 1886, C. Y. Lang, *The Swinburne Papers*, v 146.

97. EBL to John Forster, December 1863, Balfour i 144–45; Robert Lytton to John Forster, 28 December 1855, Lytton MSS, DEK c40 B.

98. Ibid., 29 July 1854, ibid.

99. EBL to Lady Murray, December 1841, Knebworth MSS, box 13; and EBL to Robert Lytton, n.d., ibid., P5, box 72.

100. Robert Lytton to ?, 1873, Huntingdon Library, Bulwer MSS.

101. Robert Lytton to EBL, 7 September 1871, Knebworth MSS, P5, box 95.

102. J. Vincent, *A Selection from the Diaries of Edward Henry Stanley, 15th Earl of Derby* (London, 1994), 443.

Notes to Chapter 5: Society

1. *LLLR*, i 327.
2. T. Macaulay, to H. Macaulay, 2 August 1833, T. Pinney, *The Letters of Thomas Babington Macaulay*, ii 289.
3. EBL, Journal, 1 June 1838, Knebworth MSS.
4. *My Novel*, book 10 chap. 9; R. Nevill, *The Reminiscences of Lady Dorothy Nevill*, 56–57.
5. Devey, 2–6.
6. *Pelham* ii chap. 7; ii chap. 8; ii chap. 16.
7. For example, the description of Marmaduke Neville in *The Last of the Barons*, book 2, chap. 1. 'His corset was of the finest cloth, sewn with seed pearls; above it, the lawn shirt, worn without collar, partially appeared, fringed with gold; over this was loosely hung a super-tunic of crimson sarcenet, slashed and pounced with a profusion of fringes. His velvet cap, turned up at the sides, extended to a point far over the forehead. His hose – under which appellation is to be understood what serves us of the modern day both for stockings and pantaloons – were of white cloth, and his shoes, very narrow, were curiously carved into chequer-work at the instep and tied with bobbins of gold thread.'
8. EBL to Lady Blessington, 31 August 1833, R. R. Madden, *The Literary Life and Correspondence of the Countess of Blessington* (London, 1855), iii 33.
9. *O'Neill*, (London, 1827).
10. *What Will He Do With It?*, book 1, chap. 1.
11. H. and M. Schwartz, *Disraeli's Reminiscences* (London, 1975), 62.
12. EBL to ?, n.d., Princeton, Parrish MSS, AM 19408; EBL to Macvey Napier, 13 March 1837, British Library, Add. MS 34618 fol. 74.
13. T. A. Jenkins, *The Parliamentary Diaries of Sir John Trelawney* (London, 1990), 247.
14. C. Dickens to John Forster, 18 April 1848, *The Letters of Charles Dickens*, v 283 and 283n.; W. Toynbee, *The Diaries of William Charles Macready* (London, 1912), i 278.
15. Lord Melbourne to Queen Victoria, 21 October 1841, A. C. Benson and Lord Esher, *The Letters of Queen Victoria* (London, 1908), i 350; Lord Teignmouth, *Reminiscences of Many Years* (Edinburgh, 1878); T. Carlyle to J. Carlyle, 27 February 1840, C. R. Saunders, *The Collected Letters of Thomas and Jane Welsh Carlyle*, xii 59.
16. *Life*, ii 17; Sir L. Ward, *Forty Years of 'Spy'* (London, 1915), 22; *Athenaeum*, 22 August 1840; Knebworth MSS, box 13.
17. T. Carlyle to J. Carlyle, 11 March 1839, Saunders, *The Collected Letters of Thomas and Jane Carlyle*, xi 48–49.
18. EBL to Rosina Lytton, 1826, Devey, 126.
19. *LLLR*, ii 378; and *Pelham*, book 1, chap. 23.
20. EBL to Lady Blessington [1834 or 5], Lytton MSS, DEK c26/35.
21. EBL to Rosina Lytton [1827]; Devey, 130.
22. S. C. Hall, *Retrospect of a Long Life* (London, 1883), i 225–26.

23. Chalon, 144–45.
24. G. Eliot to S. Hennell, 2 March 1858, *The George Eliot Letters*, ii 439.
25. A. Kenealy, *Memoirs of Edward Vaughn Kenealy* (London, 1908), 229–30.
26. EBL to Mrs Cosway [*c*. 1871], Lytton MSS, DEK c26/18.
27. *Cornhill Magazine*, autumn 1873.
28. EBL to John Forster, n.d., Lytton MSS, DEK c23.
29. EBL to John Forster [17 August 1840], ibid., c27.
30. *Cornhill*, no. 1077, 1873.
31. EBL to Lord Houghton [1871], Trinity College, Cambridge, Houghton MSS, 15/178 and 15/180.
32. Knebworth MSS, box 53.
33. *New Monthly Magazine*, no. 37, 30.
34. EBL to John Forster [26 September and 12 December 1840], Lytton MSS, DEK c27; *Life*, ii 191; EBL to Lady Blessington n.d., Lytton MSS, c26/34.
35. EBL to Mlle de Bourgand, 27 April 1857, Princeton, Parrish MSS.
36. EBL to Dr ?, 4 February 1867, Huntingdon Library, Bulwer MSS, 7912; Knebworth MSS, box 53.
37. EBL to Dr Garrett, 6 January 1866, Lytton MSS, DEK c28/1; EBL to John Forster [22 August 1840], ibid., c27.
38. EBL to Lady Murray, 8 August 1840, Knebworth MSS, box 13; EBL to C. d'Eyncourt [December 1844], Lytton MSS, c26/21.
39. *The Coming Race*, chap. 15.
40. *New Monthly Magazine*, vol. 75, September 1845; EBL to John Forster, 18 June 1844, Lytton MSS, DEK c27; *LLLR*, ii 167. EBL to Lady Blessington, June 1844; R. R. Madden, *The Literary Life and Correspondence of the Countess of Blessington*, iii 46–47; Chalon 274.
41. C. Luther, *Sir Edward Bulwer Lytton and Homeopathy* (London, 1853).
42. Lady Granville to Duchess of Devonshire, 29 November 1844, F. Leveson Gower, *Letters of Harriet, Countess Granville* (London, 1894), ii 389.
43. Lord Macaulay's Journal, 31 December 1838. I am most grateful to W. E. S. Thomas for this reference.
44. *The Parisians*, book 3, chap. 4.
45. *Pausanias*, book, 1 chap. 1.
46. *Lucretia*, part 2, prologue.
47. Edward IV in *The Last of the Barons*, book 2, chap. 2; Lepidus in *The Last Days of Pompeii*, book 2, chap. 3; Giulio Franzini in *My Novel*, book 8, chap. 2.
48. EBL to Lady Cunningham, 25 June 1826, *LLLR*, ii 127.
49. *LLLR*, ii 195.
50. *England and the English*, book 4, section 2.
51. Rosina Lytton to A. E. Chalon, 10 February 1855, Chalon, 124.
52. EBL to Macvey Napier, 19 December 1835, British Library, Add. MS 34617, fol. 576.
53. EBL to Durham [1836], S. J. Reid, *Life and Letters of the First Earl of Durham* (London, 1906), ii 97.

54. G. Storey, *The Letters of Charles Dickens*, ii 58 n. 3; Chalon 155. Rosina's annotations to the Blessington Life and Correspondence in Knebworth Library.

55. Lady Blessington to Benjamin Disraeli [1836], Bodleian Library, Hughenden MSS, 119/2, fol. 87.

56. M. Sadleir, *Blessington d'Orsay* (London, 1933), 203–4; Lady Blessington to EBL [1831], Lytton MSS, DEK c9, fol. 7.

57. Ibid., fol. 1.

58. Sadleir, *Blessington d'Orsay*, 243–54.

59. EBL to Mrs W. Lewis, n.d., Bodleian Library, Hughenden MSS, 190/3, fol. 105.

60. Lady Blessington to Henry Bulwer, 6 November 1834, R. R. Madden, *The Literary Life and Correspondence of the Countess of Blessington*, iii 67.

61. EBL to Lady Blessington, n.d. and 23 October 1834, Lytton MSS, DEK c26/35.

62. Lady Blessington to EBL [c. 1835], ibid.

63. *Godolphin*, preface.

64. Ibid., chap. 8; *Ernest Maltravers*, book 2, chap. 4; *What Will He Do With It?*, book 2, chap. 9.

65. Benjamin Disraeli to Lady Blessington [12 January 1837], *Life*, i 530–31; A. Fonblanque to EBL, 19 December 1835, Lytton MSS, DEK c1; A. d'Orsay to Mrs Disraeli [19 April 1845], Bodleian Library, Hughenden MSS, 189/1, fol. 266.

66. A. d'Orsay to EBL, n.d., Lytton MSS, DEK c22/154.

67. *The Siamese Twins*, book 2, chap. 2.

68. *What Will He Do With It?*, book 1, chaps 14 and 17.

69. EBL to Lady Blessington, 2 April 1849, Lytton MSS, DEK c26/34; Lady Blessington to EBL, 30 April 1849, ibid., c9, fol. 2; *Life*, ii 116 seq.

70. EBL to Benjamin Disraeli, 22 December 1836, Bodleian Library, Hughenden MSS, 104/, fos 58–59; *Very Successful*, i 278.

71. *Ernest Maltravers*, book 1, chap. 16.

72. *LLLR*, i 331–32; F. Villiers to EBL [1831 or 1832], Lytton MSS, DEK c25/139/4; ibid., DEK c22/16.

73. *LLLR*, i 363; *Bentley's Miscellany*, July 1848, no. 24, 5.

74. Devey, 316.

75. *Cheveley*, iii 36, 190.

76. EBL annotation to C. H. Townshend to EBL, 29 February 1840, Lytton MSS, DEK c6, fol. 11; *LLLR*, i 172 n i.

77. *LLLR*, i 169.

78. C. H. Townshend to EBL, 29 February 1840, Lytton MSS, DEK c6, fol. 11.

79. Devey, 263; EBL to Benjamin Disraeli, 26 July 1829, Bodleian Library, Hughenden MSS, 104/1, fol. 6.

80. H. and M. Schwartz, *Disraeli's Reminiscences*, 12.0.

81. Lady Blessington to Benjamin Disraeli, 4 September 1834, Bodleian Library, Hughenden MSS, 119/2, fol. 39.

82. Disraeli's Commonplace Book, ibid., A26/2 fol. 133.

83. Robert Lytton to Benjamin Disraeli, 6 February 1873, ibid. 105/1, fol. 6.

84. *LLLR*, ii 327.

85. EBL to Benjamin Disraeli, 6 March 1834, Bodleian Library, Hughenden MSS, 104/1, fol. 44.
86. EBL to Benjamin Disraeli [1831]; ibid., 104/1, fos 25–27.
87. EBL to I. Disraeli, 20 August 1836, ibid., 224/5, fol. 95; Benjamin Disraeli to EBL, 14 November 1834, Lytton MSS, DEK c1, fol. 100.
88. EBL to Benjamin Disraeli [1831], 17 June 1832, 8 March 1856, 12 August 1868; Bodleian Library, Hughenden MSS, 104/1, fos 29, 32, 180, and 104/3, fos 36–38.
89. EBL to W. Kent [4 August 1868], Boston Public Library, MS C.1.41.106.
90. EBL to Benjamin Disraeli, 10 April 1830, Bodleian Library, Hughenden MSS, 104/1, fos 11–12.
91. EBL to John Forster, n.d., Lytton MSS, DEK c23.
92. Ibid., n.d.; ibid., c27; *The Disowned*, book 1, chap 8.
93. H. and M. Schwartz, *Disraeli's Reminiscences*, 61–62.
94. Rosina Lytton to L. Devey, 19 April 1881, Knebworth MSS, 01585.
95. Rosina Lytton to A. E. Chalon, 6 March 1852 and 8 February 1856, Chalon 58 and 233–34.
96. Rosina's annotation of *The Literary Life and Correspondence of the Countess of Blessington* in Knebworth Library.
97. R. Blake, *Disraeli*, 155.
98. Anon., *Literary Daguerreotypes of the Nineteenth Century*, Knebworth V2/21.
99. Dr J. Connolly to ?, 10 August 1858, Lytton MSS, DEK c22/115/10.
100. Benjamin Disraeli to EBL, 1858, ibid., c22/149/2; A Kenealy, *Memoirs of Edward Vaughn Kenealy* (London, 1908), 229.
101. P. Rose to EBL, 18 October 1864, Lytton MSS, DEK c17, fol. 119.
102. John Forster to EBL, 10 July 1848, Lytton MSS, DEK c14, fol. 90.
103. Ibid., c14, fol. 1. See also EBL to John Forster [1841], ibid. c23; and ibid., n.d., c27, fol. 335.
104. 26 February 1841; Victoria and Albert Museum, Forster MSS, 5557.
105. J. A. Davies, *John Forster: A Literary Life* (Leicester, 1983), 39.
106. EBL to John Forster, n.d., Lytton MSS, DEK c23.
107. J. A. Davies, *John Forster*, chap. 4.
108. EBL to W. Kent, 25 August 1869, Boston Public Library, MS C.1.41.116; and EBL to Robert Lytton., n.d., Knebworth MSS, JIV 1665.
109. EBL to the editor of *Burke's Peerage*, 18 September 1844, Huntingdon Library, Bulwer MSS, 594.
110. T. H. Duncombe, *The Life and Correspondence of T. S. Duncombe*, i 139–42.
111. *The Last of the Barons*, book 1, chap. 1; *The Last Days of Pompeii*, preface; *Edinburgh Review*, 44, no 520, January 1837.
112. *In Olden Time*, 1823.
113. For example, *The Lay of the Minstrel's Heart* and *The Fairy Bride*.
114. EBL to Mrs Thomson [1844], *Life*, ii 53–54.
115. *What Will He Do With It?*, book 2, chap 14.
116. A. Trollope's commonplace book, 19 December 1840; N. J. Hall, *The Letters of Anthony Trollope* (Stanford, 1983), i 319 n. 6; ibid., ii, appendix a.

117. It should be noted, however, that Lytton could also laugh at hereditary pretension. *Hereditary Honours* tells the story of a young man, who claims 400 years of family distinction. It transpires that the distinction in question is that of being hereditary hangman. *New Monthly Magazine*, no. 30, May 1832, 433–40.
118. T. B. Macaulay to H. Macaulay, 5 August 1831, T. Pinney, *The Letters of Thomas Babington Macaulay*, ii 84.
119. T. Carlyle to J. Carlyle, 1 August 1840, C. R. Saunders, *The Collected Letters of Thomas and Jane Welsh Carlyle*, xii 211.
120. T. Carlyle, *Sartor Resartus*, book 3, chap. 10.
121. *Life*, i 236–37.
122. W. M. Thackeray, *The Yellowplush Letters*, ix. See also W. M. Thackeray to Mrs Proctor, [27] August 1847; E. F. Harden, *The Letters and Private Papers of William Makepeace Thackeray*, i 200.
123. Ibid.
124. *The Disowned*, vol. 1, chap. 6.
125. *New Monthly Magazine*, no. 38, 417–22, August 1833.
126. R. Blake, *Disraeli*, 83; EBL to Lady Blessington, 24 January 1835, R. R. Madden, *The Literary Life and Correspondence of the Countess of Blessington*, iii 36–37.
127. EBL annotations, Lytton MSS, DEK c2, fol. 9, and c6, fol. 55.
128. *What Will He Do With It?*, book 6, chap. 1.
129. *Miscellaneous Prose Works*, ii 186–90.
130. EBL to Lady Blessington, 23 October 1834; *Life*, i 459.
131. *Miscellaneous Prose Works*, ii 72.
132. EBL to Miss Bacon, 17 April [1832], Cambridge University Library, Bacon MSS, fol. 9; and EBL to W. Kent, 28 September 1872, Boston Public Library, MS C.1.41.130.
133. Bodleian Library, MS Autograph, c24, fol. 144.

Notes to Chapter 6: A Writer and the Public

1. *The Disowned*, vol. 2, chap. 48.
2. Ibid.
3. *Ernest Maltravers*, book 4, chap. 4. See also *Life*, ii 95–96.
4. T. B. Macaulay to EBL, 24 June 1842, T. Pinney, *The Letters of T. B. Macaulay*, iv 42–43.
5. EBL to Lady Cunningham-Fairlie, 25 June 1826, Lytton MSS, DEK c26/20.
6. *New Monthly Magazine*, no. 32, September 1831.
7. *The Pilgrims of the Rhine*, chap. 5; *What Will He Do With It?*, book 6, chap. 6.
8. EBL to G. H. Lewes [November 1842]; Bodleian Library, MS Eng. Lett. d40, fol. 72; EBL to Robert Lytton [7 February 1868], Knebworth MSS, Jiii 1105; EBL to M. Napier, 30 September 1830, British Library, Add. MS 34617 fol. 576.
9. Memoir of Laman Blanchard, in *Miscellaneous Prose Works*, i, pp. vii–viii.

10. EBL to Lord J. Russell [*c.* 1846], *Speeches*, preface, xxxiii–iv; C. Dickens to EBL, 12 February 1870, Knebworth MSS, V2/11.

11. EBL to Robert Lytton [*c.* 20 January 1857], *Life*, ii 249.

12. C. W. Snyder, *Liberty and Morality: A Political Biography of Edward Bulwer Lytton* (New York, 1995), 89.

13. *New Monthly Magazine*, no. 35, 418–22, November 1832.

14. 'The Master and the Scholar'.

15. In 1838, as co-editor of the *Monthly Chronicle*, he published *Zicci* in that journal, republished later as *Zanoni*. In 1849–53, he gave *The Caxtons* and *My Novel* to Blackwoods, followed by *What Will He Do With It?* in 1859. As a favour to Dickens, *A Strange Story* appeared in *All The Year Round* in 1862.

16. *England and the English*, book 4, chap. 5; EBL to R. Bentley, 14 August 1851, Bodleian Library, MS Eng. Lett. d 90, fol. 217.

17. EBL to Robert Lytton, 28 February 1858; Knebworth MSS, Jiii 1107.

18. EBL to Mary Braddon, 13 December 1864, *Harvard Library Bulletin*, 12 (1974), 29.

19. 'On the Spirit of Criticism', *LLLR*, ii 267–68.

20. *New Monthly Magazine*, no. 37, January 1833, 82–87.

21. *The Last of the Barons*, book 6, chap. 6; *Paul Clifford*, chap. 2.

22. EBL to Macvey Napier, 8 September 1830, British Library, Add. MS 34614, fol. 386; and EBL to ?, n.d., Princeton, Parrish MSS, AM 9299.

23. EBL to John Forster, 21 January 1864, Lytton MSS, DEK c27; and EBL to Macvey Napier, 1 March 1834, British Library, Add. MS 34615, fol. 19.

24. EBL to John Forster, 26 April 1838, Lytton MSS, DEK c27.

25. *New Monthly Magazine*, no. 32, December 1831.

26. EBL to Lady Sherborne, December 1872, Lytton MSS, DEK c26/29.

27. EBL to Mrs Cosway [*c.* December 1870], *Life*, ii 472; S. C. Hall, *Retrospect of a Long Life*, i 272–75.

28. EBL to John Forster, 1 January 1847, Lytton MSS, DEK c27/15–21.

29. EBL to W. Kent, 17 November 1867, Boston Public Library, MS C.1.41.101.

30. *New Monthly Magazine*, no. 35, November 1832, 403.

31. EBL to W. Kent, 8 October 1868, Boston Public Library, MS C.1.41.107; and EBL to Robert Lytton., n.d., Knebworth MSS, Jiv 1780.

32. Mrs Hughes to Mrs Southey, n.d., S. M. Ellis, *William Harrison Ainsworth and his Friends* (London, 1911), 63.

33. K. Hollingsworth, *The Newgate Novel* (Detroit, 1963), 202–22.

34. EBL to C. Norton [*c.* 1846], Princeton, Parrish MSS, 5/3/56; and EBL to John Forster, 20 December 1846, Lytton MSS, DEK c27.

35. H. Smith to EBL, 26 May 1846, ibid., c2, and *Life*, ii 86.

36. EBL to G. H. Lewes, 24 December 1846, Bodleian Library, MS Eng. Lett. d 40, fol. 80.

37. EBL to Lady Blessington, 20 December 1846, Lytton MSS, DEK c26/34.

38. *Life*, ii 86.

39. *A Word to the Public* (London, 1847).

40. H. Martineau to EBL, 26 January 1844, Lytton MSS, DEK c4, fol. 5.

41. EBL to John Forster, n.d., ibid., DEK c27, fol. 329; EBL to W. Kent [c. 1858], Boston Public Library, MS C.1.41.137; W. P. Frith, *My Autobiography and Reminiscences*, iii 103–4.

42. *LLLR*, ii 281.

43. *New Monthly Magazine*, December 1831, no. 32, 577.

44. *Fraser's Magazine*, 4 December 1831, 520–25.

45. EBL to John Forster, 12 January 132, Lytton MSS, DEK c27, fol. 502.

46. S. C. Hall, *Retrospect of a Long Life*, i 317. Lytton himself could sometimes admit that he was 'too warm' on the pages of his journal: EBL to Lady Blessington, n.d., Lytton MSS, DEK c26/35.

47. EBL to John Forster, January 1847, ibid., c27, fos 22–23.

48. W. M. Thackeray to J. Hannay, 29 January 1849; G. N. Ray, *The Letters and Private Papers of William Makepeace Thackeray*, ii 554; *LLLR*, ii 276.

49. G. Storey, *The Letters of Charles Dickens*, vi 662.

50. G. Hogarth to J. T. Fields, 1873, Knebworth MSS, A5/10.

51. EBL to Lady Blessington, 24 December 1846, Lytton MSS, DEK c26/34.

52. EBL to Robert Lytton, 21 November 1862, Knebworth MSS, J2 i 424.

53. EBL to John Forster, n.d., Lytton MSS, DEK c27, fos 333, 754, 911.

54. EBL to Robert Lytton, 22 November 1867, Knebworth MSS, Jii 1075.

55. Ibid., 3 November 1869; ibid., J iii 1386.

56. EBL to ?, n.d., Bodleian Library, MS Eng. Lett., b 26, fol. 3.

57. John Forster to A. Tennyson, 18 February 1846, C. Y. Lang, *The Letters of Alfred, Lord Tennyson*, i 251–52.

58. *New Monthly Magazine*, January 1833, no. 37, 70.

59. EBL to Robert Lytton, 12 December 1864, Knebworth MSS, J2 ii 713; EBL to John Forster, 26 November 1870, Lytton MSS, DEK c27, fol. 505, and EBL to John Forster, 9 June 1842; ibid., fol. 491.

60. EBL to G. H. Lewes, n.d., Bodleian Library, MS Eng. Lett., d 40, fol. 72.

61. EBL to John Forster, 15 March 1846, *Life*, ii 73–74.

62. *The New Timon* and *The New Timon and the Poets*.

63. EBL to H. Bulwer, 1 February 1849, Knebworth MSS, P4 69.

64. G. Eliot to J. Blackwood, 23 February 1860; G. S. Haight, *The George Eliot Letters* (New Haven, 1954–78), iii 264; and EBL to Robert Lytton, 8 June 1868, Knebworth J iii 1145.

65. EBL journal, 26 May 1838, Knebworth MSS, bundle 22.

66. *Ernest Maltravers*, book 8, chap. 6; *My Novel*, book 2, chap. 4; *Eugene Aram*, book 4, chap. 5.

67. T. B. Macaulay to H. Macaulay, 23 June 1832, T. Pinney, *The Letters of T. B. Macaulay*, ii 139; *Life*, i 447–8; EBL to John Forster, various dates, Lytton MSS, DEK c27, fos 353, 494, 497, 505; Leigh Hunt to EBL, n.d., ibid., c11 fol. 126; E. J. Stanley to EBL, 16 April 1838, British Library, Add. MS 38109, fol. 199.

68. A. C. Swinburne to A. Swinburne, 28 August [1866], C. Y. Lang, *The Swinburne Letters*, i 178.

69. EBL to L. Landon, 1838, Lytton MSS, DEK c1, fos 222–23; ibid., c24/26; ibid., c22/63/1; EBL to Mrs Disraeli, 23 February 1840, Bodleian Library, Hughenden MSS, 190/3, fol. 106.

70. T. Hood to F. O. Ward, July 1844, P. F. Morgan, *The Letters of Thomas Hood*, 632; T. Hood to EBL, 30 October 1844, British Library, Add. MS 30262, fol. 91.

71. EBL to C. Babbage, n.d., British Library, Add. MS 37200, fol. 40.

72. J. Forster, *The Life of Charles Dickens*, 821.

73. *Life*, ii 139 seq.; G. Storey, *The Letters of Charles Dickens*, vii 268 n 3.

74. H. and M. Schwartz, *Disraeli's Reminiscences*, 65.

75. Robert Lytton to R. Browning, 23 July 1887, Baylor University, Browning MSS, 87167.

76. *Monthly Chronicle*, i 168, April 1838.

77. EBL to John Forster, 25 November 1847, Lytton MSS, DEK c27, fos 108–11. See also DEK c22/157. EBL to I. Disraeli, 20 April 1832, Bodleian Library, Hughenden MSS, 244/5, fos 69–70.

78. F. Diener to EBL, 6 February 1841, Lytton MSS, DEK c2, fol. 193.

79. EBL to ?, n.d., Bodleian Library, MS Eng. Lett., d 90, fol. 216.

80. EBL to Sir J. Crampton, 25 August 1852, Bodleian Library, Crampton MS 5, fol. 2791. See also Lytton MSS, DEK c27, fos 383–88.

81. G. Storey, *The Letters of Charles Dickens*, iii 86 n 3.

82. *What Will He Do With It?*, book 3, chap. 23; *Godolphin*, chap. 8.

83. EBL to Lady Dacre, 21 November 1850, G. Lyster, *A Family Chronicle*, 257–58. See also C. Dickens to EBL, 3 November 1850, G. Storey, *The Letters of Charles Dickens*, vi 216.

84. *The Parisians*, book 4, chap. 6.

85. The vivid friendship between Lytton and Macready may be followed in Sir F. Pollack, *Macready's Reminiscences* (London, 1875); W. Toynbee, *The Diaries of William Charles Macready* (London, 1912); W. Marston, *Our Recent Actors* (London, 1888); *Life*, passim; C. H. Shattuck, *Bulwer and Macready* (Illinois, 1958).

86. *Speeches*, i 85.

87. *New Monthly Magazine*, no. 34, 131–35, February 1832.

88. *Parliamentary Debates*, no. 95, 244, 31 May 1832.

89. Ibid., no. 98, 561–64, 12 March 1833; and EBL to T. Duncombe, 3 October 1832, T. H. Duncombe, *The Life and Correspondence of T. S. Duncombe*, ii 29.

90. EBL to Mrs Bulwer, 24 July 1830, Knebworth MSS, P5, box 68.

91. EBL to Emily Lytton [November 1847], ibid., P5, box 88.

92. EBL to Macvey Napier [3 June 1835], British Library, Add. MS 34617, fol. 113; EBL to J. Blackwood [1848], National Library of Scotland, Blackwood MSS, 4084, fol. 218. See also, M. Oliphant, *Annals of a Publishing House*, passim.

93. A. M. Brown, 'The Metaphysical Novels of Edward Bulwer Lytton' (unpublished Ph.D. thesis, Cambridge University, 1979).

94. EBL to H. Colburn [31 October 1831], Bodleian Library, MS Eng. Lett., d 90, fol. 15.

95. EBL to R. Bentley, Bodleian Library, MS Eng. Lett., d 90; EBL to John Forster, 10 and 16 September and 19 October 1838, Lytton MSS, DEK c27, fos 587, 595, 608; R. Bentley to EBL, n.d., ibid., c22/37; and many other examples.
96. EBL annotation; ibid. c15; EBL to John Forster, n.d., ibid., c27, fol. 302.
97. EBL to John Forster, n.d., ibid., c27, fol. 304; EBL to Rosina Lytton [1826], Knebworth MSS, P4, box 70. See also a series of letters to Chapman and Hall in the J. P. Morgan Library in New York.

Notes to Chapter 7: Ghosts and Artists

1. *Godolphin*, chap. 28.
2. *Blackwood's Magazine*, no. 86, 358–59, September 1859.
3. *Light*, 11 September 1915; Knebworth MSS, V2/58.
4. EBL to Robert Lytton, 3 August 1871, Lytton MSS, DEK c28/34.
5. *Cornhill Magazine*, no. 27, 348, January 1873.
6. EBL to Lord Stanhope, 30 June 1867, Kent Record Office, Stanhope MSS, U1590 c347.
7. *New Monthly Magazine*, no. 25, 152, August 1832.
8. *The Pilgrims of the Rhine*, preface.
9. M. M. Roberts, *Gothic Immortals*, 182–83. This chapter, pp. 150–98, is a very good account of Lytton's search for the ideal.
10. EBL to Lord Walpole, 25 March 1850, Lytton MSS, DEK c26/59/45.
11. EBL to Lady Blessington, 5 January 1836, R. P. Madden, *The Literary Life and Correspondence of the Countess of Blessington*, iii 40–41; A. C. Christensen, *Edward Bulwer Lytton*, 3.
12. Ibid., 9.
13. H. Martineau to EBL, 8 February 1844, Lytton MSS, DEK c4, fol. 8.
14. 'Sculpture' (London, 1825).
15. *Rienzi*, book 7, chap. 7; *Parliamentary Debates*, no. 42, 1181, 15 February 1838.
16. EBL to John Forster [1842], Lytton MSS, DEK c27, fol. 784.
17. *Life*, ii 419–38.
18. R. A. Zipser, *Edward Bulwer Lytton and Germany*, 97. In 1844 he published *The Poems and Ballads of Schiller*, with a long, biographical preface.
19. *Rienzi*, book 1, chap. 8.
20. *Zanoni*, preface to the 1853 edition.
21. *Life*, ii 33–35.
22. EBL to John Forster, n.d., Lytton MSS, DEK c27, fol. 283.
23. C. H. Beale, *Reminiscences of a Gentlewoman of the Last Century*, 211.
24. *Life*, ii 37. Its German character may have been the reason why it was one of the few Lytton novels to meet with Carlyle's approval. T. Carlyle to EBL, 23 February 1842, Lytton MSS, DEK c2, fol. 24.
25. EBL to Benjamin Disraeli, February 1842, Bodleian Library, Hughenden MSS, 224/5, fol. 99.
26. H. Martineau to EBL, August 1844, Lytton MSS, DEK c4, fol. 17.

27. *Zanoni*, book 4, chap. 2.

28. EBL to W. Kent [27 September 1861], Boston Public Library, MS C.1.41.41.

29. *A Strange Story*, preface.

30. Ibid.

31. *What Will He Do With It?*, book 8, chap. 1.

32. EBL to W. Macready, 27 April [1853]; C. H. Shattuck, *Bulwer and Macready*, 250.

33. EBL to W. Drury, 12 November [1834], Princeton, Parrish MSS, AM 19764; EBL to ?, n.d., ibid., AM 8437.

34. EBL to Lady Blessington, 22 November 1844, Lytton MSS, DEK c26/4. See also EBL to Miss Greene, 3 January 1863, ibid., c28/3/9.

35. EBL to Lady Sherborne, 5 January 1873, ibid., c26/29.

36. EBL to Robert Lytton, 22 January 1862, *Life*, ii 410–11.

37. EBL to Robert Lytton, 19 November 1861, *Life*, ii 400–401. See also *Kenelm Chillingly*, book 3, chap. 7, and EBL to ?, 2 June 1871, Lytton MSS, DEK c28/61.

38. *Life*, ii 403.

39. Lady Blessington to EBL, 26 November 1844, Lytton MSS, DEK c9, fol. 1. See also Robert Lytton to EBL, 16 January 1862, Balfour, i 136.

40. EBL to Robert Lytton, 17 December 1861, Knebworth MSS, J2 vol. i, fol. 241.

41. C. N. Stewart, *Bulwer Lytton as Occultist*, 32.

42. William Bulwer to EBL, n.d., Knebworth MSS, box 56; Robert Lytton to R. Browning, 7 January 1853, Baylor University, Browning MSS, 54020.

43. *Monthly Chronicle*, ii 29–30, June 1838.

44. EBL to W. Macready, 27 April [1853], Shattuck, *Bulwer and Macready*, 250.

45. EBL to Robert Lytton, 11 December 1861, Knebworth MSS, J2 i 225.

46. *Blackwood's Magazine*, no. 86, 236, August 1859.

47. *Zanoni*, book 2, chap. 6.

48. *The Coming Race*, chap. 7. The properties of Vril were so potent that the makers of Bovril incorporated the word into the name of their product.

49. *A Strange Story*, chap. 71.

50. *Life*, ii 345. See also ibid., 348.

51. I am most grateful to Knebworth's Archivist, Clare Fleck, for help in establishing these points.

52. R. L. Wolff, *Strange Stories and Other Exploration in Victorian Literature* (Boston 1971), pp. 264 seq.; *A Strange Story*, chap. 24.

53. EBL to Dr John Elliotson [October 1846]; R. L. Wolff, *Strange Stories*, 237.

54. R.L. to R. Browning, 22 April 1854; Baylor University, Browning MSS, 54063.

55. *Life*, ii 456, and Knebworth MSS, J2 ii 579–80.

56. EBL to ?, 30 September 1871, Huntingdon Library, Bulwer MSS, 7904.

57. EBL to Lord Stanhope, 21 January 1854, Kent Record Office, Stanhope MSS, U1590 c347; and EBL to Robert Lytton, 25 January 1865, Knebworth MSS, J2 ii 756.

58. EBL to J. Blackwood, 1854, National Library of Scotland, Blackwood MSS, 4106, fol. 107.

59. *Life*, ii 50.

60. EBL to ?, 15 March 1870, Lytton MSS, DEK c28/61.

61. T. H. S. Escott, *Edward Bulwer, First Baron Lytton*, 41; EBL to C. H. Townshend, n.d., Wisbech and Fenland Museum, Townshend MSS, iv 45.

62. G. Storey, *The Letters of Charles Dickens*, ii 110 n. 1.

63. EBL to Rosina Lytton [1826], Knebworth MSS, P4, box 70; *Eugene Aram*, book 5, chap. 5.

64. EBL to Emily Lytton [22 March 1843], Knebworth MSS, P5, box 88.

65. EBL to John Forster [1844], Lytton MSS, DEK c27, fol. 849; EBL to Lady Blessington [1843], ibid., c26/34.

66. H. Martineau to EBL, 26 January and 8 February 1844, ibid., c24/66/2 and 11.

67. Lady Hills-Johnes, Recollections of a Visit to Knebworth, 1857, National Library of Wales, Dolaucothi MSS, 8103.

68. T. H. S. Escott, *Edward Bulwer, First Baron Lytton*, 231–32.

69. H. Martineau to EBL, 27 November [1844], Lytton MSS, DEK c4, fol. 19.

70. EBL to W. Kent [24 October 1853], Boston Public Library, MS C.1.41.12; and EBL to L. Blanchard, n.d., Princeton, Parrish MSS, AM 19808.

71. EBL to W. Kent, 6 January 1866, Boston Public Library, MS C.1.41.71; and EBL to Robert Lyton, n.d.; Knebworth MSS, J2 I, fol. 99.

72. M. Oliphant, *Annals of a Publishing House*, iii 84.

73. EBL to Lord Walpole, 19 June 1853, Lytton MSS, DEK c28/59/144.

74. Lady Hills-Johnes, Recollections of a Visit to Knebworth, 1857, National Library of Wales, Dolaucothi MSS, 8103.

75. W. P. Frith, *My Autobiography and Reminiscences*, ii 309–11.

76. Knebworth MSS, box 53, June 1852 and July 1853.

77. EBL to Lord Houghton, n.d., Trinity College, Cambridge, Houghton MSS, 15/145; EBL to Lord Carvarvon, 30 October 1857, British Library, Add. MS 60780, fol. 6; Carnarvon to EBL, 2 November 1857, Lytton MSS, DEK c11, fol. 4.

78. EBL to Robert Lytton, 15 September 1853, Knebworth MSS, J4 2047–48.

79. EBL to Miss Johnes [c. 1858], Knebworth MSS, box 13; *Extract from Lord Halifax's Ghost Book*, ibid.; Lady Hills-Johnes, Recollections of a Visit to Knebworth, National Library of Wales, Dolaucothi MSS, 8103.

80. F. Parkes to EBL, n.d., Lytton MSS, DEK c6 fol. 27; EBL to Mrs Duncombe, n.d., Princeton, Parrish MSS, AM 20759.

81. EBL to Robert Lytton, December 1853, Knebworth MSS, J4 1968; Robert Lytton to EBL [1843], Lytton MSS, DEK c41; S. C. Hall, *Retrospect of a Long Life*, i 278.

82. Robert Lytton to John Forster [February 1855], Lytton MSS, DEK c40.

83. Accounts of these séances may be found in *Life*, ii 43–44; Robert Lytton to R. Browning, 19 July 1854, Baylor Univ., Browning MSS, 54090; W. Elwin to ?, 25 July 1854, Knebworth MSS, V2/54.

84. D. D. Hone, *Incidents in My Life* (London, 1863), 65; Mrs D. Hone, *D. D. Hone: His Life and Mission*, (London, 1888), 50.

85. Mrs D. Hone, *The Gift of D. D. Hone* (London, 1890), 34–36.
86. EBL to Robert Lytton [1853], *Life*, ii 42–43.
87. EBL to W. Macready [March 1853], G. Storey, *The Letters of Charles Dickens*, vi 281 n. 7.
88. Stewart, *Bulwer Lytton as Occultist*, passim; Lord F. Hamilton, *The Days Before Yesterday*, 228.
89. EBL to Lady Sherborne, n.d., Lytton MSS, DEK c26/29.
90. Rosina Lytton, *Not Very Successful*, notice to vol. 2; C. Dickens to Rev. J. White, 7 March 1854, G. Storey, *The Letters of Charles Dickens*, vii 286.
91. Lady Stafford, *Leaves from the Diary of Henry Greville*, 36–37.
92. G. Eliot to S. Hennell, 6 December 1861, G. S. Haight, *The George Eliot Letters*, iii 468.
93. *The Times*, 30 June 1863; S. Ballantine, *Some Experiences of a Barrister's Life*, ii 82–85.
94. C. Dickens to EBL, 12 May 1861, G. Storey, *The Letters of Charles Dickens*, ix 412–14; *Life*, ii 351; and EBL to John Forster [April 1862], Lytton MSS, DEK c27.
95. Ibid. [*c.* 1853], ibid., c23.

Notes to Chapter 8: Europe

1. *England and the English*, book 1, chap. 3.
2. EBL to Macvey Napier, 1 March 1831, British Library, Add. MS 34615, fol. 50.
3. EBL to Robert Lytton, 24 November [?], Knebworth MSS, P5, box 88.
4. EBL to John Forster, n.d., Lytton MSS, DEK c27, fol. 255.
5. EBL to ?, 23 May [?], Princeton, Parrish MSS, AM 21037.
6. L. Blanc to EBL, 1 October 1863, Lytton MSS, DEK c4, fol. 120.
7. EBL to ?, 12 January 1856, Princeton, Parrish MSS, AM 81119.
8. EBL to M. Julien, 4 January 1829, British Library, Add. MS 33964, fol. 279.
9. *Spanish Song*, 1823.
10. EBL to Robert Lytton [1870]; Knebworth MSS, P5, box 72.
11. EBL to John Forster, n.d., Lytton MSS, DEK c27, fol. 360.
12. EBL to Lady Murray, March 1845, Knebworth MSS, box 13.
13. EBL to Robert Lytton, 19 December 1863, ibid., J2 ii, fol. 735.
14. EBL to Miss C. Hutton, April 1842, C. H. Beale, *Reminiscences of a Gentlewoman of the Last Century*, 212.
15. EBL to J. Blackwood [*c.* 1850], National Library of Scotland, Blackwood MSS, 4722, fol. 226.
16. *Speeches*, ii 296, 2 August 1860.
17. Ibid., i 46 [1857].
18. EBL to J. Blackwood, 27 February 1863, National Library of Scotland, Blackwood MSS, 4183, fol. 61.
19. T. H. S. Escott, *Edward Bulwer, First Baron Lytton*, 254.
20. EBL to Robert Lytton, 19 August 1871, Knebworth MSS, J3 1550.
21. Lord Lytton, *Miscellaneous Prose Works*, i 4–5.

22. EBL to John Forster, 1 June 1842, Lytton MSS, DEK c27, fol. 489.

23. *What Will He Do With It?*, book 7, chap. 9.

24. *Alice*, book 6, chap. 2.

25. EBL to Lady Blessington, 5 January 1836, *The Literary Life and Correspondence of the Countess of Blessington*, iii 41. See also ibid., 20 March 1838, Lytton MSS, DEK c26/34.

26. EBL to Lord Durham, 1836, S. J. Reid, *Life and Letters of the First Earl of Durham*, ii 97–98.

27. EBL to Lady Blessington, 31 August 1833, Blessington, *Literary Life*, iii 33.

28. 'One of the Crowd', 1 January 1836, ibid., iii 53–63.

29. EBL to John Forster, 1 March 1848, *Life*, ii 98.

30. Ibid., 10 April 1846, ibid. ii 84; and EBL to Mrs Cosway, 27 December 1871, Lytton MSS, DEK c26/18.

31. EBL to J. Blackwood, 22 July 1859, National Library of Scotland, Blackwood MSS, 4140, fol. 262. See also EBL to J. Blackwood [1850], ibid., 4722, fol. 169.

32. EBL to Robert Lytton, 22 February 1871, Knebworth MSS, J4 1625.

33. *The Parisians*, book 8 chap. 1. See also ibid., book 5, chap. 3.

34. EBL to Mrs Cosway, 27 December 1871, Lytton MSS, DEK c26/18.

35. EBL to John Forster, 26 January 1846, *Life*, ii 79–80. See also EBL to Lady Blessington, 26 November 1833, *The Literary Life and Correspondence of the Countess of Blessington*, iii 35–36.

36. *Godolphin*, chap. 37.

37. *Rienzi*, preface to the 1848 edition.

38. EBL to John Forster, 26 October 1849, *Life*, ii 121.

39. *Rienzi*, preface to the 1848 edition.

40. EBL to Lady Blessington, 10 April 1846, Lytton MSS, DEK c26/34.

41. EBL to J. Blackwood, 27 October 1849, National Library of Scotland, Blackwood MSS, 4086, fol. 163.

42. 'Speech on Italy' [c. 1859], Huntingdon Library, Bulwer MSS; and EBL to W. E. Gladstone, 26 December 1860, Lytton MSS, DEK 659 2/20.

43. *England and the English*, book 5, section 8.

44. EBL to C. d'Eyncourt, Novmber 1848, Lytton MSS, DEK c26/21; EBL to J. Blackwood, 6 October 1848; National Library of Scotland, Blackwood MSS, 4081, fol. 224.

45. EBL to John Forster, 25 August 1849, Lytton MSS, DEK c27, fol. 275.

46. *Parliamentary Debates*, 19 December 1854, no. 238, 526–27.

47. EBL to J. Blackwood, 5 and 16 January 1864, National Library of Scotland, Blackwood MSS, fos 287 and 289. See also *Life*, ii 358.

48. EBL to Edith Lytton [1870], Knebworth MSS, P5, box 72.

49. *The Parisians*, book 11, chap. 12.

50. EBL to John Forster, 3 October 1838, Lytton MSS, DEK c27, fos 602–3; EBL to John Forster, 3 October 1840, ibid., fol. 710; EBL to J. Blackwood, 9 July 1842, National Library of Scotland, Blackwood MSS, 4061, fol. 278; *Blackwood's Magazine*, September 1842, no. 52, 286.

51. Ibid., August 1843, no. 54, 139.
52. EBL to T. Carlyle [1844], National Library of Scotland, MS 5509, fol. 121.
53. EBL to Robert Lytton, 20 November 1869, Knebworth MSS, J3 1369.
54. EBL to ?, 27 July 1844, Bodleian Library, MS Eng. Misc. c107, fos 110–12; Lord Lytton, *Miscellaneous Prose Works*, i 402–3.
55. A. M. Brown, 'The Metaphysical Novels of Edward Bulwer Lytton' (unpublished Cambridge Ph.D. thesis), 257.
56. For an authoritative account of German influence, see R. A. Zipser, *Edward Bulwer Lytton and Germany*, particularly chap. 2.
57. *Ernest Maltravers*, preface.
58. C. H. Shattuck, *Bulwer and Macready*, 50–51.
59. Louis Napoleon to EBL, 28 September 1839, Lytton MSS, DEK c2, fol. 114; M Braddon to EBL, 7 January 1864, *Harvard Library Bulletin*, no. 12, 20 (1974).
60. C. Norton to EBL, n.d., Lytton MSS, DEK c24/99/10.
61. EBL to Sir C. Babbage, n.d., British Library, Add. MS 37200, fol. 512.
62. J. Murray to EBL, 25 July [1831?], Lytton MSS, DEK c1, fos 119–20; EBL to H. Sillern, 14 October 1846, ibid., D/25 c61.
63. Zipser, *Edward Bulwer Lytton and Germany*, 187.
64. J. Murray to EBL, 24 December [1831], Lytton MSS, DEK c1, fol. 122.
65. Zipser, *Edward Bulwer Lytton and Germany*, 13.
66. T. Hood to C. W. Dilke, 20 June 1836, P. F. Morgan, *The Letters of Thomas Hood*, 249.
67. *Bentley's Miscellany*, 24 July 1848, xxiv 1–2.
68. EBL to G. H. Lewes, n.d., Bodleian Library, MS Eng. Lett., d40, fol. 66.
69. EBL to Lady Blessington, 26 November 1833, *The Literary Life and Correspondence of the Countess of Blessington*, iii 35–36; speech given at the Hertford Literary Society, Lytton MSS, DEK 57459.
70. EBL to Lady Blessington, 25 January 1835, ibid., c26/35.
71. EBL to C. d'Eyncourt, 20 October 1852, Lincolnshire Record Office, d'Eyncourt MSS, T d'E/H/160/10; EBL to Benjamin Disraeli, 12 October 1834, Bodleian Library, Hughenden MSS, box 104/I, fos 52–53.
72. EBL to John Forster, 18 October 1848, Lytton MSS, DEK c27, fos 198–99.
73. EBL to Lady Stanhope, 26 October 1867, Kent Record Office, Stanhope MSS, U1590 c347.
74. *England and the English*, book 3, section 3.
75. *What Will He Do With It?*, book 5, chap. 10.
76. EBL to Emily Lytton, n.d., Knebworth MSS, P5, box 88.
77. *New Monthly Magazine*, no. 35, 545–553, December 1832.
78. *Pelham*, vol. 1, chap. 9.
79. *New Monthly Magazine*, no. 34, 227–232, March 1832.
80. Ibid., no. 33, December 1831, 545.
81. *Ernest Maltravers*, book 5, chap. 8.
82. EBL to Benjamin Disraeli, 12 October 1834, Bodleian Library, Hughenden MSS, box 104/I, fol. 153.

83. EBL to J. Blackwood, n.d., M. Oliphant, *Annals of a Publishing House*, ii 429.
84. *LLLR*, ii 335–36.
85. *England and the English*, book 3, section 4.
86. *Edinburgh Review*, no. 52, 375, January 1831.
87. *New Monthly Magazine*, no. 34, 22, January 1832.
88. *England and the English*, book 2, chap. 1.
89. Ibid., book 2, chap. 2.
90. *New Monthly Magazine*, no. 28, 330–31, April 1830.
91. EBL to John Forster, 20 May 1850; *Life*, ii 129.
92. *The Pilgrims of the Rhine*, chap. 10.

Notes to Chapter 9: Radical

1. EBL to Mrs Bulwer, 1831 and 17 November 1834, Knebworth MSS, P5, box 68.
2. EBL to Rosina Lytton, 6 September 1826, ibid., P4, box 70.
3. Ibid. [*c.* 1826], ibid.
4. *Edinburgh Review*, no. 65, 116, July 1837.
5. A. M. Brown, 'The Metaphysical Works of Edward Bulwer Lytton' (unpublished Ph.D. thesis, Cambridge University), chap. 4.
6. *Dublin University Magazine*, no. 15, 267, March 1840.
7. EBL to W. Tait, 15 June 1834, National Library of Scotland, Blackwood MSS, 3713, fol. 56.
8. *LLLR*, i 240–42, 261–67.
9. Ibid., i 301–3.
10. EBL to T. Alsop, 13 January 1832, Princeton, Parrish MSS, AM 19571.
11. *New Monthly Magazine*, no. 28, 467–68, May 1830.
12. *Life*, i 371.
13. J. S. Mill to EBL, 23 November 1836, Lytton MSS, DEK c1, fol. 23; EBL to Lady Cunningham, May 1826, *LLLR*, 124.
14. *Parliamentary Debates*, no. 125, 316, 30 April 1834; no. 39, 893, 7 April 1837; no. 140, 512, 4 May 1837.
15. Ibid., no. 145, 110, 22 May 1838; *Reformer*, 4 August 1838.
16. *New Monthly Magazine*, no. 29 April 1831; no. 32, 514, December 1831.
17. *The Pilgrims of the Rhine*, chap. 1.
18. EBL to Mrs Bulwer, 23 October 1834, Knebworth MSS, P5, box 68.
19. *What Will He Do With It?*, book 3, chap. 10.
20. EBL to Benjamin Disraeli, 12 October 1834, *Life*, i 454.
21. *Parliamentary Debates*, no. 135, 1357, 2 June 1836; no. 138, 801, 21 February 1837.
22. *O'Neill*, 1827.
23. EBL to Lord Stanhope, 7 April 1870, Kent Record Office, Stanhope MSS, U1590 c347. See also EBL to Lady Blessington, n.d., Lytton MSS, DEK c26/35.
24. *Parliamentary Debates*, no. 118, 239, 6 February 1833; ibid., 1236, 27 February 1833.
25. *Life*, i 152.
26. EBL to M. Napier, 1 March 1831, British Library, Add MS 34616, fol. 51.

27. *Parliamentary Debates*, no. 106, 756, 5 July 1831.

28. Ibid., no. 108, 609, 25 August 1831; *New Monthly Magazine*, no. 34, 105–11, February 1832.

29. *Parliamentary Debates*, no. 107, 577, 30 July 1831; *New Monthly Magazine*, no. 32, November 1831; *England and the English*, book 1, chap. 3.

30. *Parliamentary Debates*, no. 138, 1082, 27 February 1837.

31. *England and the English*, book 2, chap. 5.

32. *Paul Clifford*, preface to 1848 edition.

33. EBL to John Forster, 18 January 1841, Lytton MSS, DEK c27, fol. 735.

34. *Night and Morning*, preface.

35. Diary, 6 May 1832, G. N. Ray, *The Letters and Private Papers of William Makepeace Thackeray* (London 1994), i 198.

36. *Catherine*, chap. 3.

37. EBL to John Forster, 18 January 1841, Lytton MSS, DEK c27, fol. 737.

38. EBL to Rosina Lytton [*c.* 1826], Devey, 25.

39. T. H. S. Escott, *Edward Bulwer Lytton*, 10; S. Ballantine, *Some Experiences of a Barrister's Life*, i 309.

40. *Lucretia*, 1853 edn, preface. For an authoritative account of Newgate writing, see K. Hollingsworth, *The Newgate Novel* (Detroit, 1963).

41. EBL to H. Colburn, n.d., Bodleian Library, MS Eng. Lett., d 90, fol. 29; Escott, *Edward Bulwer Lytton*, 169–70; and W. Godwin to EBL, 13 May 1830, *Life*, ii 258.

42. *Night and Morning*, preface.

43. *Paul Clifford*, chap. 31.

44. *Lucretia*, part 2, chap. 1, and part 2, chap. 6. See also Hollingsworth, *The Newgate Novel*, 65. Lytton's interest in poverty and crime as literary themes may once again suggest German influences, particularly Schiller's *Verbrecher aus Infamie* and *Die Raüber*. See Zipser, *Edward Bulwer Lytton and Germany*, chap. 3.

45. *Paul Clifford*, chap. 18, and *Night and Morning*, book 2, chap. 2.

46. Ibid., preface to 1848 edition.

47. EBL to John Forster [*c.* 1832], Lytton MSS, DEK c23. See also EBL to M. Napier, British Library, Add. MS 34618, fol. 135.

48. *Falkland*, book 1; *New Monthly Magazine*, no. 28, 339, April 1830.

49. *England and the English*, book 1, chap. 5.

50. *Almacks*, 1825.

51. EBL to W. Rose, 25 January ?, Bodleian Library, MS Autograph d 21, fos 128–30.

52. *Godolphin*, chap. 16, character of Lord Erpingham.

53. *The Siamese Twins*, book 4, chap. 1.

54. EBL to Lady Holland, 29 May 1835 and 2 January 1836, Biltmore MSS, and *Life*, i 252.

55. EBL to Dr Parr [1820], Bodleian Library, MS Eng. Misc. d 590, fol. 27; and EBL to Melbourne, 15 August 1837, Princeton, Parrish MSS, AM 16870.

56. Lord Melbourne to EBL, 6 April 1831 and 28 November 1834, Lytton MSS, DEK c24/22/1 and c6, fol. 104; *Life*, i 488.

57. EBL Journal, 25 May 1838, Knebworth MSS, bundle 22.

58. EBL to Lord Cowper, n.d., Boston Public Library, MS Eng. 86; *Quarterly Review*, no. 97, 529, September 1855.

59. *Life*, ii 13.

60. M. Rochester, *The Derby Ministry* (London, 1858), 171.

61. *England and the English*, book 5, section 1.

62. EBL to W. Drury, 12 November [1834], Princeton, Parrish MSS, AM 19764.

63. EBL to A. Fonblanque, 22 January 1836, Lytton MSS, DEK c26/32; EBL to Lord Durham, 1836, S. J. Reid, *Life and Letters of the First Earl of Durham*, ii 118–19.

64. EBL to Lord Durham, 13 January 1835, Lytton MSS, DEK c28/31.

65. J. S. Mill to EBL, 3 March 1838, ibid., DEK c1, fol. 235.

66. EBL to W. Drury, 12 November [1834], Princeton, Parrish MSS, AM 19764.

67. Ibid., 26 November 1834, C. W. Snyder, *Liberty and Morality: A Political Biography of Edward Bulwer Lytton* (New York, 1995), 54.

68. *A Letter to a Cabinet Minister*, 1834; EBL to Lady Blessington, 1 November 1834, Lytton MSS, DEK c26/35; *Life*, i 473–74; EBL, annotations, Lytton MSS, DEK c7, fol. 32.

69. *A Calm Consideration on the Present State of Public Affairs* (1835).

70. EBL to W. Drury, April 1835, Princeton, Parrish MSS, AM 8696; and EBL to John Forster, 18 January 1841, Lytton MSS, DEK c23.

71. EBL to Lord ?, 15 September 1839, Lytton MSS, DEK c28/61; and EBL to M. Napier, 26 August 1839, British Library, Add. MS 34620, fol. 335.

72. Ibid., 12 October 1839, fol. 429.

73. *Edinburgh Review*, no. 70, 245–81, October 1839.

74. Journal, 22 May 1838, Knebworth MSS, bundle 22; EBL to ?, n.d., Princeton, Parrish MSS, AM 17260; W. Toynbee, *The Diaries of William Charles Macready*, i 459.

75. T. A. Jenkins, *The Parliamentary Diaries of Sir John Trelawny*, 18 February [1855], 24. In return, EBL condemned Palmerston for making speeches that were full of 'indecorous gesticulations', EBL to Robert Lytton, 2 February 1858, Knebworth MSS, J2 vol. I, fol. 109.

76. W. White, *The Inner Life of the House of Commons* (London 1897), i 9.

77. T. B. Macaulay to T. F. Ellis, 24 March 1859, T. Pinney, *The Letters of Thomas Babington Macaulay*, vi 203; and *Speeches*, i, preface cxv–vi.

78. EBL to W. Kent [*c.* 1855], Boston Public Library, MS C.1.41.134.

79. Ibid., 14 December 1852, 9. See also Lytton MSS, DEK W100.

80. EBL to H. Bulwer, March 1859, Norfolk Record Office, Bulwer MSS, BUL 1/255/13. See also EBL to Robert Lytton, n.d., Knebworth MSS, J2 ii 752–53.

81. EBL to Robert Lytton, 10 February 1865, ibid., 767.

82. EBL to A. Fonblanque, n.d., Lytton MSS, DEK c26/32; and EBL to E. Chadwick [*c.* 1831], University College London, Chadwick MSS, 3.

83. *Parliamentary Debates*, no. 109, 58, 15 September 1831; no. 115, 619, 14 June 1832; no. 125, 1193, 22 May 1834; and no. 132, 835, 21 August 1835; *New Monthly Magazine*, no. 34, 1–3, January 1832; *England and the English*, book 4, section 1.

84. *Parliamentary Debates*, no. 238, 1117, 26 March 1855. See also G. J. Holyoake, *Sixty Years of an Agitator's Life* (London, 1892), i 293–95.

85. EBL to Emily Lytton, n.d., Knebworth MSS, P5, box 88; EBL to Mrs Bulwer, 8 March 1831, ibid., Devey, 228, *LLLR*, ii 300–4; EBL to W. Jerdan [28 July 1830], Bodleian Library, MS Eng. Lett., d 114, fol. 56; W. Cowper to EBL, 17 May [*c.* 1831], Lytton MSS, DEK O23/91–2.

86. *My Novel*, book 12, chap. 19.

87. EBL to Lady Blessington, 1 November 1834, Lytton MSS, DEK c26/35.

88. EBL to H Brougham, 5 December 1834, University College London, Brougham MSS, 14, 561; and EBL to Durham [1834], A. Aspinall, *Lord Brougham and the Whig Party*, 210.

89. EBL to Durham, 21 January 1835, Lytton MSS, DEK c28/31.

90. *England and the English*, book 5, chap. 7.

91. Durham to EBL, 26 January 1835, Lytton MSS, DEK c6, fol. 140; Report of the Proceedings at the Lincoln Dinner, 1838, ibid., W100; and J. S. Mill to EBL, 5 March 1838, ibid., c1, fol. 238.

92. S. C. Hall, *Retrospect of a Long Life*, i 271.

93. *The Disowned*, vol. 1, chap. 17, and vol. 2, chap. 75.

94. *Life*, ii 306–7.

95. *Parliamentary Debates*, no. 42, 1175, 15 February 1838.

96. Ibid., no. 124, 118–19, 28 April 1834.

97. *Monthly Chronicle*, i 3, March 1838, and ii 297, October 1838.

98. *Life*, ii 96.

99. *Parliamentary Debates*, no. 125, 386, 1 May 1834.

100. EBL to Emily Lytton, n.d., Knebworth MSS, P5, box 88; EBL to John Forster [26 January 1841], Lytton MSS, DEK c27, fos 742–43.

Notes to Chapter 10: Tory

1. W. Macready to EBL, 8 August 1853, Lytton MSS, DEK 24/61.

2. EBL to Lord Walpole, 25 March 1850, *Life*, ii 128–29.

3. EBL to C. d'Eyncourt, 31 March 1851, Lytton MSS, c26/21.

4. EBL to M. Aytoun [*c.* 1853], National Library of Scotland, Blackwood MSS, 4896, fos 252–54.

5. EBL to J. Blackwood [*c.* 1850], ibid., 4722, fol. 165.

6. *The Letters of Manilius*, 31.

7. EBL to ?, n.d., National Library of Scotland, Blackwood MSS, 3925, fol. 127.

8. *The Letters of Manilius*, 12, 48.

9. Ibid., 45.

10. *Life*, ii 309.

11. *New Monthly Magazine*, no. 35, 303, October 1832.

12. *The Last of the Barons*, book 5, chap. 1.

13. Ibid., book 2, chap. 3, and book 5, chap. 3.

14. *Alice*, book 2, chap. 7, and book 4, chap. 2.

15. *Lucretia*, part i, epilogue.

16. EBL to J. Blackwood, 12 November 1849 and [23 June 1850], National Library of Scotland, Blackwood MSS, 4086, fol. 166, and 4089, fol. 289.

17. *My Novel*, book 2, chap. 7.

18. EBL to Rosina Lytton [1826], Devey, 50; *Kenelm Chillingly*, book 3, chap. 3; *Parliamentary Debates*, no. 235, 371, 15 May 1854.

19. *Money*, act 1, scene 5.

20. *Life*, i 161.

21. EBL to J. Blackwood [1853], National Library of Scotland, Blackwood MSS, 4722 fol. 121.

22. *England and the English*, book 4, section 4.

23. *Parliamentary Debates*, no. 225, 1230, 10 December 1852.

24. Ibid., 1223. For an authoritative study on the continuing impact of the Corn Law debate after 1846, see A. Gambles, *Protection and Politics* (London, 1999).

25. EBL to ?, [1857], Lytton MSS, DEK c28/61.

26. EBL to C. Griffin, 2 January 1860, British Library, Add. MS 28511, fol. 83.

27. EBL to Lady Blessington [c. 1847], *The Literary Life and Correspondence of the Countess of Blessington*, iii 45; EBL to Durham, 2 February 1835, Lytton MSS, DEK c28/31.

28. *Bucks Gazette*, 4 October 1845.

29. EBL to Lady Blessington, 12 February 1846, Lytton MSS, DEK c26/34; and EBL to John Forster, 18 July 1846, ibid., c27, fol. 941.

30. Ibid., 15 December 1845, fol. 905.

31. *Life*, appendix.

32. EBL to Henry Bulwer, 17 January 1846, Knebworth MSS, P4, box 69.

33. C. F. Gore to EBL [1846], Lytton MSS, DEK c1 172–73.

34. H. Brougham to EBL, 19 April 1852, Lytton MSS, DEK c22/64/2.

35. EBL to Robert Lytton, 21 January 1851, Knebworth MSS, J2 i fol. 19; and EBL to Benjamin Disraeli [19 October 1850], Bodleian Library, Hughenden MSS, 104/1, fol. 101.

36. A. Gambles, *Protection and Politics*.

37. EBL to H. Bulwer, 17 January 1850, Knebworth MSS, P4 69.

38. EBL to [W. Pollard], 7 April 1852, C. W. Snyder, *Liberty and Morality: A Political Biography of Edward Bulwer Lytton* (New York, 1995), 104.

39. EBL to Lord Walpole, 3 March 1850, Lytton MSS, DEK c28/59/42; EBL to John Forster, n.d., ibid., c27, fos 297 and 315.

40. J. R. McCulloch to EBL, 22 April 1851, ibid., c24/55/2.

41. EBL to J. Blackwood, 6 November [1851 or 1852], National Library of Scotland, Blackwood MSS, 4722, fol. 32.

42. Benjamin Disraeli to EBL, 2 May 1851, Lytton MSS, DEK c5, fol. 41.

43. *Life*, ii 163–64; *Letters to John Bull*, i 6–7, 12. For the pamphlet's reception, see EBL to J. Blackwood, 20 March 1851, National Library of Scotland, Blackwood MSS, 4094, fol. 21; EBL to Lord Salisbury [1851], Lytton MSS, DEK O23, fol. 27; and Anon., *A Few Words to John Bull*.

44. *Athens* (London, 1847), ii 388.

45. EBL to Mr Bacon, 10 January 1832, Cambridge University Library, Bacon MSS, fol. 14.

46. EBL to J. Blackwood, 27 September 1851, National Library of Scotland, Blackwood MSS, 4094, fol. 205; and EBL to J. Blackwood, n.d., ibid., 4722, fos 70–71.

47. EBL to John Forster [January 1846], Lytton MSS, DEK c27, fos 920–21.

48. EBL to Lady Blessington, 12 February 1846, ibid., c26/34.

49. EBL to ?, 26 July 1857, ibid., DEK c28/61.

50. *The Crisis*, 1845.

51. EBL to Lord Lansdowne, 6 January 1852, Lytton MSS, DEK 023, fol. 31.

52. C. Dickens to John Forster [5 July 1841], G. Storey, *The Letters of Charles Dickens*, iii 323.

53. EBL to Lord Cowper, n.d., Princeton, Parrish MSS, AM 19149; EBL to John Forster, 20 July 1847, Lytton MSS, DEK c27, fos 71–73; and Snyder, *Liberty and Morality*, 83–86.

54. W. Loaden to EBL, 16 June 1847, Lytton MSS, DEK 023, fol. 5.

55. EBL to John Forster, n.d.; ibid., c27, fol. 279; W. Loaden to EBL, 30 July 1847, ibid., 023, fol. 136.

56. EBL to Sir J. Hobhouse, 12 March 1848, British Library, Add. MS 36471, fol. 364. See also T. M. Hobhouse to Sir J. Hobhouse, 14 March 1848, ibid., fol. 377; and EBL to John Forster, 24 March 1848, Lytton MSS, DEK c27, fos 138–40.

57. Lord J. Russell to EBL, 26 September 1847, Bodleian Library, MS Eng. Lett., d 307, fos 73–74.

58. EBL to Lord Walpole, 20 December 1848, Lytton MSS, DEK c28/59/5; and EBL to the Electors of Leominster, 22 January 1849, ibid., DEK 023.

59. EBL to John Forster, 1848, ibid., DEK c27, fol. 120; and EBL to C. d'Eyncourt, 5 August 1849, ibid., DEK c26/21.

60. Ibid. [18 May 1847], Lincolnshire Record Office, d'Eyncourt MSS, 2 TdE/H/61/8; and ibid., 17.

61. EBL to W. Kent [11 July 1865], Boston Public Library, MS C.1.41.60.

62. EBL to C d'Eyncourt, 2 March 1852, Lincolnshire Record Office, d'Eyncourt MSS, 2 TdE/H/160/33.

63. EBL to John Forster, 29 October 1847, Lytton MSS, DEK c27, fos 88–92.

64. EBL to W. Kent, 23 July 1853, Boston Public Library, MS C.1.41.6. See also C. Pearson to EBL, 5 April 1859, Lytton MSS, DEK 023 138.

65. EBL to John Forster, 5 November 1851, ibid., c27, fol. 845.

66. *St Stephen's*.

67. EBL to Robert Lytton, 4 April 1851, Lytton MSS, DEK c28/34.

68. Sir A. West, *Recollections* (London, 1899), 406.

69. *The New Timon*, part i.

70. EBL to Lord Walpole, 10 May 1850, Lytton MSS, DEK c28/59; EBL to J. Blackwood [1852], National Library of Scotland, Blackwood MSS, 4099, fol. 101; EBL to W. Kent, 20 February and 31 October 1868, Boston Public Library, MS C.1.41.102 and 108.

71. EBL to John Forster [1855], Lytton MSS, DEK c27, fol. 429; EBL to Lord Houghton, 19 October 1854; Trinity College Cambridge, Houghton MSS, 15/157.

72. EBL to J. Blackwood, 21 November 1856, National Library of Scotland, Blackwood MSS, 4118, fol. 137.

73. *Parliamentary Debates*, no. 238, 1169, 29 January 1855.

74. Ibid., no. 240, 2119, 5 June 1855.

75. British Library, Add. MS 56445, fol. 22, 15 June 1855.

76. *Parliamentary Debates*, no. 243, 1819, 1 May 1856.

77. C. F. C. Greville, *A Journal of the Reigns of King George IV, King William IV and Queen Victoria*, vii 279.

78. EBL to ?, 26 April 1855, Princeton, Parrish MSS, AM 19407.

79. C. W. Snyder, *Liberty and Morality*, 136. *Parliamentary Debates*, no. 240, 1378, 4 June 1855.

80. EBL to D. Radcliffe, 12 November 1855, Lytton MSS, DEK 57473.

81. EBL to J. Blackwood, 2 May 1855, M. Oliphant, *Annals of a Publishing House*, ii 431; EBL to H. Brougham, 10 November 1855, University College London, Brougham MSS, 4208; EBL to J. Blackwood, 1855, National Library of Scotland, Blackwood MSS, 4111, fol. 108–9.

82. Benjamin Disraeli to EBL, 6 January 1855, Lytton MSS, DEK c5, fol. 50.

83. EBL to Benjamin Disraeli, 15 October and [12 November] 1855, Bodleian Library, Hughenden MSS, box 104/1, fos 164, 166; ibid. [9 November 1855], Lytton MSS, DEK c5, fol. 151; EBL to J. Blackwood [1855], National Library of Scotland, Blackwood MSS, 4722, fos 248–49.

84. *Athens*, i 252.

85. *Godolphin*, chap. 64.

86. EBL to Lord J. Russell [1846], *Speeches*, i preface xv; EBL to Lord Walpole, 17 November 1857, Lytton MSS, DEK c28/59/107.

87. EBL to W. Kent, 15 May 1860 [17 April 1865] and [10 February 1869], Boston Public Library, MS C.1.41/38, 58, 114.

88. *Parliamentary Debates*, no. 255, 558, 22 March 1859.

89. *Hertford Mercury*, 12 June 1858; Lord Malmesbury to Benjamin Disraeli, 3 December 1858 and Benjamin Disraeli to Queen Victoria, 22 March 1859, W. F. Monypenny and G. E. Buckle, *The Life of Benjamin Disraeli*, iv 189 and 206.

90. EBL to W. Kent, 16 May 1866 and 27 January 1867, Boston Public Library, MS C.1.41.77 and 86.

91. EBL to ?, n.d.; *Life*, ii 309–10.

Notes to Chapter 11: Cabinet Minister

1. Lady Hills-Johnes, Recollections of a Visit, 1857, National Library of Wales, Dolaucothi MSS, 8103.

2. EBL to Miss Johnes, October 1858, ibid., 8099.

3. John Forster to EBL, 24 February 1858, Harvard, Houghton Library, Autograph File.

4. Lord Derby to Benjamin Disraeli, 25 February 1858, Bodleian Library, Hughenden MSS, 109/2, fol. 161.

5. Henry Bulwer to Robert Lytton, n.d., Knebworth MSS, box 58; Henry Bulwer to EBL, 14 March 1858, Knebworth MSS, ibid.

6. R. Blake, *Disraeli*, 386; EBL to Benjamin Disraeli [30 May 1858], Bodleian Library, Hughenden MSS, 140/2, fos 5–6.

7. Rosina Lytton to Dr Price, 8 May 1859, Devey, 344; A Kenealy, *Memoirs of Edward Vaughn Kenealy*, 202–3.

8. EBL to Benjamin Disraeli [1858], Bodleian Library, Hughenden MSS, 104/2, fol. 69.

9. R. Blake, *Disraeli*, 398.

10. T. B. Macaulay to EBL, 27 April 1859, T. Pinney, *The Letters of Thomas Babington Macaulay*, vi 209–10 and n. 2.

11. EBL to Benjamin Disraeli, 22 December 1858, Bodleian Library, Hughenden MSS, 104/2, fos 61–62. See also EBL to W. Kent, 27 December 1858, Boston Public Library, MS C.1.41.31.

12. Lytton MSS, DEK c27, fol. 479.

13. Lord Derby to Benjamin Disraeli, 30 December 1858, Bodleian Library, Hughenden MSS, 109/2, fos 278 and 244.

14. EBL to Benjamin Disraeli, 4 April 1859, ibid., 104/2, fos 86–87; R. Blake, *Disraeli*, 398–99.

15. EBL to Benjamin Disraeli, 6 April 1859, Lytton MSS, DEK c25/96.

16. EBL to Robert Lytton [1859], *Life*, ii 305.

17. EBL to Lord Derby, 1 April 1859, Lytton MSS, DEK c28/55.

18. *Speeches*, ii 317, 4 March 1862.

19. Report of Proceedings at the Lincoln Dinner, 1838, Lytton MSS, DEK w100.

20. EBL to ?, Princeton, Parrish MSS, 4 September [1857 or 1858]; *Parliamentary Debates*, 250, 18 February 1858, 1676 seq.

21. *My Novel*, book 7, chap. 22.

22. *Parliamentary Debates*, no. 246, 1434–46, 26 February 1857; EBL to J. Blackwood, 4 April 1857, Blackwoods MSS, 4125, fol. 161.

23. EBL to Lord Derby, 26 November 1858, Lytton MSS, DEK c28/55.

24. EBL to Lord Carnarvon [29 July 1858], British Library, Add. MS 60780. fol. 9.

25. EBL to Sir G. Bowen, 29 April 1859, Lytton MSS, DEK 028, fos 125–30.

26. Ibid., 6 March 1860, S. Lane-Poole, *The Official Papers of Sir George Bowen*, i 109.

27. Ibid., i 6–7.

28. *Parliamentary Debates*, no. 42, 398, 23 January 1838.

29. EBL to Benjamin Disraeli [14 December 1858], Bodleian Library, Hughenden MSS, 104/2, fos 49–50.

30. EBL to W. Kent [10 March 1869], Boston Public Library, MS C.1.41.115.

31. *Parliamentary Debates*, no. 253, 1101, 8 July 1858.

32. Ibid., 1815, 20 July 1858.

33. E. E. Rich, *The Hudson's Bay Company*, iii 783.

34. *Parliamentary Debates*, no. 253, 1817, 20 July 1858; ibid., 1102, 8 July 1858.
35. *Life*, ii 292–93.
36. British Library, Add. MS 60783. The whole volume details Lytton's handling of the Ionian Islands question.
37. EBL to W. Gladstone, 9 October 1858, Bodleian Library, Hughenden MSS, 104/2, fos 39–40.
38. Ibid., 5 and 9 October 1858, British Library, Add. MS 44241, fos 5 and 9.
39. EBL to W. Gladstone, 11 December 1858, ibid., fol. 101.
40. Ibid., 14 February 1859, Lytton MSS, DEK 028, fol. 87. See also ibid., 12 August 1861, British Library, Add. MS 44241, fol. 282; and EBL to Benjamin Disraeli [1858], Bodleian Library, Hughenden MSS, 104/2, fos 43–44.
41. EBL to 'R', n.d.; Huntingdon Library, Bulwer MSS.
42. EBL to Sir G. Bowen, 12 August 1860, Lytton MSS, DEK c26/7.
43. EBL to Robert Lytton, 24 October 1860, *Life* ii 339–40.
44. EBL to John Forster, 18 March 1863, Lytton MSS, DEK c27.
45. EBL to Robert Lytton, 5 January 1863, Knebworth MSS, J2 i 455. *Life*, 355.
46. EBL to Lord J. Manners, 17 May 1859, Lytton MSS, DEK c28/36.
47. EBL, Annotations, ibid., DEK c13, fol. 21.
48. T. A. Jenkins, *The Parliamentary Diaries of Sir John Trelawny*, 71 and 75.
49. M. Oliphant, *Annals of a Publishing House*, iii 81.
50. H. Bulwer to EBL, 3 September 1858, Norfolk Record Office, Bulwer MSS, BUL 1/255/16.
51. W. Bulwer to EBL, 3 March [1858 or 1859], Knebworth MSS, box 56, and G. Storey, *The Letters of Charles Dickens*, ix 5.
52. *Life*, ii 281 and 305.
53. Lord Carnarvon to EBL, 1870, Lytton MSS, DEK c19, fos 22–40.
54. EBL, annotation, ibid., c11 fol. 1.
55. EBL to Lord Carnarvon [14 and 17 April 1859], British Library, Add. MS 60780, fos 89 and 91.
56. British Library, Add. MS 60783, fos 67 seq.
57. EBL to Robert Lytton, 28 July 1859, Knebworth MSS, J2 I, fol. 117.

Notes to Chapter 12: Prophet

1. *The Parisians*, preface to 1873 edition.
2. EBL to John Forster, 20 May 1850, Lytton MSS, DEK c27, fol. 375.
3. *The Caxtons*, part 13, chap. 4.
4. EBL to W. Kent, 30 October 1867, Boston Public Library, MS C.1.41.99.
5. EBL to J. Blackwood, 4 May 1872, National Library of Scotland, Blackwood MSS, 4293, fol. 153.
6. Robert Lytton to EBL, 27 May 1871, Knebworth MSS, P5, box 95.
7. *The Parisians*, book 8, chap. 1.
8. EBL to J. Blackwood, 9 January 1872, National Library of Scotland, Blackwood MSS, 4293, fol. 135.

9. *Ernest Maltravers*, book 2, chap. 12.

10. *Night and Morning*, book 4, chap. 5.

11. *Quarterly Review*, no. 97, 567, September 1855.

12. *Rienzi*, appendix; *The Parisians*, book 5, chap. 5.

13. *Rienzi*, book 5, chap. 3.

14. *The Parisians*, book 5, chap. 6.

15. Ibid., book 2, chap. 6; EBL to J. Blackwood, 19 July 1866, National Library of Scotland, Blackwood MSS, 421, fol. 177.

16. EBL to Robert Lytton, 18 November 1868; Lytton MSS, DEK c28/34.

17. Address to the Hertfordshire Agricultural Society, October 1861, ibid., DEX 659 2/20.

18. *Speeches*, i 172, 25 January 1854.

19. *Quarterly Review*, no. 120, 559, October 1866.

20. *Life*, ii 195, 18 January 1854; EBL to Sir H. Drummond Wolff, 1 April 1859, Knebworth MSS, box 13.

21. EBL to Robert Lytton, 29 January 1871, Knebworth MSS, Jiv 1805.

22. *Life*, ii 80, 26 January 1846.

23. *Speeches*, i 188, 25 January 1854.

24. Edith Lytton to Robert Lytton, 28 July 1865, Lady E. Lutyens, *The Birth of Rowland*, 97.

25. *Life* [1869], ii 454–55. See also EBL to Robert Lytton, 25 May and 16 June 1869, Knebworth MS, Jiii 1323 and 1316; and EBL to J. Blackwood [1868], National Library of Scotland, Blackwood MSS, 4236, fos 109 seq.

26. EBL to Robert Lytton, 9 May 1866, Knebworth MSS, Jii 975.

27. EBL to Henry Bulwer, 25 May 1857, Knebworth MSS, P4, box 69.

28. EBL to Robert Lytton, 1864, Balfour, i 291.

29. 'The Genius of Conservatism' [1858], *Speeches*, i p. lxxxvi.

30. EBL to J. Blackwood, 1869, National Library of Scotland, Blackwood MSS, 4249, fol. 192. EBL to Robert Lytton, 11 May 1868, Knebworth MSS, Jiii 1132–33.

31. EBL to John Forster, 12 December 1868, Lytton MSS, DEK c27, fol. 333.

32. EBL to J. Meynell, 29 November 1868, ibid., c28/38.

33. EBL to J. Blackwood [1869], National Library of Scotland, Blackwood MSS, 4249, fol. 151.

34. EBL to Robert Lytton [1866?], Knebworth MSS, Jii 924; see also 918.

35. *Parliamentary Debates*, no. 260, 143 seq., 26 April 1860. See also EBL to Robert Lytton, 9 May 1860, Knebworth MSS, P5, box 72; and EBL to John Forster, 19 April 1860, Lytton MSS, DEK c27, fol. 622.

36. *Parliamentary Debates*, no. 284, 1237 seq., 13 April 1866. See also EBL to Robert Lytton, 11 March 1867, Knebworth MSS, Jii 1047; and EBL to J. Blackwood, 12 May and 1 August 1867, National Library of Scotland, Blackwood MSS, 4222, fos 183 and 195.

37. *Life*, ii 318–19.

38. EBL to J. Blackwood, 15 February 1868, National Library. of Scotland, Blackwood MSS, 4236, fol. 87.

39. Ibid. [1871], ibid., 4278, fos 219–20. The book is dedicated to the philologist Max Muller.

40. *The Coming Race*, chap. 17.

41. Ibid., chap. 9.

42. Ibid., chap. 20.

43. Ibid., chap. 17.

44. Ibid., chap. 26.

45. EBL to John Forster, 15 March 1870, Lytton MSS, DEK c27, fol. 450.

46. Robert Lytton to EBL [*c.* 1870], Knebworth MSS, P5, box 95.

47. EBL to John Forster, 20 March 1870, Lytton MSS, DEK c27, fol. 460.

48. Ibid., 15 March 1870, *Life*, ii 465.

49. EBL to J. Blackwood, 26 February 1860, National Library of Scotland, Blackwood MSS, 4151, fol. 14.

50. Henry Bulwer to Robert Lytton, 7 July [1868], Knebworth MSS, P4, box 58.

51. EBL to H. Brougham [February 1863], University College London, Brougham MSS, 18351. Brougham annotated this letter with the remark, 'Most ridiculous letter from Bulwer'.

52. *Life*, ii 368–69

53. EBL to John Forster [1866], Lytton MSS, DEK c27.

54. EBL to Robert Lytton, 19 May 1871, *Life*, ii 477.

55. *Kenelm Chillingly*, book 4, chap. 9.

56. Schiller, *Das Ideal und das Leben*.

57. A. C. Christenson, *Edward Bulwer Lytton*, 198.

58. Robert Lytton to EBL, 19 January [1871 or 1872], Knebworth MSS, P5, box 95.

59. EBL to Robert Lytton, July 1868, *Life*, ii 448.

60. Edith Lytton's account of Bulwer Lytton's death, 1874 or 1875, Knebworth MSS, V9.

61. B. Jowett to A. P. Stanley, 19 January 1873, E. Abbott and L. Campbell, *The Letters of Benjamin Jowett*, 184.

62. EBL to J. Blackwood, 13 January 1873, National Library of Scotland, Blackwood MSS, 4307, fol. 6.

63. M. Halliday to J. Blackwood [1873], National Library of Scotland, Blackwood MSS, 4304, fol. 63. Dr Hall, 'Last Moments of Lord Lytton', 1873, Knebworth MSS, P2 40A, *Life*, ii 487.

64. EBL's wills, March 1848 and 15 April 1854, Knebworth MSS, box 40.

65. 'Gertrude' to EBL, 18 January 1870 or 1871 and 1873, ibid., box 117.

66. Will read 4 March 1873, ibid., V10/2. According to Rosina, the two Lowndes children were the products of his liaison with the Swiss governess, Mlle Pion, in 1828. Rosina Lytton to editor of *Once a Week*, 14 December 1872, J. P. Morgan Library, M.A. unassigned.

67. C. Y. Lang, *The Swinburne Letters*, ii 255.

68. B. Jowett, *Lord Lytton*, 8.

69. Lady Sherborne to Lord Houghton, 23 January 1873, Trinity College, Cambridge, Houghton MSS, 185/1.

70. J. Vincent, *A Selection from Lord Derby's Diaries*, 124.

71. S. C. Hall, *Retrospect of a Long Life*, i 269.

72. EBL to Robert Lytton [*c.* 1860], Knebworth MSS, Jiv 1985.

73. *Ernest Maltravers*, book 1, chaps 8 and 12.

74. *Pausanias*, book 2, chap. 5.

75. EBL to Laman Blanchard [March 1843], J. P. Morgan Library, M.A., 4500.

76. EBL to Lady Morgan, 4 November 1857, Princeton, Parrish MSS, AM20225.

Bibliography

MANUSCRIPTS

Aberystwyth, National Library of Wales
Correspondence of the Johnes family

Birmingham, City Archives
Correspondence of Catherine Hutton

Boston, Public Library
Correspondence of W. Kent

Cambridge, England, Trinity College
Correspondence of Lord Houghton

Cambridge, England, University Library
Correspondence of Lord Lytton

Cambridge Massachusetts, Harvard University, Houghton Library
Lord Lytton Correspondence

Edinburgh, National Library of Scotland
Correspondence of the Blackwood Family

Hertford, Hertfordshire Record Office
Correspondence of Lord Lytton and other members of the Lytton family

Knebworth House, Hertsfordshire

Correspondence of Lord Lytton and other members of the Lytton family

Lincoln, Lincolnshire Record Office

Correspondence of the Tennyson d'Eyncourt family

London, British Library

Aberdeen MSS, Correspondence of the 4th Earl of Aberdeen
Babbage MSS, Correspondence of Sir Charles Babbage
Carnarvon MSS, Correspondence of the 4th Earl of Carnarvon
Gladstone MSS, Correspondence of W. E. Gladstone
Hobhouse MSS, Correspondence of Sir John Hobhouse
Hunt MSS, Correspondence of Leigh Hunt
Napier MSS, Correspondence of Macvey Napier

London, University College

Correspondence of Henry Brougham
Correspondence of Edwin Chadwick

London, Victoria and Albert Museum

Correspondence and Papers of John Forster

Los Angeles, Huntingdon Library

Correspondence of Edward and Rosina Lytton

Maidstone, Centre for Kentish Studies

Correspondence of the 5th Lord and Lady Stanhope

New York, J. P. Morgan Library

Correspondence of Lord and Lady Lytton

Norwich, Norfolk Record Office

Correspondence of Henry Bulwer

Oxford, Bodleian Library

Hughenden MSS, Correspondence of Benjamin, Isaac and Mary Ann Disraeli
Crampton MSS, Correspondence of Sir John Crampton
MSS Eng. Lett. d 90, Correspondence of R. Bentley and H. Colburn

Princeton, New Jersey, Princeton University Library

Correspondence and Papers of M. L. Parrish

Waco, Texas, Baylor University Library

Correspondence of Robert Browning

Wisbech, Lincs, Wisbech and Fenland Museum

Correspondence of C. H. Townshend

PRINTED SOURCES

Works by Edward Bulwer Lytton

Weeds and Wildflowers (London, 1826).
Falkland (London, 1827).
Pelham (London, 1828).
The Disowned (London, 1829).
Devereux (London, 1829).
Paul Clifford (London, 1830).
The Siamese Twins (London, 1831).
Eugene Aram (London, 1832).
Godolphin (London, 1833).
A Letter to a Late Cabinet Minister (London, 1834).
Pilgrims of the Rhine (London, 1834).
The Last Days of Pompeii (London, 1834).
Rienzi (London, 1835).
Ernest Maltravers (London, 1837).
Alice (London, 1838).
Leila (London, 1838).
Night and Morning (London, 1841).
Zanoni (London, 1842).

The Last of the Barons (London, 1843).

The Crisis (London, 1845).

Lucretia (London, 1846).

The New Timon (London, 1846).

A Word to The Public (London, 1847).

Athens (London, 1847).

Harold (London, 1848).

The Caxtons (London, 1849).

Letters to John Bull (London, 1851).

My Novel (London, 1853).

The Press (London, 1853).

Inaugural Address Delivered at Glasgow University (London, 1857).

What Will He Do With It? (London, 1859).

A Strange Story (London, 1862).

The Coming Race (London, 1871).

The Parisians (London, 1873).

Kenelm Chillingly (London, 1873).

Works by or on Rosina Lytton

Cheveley: or The Man of Honour (London, 1839).

The Budget of the Bubble Family (London, 1840).

Miriam Sedley (London, 1851).

The School for Husbands (London, 1852).

Very Successful (London, 1856).

Appeal to the Justice and Charity of the English Public (London, 1857).

The World and his Wife (London, 1858).

Shells from the Sands of Time (London, 1876).

A Blighted Life (London, 1880).

Unpublished Letters of Lady Lytton and A. E. Chalon (London, n.d.).

L. Devey, *Letters of the Late Edward Bulwer, Lord Lytton, to his Wife* (London, 1884).

Life of Rosina, Lady Lytton (London, 1887).

Works by or Edited by Robert Lytton

Miscellaneous Prose Works by Edward Bulwer, Lord Lytton (London, 1868).

Speeches of Edward, Lord Lytton (London, 1874).

The Life, Letters and Literary Remains of Edward Bulwer, Lord Lytton (London, 1883).

Works on Edward Bulwer Lytton

R. Blake, 'Bulwer Lytton', *Cornhill Magazine*, September 1973.

A. M. Brown, 'The Metaphysical Novels of Edward Bulwer Lytton' (unpublished Ph.D. thesis, Cambridge University, 1979).

A. Caswell, *A Letter to Edward Lytton Bulwer on the Present Crisis* (London, 1834).

A. C. Christensen, *Edward Bulwer Lytton* (Athens, Georgia, 1976).

T. Cooper, *Lord Lytton* (London, 1873).

T. H. S. Escott, *Edward Bulwer, First Baron Lytton* (London, 1910).

B. Jowett, *Lord Lytton* (London, 1873).

C. Luther, *Sir Edward Bulwer Lytton and Homeopathy* (London, 1853).

Victor, 3rd Lord Lytton, *The Life of Edward Bulwer Lytton* (London, 1913).

C. H. Shattuck, *Bulwer and Macready* (Illinois, 1958).

C. W. Snyder, *Liberty and Morality: a Political Biography of Edward Bulwer Lytton* (New York, 1995).

Sir Leslie Stephen, 'The Late Lord Lytton as a Novelist', *Cornhill Magazine*, March 1873.

C. N. Stewart, *Bulwer Lytton as Occultist* (London, 1927).

R. A. Zipser, *Edward Bulwer Lytton and Germany* (Berne, 1974).

R. L. Wolff, 'Edward Bulwer Lytton', *Harvard Literary Bulletin*, 22 (1974).

Newspapers and Magazines

Bentley's Magazine
Dublin University Magazine
Edinburgh Review
Fraser's Magazine
London and Westminster Review
Monthly Chronicle
New Monthly Magazine
Parliamentary Debates
Quarterly Review
The Times

Secondary Works

Anon., *A Calm Consideration of the State of Public Affairs* (London, 1835).
—, *Letter to Sir E. Bulwer Lytton* (London, 1851).
—, *A Few Words from John Bull* (London, 1851).
E. Abbot and L. Campbell, *Letters of Benjamin Jowett* (London, 1899).

A. Aspinall, *Lord Brougham and the Whig Party* (London, 1972).

Lady Balfour, *Personal and Literary Letters of Robert, First Earl of Lytton* (London, 1906).

S. Ballantine, *Some Experiences of a Barrister's Life* (London, 1882).

C. H. Beale, *Reminiscences of a Gentlewoman of the Last Century* (London, 1891).

A. C. Benson and Lord Esher, *The Letters of Queen Victoria* (London, 1908).

W. Besant, *Essays and Historiettes* (London, 1903).

R. Blake, *Disraeli* (London, 1966).

L. Blanchard, *Sketches from Life* (London, 1846).

J. A. Davies, *John Forster: A Literary Life* (Leicester, 1983).

R. Disraeli, *Lord Beaconsfield's Correspondence with his Sister, 1832–52* (London, 1886).

T. H. Duncombe, *The Life and Correspondence of T. H. Duncombe* (London, 1868).

S. M. Ellis, *William Harrison Ainsworth and his Friends* (London, 1911).

J. Forster, *The Life of Charles Dickens* (London, 1928).

W. P. Frith, *My Autobiography and Reminiscences* (London, 1898).

C. F. C. Greville, *A Journal of the Reigns of King George IV, King William IV and Queen Victoria* (London, 1888).

G. S. Haight, *The George Eliot Letters* (New Haven, Connecticut, 1954–78).

N. J. Hall, *The Letters of Anthony Trollope* (Stanford, California, 1983).

S. C. Hall, *Retrospect of a Long Life* (London, 1883).

Lord F. Hamilton, *The Days Before Yesterday* (London, 1937).

E. F. Harden, *The Letters and Private Papers of William Makepeace Thackeray* (London, 1994).

J. O. Hoge and C. Olney, *The Letters of Caroline Norton to Lord Melbourne* (Ohio, 1974).

K. Hollingsworth, *The Newgate Novel* (Detroit, Michigan, 1963).

G. J. Holyoake, *Sixty Years of an Agitator's Life* (London, 1892).

D. D. Home, *Incidents in My Life* (London, 1863).

Mrs D. Home, *D. D. Home: His Life and Mission* (London, 1888).

—, *The Gift of D. D. Home* (London, 1890).

L. Hunt, *Autobiography* (London, 1960).

T. A. Jenkins, *The Parliamentary Diaries of Sir John Trelawny* (London, 1990).

A Kenealy, *Memoirs of Edward Vaughn Kenealy* (London, 1908).

S. Lane-Poole, *The Official Papers of Sir G. F. Bowen* (London, 1899).

C. Y. Lang, *The Swinburne Letters* (New Haven, 1959–62).

—, *The Letters of Alfred Lord Tennyson* (Oxford, 1982–90).

F. Leveson Gower, *Letters of Harriet, Countess Granville* (London, 1894).

Lady E. Lutyens, *The Birth of Rowland* (London, 1956).

G. Lyster, *A Family Chronicle* (London, 1908).

R. P. Madden, *The Literary Life and Correspondence of the Countess of Blessington* (London, 1855).

W. Marston, *Our Recent Actors* (London, 1888).

L. G. Mitchell, *Lord Melbourne* (Oxford, 1997).

W. F. Monypenny and G. E. Buckle, *The Life of Benjamin Disraeli* (London, 1910–1920).

P. F. Morgan, *The Letters of Thomas Hood* (Edinburgh, 1973).

A. Morrison, *The Blessington Papers* (London, 1895).

R. Nevill, *The Reminiscences of Lady Dorothy Nevill* (London, 1906).

M. Oliphant, *Annals of a Publishing House* (London, 1897).

Mrs Osborne, *Memorials of the Life and Character of Lady Osborne* (Dublin, 1870).

T. Pinney, *The Letters of Thomas Babington Macaulay* (Cambridge, 1974–81).

Sir F. Pollack, *Macready's Reminiscences* (London, 1875).

J. Preston, *That Odd Rich Old Woman* (Dorchester, 1995).

G. N. Ray, *The Letters and Private Papers of William Makepeace Thackeray* (London, 1945–46).

S. J. Reid, *Life and Letters of the First Earl of Durham* (London, 1906).

E. E. Rich, *The Hudson's Bay Company* (Glasgow, 1960).

Lady Ridley, *The Life and Letters of Cecilia Ridley* (London, 1978).

M. M. Roberts, *Gothic Immortals* (London, 1990).

M. Rochester, *The Derby Ministry* (London, 1858).

M. Sadleir, *Blessington d'Orsay* (London, 1933).

C. R. Sanders, *The Collected Letters of Thomas and Jane Welsh Carlyle* (Durham, North Carolina, 1970–97).

H. and M. Schwartz, *Disraeli's Reminiscences* (London, 1975).

Lady Stafford, *Leaves from the Diary of Henry Greville* (London, 1905).

G. Storey, *The Letters of Charles Dickens* (Oxford, 1965–98).

Lord Teignmouth, *Reminiscences of Many Years* (Edinburgh, 1878).

W. Toynbee, *The Diaries of William Charles Macready* (London, 1912).

F. E. Trollope, *Frances Trollope* (London, 1895).

J. Vincent, *A Selection from the Derby Diaries* (London, 1994).

Sir L. Ward, *Forty Years of Spy* (London, 1915).

Sir A. West, *Recollections* (London, 1899).

W. White, *The Inner Life of the House of Commons* (London, 1897).

N. P. Willis, *Pencillings by the Way* (London, 1835).

R. L. Wolff, *Strange Stories and Other Exploration in Victorian Literature* (Boston, 1971).

Index